The
Abbey Fields

Robin D. Leach

Published by Rookfield Publications
Kenilworth, 2017

www.VictorianKenilworth.co.uk
www.Kenilworth-ww2.co.uk

Front cover: *17ᵗʰ April 2016*

Back Cover: *15ᵗʰ March 2017*

Opposite: Looking down the diagonal path from Abbey Hill towards Rosemary Hill; the Rosemary Hill field has an additional fence across it. The photograph is dated *c*1892, although there is no record of any seats being placed in the Abbey Fields until the celebration of Queen Victoria's jubilee in 1897 *(FF)*

© Robin D Leach

Published by Rookfield Publications

Printed in Kenilworth by Emmerson Press

ISBN: 978-0-9552646-4-1

Contents

Acknowledgments *Page 4*

Chapter 1   *Public Walks and Pleasure Grounds*   *Page 5*
Landform; the Priory is built, the Abbey destroyed; animals graze; a park created; the Abbey excavated; a swimming pool built; houses appear on the estate; a club builds a bowling green.

Chapter 2   *To Benefit the Community*   *Page 57*
The Great War; more land donated; tennis courts and a children's playground are built; more of the Abbey excavated; sports pitches are created; the swimming pool becomes a lido; a museum; another land donation, but some land lost.

Chapter 3   *Privileges of the Abbey Fields*   *Page 99*
The second World War; a showground created; land is lost; a temporary car park is made; grazing ends; the swimming pool improved; pitch & putt; two new areas of land added.

Chapter 4   *A Municipal Park or Rural Open Countryside*   *Page 155*
Abbey Fields no longer belongs to Kenilworth; a new museum; more ruin excavations; a lake at last; amenities lost; a new indoor pool; groups and societies become involved; the car park becomes permanent; play equipment extended.

Addendum *Page 197*

Index *Page 200*

Also by this author *Page 204*

Acknowledgments

I am indebted to a great many people for their assistance in the compilation of this book:

All staff at Warwick County Records Office are thanked for their first class service, but Robert Eyre, Senior Archivist, in particular for permission to publish images from their collections.
Keith Grierson, Churchwarden, gave permission for the use of St Nicholas church archives held at the County Records Office.
Chris Lillington, Editor, for allowing the reproduction of photographs from the *Kenilworth Weekly News* and *Leamington Courier*.
Louise Essex, Senior Librarian, Local Studies, and Linda Young, Library and Information Advisor, Kenilworth Library, for the use of photographs from the Kenilworth Library collection and providing copying facilities.
Kevin Carty, Warwick District Council Sports Facilities Area Manager, and Paul Murphy, Operations Manager Abbey Fields Swimming Pool, for statistics and access for photography.
The original Abbey Fields conveyances held by Warwick District Council have been studied; illustrations marked *WDC* are taken from these, followed by their own reference number. Thanks are due to Warwick District Council Estates Manager Chris Makasis for making them available and providing studying and copying facilities.
Norman Stevens provided guidance and information as regards mediaeval Kenilworth.
Neil Eaton, Kenilworth Deputy Town Clerk, retrieved documents from the Council archives.
Sandra Whitlock shared the early history of Friends of Abbey Fields.
Sue Newman provided sound editorial advice.
Other contributions are by Alan Edmunds, Shelagh Hubbard, Joanna Illingworth and Steven Wallsgrove.

The source of illustrations and their notations are as follows:

Copyright the Francis Frith Collection *(FF)*, Friends of Abbey Fields *(FoAF)*, Copyright Historic England Collection, Aerofilms Archive *(HE)*, John H Drew Collection at Kenilworth Library *(JHD)*, Kenilworth Fire Brigade *(KFB)*, Kenilworth History & Archaeology Society *(KHAS)*, Kenilworth Library *(KL)*, Kenilworth Weekly News *(KWN)*, Courtesy Alice Swatton, Curator, Leamington Spa Art Gallery & Museum *(LAG&M)*, Leamington Courier *(LC)*, Peter James *(PJ)*, Sally Taylor *(SaT)*, Susan Tall *(SuT)*, Warwickshire County Records Office *(WCRO)*, Warwick District Council *(WDC)*.

I am particularly grateful to Helen Scott *(HS)* for once more making her extraordinary collection of postcards and photographs available.

Unaccredited photographs are taken by the author (post 1980), or are from his collection (pre 1980).

Some photographs are included for their interest and rarity rather than quality and include a number scanned from newspapers, and several copied from film-photographs of elderly, but now lost, originals. All image editing is by the author.

Quotes in italics are from newspapers, mostly the *Kenilworth Advertiser*, *Kenilworth Weekly News*, & *Leamington Courier*; quotes not in italics are, unless credited, from minutes of Vestry, Local Board of Health, or Kenilworth Urban District Council meetings. Quotes in alterative type are from legal documents.

In places, monetary values in italics are added in brackets; this is the modern equivalent calculated using the Bank of England Inflation Calculator for the year 2016.

Chapter titles are quotations taken from the text.

Although many works were consulted, the reader may find these publications of particular interest:

Archaeology Warwickshire, Report 1353, September 2013, and *Report 1417*, February 2014
Conservation Plan, Abbey Fields, Kenilworth Abbey Advisory Committee, 2005
Kenilworth History, in addition to references to specific editions in the text, the annual publication of the Kenilworth History & Archaeology Society is recommended reading.
Recent Research into the Lost History of Kenilworth, Graham Gould, self published, 2014
The Story of the Abbey, Harry Sunley & Norman Stevens, Pleasaunce Press, second edition 2015

Chapter 1: *Public Walks and Pleasure Grounds*

The origin of the physical formation of the Abbey Fields is best described by Geoff Hilton in his article Kenilworth History and Landform, *Kenilworth History 2004/5,* published by the Kenilworth History & Archaeology Society:

> The Finham Brook is confined by two parallel ridges of Kenilworth sandstone supporting High Street-New Street and Abbey Hill-Albion Street. The flow of Finham Brook was impeded by a barrier of glacial deposits (or possibly a tongue of ice) lying between Highland Road and Knowle Hill, and a small lake formed in the region of the (later) Castle Mere and Abbey Fields. This was fed by immense quantities of melt-water from the retreating ice. The accumulating water was sufficiently powerful to overflow the barrier and cut through to form a two to three kilometre long water channel, the 'Kenilworth Gorge'.
>
> The ridges of Kenilworth sandstone resist erosion, but in the Abbey Fields they are separated by a band of softer Kenilworth mudstone and this layer has been eroded by the Finham Brook resulting in the bowl-shaped Abbey Fields. At some time in the drainage of the glacial lake, a terrace fan of sands and gravels formed on the northern side and this provided the flatter, elevated area.

Around Kenilworth, Bronze Age artefacts have been found and the Romans were active in brick and tile making; historians thus speculate that remnants of Roman buildings may one day be found in the Abbey Fields or elsewhere. In all probability people were living in the district throughout the first millennium but recorded history in Kenilworth does not start until after the Norman invasion. In 1086, Kenilworth's entry in the Domesday Book can be summarised thus: 'Richard the Forester holds 90 acres of lands from the king. There are ten villagers and seven smallholders with three ploughs. The woodland is four furlongs wide'. The woodland most likely spread westward towards Honiley and was a remnant of the Forest of Arden. Ninety acres was a small community for Domesday Warwickshire, 620 acres being the average. The derivation of the town's name as recorded in 1086, Chinewrde (pronounced *kinny-worth*), was 'the farm of a woman called Cynehild'. The farm's location is unknown, but was likely to have been alongside a water course; if it was today's Finham Brook, perhaps at least part of the farm was in what was to become the Abbey Fields which also provided south-facing slopes, although the marshy nature of the lower ground may preclude this area. The higher and thus drier ground north of Castle Green, with a stream to the west, is the popular hypothesis.

Geoffrey de Clinton, probably taking his surname from Glympton in Oxfordshire where he held the Manor by 1120, was an Anglo-French nobleman of uncertain ancestry. By this time, he was treasurer to King Henry I and *c*1121 he was appointed Sheriff of Warwickshire; to cement the strength of his position he founded a Castle at Kenilworth. Further down the watercourse alongside which his Castle was being built, de Clinton also founded a Priory, dedicated to St Mary, on the aforementioned terrace of the sand and gravel deposited about 30,000 years ago; it was one of the earliest Augustinian Priories, eventually to number 251. Written evidence by the chronicler John Strecche, Canon at St Mary's, claims the Priory was founded in 1119; this adds to the unresolved discussions as to the founding dates of both Castle and Priory, as the Castle would certainly have been established first. It is quite possible the Priory may have been built on the site of an earlier farm or smallholding; it was also quite common for a Priory to be constructed on a site of Roman buildings although no evidence has yet been found to substantiate either scenario. It is probable that from the outset the Priory would have included all the land that we know today as the Abbey Fields; its status and permanence ensured the local road system circumnavigated its boundaries.

The reason that such a thinly populated area was chosen for the Castle and Priory was due not only to a favourable location and landscape, but also that outcrops revealed a source of building material, the local red sandstone. It is possible that some of the stone for the building of the Castle and/or Priory came from the Abbey Fields (there is speculation that the rocky outcrop on the southern side of the valley could have been quarried, although this may have been at a later date), but other areas away from the fields certainly provided the majority of stone (in the vicinity of Grounds Farm, Berkeley Road, Malthouse Lane and Fieldgate Lane); masons are thought to have been at work between the two building sites in an area later known as Little Virginia. The simultaneous building of the Castle and Priory, and associated quarrying, obviously attracted a large workforce to the area leading to the establishment of a true village. It is likely that there was already a parochial chapel for villagers; an interesting hypothesis suggests the foundations of today's 12 & 13 Castle Green may have supported such a structure.

The southern part of the town was established as a borough by 1147 alongside an existing straight north-south trackway forming today's Warwick Road and The Square; the Priory and Castle lands following Finham Brook to the Common created a demarcation line between the two distinct parts of the growing village.

During the Great Siege in 1266, King Henry III is likely to have spent much of his time in Kenilworth in the comfortable surrounds of the Priory, particularly as he was its patron. The fields would have been ravaged for the Priory's food by both sides before and during the siege. The supposed earlier chapel would not have survived the confrontation and this led to the building of a parish church, St Nicholas, known to exist by 1291, close to the Priory church and on the same alignment. Although built on land given up by the Priory, there would have been no direct access between the two; a wall, perhaps connecting to the Tantara Gatehouse, would have ensured the Priory's privacy. The new churchyard would have been established between St Nicholas Church and High Street. There are substantial mediaeval foundations and stonework under High Street buildings that suggest the location of the Priory's boundary wall and/or the St Nicholas almonry. The original size of St Nicholas Church is uncertain but its entrance was on its northern side, accessed directly from High Street; its final form was probably reached in the later 14th century but it was still less than half the length of the Priory church. Other buildings were constructed in the immediate High Street area, giving a new focal point to the developing village.

The Priory gained a great deal of wealth and land across Warwickshire (and beyond) with only the Earl of Warwick and Coventry Priory holding more at one time, and in 1447 its status was, unusually, upgraded to Abbey. Its newly found prominence was comparatively short lived; its fate was sealed by the 1534 Act of Supremacy and it became one of 825 religious communities dissolved by Henry VIII, succumbing in April 1538. Henry gave the Abbey site to Sir Andrew Flammock. The valuable lead roof was quickly removed, melted into 'pigs' weighing half a ton for use elsewhere, and this ensured the rapid deterioration of the buildings; the stonework began to be dismantled for use in other structures around the village, including the Castle, but also further away such as Rowington Church. Carved stones from the Abbey's doors and windows which would have been useless for structural work were incorporated in the magnificent west doorway of St Nicholas Church, installed between 1550 and 1640.

The assets of the Abbey at the time of its suppression were listed in 1547. It was described as having 20 acres enclosed by a stone wall, and included a 5 acre 'great orchard' (*note:* another transcription dated 1538 records this orchard as '10 acres over and besides the wood within the same growing'), a 1 acre pasture called the sextery, the fermery garden with a pool and orchard totalling 1 acre, a vineyard of 1 acre and a 3 acre 'young orchard' that included a pool next to the 'bake-house pool'. This gives a total acreage of about 11 (the difference from the mentioned 20 acres could be accounted for by the Abbey Pool on the later-named Oxpen Meadow) and all would be located close to the Abbey on the northern side of the brook, the pools being alongside the brook itself; the Estate Map of 1692 by James Fish (see page 8) does show this as an area of 11 acres. These are however just the amenities in the immediate vicinity of the Abbey; there is little doubt that the fields on the opposite side of the brook were also incorporated.

In 1560, Sir William Flammock, who had inherited the site of the Abbey from his father in 1549, died and it passed to his daughter Catherine, then aged just 2. Her eventual husband, John Colburn, sold it on to Robert Dudley, Earl of Leicester, in about 1570, soon after he had been given possession of the Castle. Despite the single ownership, the Abbey and Castle manors remained distinct, creating the districts Abbey End and Castle End.

There was a Civil War skirmish in Kenilworth in 1642, perhaps contributing to the musket shot marks still visible on the walls of the Tantara Gatehouse and the Barn (see back cover). With King Charles' position continuing to decline, in the third year of the Civil War, 1644, his army lodged in St Nicholas Church and presumably also in any usable remnants of the Abbey; the following year Cromwell's army was hosted. Weapon sharpening evidence on gravestones and external church walls are likely to be from these visits.

In 1665 the Crown granted the Castle and Manors, including the Abbey Fields, to Laurence Hyde, later created Earl of Rochester, son of the 1st Earl of Clarendon; at his death the estate passed to his son Henry Hyde, the Earl of Rochester & 4th Earl of Clarendon, and when he died in 1753 leaving no heir, all his honours became extinct. The estates of the now derelict Castle and Abbey thus passed to the Hon Thomas Villiers, later 1st Earl of Clarendon of the second creation, who had married Charlotte, granddaughter of the aforementioned Henry Hyde; in 1785 they passed to Thomas, 2nd Earl of Clarendon, and the estates subsequently descended with the Earldom.

Over time, the Abbey, and therefore its grounds, had been visited either certainly, or in some cases probably, by 8 monarchs: Henry III, Edward II & III, Henry V & VI, Richard III, Henry VII, and of course Elizabeth I who famously worshipped at St Nicholas Church, are all believed to have walked the grounds of the Abbey.

At the time the Priory was built, the course of the meandering Finham Brook was more central to the valley but this was to change as a water system to suit the needs of the Priory, and later Abbey, was developed. A dam across the approximate centre of the fields was first constructed $c1200$ and produced a large lake flooding the area back along Finham Brook to today's Castle Ford, and along Luzley Brook perhaps as far as today's Castle Farm sports centre. Probably at around the same time, at the southern end of the dam a mill was constructed, necessitating the coursing of the brook as a millstream and producing the dog-leg in the centre and the straightened course (the mill race) towards Bridge Street. The level of the lake was later lowered and an overflow was constructed towards the northern end of the dam; it was then similar to the level of today's lake but still also stretched along the course of Luzley Brook almost to Borrowell Lane.

The mound alongside Finham Brook, now about 8ft high and 50ft across at its base, has been identified as a potential surveying position for the construction of the Abbey water system; such a place would have been necessary and it is sited in an advantageous position with a clear view upstream and downstream, southwards along the Luzley Brook, and also overlooks the site of the Abbey pool. If this is the case, then it would have been built $c1200$ *(6th February 2017)*

It is quite probable that the Abbey's fields were entirely enclosed by a substantial wall, perhaps 10ft high, to ensure privacy. Known remnants include a probable length through the middle of the later Little Virginia and along the High Street boundary and this probably continued through the alignment of today's buildings on the south side of High Street; the demolition of this wall too would have provided substantial amounts of building material for local projects. No evidence of a wall has yet been found on the southern part of the fields.

At some time, $c1650$ is the popular estimate, the Abbey lake was drained and a new course for Finham Brook to the west of the central dam was dug, the excavated material being used to construct a raised embankment to contain it on the northern side to prevent permanent flooding of the former lake; on the James Fish map the area is shown as the Abbey Meadow so draining must have been at least partially successful, but springs on the northern slopes kept some wetness in the area.

There would have been a bridge of some sort in the vicinity of the mill for much of its existence, but the stone built Abbey Bridge, referred to as a packsaddle bridge due to its form, was on the dam alignment after the lake was drained. This alignment raised the pathway above flood level and there is likely to have been an embankment on the southern shore of the brook. The bridge was destroyed by floods in 1673; its later replacement, the current Iron Bridge, was built a little further to the east at an unknown date.

For a full explanation of the historic water system of the Abbey Fields, I thoroughly recommend the pioneering work of David Brock, and his articles in *Kenilworth History*, 2004/5, 2005/6, 2006/7 and 2012, published by the Kenilworth History & Archaeology Society.

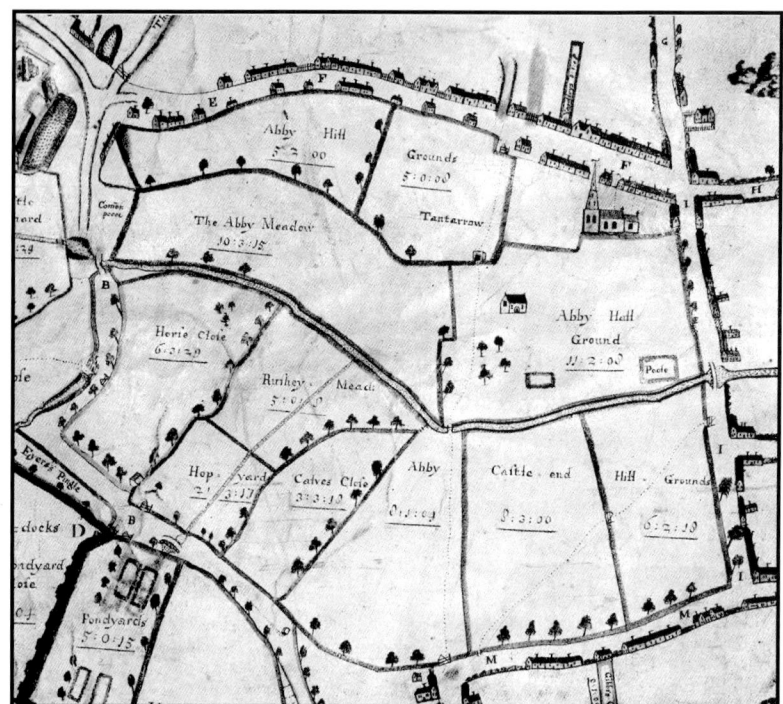

An extract of the Estate Map of 1692 by James Fish. The Abbey Fields division into 11 fields is indicative of farming; these field partitions remained, with additions, into the 20th century *(KHAS; WCRO, CR 143/1)*

After the dissolution, Abbey land alongside its enclosing roads became available for building purposes. The estate map shows numerous cottages along the fields' northern edge; those at the later-called Little Virginia were built probably in the early 17th century so are likely to include stone from the Abbey, or its substantial perimeter wall that had passed either through the centre or alongside the group. The site was located with a sharp drop behind the cottages into the fields.

At the time of the Abbey, the fields would have been out of bounds for the public, but a north-south path across them is likely to have been established before the Priory was built, and perhaps became a right of way; its alignment continued to the south where the new borough was founded in 1147, and northwards as seen in the James Fish map, although today this is less distinct. Its course, past the mill and over the Abbey Bridge, took it alongside the Tantara Gatehouse, and possibly helps to explain the location of the latter. The north-south path would have been the only established route across the Abbey lands and connected the two parts of the town.

Although not shown on the 1692 map, it is believed a path probably existed from the centre of the fields running around the hill towards Borrowell Lane; Victorian writers believed it to be an old *'offertory path, so called because money was donated to it from church collections'*. However, it may have been established by beast-hauled traffic following the contour from the vicinity of today's The Square to avoid climbing the hill. Another probable path was from Little Virginia to the fields' centre, perhaps established as a route for worked stone being delivered to the Priory.

By 1700 the Abbey was a ruin. An engraving by Samuel and Nathaniel Buck in 1729 shows a range of surviving but derelict walls, up to about 15ft high, between the Tantara Gatehouse and the Chapter House wall. Two buildings had survived more or less intact from the scavenging: one, of uncertain original use, lost its lead roof at the same time as the Abbey but within a century was re-roofed and in use as a barn (the name by which it is best known today) and the other was the Tantara Gatehouse, the ground floor of which survived sufficiently for two 1787 prints to suggest it was inhabited as smoke is rising from a chimney; it is shown thatched, the thatch being over a waterproofing clay seal. The fields were by now established for use by local farmers for grazing and there is some visible evidence to suggest ridge and furrow agricultural use west of the north-south path, between the brook and southern slope (although this could be interpreted as a remnant of an orchard). As far as is known the fields were not attached to any particular farm, but only Borrowell Lane (the roads were then little more than worn tracks, perhaps with a gravel topping) separated the fields from the extensive Castle Farm. The Castle grounds, including inside the walls, were also grazed at this time.

The Abbey's destruction would have allowed the townsfolk, such that they were at that time (in 1730 the population was 792), to establish new footpaths across the fields, particularly as some could have been working the land. A branch from the north-south path led to St Nicholas Church, a necessary and regular destination that now had a long-established western entrance. The only other path James Fish marked on his map was the diagonal path from Abbey End (but from the other side of a field boundary hedge to the north-south path), down to near the bridge carrying Rosemary Hill over Finham Brook; its only purpose would seem to be 'cutting the corner', not only reducing the distance travelled but avoiding the then much steeper incline at the top of Rosemary Hill. The path joins Rosemary Hill at the start of a raised embankment for the bridge over the brook, perhaps suggesting the path post-dates the bridge (the date of origin of which is unknown, although the current structure is believed to be 18th century) or at least the embankment. At some unknown date, but its location confirming it would have been after the dissolution of the Abbey, a diagonal path was created from Bridge Street to St Nicholas Church, again from the end of the bridge embankment.

As the town developed southwards, and west to east along the northern boundaries, the Abbey Fields remained intact and became both a barrier and connection between the two distinct areas. The town was surrounded by farms, many leased out by Clarendon, and the rented Abbey Fields were an extension of the farmlands, and despite the presence of livestock for much of the year it is likely that the paths became used for perambulations in the same manner as paths across fields in the outlying districts of the town. By 1831, Kenilworth's population had risen to 3,097.

In 1834, floodwater carried away part of the mill dam in the centre of the fields, *'an act often attributed since to Oliver Cromwell'*, and in all probability removed any remaining sign of the mill dam south of the brook. The level of this flood is marked on Townpool Bridge.

In 1835, the trustees of the Leamington and Warwick to Coventry toll road proposed a short cut to avoid the troublesome Rosemary Hill, then steeper at the top and with a tighter curve than today. The suggestion was to continue the road in a straight line from Abbey End into the Abbey Fields before a curve took it to rejoin Rosemary Hill just before Townpool Bridge. The fields across which the proposed route took were rented individually from John Villiers, the 3rd Earl of Clarendon, by his land agent William Henry Butler (Field 1), William Boddington, probably a bailiff (Field 2), and High Street baker David Fancott (Field 3); all fields are described as pastureland and it is possible that horses used for transport rather than cattle were the prominent livestock, particularly in the case of David Fancott. The scheme did not come to fruition, probably due to costs; the existing road was upgraded instead.

In 1838, John Villiers died aged 81, and he was succeeded by his nephew, 38-year-old George Frederick William Villiers, the 4th Earl of Clarendon.

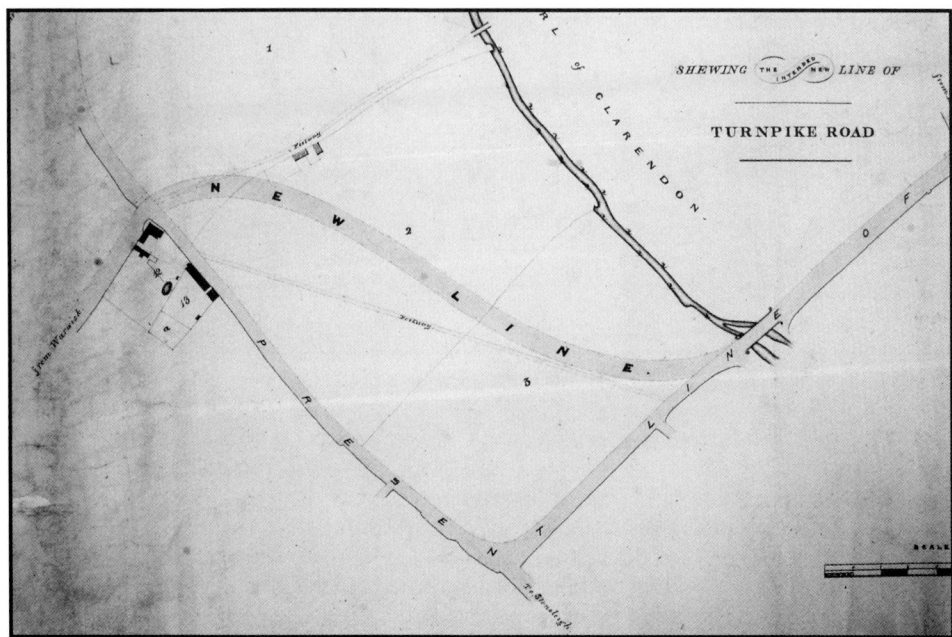

The Toll Road proposed in 1835 *(WCRO, QS 111/87)*

The **churchyard** of St Nicholas was initially just the area to the north of the church; ruins had been struck during grave digging in 1793, although it is not known if this was structural or loose stone. In 1840, the Earl of Clarendon gave an 'L' shaped area of the Abbey Fields land westwards then southwards from the church to extend the churchyard and as soon as digging began in July loose remnants of the Abbey stonework were discovered. It was decided to clear the area to a depth of 9ft to ensure future grave digging would be trouble free, and this led to a full-scale archaeological excavation during which human remains, foundations of a large octagonal building, Norman foundation stones and sepulchral slabs (one of which has a likely date of origin between 1171 and 1363, and now covers the grave of the Poole family) were discovered. (For a full account of these excavations, see *Victorian Kenilworth and its People*, page 8.) With the site cleared, refilled and levelled, the first burial, that of Mary White, took place in 1842.

A further churchyard extension into the Abbey Fields became necessary in 1866. There were two options, westwards or southwards from the church; the southern area of 1950 sq yds was the preferred choice as the church would then be more central to its yard. Surviving letters show that the 4th Earl of Clarendon came to Kenilworth in mid-August 1866, 'where I must stay for 4 or 5 days as my affairs there are in utter confusion'. It is probably no coincidence that it was at the next Vestry meeting just weeks after his visit that it is recorded Clarendon had refused permission for the preferred choice for the churchyard extension and insisted upon the westward area being used, despite it being difficult for the carrying of coffins (as no path from the church into the area existed) and had been found to contain 'bones from the Priory'. Clarendon also insisted that the Tantara Gatehouse within the area was not included and remained his, and that a 15ft wide roadway alongside was to be maintained. He also stated that this would be the last time he would give up any of his land for a churchyard extension. The extension was over an existing pathway that ran through the Tantara Gatehouse and joined High Street; this was rearranged and provided an entrance into the yard from High Street. Clarendon did:

> Freely and voluntarily give grant and convey... every part thereof to be held forever as part of the churchyard except and always reserved out of this conveyance a public footroad and right of way of width three foot six inches leading out of the High Street... such right of way to be maintained for the Parishioners of Kenilworth.

The process cost £6 6s 8d in legal fees; one of the solicitors involved was Edward Draper, who shall appear again later. By 1867, a wall of scabbard stone (likely to be loose stone from the Abbey ruins) was being built to provide a new permanent western boundary to the churchyard, the 15ft wide roadway was on the other side of it. At this time the churchyard was not fully enclosed and livestock grazed amongst the gravestones; sheep eating the flowers left on graves being particularly distressing.

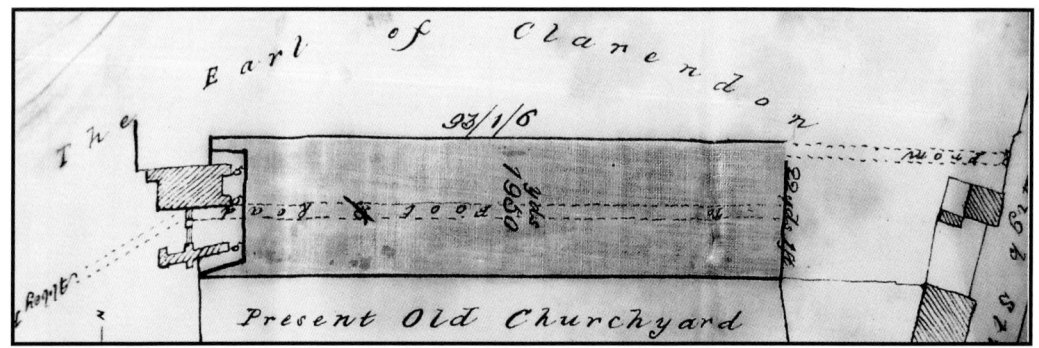

The 1867 churchyard extension, showing the right of way to it from High Street *(WCRO, DR 189/46/1)*

On 9th May 1870, the Reverend Bickmore, and Churchwardens Dr Wynter and Luke Heynes, sent a letter to the Bishop of Worcester saying the churchyard extension was ready to be consecrated, 'to separate the land for the future from the common and profane uses and consecrate and dedicate it... for the internment of the dead bodies of persons dying within the parish of Kenilworth.'

George Villiers, the 4th Earl of Clarendon, was true to his word about not allowing another extension; he was taken seriously ill during his 1866 stay in Kenilworth, never fully recovered, and died aged 71 on 27th June 1870 before another extension needed to be requested. At the time, he was serving as Foreign Secretary, a position he had held on and off since 1853. His son, Edward Hyde Villiers, who was just 24 years old, became the 5th Earl of Clarendon.

The 1867 churchyard extension had the Tantara Gatehouse at its southern end with the well-worn path, presumably the remnant of an Abbey approach dating from antiquity, leading to the main gate and clapper gate into the fields. On the right is the sedilia rescued from the Abbey; haystacks can be seen behind it. Gravestones or their absence date this photograph to between 1882 and 1886 *(HS)*

Despite the townsfolk being surrounded by farmland, much of which was owned by Clarendon, the central location made the Abbey Fields easily accessible to all and ideal to be used for other purposes, but of course dependent upon permission from Clarendon and whoever was renting the field in question for their primary use for grazing. The picturesque location with the Abbey ruins and St Nicholas Church as backdrops enhanced the attraction.

By being part of their daily lives and routines, the townsfolk became attached to the fields and think of them as a vital part of the town, perhaps in the way, but on a much larger scale, that a village green was seen in countless hamlets across the country.

In 1858, to mark the occasion of **Queen Victoria** passing through the town on the way to the railway station and Prince Albert's brief visit to the Castle, the Abbey Fields hosted a meal of meats and plum pudding for 2,000 townsfolk from mostly poor families; the population at the time was under 3,700. It was in the field rented by Kenilworth solicitor and County Coroner William Poole, but it has not been possible to trace which field this was.

In 1872 the newly re-formed **Kenilworth Cricket Club** held their first practises in the field rented by Queen & Castle licensee Joshua Blackwell, and matches were later played there; the summer of 1873 saw a North *v* South Kenilworth match.

Also in 1873, after the purchase of new equipment, the Kenilworth Volunteer **Fire Brigade** paraded through the town and spread out their apparatus for inspection in the field leased by Mr Fancott; this is thought to still be that on the southern side of the brook alongside Rosemary Hill. A demonstration of the brigade's skills followed. The following week other local brigades were invited to display in a similar fashion; as some visitors had steam powered engines, the Kenilworth brigade with its manual pump engine must have looked poorly equipped by comparison. Fire brigade drills became a common sight in the fields.

Another pastime enjoyed by many was ice skating on a field leased by farmer and miller Richard Robbins. The field in question was north-west of the central Iron Bridge and on the site of the former Priory pond, and was now known as the **Oxpen Meadow**; presumably there was a means of control to allow the field to flood or otherwise. Over the winter of 1878/79, he allowed his field to be flooded and frozen and he charged 3d for a day's skating; he donated the takings to the soup kitchen that provided winter sustenance for Kenilworth's poorest people. Over 500 were recorded skating on one day in early 1879; the following winter was cold enough for skating to return on Boxing Day. The lease on the field later passed to Joseph Roberts, a High Street butcher who released cattle and/or sheep into the fields.

It is worth noting that with the exception of Richard Robbins, all those mentioned in the above paragraphs as renting an Abbey field were not farmers, again suggesting that pasturing horses was a likely common use of the fields.

Kenilworth's affairs were in the hands of the Vestry meetings, a collection of high ratepayers and Churchwardens. Their limitations became obvious when planning a sewer system in the late 1870s and it was thus decided to apply for Kenilworth to form a Local Board of Health (referred to from here-on as the Local Board) which would have greater independent powers when, for example, it came to borrowing money for projects. The official order was dated 22nd August 1877, and for the first time those taking responsibility for Kenilworth's affairs had to be elected.

Following nationwide interests in the exploits of Captain Webb, Kenilworth was no different to other places in wishing to promote the art of **swimming**, particularly for young boys; bathing in cold water was believed to be a cure-all medical treatment but the benefits of swimming as an exercise and sport were beginning to be appreciated for the first time. A committee was appointed to look into the provision of a suitable spot along the Finham Brook (the only water source other than wells and springs) for a proper and safe bathing place but the scheme quickly foundered due to the 5th Earl of Clarendon, now in his early 30s, refusing to even enter discussions about such use of his land anywhere along the local waterways. The brook, it should be mentioned, was much deeper than it generally is today, and powered the mill at Mill End. A place near the bridge at Chesford was quickly established as a popular place for a swim.

Despite Clarendon's obstinacy, in 1879 the matter was discussed at length at meetings of the new Local Board and it was suggested that part of the brook in the Abbey Fields could be simply cordoned off for the use of boys who already put the brook to that use in any case: *'The scenes in the Abbey Fields are not particularly decent... it is very shocking to see boys enjoying themselves in the water'*. There was however a problem with the water depth as it *'barely reaches the pockets of your breeches'*. Bathing here would seem to have been a long-standing pastime as William Holmes reminisced that as a small boy (he was born in the 1830s) he was once chased to his New Street home from the Abbey Fields *'in my original birthday suit.'*

The drowning near the Common in the summer of 1880 of 13-year-old William Swain, son of well-known Kenilworth builder John Swain of School Lane, resurrected the discussions of a safe bathing place and a good sum in donations was quickly raised. With Clarendon not interested in providing a site within the Abbey Fields, three places alongside the brook at School Lane, Mill End and opposite the Common were suggested, but at this time the provision of a water works to supply fresh water to all parts of the town was under way; its successful completion would mean that in theory a bathing place could be created virtually anywhere in the town and so the subject fell from discussion. Edward Swain, brother of the earlier drowning victim, drowned in July 1884 whilst fishing at a popular spot in the Abbey Fields. He was prone to fits and it was believed he simply fell in.

The probable start of what became a popular movement was a letter written to the Clerk of the Local Board by Joseph Stone Burbery in December 1880: *'May I ask if you will kindly consent to request the attention of the Local Board to the want of a* **public recreation** *or play ground for the young working-men of Kenilworth. I would suggest that the best and most effectual way of meeting this need would be to acquire a field in as central a location as possible'*, a clear inference to the Abbey Fields and its occasional sporting use. As an alternative he suggested the plateau on the Common which he thought was suitable for *'games of football, hockey etc, though somewhat small for cricket'*. The Board agreed that such a site was desirable but they were simply too committed to other projects, notably the building of the sewer system and provision of fresh water (the latter eventually provided by a private company).

In 1881, the 'embanked sewer across the meadow leading to Castle Grove (was) abandoned' and a new one planned and built. This began at a junction in the Abbey Meadow with the sewer from Castle Green, then crossed the brook near the Iron Bridge and went in a straight line to the Borrowell Lane bridge where it crossed the brook again and then to the houses at the back of Castle Grove. Excavation work for the new sewer in the Abbey Fields in November revealed worked stone with carved flowers, found at a depth of 3ft in an unrecorded location. Other relics found included unworked stone and glazed pottery. Beyond the 6ft depth of the works was found *'a subterranean passage, supposedly to Warwick'*. Part of the stonework collapsed on a Kenilworth labourer called Heath, injuring his legs.

By the end of 1881 there were concerns that within 18 months the St Nicholas **graveyard** would be full once more and with the Local Board having no money to spend on providing a cemetery, the problem would soon become critical; *'There is a necessity for immediate action'*. A committee was formed and, despite the now 35-year-old 5th Earl of Clarendon maintaining his father's position in not allowing a further extension of the churchyard, he was approached in April 1882 about selling only about 2 acres; it had the inevitable outcome.

Passing through Parliament at the time was the Settled Lands Act (becoming law on 1st January 1883) and this may have had a bearing on Clarendon's stance as in later 1882, it isn't certain when, he made it known that he was putting the entire Abbey Fields estate up for sale as building land; simple straight-line extensions of Southbank Road, Abbey End and School Lane would no doubt have provided a basis of a road system across the fields. The town was in a process of development; the railway line was being doubled and extended and a new station provided, the sewers were nearly complete, a company was intending to provide the town with fresh water, and a new road (Priory Road) was being planned that would give direct access to the proposed Abbey Fields building area from the railway station. Clarendon was selling 78 acres of the fields which included 19 cottages (those at Little Virginia, today's 81-85 High Street, and two others), a smithy (attached to number 81), and Sion House in High Street. It was feared that if bought by a private speculator, subsequent development *'would spoil Kenilworth possibly by the running up of factories and small houses'*. However, the Local Board realised that if they bought the estate they could cure their immediate need to extend the churchyard as much as they wished, then create the oft called-for permanent recreational and pleasure grounds for organised cricket and other sports, and it was already the preferred site to create a swimming baths. They would also preserve the fields for use for major events. By careful consideration they could also manage any possible building development by controlling the future sale of plots within the fields.

Burials were however the most pressing problem. At the first subsequent Local Board meeting, a Cemetery Committee was formed, comprising Richard Robbins, Frederick Slade, Dr Daniel Wynter, William Evans, George Turner, Joseph Holland Burbery and Edward Mander, to investigate 'the extension of the churchyard or formation of a cemetery'. They were obviously keeping their options open but at the same meeting the committee 'unanimously resolved that Mr Robbins be authorised to inform Mr Humbert that the Kenilworth Local Board are prepared to purchase the estate, that is to say the lands and cottages at Kenilworth shown on the plan sent by Clarendon's agent Mr Humbert, and also Sion House, at £16,000 subject to approval of the Local Government Board and to their consent being obtained to the borrowing of the money'; an additional £450 was to be paid for the value of the timber on the estate. It is not known if this was Clarendon's asking price or simply what the Local Board had decided to offer, but it was given full Board authorisation on 18th January 1883, and on 10th February the Board received a letter of acceptance from Clarendon. An Abbey Fields Estate Purchase Committee was formed comprising J H Burbery, Evans, Robbins and Luke Heynes and on 28th February the purchase of the entire estate was approved by the Board; the voting was unanimous, save for the dissenting voice of Dr Daniel Wynter. (As an indication of the proposed investment, £16,000 then is the equivalent today of *£1,766,000*.)

The offer had been accepted by Clarendon on the condition of the Board being able to raise the money by the coming 29th September, but here was a problem; the rateable value of the town, £20,000, and the existing loans of £8,000 (largely used for the building of the sewer system and new Council offices) meant that by law only £12,000 of the required £16,450 could be borrowed by the Board. The solution was to raise the difference once the fields were theirs by first selling 2 acres for £400 to the Churchwardens to extend the churchyard, and then by selling a few building plots fronting the roads around the perimeter of the fields. The borrowing of £12,000 had to be authorised by the Local Government Board, and to this end an inquiry was set for 9th March at the Institute in Bridge Street. Placards were placed around the town telling of the Board's intentions.

Dissenting Board member Dr Wynter was appalled that the Board could commit the town to borrowing such a large amount of money, and leaving no possibility of raising loans for further projects, without consulting the ratepayers and he called a meeting (held at The King's Arms Assembly Rooms on Monday 5th March, just four days before the inquiry) to gauge the views of the public. Those present included Kenilworth notables John Bagshaw, Thomas Hawley, Walter Lockhart, Thomas Birch, Edward H Mander and John Judd. The concerns Wynter put to the meeting were: that pleasure grounds were not in any way necessary as the fields surrounding the town could be used for such purposes, that adding the financial burden of the full cost would be £6,000 more than the town's rateable value and that was *'undesirable'*, the building scheme was *'speculative'* and was thus outside the province of the Board which was not there to speculate with the town's money, and that it would be *'unfair to the rural owners and occupiers in the rated area'*. There was support at the meeting for the purchase too, particularly as it would facilitate the much needed extension of the churchyard, of which many of those present doubtless expected one day to be a resident, but when put to the vote there was a *'considerable majority'* opposed to purchasing the fields. A committee was formed including Dr Wynter, Thomas Hawley, John Judd, Walter Lockhart, and John Bagshaw.

At the Public Inquiry at the Bridge Street Institute four days later on Friday 9th March 1883, Board member William Evans, a retired solicitor who had been appointed to be responsible for all legal aspects of the proposed purchase, spoke at length and stressed the great need to extend the churchyard and that the only course was to buy the entire estate as it was for sale in one lot; this in turn would provide a public park. Board Chairman Frederick Slade tried to convince the inquiry that the decision to buy the fields was unanimous, which brought laughter from those present as he had ignored Dr Wynter and the show of support he had received from the public. Slade was however correct when he continued, *'unless the land is acquired now, there would be no probability of getting it hereafter'* as it was already attracting others in the market; auctioneer James Whittindale confirmed that he was in contact with a party wishing to buy the estate who had backed off once the Kenilworth Board showed interest; Whittindale thought there would be no difficulty in selling excess plots, particularly if there could be a delay until the new railway facilities then under construction were complete. The inquiry found in favour of purchasing the estate and sanctioned the maximum permissible loan of £12,000, confirmed by a letter received on 9th May, leaving £4,450 to be raised by the selling of plots. Now confident that St Nicholas churchyard would be extended, that month improvements to it were planned by the planting of lime trees in the central walkway from the west door, and laburnums nearby; flower beds were also in the scheme.

Unfortunately, it had been overlooked that the intention to raise the £4,450 shortfall by the sale of perimeter plots was illegal; the Public Health Act of 1875 required that any sale of plots could only be used to pay off the loan and not directly towards the purchase. Once realised, this resulted in a pause in the proceedings.

In August 1883, engineer Frederick Slade resigned from the Local Board as he was leaving town; William Evans turned down the Board's motion for him to take Slade's place as Chairman and so the position went to agriculturist Samuel Forrest who farmed at The Chase but lived at Fern Bank, Ladies Hill. There was soon to be another resignation; the Town Clerk William Savage Poole, a former solicitor who had occupied the position since the Board's formation in 1877, handed in his notice on 21st November. He worked until his replacement, 31-year-old solicitor George A H Addison from Coventry, took office on 21st December.

William Evans was born in Coventry in 1825; his father was a silk and ribbon merchant and one-time MP for Coventry. William was educated at Wakefield Grammar School and afterwards articled to Wagstaff & March, Solicitors, Warrington. He later returned to Coventry where he practised as a solicitor until 1856 when he became a partner in the firm Ingleby, Wragge and then Evans. The firm had a high reputation being legal advisers to the Birmingham Canal Company, Lloyd's Bank, Birmingham Dudley & District Bank, and the South Staffordshire Waterworks Company. He also became the auditor and Parliamentary agent for the London & North Western Railway at which he particularly excelled. He was also President of the Birmingham Law Society. When aged 38 in 1863, he married 21-year-old Sarah, the daughter of Mr Bagnall of Cheltenham; their known children were Percy (born 1865), Beatrice (1867), and Gertrude (1874). He retired in 1882 and came to live at The Spring in Kenilworth arriving in late 1881, moving from 45 Augustus Road in Edgbaston (the house still survives, assuming there has been no renumbering). He then diverted his energies for the good of his new hometown and was elected to the Board in early 1882. He was appointed a JP in 1883.

In 1870, William Evans' sister Frances married William Thompson Pears who was also a solicitor; she died in 1884 and soon after, Pears moved to Kenilworth Hall; his brother-in-law living at The Spring being a likely influence on his decision.

With the Board uncertain as to how to progress with the Abbey Fields estate purchase and the original agreement date passed, on 12th December 1883 Clarendon agreed to the sale being deferred until 25th March 1884 on the understanding that £6,450 of the purchase money was paid on or about 26th December. It was unanimously agreed to and, after a delay, on 13th February 1884 the Board borrowed £6,450 at the rate of four per cent from the Leamington & Warwickshire Bank (about to move to a splendid new building in High Street) and duly paid the same to Clarendon; he signed for it on behalf of his trustees on 5th March, but no land had yet changed hands.

With the 25th March deadline approaching, the *Kenilworth Advertiser* editorial for 15th March 1884 takes up the story but first recounted the events so far. The reasons for the acquisition were threefold; the enlargement of the churchyard, the *'preservation of the recreation ground'*, and the third reason, a *'corollary'*, the enlargement of the housing accommodation. The total purchase money was to be £16,450 and of the authorised £12,000 in loans, £6,450 had been paid to Clarendon on 5th March, and the Board were to borrow another £5,000 leaving a balance of £5,000 intended to be raised by selling building plots; this however was now known not to be possible. The area of the fields the Board had earmarked for selling was that deemed the most attractive for building with frontages on Bridge Street, Rosemary Hill and Abbey Hill (the newly built Priory Road would provide a direct route to the improved railway accommodation) and it had been thought that there would be no difficulty in realising £5,000 from a sale. However, this was thought of as the most picturesque area as it provided views across to St Nicholas Church and the Castle; *'the erection of buildings* (in that area) *would spoil the view for which this part of Kenilworth has long been noted, and depreciate the picturesque scenery'*. And so in a move as individuals rather than Board members, several *'members of the Local Board with a most praiseworthy desire to preserve the beauties of the town, resolved to stay the hand of the speculative builder and by appealing to the land-owners and the general public, to obtain such a sum of money as shall for ever preserve in its integrity this charming situation'*. In short, they side-stepped their decision as a Board to potentially sell to developers, and themselves arranged to preserve that part of the fields; it also of course would reduce the amount of cash the Board would have to raise. The area (Area B, see map, page 16) was of 13 acres 1 rood 4 perches (a rood is ¼ acre, a perch 1/160th acre).

An appeal fund was set up at the Leamington Priors Bank in the name of 'Mr Samuel Forrest and Mr William Evans *re* the Abbey Fields Estate'. Money was rapidly raised and the week following the newspaper editorial, a list of donations was published: Mr Badley*, Mrs Dawes*, Henry Street* and George Turner* each gave £500; Mrs Porter* £200; Mr Brittain*, George Church*, Edward Draper*, Thomas Emery*, Mrs Morris*, William Evans and Edward Smith* £100 each; J C Carter, Joseph H Burbery, Samuel Forrest, Richard Robbins and Charles Trepplin £50 each, and lastly there was a £20 donation from the Reverend Alfred Binnie giving the Preservationists a total of £3,170 of the required £3,500. This calculates at £269 an acre. (Those marked * owned property fronting the land.)

This action seems to have instigated, or been part of, a rethink by the Board, or more accurately by William Evans; either way there was clear collusion in what followed. As a solicitor for railway and canal companies, William Evans had years of experience in dealing with land matters and found a solution to all the problems. With the delayed deadline passed, and almost three weeks after the Preservationists fund for the Abbey Hill area had been set up, he put forward a new proposal, seconded by Henry Street, at the Board meeting of 2nd April 1884 that the existing contract with Clarendon should be cancelled and in its place the Board should buy just the inner low-lying portion of 40 acres 2 roods 18 perches for £6,000 (Area A on the plan), at just £150 per acre; much of this is the Finham Brook flood plain with patches of a marshy consistency. Added to the privately preserved Abbey Hill - Bridge Street land, 53 or so acres of the fields would be saved and retain the two main footpaths across them from Abbey End. Careful calculations ensured that the annual repayments for the £6,000 loan could be met by the income generated from continuing to rent out the fields for grazing; the Board would thus purchase over half the fields, and could by arrangement have control of a further 13 acres, effectively without spending a single penny. This also negated the points of opposition raised by Wynter that had received popular support; the occupiers would stay, there would be no financial burden to the town, and there would be no speculating by the Board with the selling of building plots. The proposal was carried unanimously. The voters who took the decision to save the central area of the fields for the town in this way were Samuel Forrest, Joseph Burbery, George Turner, Henry Street, William Clarke, William Evans, Edward Mander, John Bagshaw, Luke Heynes, and Richard Robbins. The money was to be borrowed from the Prudential Assurance Company over 60 years. What became of the £6,450 already paid to Clarendon is uncertain, presumably it was cancelled along with the original contract; this is one of a number of unresolved financial anomalies associated with the estate. Within weeks, William Evans, the driving force behind the scheme, was voted to the Chair of the Board, and this time he accepted

These arrangements still left about 25 acres around the boundary of the estate available for development. This remaining land was split into four areas (Areas C, D, E, & F; see map, page 16) and Sion House, and in a move perhaps inspired by those who were saving the Abbey Hill area, another group of Board members, William Evans, Samuel Forrest, Luke Heynes and Joseph Burbery (probably the current members of the Abbey Fields Purchase Committee), took responsibility for privately purchasing these remaining areas and thus relieving the Board of potential further outlay. The group intended to retrieve their costs by later selling Sion House and as many building plots as necessary in three areas C, D & E around the extremities, and to convey *'any residue'*, presumably land or cash, to the Board. The fourth area, F, was earmarked for sale as the churchyard extension and included a narrow strip to High Street ensuring access and preserving the 15ft wide roadway insisted upon by Clarendon in 1867. There was a strict understanding that the syndicate of four were to make no profit from their privileged position of involvement in the purchase and all declared their intentions were to benefit the town. The price agreed for these areas was £6,200; this calculates at £248 an acre, but it will have perhaps more like £225 an acre for the fields as the purchase price included Sion House with a value of about £750. This process became simultaneous with the moves to purchase the central 40 acres.

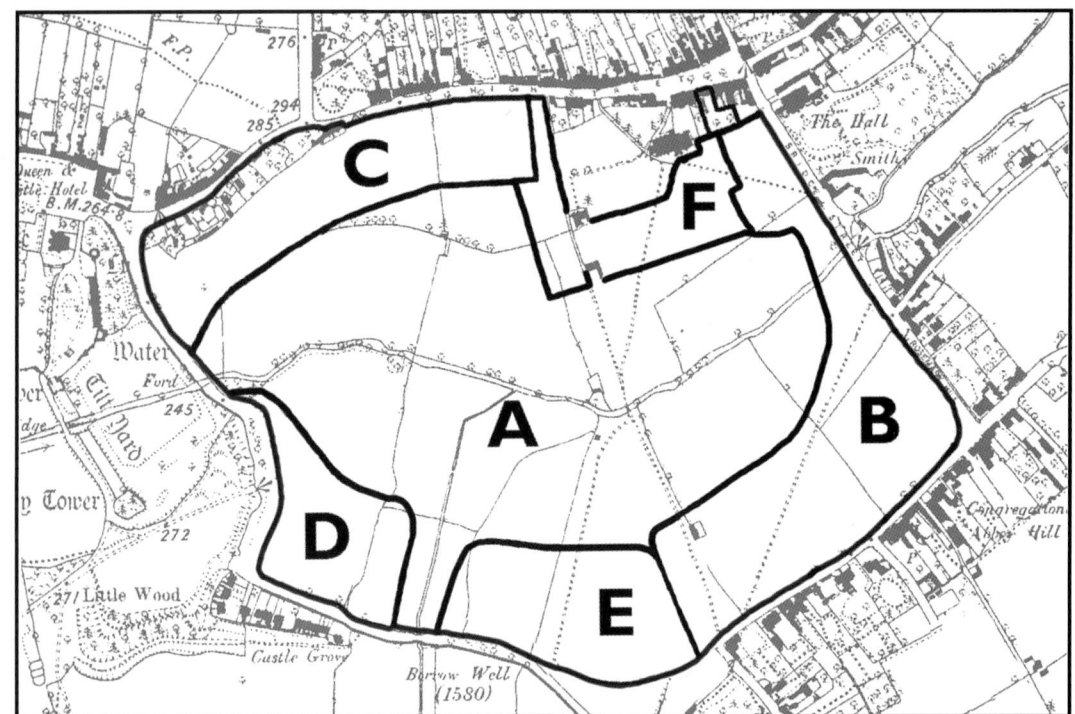

The different areas of the Abbey Fields Estate, and Sion House, as split into individual plots for sale by Clarendon; the reference letters are the author's as used in the text. Why some field areas were such convoluted shapes is unestablished. The map is from the 1886 First Edition Ordnance Survey, with some alterations to resemble 1884

It appears that the same bank account was used by this Syndicate as was used by the Preservationists when purchasing the Abbey Hill area:

> That the said sum of £6,200 paid by the parties thereto as the purchase money of the said hereditaments together with other monies had with the occurrence of the other persons thereto been borrowed by the said William Evans and Samuel Forrest from the Leamington Priors & Warwickshire Banking Co and debited to an account opened by them with that company under the title Mr Sam Forrest and Mr William Evans re- the Abbey Fields estate and other monies might from time to time be borrowed relative to that estate from the said banking Co and charged to that account.

On 10th May 1884, the Board received the £6,000 loan money for the cost of Area A from the Prudential Assurance Co and a special meeting was arranged just for the cheque signing; interestingly, the only four members of the Board that were present were the four members of the Syndicate. Two days later on 12th May the fields were conveyed from Clarendon and his father's trustees to the three factions. The purchase of the main central area was completed by new Town Clerk George Addison, the Abbey Hill - Bridge Street area was bought in the names of two Board members 'partly (in the names of) Street and Turner, and partly by persons interested in the messuages opposite the said pieces of land', and the rest of the fields in the names of the four Board members who belonged to the Syndicate, Joseph Burbery, William Evans, Samuel Forrest and Luke Heynes. The cost to the Board was the £6,000 loan, and to individuals £9,700, a final total of £15,700 for Clarendon (*£1,733,000*).

Despite the sale of the entire estate, it was just over half, the central 40 acres, that were owned by the Local Board. That conveyance included a covenant to ensure its future as recreational land:

> ... the said pieces or parcels of land and premises hereinbefore expressed to be hereby conveyed shall forever hereafter be solely used as public walks or pleasure grounds under the control of the said Board and that the said pieces or parcels of land shall not nor shall any part thereof at any time hereafter be sold leased or otherwise disposed of for any other purpose inconsistent with the same being solely used as aforesaid.

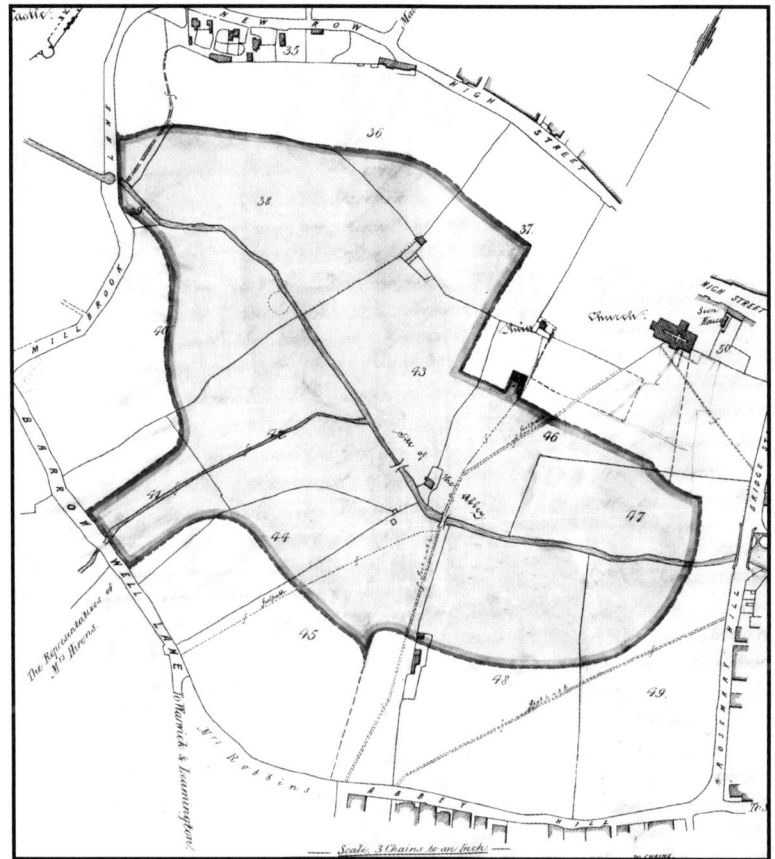

The central 40 acres of land purchased by the Local Board. The areas bought by Preservationists (alongside Abbey Hill and Rosemary Hill) and the Syndicate (around the churchyard, alongside High Street and New Row, by Millbrook Lane and Mr Robbins land) can be discerned

(WDC 129)

It is worth noting that it is the seller that inserts any Covenants for the land; Clarendon at one time wishing to sell the land to be built upon was now ensuring that it never would be and that the Board could not re-sell to make a profit on the cheap price per acre. The conveyance also specifically mentioned the inclusion of the ruins and thus the ownership of the Abbey and its land separated from the Castle for the first time in over 300 years. Appearing on the surviving conveyance documents from the 5th Earl of Clarendon are the Right Honourable Frederick Arthur Stanley and the Right Honourable Edward Earl of Lathom who were the executors of the 4th Earl of Clarendon's estate. Stanley was the 16th Earl of Derby, an MP, Governor of Canada, and donator of the Stanley Cup; Lathom was a Conservative MP who had served in every Conservative administration since 1866. Each was married to one of the 5th Earl's elder sisters; Stanley to Lady Constance Villiers, and Lathom to Lady Alice Villiers. As was the convention of the time, even Ladies were not trusted in such family matters but their husbands were.

Just four weeks later, on Monday 9th June 1884, the Syndicate began the process to reduce its debt at an auction held by James Whittindale at The King's Arms. Lot 1 was Sion House and its gardens. Nearby, about half of Area C was split into 12 building plots (lots 2-13), including the three cottages and a smithy within the plots but avoiding Little Virginia and the land behind which were not included in this auction. The plot boundary lines passed through the three cottages at random; they were obviously deemed expendable. The High Street plots were described as *'Suitable for first class villa residencies, having an elevated position, the most desirable building sites offered to the public anywhere in the Midlands'*, and had frontages of between 80 and 120ft, and areas from 2,000 to 3,000 sq yds.

The roadside part of Area D was split into five lots (Plots 14-18) in Millbrook Lane each with a frontage of 40ft and an area of about 450 sq yds, and ten lots (Plots 19-28) in Borrowell Lane, each with a frontage of 22ft 6ins and an area of about 312 sq yds *'suitable for small villa residencies'*. The sale advertisement commented, *'Most of these plots command views of the Public park, the Abbey Church, Fields and Castle'*.

At the auction, Lot 1 Sion House was bought by George Church for £750, and he also bought Plots 19-28 (a total of 3,120 sq yds at 2s 6d a yd - £390); Mr Robbins bought Plots 17 (437 sq yds at 3s a yd - £65 11s) and 18 (466 sq yds at 3s 5d a yd - £79 12s 2d). The Syndicate had recouped £1,385 3s 2d of its £6,200 liability. Plots 2-13 alongside High Street and 14-16 at Millbrook Lane were withdrawn, more of which later.

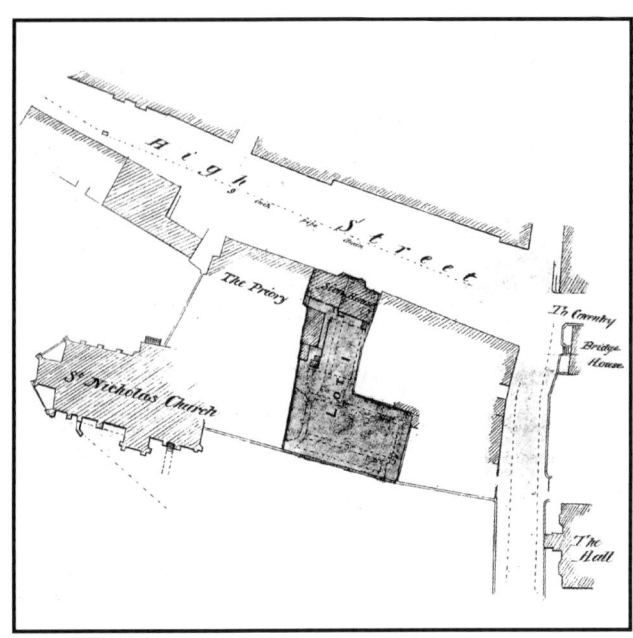

Lot 1, Sion House *(WCRO, CR 1525/94/2)*

Area E, of just under 6 acres and in the possession of the Syndicate of Burbery, Evans, Forrest and Heynes, only partially had a road frontage and so was omitted from the 9th June building plots auction, but in early August 1884, it was suggested that a new road should be cut from the right-angled Abbey Hill - Abbey End junction to a point near the bridge carrying Borrowell Lane over the Luzley Brook. The course of the road was across part of Area E and would have several advantages; it would replace a trackway described as *'one of the ugliest, dirtiest and most dangerous bye-paths that could be imagined'*, provide a continuous carriage drive around the perimeter of the fields and perhaps more importantly open up the plot for building. Construction was to be paid for by the Syndicate but work carried out by the Local Board workmen. The proposed name, Abbey Hill Road, was unsurprising.

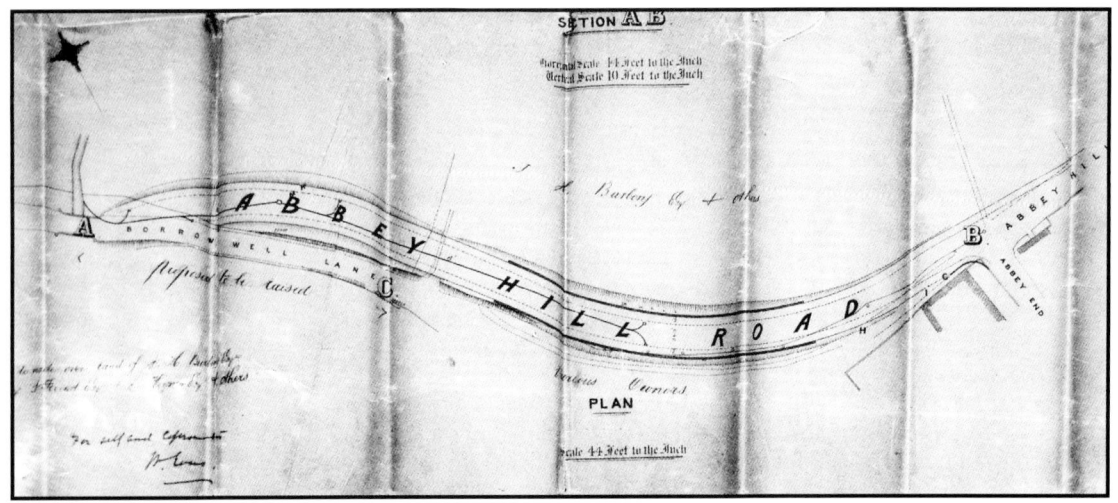

The fragile surviving plans for Abbey Hill Road built by the Syndicate on part of the Abbey Fields. The Syndicate's land, Area E, is described as being that of 'J H Burbery and others' *(WCRO, CR 2487/1/1/28)*

A couple of weeks after the announcement of the planned new road, on 27th August 1884 Area E was put up for auction at The King's Arms, split into sizeable building plots of between 3030 sq yds and 5520 sq yds. The land was described as providing an elevated position overlooking the Castle, church, and Abbey ruins, and that the plots *'afford exceptional sites for excellent residences of superior quality, with frontages to a proposed handsome new road'*. The sub-soil was of sand and gravel. No plots were sold but despite this, the building of the road went ahead; once built it would of course create interest in the building land. A great deal of earthworks was required for the road; to ease the gradient, part of Borrowell Lane needed to be raised for the junction and both a cutting and embankment built for the road itself, creating features in the fields. Also, so the road could have a decent width at its entrance, Abbey Hill itself needed to be widened and realigned, causing 34 perches of land to be taken from Area B of the fields (it is not known if any compensation was paid); the plans (and later maps) show the new pavement on the Abbey Fields side of the new road was extended along Abbey Hill only as far as the end of the diagonal footpath down to Bridge Street. The work uncovered *'rounded stones, suggestive of huge stone bullets'* thought to be relics of the great siege.

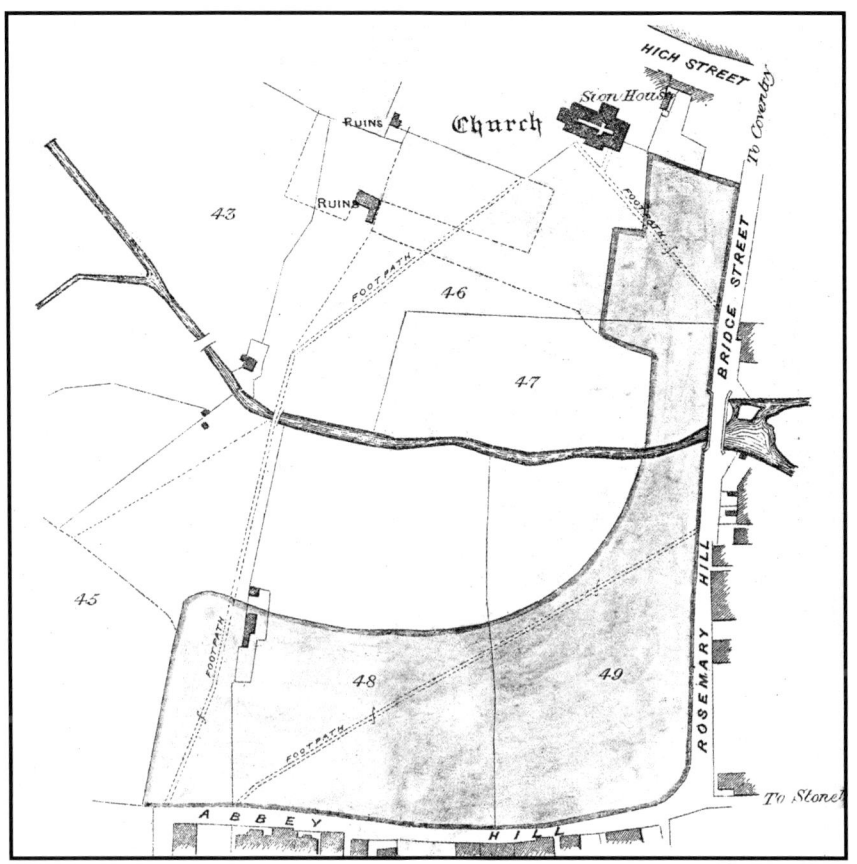

Area B, the 13 acres of the fields preserved by public donations

(WCRO, CR 1901)

Some six months after its purchase by donations from at least 18 inhabitants, the preserved 13 or so acres alongside Abbey Hill to Bridge Street were re-conveyed on the 28th November 1884 to William Evans and Joseph Roberts (a butcher) in their capacity as Churchwardens to be Trustees for public grounds, but the land to be managed by the Local Board in conjunction with the central area. Quite why it was not conveyed to the Board is undiscovered, but the 6 months since the purchase from Clarendon had allowed time for careful consideration by the many donation contributors; they had paid the highest price per acre of any part of the estate and wished to protect their investment. The Conveyance was carefully worded; the central area had just one proviso, to be used forever as 'pleasure grounds', but the Preservationists inserted a number of restrictions to protect the land, and their view across it:

> Whereas it would be of great benefit to the inhabitants of Kenilworth that the public grounds dedicated to their use should be of greater extent than the lands so vested in the Board... that the said pieces of land hereinafter described and intended to be conveyed... should forever remain unbuilt upon... for the purposes of the Recreation Grounds Act 1859. The management and direction of the said pieces of land... shall remain in the Kenilworth Local Board to the intent that the same be managed in connection with the public grounds so vested in the said Board. And it is hereby declared that no building or erection shall at any time hereafter be built or erected upon any part of the premises... except such boundary walls or fences as may be considered desirable for separating the said premises from adjoining roads, and except also such gates and gatehouses as may be considered desirable for proving convenient access thereto, the said premises shall for ever remain as open public grounds for the purposes of the said act.
>
> If at any time or times hereafter the said Board shall consider it desirable to widen the public roads, or any of the public roads adjoining the said pieces of land, the Trustees hereof for the time being shall permit the said Board to add to the said public roads, or any of them, and dedicate to the public as roads such portions of the said pieces of land as the said Board shall consider necessary for bringing such road or roads to a convenient width.

The opening line of the referred to Recreation Grounds Act of 1859, states 'Any lands may be lawfully conveyed to trustees, to be held by them as open public grounds for the resort and recreation of adults, and as playgrounds for children and youth, or either of such purposes, and for any estate, and subject to any reservation, restrictions, and conditions which the donor or grantor may think fit.'

The total area now under the management, but not all in ownership, of the Board was 53a 3r 22p.

The Board could now negotiate rents for the fields under its command, and from 10th December 1884, agreements were made as in the following table; how this differs from the agreements under Clarendon is unknown, as is any arrangement made with the Syndicate or Preservationists. The fields would produce an annual rent of about £150. The way in which the 53 acres of the fields, well defined by hedges and fences, were broken by the delineation of the areas bought by the separate factions, led to an involved listing; reference to the conveyance plan on page 17 reveals the complications. The agreements were reviewed annually, and some fields regularly changed hands.

Field	Tenant	Area			Rent
Part of 36	Mary Draper	1 acre	3 rood	12 perch	
Part of 38	" "	5	2	28	£20 12s 6d
Part of 37	Richard Robbins	1	2	15	
Part of 42	" "	5	0	29	
Part of 43	" "	4	2	25	
Part of 44	" "	1	3	1	£19 15s 7d
Part of 39	Trepplin	0	0	20	
Part of 40	"	3	0	14	
Part of 41	"	1	2	36	£8 12s 10d
Part of 45	Davis	3	0	34	
Part of 48	"	3	1	9	£23 6s 8d
Part 45 & 48	Davis	6	0	18	£21 17s 7d
Part of 46	Roberts	1	1	21	
Part of 47	"	3	0	36	£18 7s 4d
Part 46 & 47	Roberts	2	0	39	£8 18s 3d
Part 49	Fancott	2	1	4	£9 9s 8d
"	"	4	3	27	£20 10s 4d
Totals:		52a	0r	48p	£151 10s 9d

Almost a year later, in October 1885, Mr Robbins leased North Abbey Field, the Oxpen and Whittons meadows, and Calves Close. The owners were given as the Local Board but also 'in part by Evans, Burbery and others'; this suggests that at this time some of the Syndicate's land was being used to raise rents for the Local Board coffers, confirmed by the increase in rent received to £172.

As mentioned, the Area C Plots 2-13 along High Street were withdrawn from the June 1884 sale but all changed hands certainly by, but probably on, 24th December 1884; with that date there are references in later documents to the Syndicate 'on the one part' and 'the several persons whose names were thereunto subscribed and whose seals were thereunto affixed in the schedule thereunto of the other part'. The twelve plots had restrictions on constructions: 'Nor shall any building be erected on any of the same lots extending to the southerly side of the building line E-F. No buildings shall be erected on any of the plots except dwelling houses with out-buildings, nor shall any trade, business or manufacture or any noxious or dangerous or offensive process be carried out'. Not more than one dwelling house or a pair of semi-detached houses could be erected on any one plot; the only exception was for an entrance lodge.

The surviving documents for December 1884 reveal High Street Plots 2 & 3 were recorded in the name of William Evans, 4 & 5 and 9-13 in George Marshall Turner's, 6 in Edward Herbert Draper's and 7 & 8 in his mother's, Mary Draper; Mary and her husband Charles had moved in to High Street's Clinton House by 1854 but Charles died in 1879 and their son Edward moved away, living in London at this time. The three plots mother and son had bought were those directly opposite Clinton House and thus they preserved the view from it across the fields by ensuring no houses would be built. Mary was also renting the fields 36 & 38 beyond those plots, extending her command of her outlook. A Covenant dated 24th December 1884 states each owner's responsibility for fencing his land from his neighbours; an additional Covenant stated the two separate Draper owners did not need to fence their common boundary.

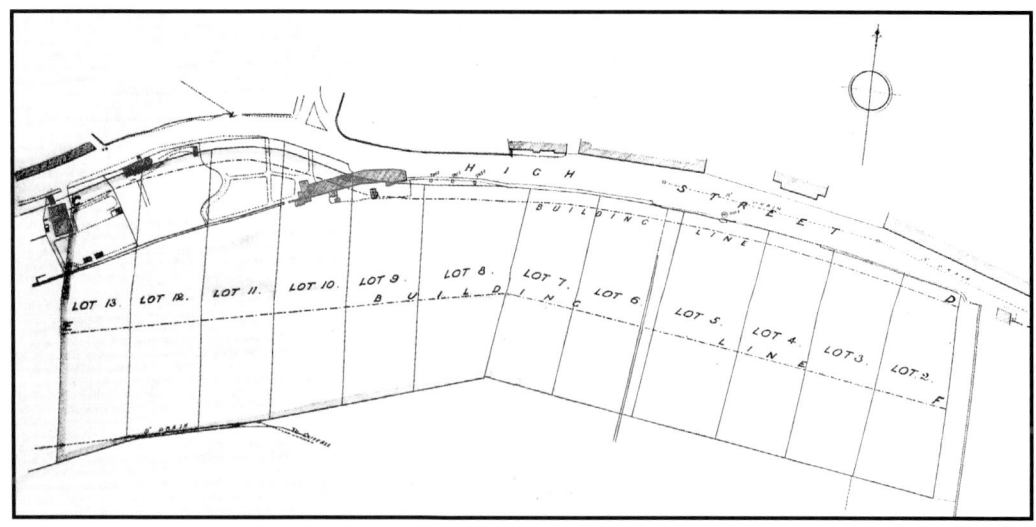

The plots on part of Area C and also showing the expendable 81-85 High Street and the smithy (on Plots 9 & 10) with the probable Abbey land's boundary wall emanating either side. Two building lines, C-D & E-F, within which any dwellings had to be contained, run across the plots *(WCRO, CR 1525/94/3)*

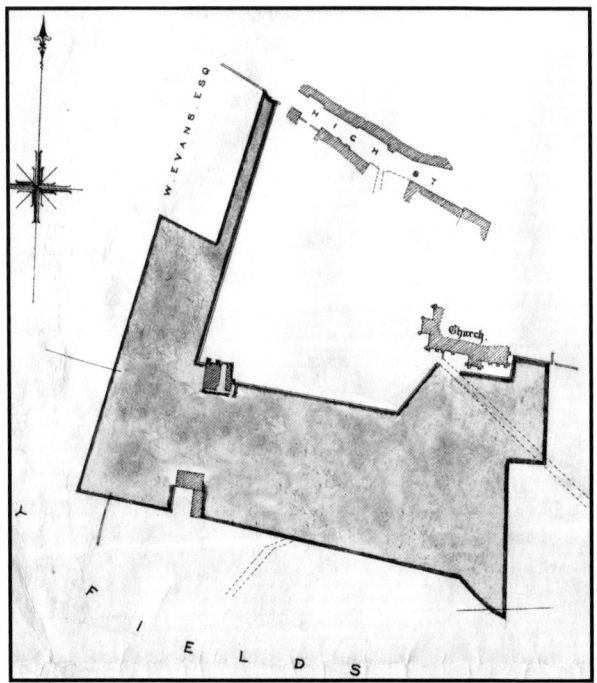

The extension of the **churchyard**, the stimulus for the purchase of the fields, could now proceed. The Syndicate had purchased an irregular shaped 5 acre plot, Area F, around the churchyard specifically for the purpose; it contained virtually all the rest of the Abbey ruins and much of the area expected to cover the cloisters. But there had been an oversight; it was discovered that by law the churchyard could only be extended by another 2 acres (as had in any case, been originally suggested in 1882).

With several different ways submitted as to how best to use 2 acres of the plot, the preferred scheme extended the existing yard *'South West by East'* and it was proposed to build a *'dwarf wall with iron pallisadings'* around the new area so the entire churchyard, and the church, would be enclosed for the first time.

The 5 acre Area F around the churchyard from which 2 acres were taken

(Plan reconstructed from WDC 131)

This was agreed but resulted in the Abbey remains having three owners; the churchyard included the nave, central tower, north transept and much of the cloisters, and the Abbey Fields (partly in land owned by the Syndicate, and partly by the Local Board) containing the choir, high alter, south transept, Chapter House and outbuildings, although the precise complete layout was at this time unknown.

The cost of purchasing the land from the Syndicate was £300 with a further £300 required for the alterations; this was to be raised by a voluntary rate of 4d and a subscription list was also opened with John Judd £10, Edward Mander, Joseph Roberts and Mr Barton, £5 each, contributing to the £60 raised at a meeting to discuss the proposals in December 1884. The extension left about 3 acres between the yard and Board-bought portion of the fields in the hands of the Syndicate that was quite unsuitable for sale as building plots.

By February 1885, the 2 acres had been acquired and work started. Initially there had been a favourable response to the voluntary rate, but there were concerns that too much cost had been incurred by the *'elaborateness'* of the wall and the unsightly *'zig-zag'* of the path, and this was eventually blamed for the ultimate shortfall in the voluntary rate collection, and it would be several years until the wall was completed. The zig-zag was partly caused by the lower part of the path following that which already existed and a dog-leg being required to take it on to the new alignment around the extension; closer to the church was a large mound covering Abbey ruins which caused another bend in the path (see map, page 24). There were compliments for the scheme too and it was said that by comparison the earlier western 1867 extension looked *'like a cattle pound'*.

In the top left corner, the Abbey Hotel is under construction, dating this photograph to 1885-86, the early days of the park at the time the churchyard was being extended; the foreground belongs to the Syndicate. On the southern slope, Field 49 appears to be pasture, and Field 48 to have been harvested, in all probability for hay *(WCRO, PH 77/35)*

The new churchyard extension was consecrated on 28th May 1885. On the day of the ceremony, the antics of a group of 9 to 15 years old boys, swimming alongside the Iron Bridge caused concerns: *'In addition to the indecency of youths bathing at a point where there are persons passing at all times, the language of the bathers was filthy in the extreme'*. There were hopes that *'steps will be taken to prevent a repetition of this reprehensible practise of bathing at midday in such a public place'*. This again started the debate about the provision of public baths, and continual incidents in the Abbey Fields prompted claims that they were required out of common decency: *'Let our* (Board) *members walk by the Iron Bridge any afternoon or evening with their lady friends and the matter will be promptly dealt with'*, but another incident suggests that perhaps the *'lady friends'* would not have be so offended as predicted; *'The young men having divested themselves of such garments as Adam scorned, were enjoying unadorned the freedom of nature, when some horrid frolicsome fellow seized upon their garments and was making off with them. They rushed from their river to give chase to their would be robber, when a lady stood face to face without the semblance of a blush, gazing upon their watery and dripping forms, thoroughly enjoying these poor fellows embarrassment.'*

After the Board meeting on 15th April 1885, Syndicate member Luke Heynes was found dead in one of the Board's offices; such was his responsible attitude to his duties, he had been the only member of the Board to attend all 15 meetings of his final year in office. Just a few weeks later, as work progressed on Abbey Hill Road, another member of the Syndicate, Samuel Forrest, died on 4th May 1885 aged just 36, and it was decided to rename the road in his honour. Forrest Road was completed in November 1885 at a cost to the Syndicate of £108 1s 3½d *(£12,730)*.

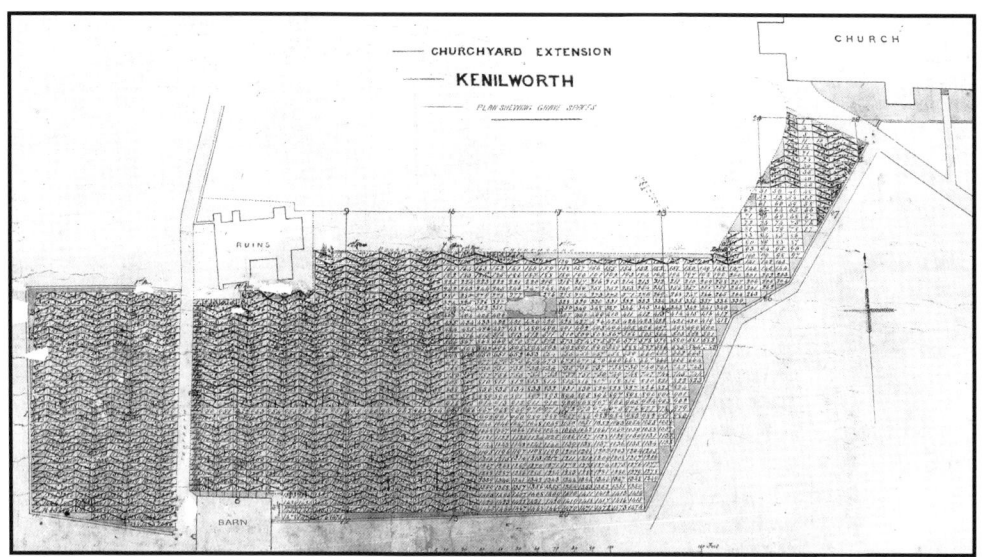

The 1885 Churchyard extension into the park with 1486 burial plots drawn in *(WCRO, DR 607/1)*

With two of the original four Syndicate members now dead, on 23rd May 1885 a new agreement was drawn up in the names of the two survivors, Evans and Burbery, and two new members, also both Local Board members, George Marshall Turner and John Bagshaw; the latter was once on the committee opposed to the purchase. The precise financial terms of the arrangement, if any, remain undiscovered although a new bank account was opened in the name of the four, and the outstanding debt transferred to it from the original. The new agreement stated that the members of the Syndicate:

> Purchased the heriditaments... with the intention that the surplus proceeds of the sale thereof should be devoted to public purposes (and were) joint tenants in equity as well as in law. On the death of any one of them the whole beneficial interest in the surplus proceeds of sale should belong to the survivors of them... they and the survivors or survivor of them might be in a position to dispose of the surplus proceeds of the sale of the same heriditaments for public purposes if they or he should think fit so to do, but might not be under any obligation so to dispose thereof and so that their right to deal with such surplus proceeds might not be in any manner affected. It is not the intention of any of the parties to derive any personal benefit from the property if they should think fit so to do.

But as has been seen, far from having 'surplus proceeds', they were at this time very much in debt.

It had been expected that once purchased, the development of the Abbey Fields into a park would be swift but with the saving of the fields taking precedent the practical aspects of enhancing them had been neglected. As they needed to be rented out to raise the income to pay off the loan, no major alterations could take place and the public could not be allowed access to them. The footpaths however were in constant use as supposed rights of way.

The town, along with much of the country, was in a general state of depression and with Kenilworth's *'trade stagnant'* and *'enterprise dead'*, suggestions and comments soon began to appear in the *Kenilworth Advertiser*. The Abbey Fields purchase was a lot of effort and expenditure for no obvious return and although they were being paid for by rent income from grazing, the amount borrowed restricted further loans for new town projects, including developing the fields into a park. An example as to how the fields could benefit the poorer classes was that one of the fields, adjoining Area D and still known by its historic name of Horse Close, was rented from the Board for *'an inconsiderable sum'* by Ernest Trepplin and it was suggested that as he did not really need it, it could be turned into allotments for the growing of fruit and vegetables for the needy. Always not far away was the regular suggestion that as there was so much spare cheap labour available, a start could be made on the long contemplated swimming baths.

As can be seen on the Conveyance map (see page 17), the **footpath** from the Iron Bridge at the field's centre to Borrowell Lane traversed part of the field owned by the Syndicate, and was thus no longer available to the public. A new path to replace it was made on the Board's land in July 1885: *'The Local Board or* *somebody else has made a road to the Iron Bridge from Borrowell Lane but I do not think that they ought to expect the public who use that way to get over a style. There was no style before and they ought to make the road as easy to travel as the one they took away.'*

From the beginning, there were calls for the fields to be developed for the **recreational purposes** outlined in the loan inquiries. Always top of the list were a swimming baths of some description and a cricket pitch; the Kenilworth Cricket Club that had used the fields in the past had just lost its 'home' ground due to Priory Road being built across it and were looking for somewhere to play. At the June 1885 Local Board meeting, it was decided the question of providing swimming baths and a cricket pitch was to be discussed at a subsequent meeting, the same was decided in July. In August, a committee was formed to 'inspect the Abbey Fields estate with a view in ascertaining its fitness for the constructing of a swimming baths and the probable cost thereof'; there was no mention of the cricket pitch, or the popular calls for a lake (often discussed by the public but not by the Board).

'At last these much wanted baths are within a measurable distance of realisation. I do hope the committee do not get up an expansive scheme so the baths cannot be made owing to the cost'; that same week, *'two boys were bathing near the Iron Bridge near the new path to Borrowell Lane. The new baths will do away with that sort of exhibition'*. Still no action was forthcoming and in April 1886 the *Kenilworth Advertiser* provided a possible reason; *'I fear another summer will pass and no public baths for Kenilworth, why this is we can only guess; no doubt it is something to do with the non-letting or selling of the outer portions of the fields, perhaps the Board think it might be prejudicial to the sale of land for building purposes'*, suggesting that the Local Board members saw the provision of facilities and development in to a park as detrimental to their efforts as individuals to sell building plots around the perimeter. By the following year, the writer seems more convinced as to where the problem was; *'How goes the lake scheme? I am afraid we do not have the right men on the Board to push the matter. Firstly it would find work for the unemployed over the winter; secondly the skating would bring in a large amount of money that would repay the outlay, and thirdly, boating and fishing in other parts of the year would also help to pay off the debt'*.

A plan hanging in the Board offices, of unknown date but surveyed and drawn for a reported £100, showed a lake with boats upon it and the park laid out with a cricket field, but no swimming pool; the Board had ideas and plans but appear to have lacked the drive and resources to achieve them, the chances of promises coming to fruition were already receding.

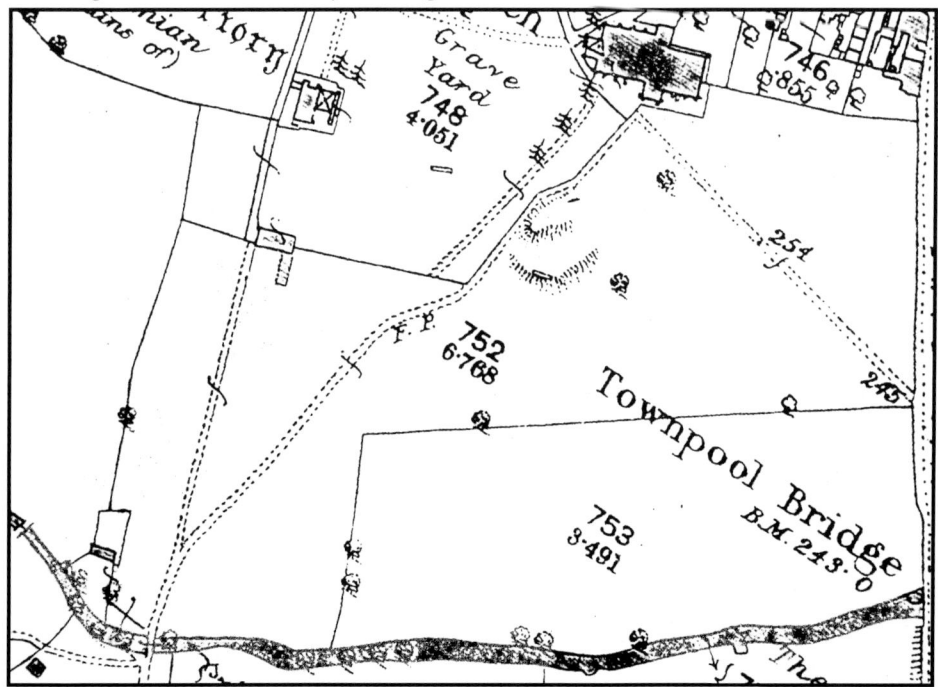

First Edition Ordnance Survey map of 1886 showing the churchyard extension and the path diverted around it alongside the undulations of the buried Abbey ruins, causing two zig-zags. The original path is still shown. The barn in the enclosure near the Iron Bridge was demolished in July 1888

In April 1887, William Evans brought to the Board's attention that part of the **ruins** in the fields near the church were in a dangerous condition, and as children climbed upon them they ought to be made safe. He and Mr Burbery investigated and the repairs were swiftly carried out.

Suggestions as to how best to celebrate **Queen Victoria's Golden Jubilee** in 1887 inevitably involved the Abbey Fields and the Local Board committee entrusted with making suggestions came up with several. One was to take the first step in making the fields the intended pleasure grounds by the building of a promenade alongside Abbey Hill; it was described as *'a ridiculous idea'* for the benefit only of the wealthiest locals. Other suggestions for the fields included making the boating lake, *'the pond exists, all we need is the water'*, the creation of paths and walkways, and of course the building of a swimming baths, but within weeks the idea of any permanent jubilee memorial in the fields had been discarded. In the event, the fields were used on Jubilee Day for well-contested sports in front of a large audience.

In late July 1888, the demolition of an old barn just north of the Iron Bridge led to the hope that it was the start of work to create a swimming pool at the spot, but it wasn't to be.

On 1st February 1888, the **Syndicate** now of Bagshaw, Burbery, Evans and Turner, paid off their debt of £5,558 1s 6d owed to the Leamington Priors & Warwickshire Bank Co (who had been taken over by the Birmingham Banking Co) with the same sum borrowed from Lloyd's Barnett's & Bosanquet's Bank Ltd (who had opened a Kenilworth branch in 1884). It is again difficult to qualify the figures; the amount owed is only £642 or so less than they had spent on purchasing their areas of the fields and raises the question, what happened to the £300 raised from the churchyard sale, the £1,385 3s 2d raised at the June 1884 auction of Sion House and plots in Area D, and apparent sale of plots along the High Street? It may be that the Preservationists failed to raise the full £3,500 for the purchase of Area B and that the Syndicate took on that shortfall too. As will be seen later, these outer areas also brought in about £95 annually from rents; this alone would be an income of over £400 since they were purchased that should also have gone towards paying off the debt, but perhaps this could again suggest that at least some of the rents for these areas were at this time going to the Board. There would also, of course, have been additions for interest payments.

About ten weeks later on Thursday 26th April 1888 at The King's Arms, a new attempt was made by the Syndicate to sell off all their building plots around the fields. On offer was 22,070 sq yds along the High Street frontage, 14,709 sq yds facing New Row (Little Virginia, and the area behind, offered for the first time), 27,739 sq yds (5.73 acres) facing Forrest Road, 6,151 sq yds at Millbrook Lane, and 11,187 sq yds on the 'new road'; the new road was proposed along the boundary of Area D with the Abbey Fields so that new houses would face the fields. In all there were 17 acres offered in only *'3 or 4'* lots rather than individual house plots. *'Circumstances render the estate unusually attractive. Contiguous to an area of about 50 acres preserved as a public park'*. The surplus land around the churchyard was not on offer as it was not suitable for building upon.

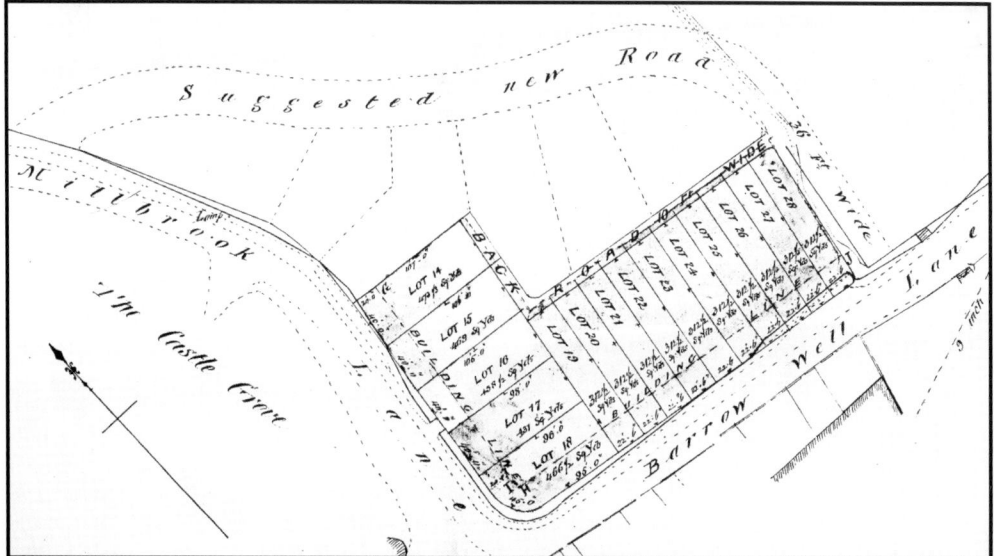

Area D showing the original auction Plots 14-28, and the proposed new road and associated building plots
(WCRO, CR 1525/94/2)

Of the areas listed above, The High Street 22,070 sq yds must have been the 9 building plots that were in the names of the Syndicate; only the three in the hands of the Drapers were not for sale at this time. The total acreage the Syndicate bought was about 25; allowing for the 5 acres around the churchyard and the 17 acres now up for sale, it means that only three acres or so had actually been sold. This suggests the Syndicate members may have simply had the plots that were in their name allocated to them but in struggling to recoup their outlay now decided they too could be sold. However, the following week's report of the auction simply states, *'No offer was made for the land.'*

The reason that the 19 cottages and smithy in New Row were not for sale as habitations was simply that as they fronted the roads it would prevent the land behind them being saleable for building purposes. Also as they were not in good condition they could entail costly repairs; when the smithy attached to number 81 was demolished in 1890 it was described thus; *'the ugliest of our landmarks has disappeared, and no one sighs for its return. The poor tumble-down cottage which depended upon the old smithy for its support is simply kept from coming to the ground by unsightly props'*; what the *'lone widow'* renting the cottage thought can only be imagined. There was little interest in building houses on other plots around the Abbey Fields because at this time there was already much potential for the building of 'villas' in the town with plots available along the new Priory Road, Waverley Road and Bertie Road, as well as Southbank Road and many open spaces along Warwick Road, and of course the recently sold Abbey Fields land fronting onto Borrowell Lane. Some of the area fronting Forrest Road also had a difficult topography for building. This is often thought of as a boom time for the town attracting industrialists and others from Birmingham, Coventry and elsewhere due to improved rail facilities, but this is erroneous; as mentioned, it was a time of uncertain trading nationally, the town was in something of a slump, many from the working class were emigrating, and there was simply no market for more larger houses. The population grew only by 23 between 1881 (4,150) and 1891 (4,173) but by over 300 in each of the decades either side.

With the building plots not selling, it left Bagshaw, Burbery, Evans and Turner out of pocket and the intention to donate excess monies from sales to town causes had all but gone. With limited options, just a couple of weeks after the attempted sale, on 9th May 1888 the Syndicate suggested the Board may wish to buy the unsold building plots to add to their park, and that perhaps there may be some obligation to do so. The Syndicate were now willing to sell their remaining 17 acres of building land and 3 acres around the churchyard for the value of their current losses. The Board set up a committee of Evans, Bagshaw, Thomas Hawley and Frederick Wyer to look into the circumstances of the fields' purchase and their current status; the inclusion of two of the Syndicate suggests trust and integrity took precedent over the obvious conflict of interest. The committee reported back to the full Board on Wednesday 18th May. In recounting the story, the report revealed that the 53 acres or so then under the control of the Board (Areas A & B) produced an annual rent of £150; this compared favourably to the loan repayments of just £115 per annum making a profit for the Board from the fields of about £35 each year. Extending the churchyard had saved in the region of an annual cost of £300 to provide a cemetery. The total cost to the Syndicate of buying the building land was £10,781 16s 1d* of which, at 1st February, £5,560 7s 4d had yet to be recouped. These areas brought in about £95 per annum (presumably for the Syndicate), from renting the cottages but perhaps also from grazing. (* The figure of £10,781 16s 1d must include the cost of Area B, building Forrest Road, and legal fees.)

William Evans, as both spokesperson for the Syndicate and Board Chairman, said he was disappointed that *'the times had been such that the owners had not been able to realise* (their outlay)*'*. They had *'no interest in the property except that common interest of all members to benefit the community'*. During discussions it became clear that no one on the Board thought it likely that a further loan would be approved for purchasing all the remaining areas of the fields. A proposition was thus put forward by Thomas Hawley: *'That having regard for all circumstances of the case, the committee regret that they cannot advise the Local Board to take a conveyance of the property and they must therefore leave Mr Burbery and his co-proprietors free to deal with it as they may think best in their own interests'*, and after the Syndicate members had left the room, the motion was carried by four votes to two. Bagshaw, Burbery, Evans and Turner were thus still left with unsalable land and a large debt *(*the equivalent of *£663,000).*

As the grave of Kenilworth builder Edward Smith was being dug alongside the Tantara Gatehouse in April 1886, **Abbey remains** were found *'consisting of a chamber with a very fine groined roof with three passages leading out of it, one of them going to the old Monks hole'*. Despite great local interest, these were covered before a local antiquary could inspect them. It was inevitable that as graves were dug in the most recent **churchyard** extension, more Abbey relics would be found; when the first grave of 1887 was dug, a skeleton was found *'the position of which proved conclusively that it was not the remains of a priest'*. In the autumn of 1888, more discoveries were made whilst digging graves in the old part of the churchyard;

window jambs, mullions and tracery, stained glass rich in ruby, amber and other colours were found, and they were put in the Tantara Gatehouse. When the foundations of a wall running at right angles to the Gatehouse were found, it was quickly suggested that a full excavation should be made, and so digging continued. On Wednesday 10th April 1889, the Abbey's church boundary wall with a doorway was uncovered in which were found pieces of tile, one was *'beautifully ornamented'*, and a clay jug which unfortunately broke as it was moved. There was much anticipation as to what might be found in the passageway behind the door and the following week it was dug out to expose the Abbey's outer wall.

To some extent, these discoveries were expected, but the next certainly was not. In the first week of July 1889, whilst a grave was being dug, a large canoe-shaped pig of lead was found, part of the melted down Abbey roof. Measuring 4ft 3½ins by 1ft 3½ins at its greatest breadth and 7½ins at its thickest, it weighed just over half a ton. According to Mr Fretton of Coventry, it had been roughly cast in a hollow of loose sand. Fretton was of the opinion that the whole area should be subject to a proper excavation with relics removed and walls left as found, so that a plan could be made.

The news of the discoveries spread, articles appeared in newspapers, and archaeologists became regular visitors amongst the many sightseers. By August 1889, it was *'possible to trace in a direct line the stone boundary wall of the old Priory, partly to the hospice or guest house. In another portion of the churchyard an arched passage, with mullioned stone walls and well preserved finials, has been laid open. A chamber of square dimensions, which was found some time ago, has been railed and affords a striking example of the skill and patience of the original builders'*. By now, it had been decided to keep burials to another part of the churchyard and leave the excavations to archaeologists. On the last Wednesday of October, the site was visited by Mr Hope, Honorary Secretary of the Royal Archaeology Society, and he made a tour accompanied by Reverend Alfred Binnie, the Churchwardens William Evans and Joseph Roberts, and Mr Fretton. Mr Hope agreed as to the source of the block of lead and mentioned that it was the second found there; another found on the site previously was preserved at Stonyhurst College. (This author's enquiry to the college failed to confirm this.) All the excavations took place within the churchyard.

Just months after declining to buy all the Syndicate's excess land in May 1888, the Board did discuss the purchase of one area the Syndicate owned, the remnants of **Area F**, reduced by the churchyard extension and now split in two by the Barn. With the discoveries made in the churchyard extension, it is probably not coincidental that the area discussed contained the known extent of the Abbey church and would bring ownership of its ruins out of private hands. The Highway Committee proposed to the full Board that for £400 they purchased the left over area around the churchyard of 3a 1r 4p, which included not only much of the area covering the Abbey remains but also the Tantara Gatehouse. *'The land in question lies between the burial ground and the park and was originally intended to form part of the burial ground, only the churchyard then would have been larger than permitted by law. A better shape would be given to the park by the absorption of the land'*. One particular attraction of this additional area was that it included the 15ft wide access insisted upon by Clarendon in 1867 and would enable the Board to make a road into the park from High Street, just outside the churchyard wall; again it was rumoured that if the Board did not buy this piece of land then a builder would, blocking off a potential access to the fields. On 8th August 1888 the Board agreed (the Syndicate members left the room during voting) and the Syndicate would thus recoup in total £700 for their 5 acre plot around the churchyard; at £140 per acre it was well below the average £248 per acre they had paid.

The Board decided to borrow another £425 and so another inquiry was held, this time at the Board's offices on 31st January 1889 and chaired by J T Harrison. Harrison was somewhat bemused when discovering the main part of the fields had yet to be thrown open to the public who did not even have the legal right to cross them, and at the cost of repayments of £125 per annum. His question, *'Do I understand that the rates are burdened £125 a year for no good to the public?'* received applause, but he had ignored the income from renting when asking the question. He did not see what benefit to the town the land was except for the pleasure of paying for it for future generations; *'If I were an inhabitant, I would like to enjoy it now'*. He was also unsure whether the Board could legally exclude the public and his comments brought both applause and laughter from the audience. It was beginning to look as though the Board may have miscalculated, and their efforts unappreciated.

Mr Bagshaw tried to retrieve the situation by saying that the Board's entire planned scheme (presumably that hanging on their office wall, including a lake, cricket pitch and ornamental walks) would cost a shilling rate and that was why the fields had not been turned into a park. He added that there was no real opposition to the new application but the majority thought money would be better spent on building swimming baths. The Clerk, Mr Addison, assured Harrison that a public meeting would soon be taking place.

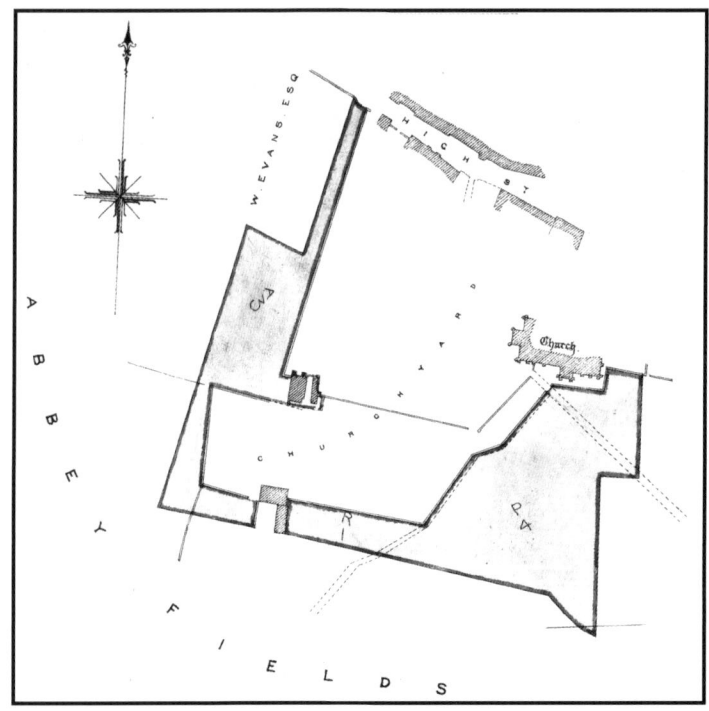

The irregular 3 acres of land purchased by the Local Board for £400 on 14th March 1889. Note the original Plot 2 alongside High Street in the name of William Evans

(WDC 131)

Despite the Board's shortcomings and Harrison's reservations, the Local Government Board granted the application and the loan was arranged with the Prudential Insurance Company at a rate of 3¾ per cent over 50 years, amounting to repayments of £18 18s 11d a year. On 13th March 1889, it was 'Resolved that the piece of land containing 3 acres 1 rood 2 perches, forming part of the Abbey Fields agreed to be purchased by the Board at the price of £400 be kept and used solely for the purpose of walks and pleasure grounds jointly with the other portions of the Abbey Fields purchased by the Board'; the conveyance is dated 14th March 1889 and incorporated the same covenant as that for the purchase of the central 40 acres:

> ... shall forever hereafter be solely used for public walks and pleasure grounds under the control of the council and the same shall not nor shall any part thereof at any time hereafter be sold leased or disposed of for any other purpose inconsistent with the same being solely used as aforesaid.

And so a second area of the Abbey Fields was conveyed to the Board, making 57a 26p under their control and the Syndicate were now in debt to the bank by a little over £5,000. Following Harrison's uncertainty over whether the leasing of the fields for grazing and associated exclusion of the public was legal, the Board's Clerk Mr Addison wrote to the Secretary of the Local Government Board in Whitehall, asking for clarification:

> I have to inform your Honourable Board that the Kenilworth Local Board are desirous of letting upon yearly tenancies as pasture land the lands recently acquired by them for the purpose of Public Walks and Pleasure Grounds until such time as in the opinion of my Board it will advantageous to the inhabitants of Kenilworth and the public generally that such lands should be laid out as public walks or pleasure grounds. My Board will therefore be glad to hear that your Honourable Board sees no objection to this being done and that your Honourable Board consent to the letting of such lands accordingly.

The reply was quickly received: 'Under section 177 of the Public Health Act, 1875 (the Secretary) hereby consents to the letting by the Kenilworth Local Board of the lands recently acquired for public walks and pleasure grounds'. The referred to section of the Act states, 'Any Local Authority may with the consent of the Local Government Board, let for any term any lands they possess, as and when they can conveniently spare the same'; as they did not already have the required consent, until that point the Kenilworth Local Board had clearly broken the rules for five years by renting out the fields. The new request that the land be let until 'it will be advantageous' to turn the grounds into a park can be interpreted different ways; it would of course be immediately advantageous to the townsfolk to have their 'Pleasure Grounds', but to the Board it would only become so when it was financially 'advantageous' to no longer need the income from the rents.

Undoubtedly due to the failure to sell any more of the plots, whilst the sale of the area around the churchyard was progressing a new agreement was drawn up by the **Syndicate** and signed on 15th October 1888. Three of the four members, John Bagshaw being the one to miss out, each took ownership of one of the three remaining areas of the Syndicate's land: Area C which included Little Virginia became George Marshall Turner's (the adjacent Plots 9-13 were already in his name), Area E facing Forrest Road became William Evans', and the land in between, Area D, some of which had been sold for development, became Joseph Burbery's (Plots 14-16 were already in his name, perhaps the reason for their withdrawal from sale in June 1884). It appears that at this point the three paid off their joint loan debt; payments made by Burbery and Evans are unknown but George Turner paid £1,891 *(£225,000)* for his share. The three acres or so around the churchyard extension remained in the name of all four as that sale progressed.

The separation document also states that the four had been 'tenants', but the land was 'Recently sold in the manner following; the portion coloured red (Area D) to Joseph Holland Burbery, blue (Area E) to William Evans and green (Area C) to George Marshall Turner', before continuing by saying they must abide by the Covenants now they are owners. This suggests that although the purchase bank account and loan were in the names of the Syndicate, they were perhaps seen as trustees and administrators to this point; being responsible for the debt, they simply paid it off and thus became owners.

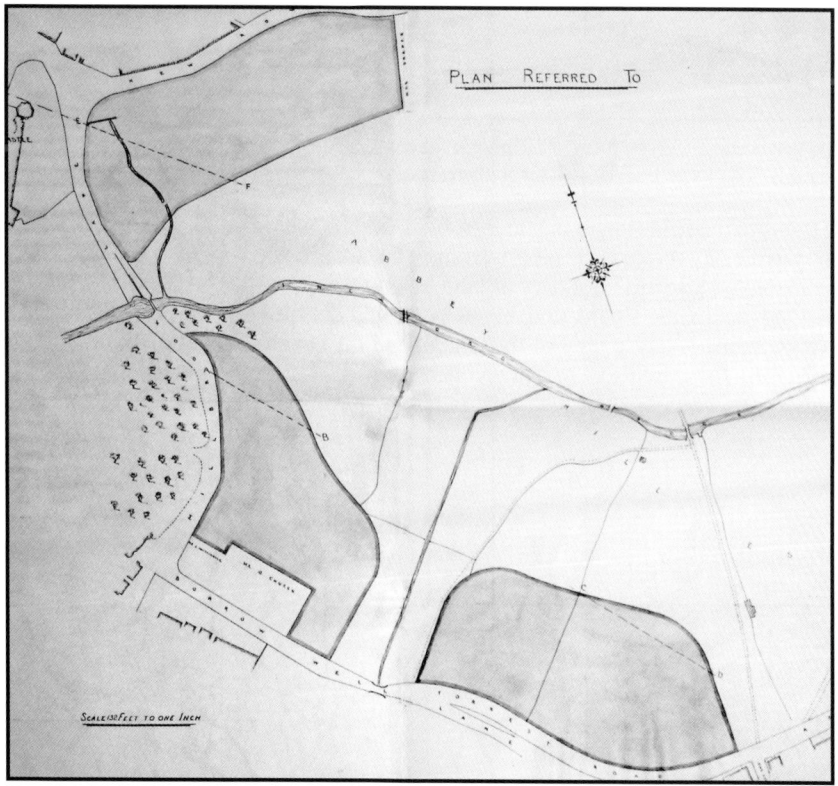

The plan included with the separation agreement, showing the areas allocated to the three syndicate members. Turner gained Area C to the north, Burbery the central Area D (with some plots showing having been sold), and Evans the southern Area E. Each area has restrictive building lines *(WCRO, CR 1525/94/6)*

The separation agreement included building restrictions. In Turner's northern area, no building greater than 2 storeys high including attic rooms, or a total 35ft high, could be erected to the west or south-west of the line E-F. In the central Burbery area, no buildings were allowed east or north-east of the line A-B as they would interfere with the view of the Castle from the Abbey Hill house of the Reverend Thomas Jeffcoat, known as Manor House (today it is Belmont), or any other house east of that on Abbey Hill. In the area alongside Forrest Road allocated to William Evans, no building east or south-east of the line C-D was to interfere, again, with the Reverend Jeffcoat's view.

As an example, the precise wording for the restrictions for Burbery's Area D included:

> That no building upon the land shall be erected on the easterly or north easterly side of the line marked A-B so as to intercept the view of the ruins from the house on Abbey Hill belonging to the Reverend Thomas Jeffcoat and known as The Manor House... and that no steam engine shall be erected or used nor shall any noxious dangerous or offensive process be carried on upon the said piece of land.

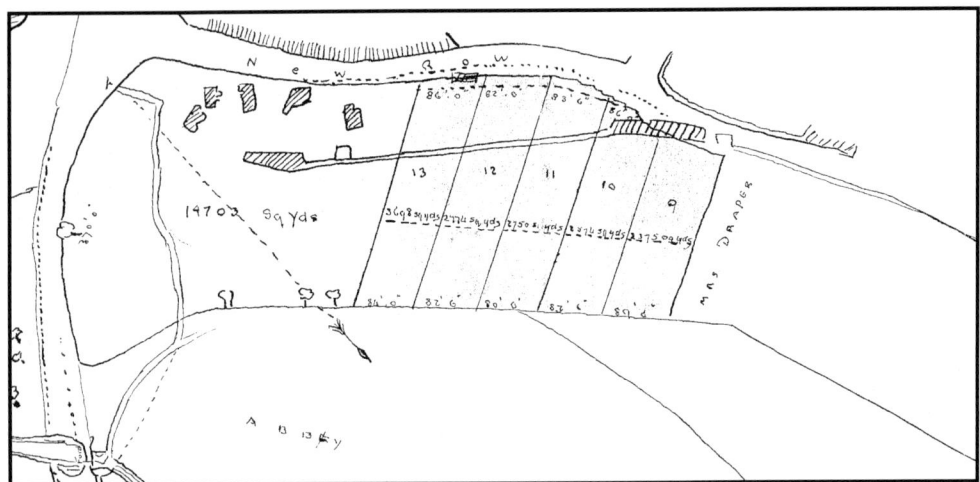

The area of land that became George Marshall Turner's showing the unsold auction Plots 9-13, and Little Virginia with the land behind as one plot of 14,703 sq yds. Of interest is a probable remnant of the Abbey's boundary wall *(PJ)*

With the status of the fields beginning to look final, on 18th March 1889 agreements were made to fence and separate the private plots around the perimeter from the areas in the hands of the Board. An 'unclimbable' fence was built along the 90-yard boundary of land belonging to Mrs Draper and Mr E H Draper off High Street, the cost to be met by the Board, and an oak posts and double-rail fence to the land owned by Evans, Burbery and Turner respectively, a total of 992 yards; half the cost to be met by the Board, and half by the three. If any rents from these fields were being collected by the Board, it now ended. These actions seemed to draw a line under any further expansion of the public ownership of the fields.

A photograph by the Amos Elkington studio, between late 1905 and April 1909. Across and just below the centre, either side of the darker line of Luzley Brook, can be seen the parallel fences enclosing the park and grazing cattle, separating it from the privately owned Area E (foreground) of William Evans, and Area D, part of which has been built upon. The relevance of the mound in the centre, and two apparent trackways leading from it to the right, is undiscovered; one of the trackways appears to be shown on the plan on page 25 *(WCRO, PH 350/1032)*

It was becoming obvious that a more scientific and organised excavation of the **churchyard** was needed and to this end, a meeting was held on 1st March 1890. The Society of Antiquaries Secretary, W H St John Hope, had by now prepared an extensive report and suggested removing all the debris down to the floor level of the Abbey. The vicar announced that his Bishop had no objections provided no damage was done to any of the remains, and suggested that the cost of excavations should be met by public subscription; the lack of church or Board funds to finance the venture was lamented.

Work continued under Fretton. The west and south walls of the Abbey had been cleared down to the base, *'the tiled floor being found nearly perfect'*, and test excavations continued in an attempt to discover the layout of the buildings. The tender for the excavation proper was let locally, Edward Smith & Son, in the hands of Joseph Smith, for £140 was successful; Smith already had the contract for building the churchyard's enclosing walls. It was apt that Joseph Smith was to undertake the task as it was the burial of his father that uncovered stonework that excited so much initial interest. Plans and specifications for the excavating were drawn up by Thomas Whitley, architect and surveyor of Coventry. He had already estimated that about 3,000 cartloads of material would have to be removed.

The dispersal of **relics** prompted some honest observations: *'If the halls of the county and the homes of Kenilworth and the outhouses for ten miles around gave up their relics, the monastery might comfortably be rebuilt. A hundred and fifty years ago the main walls were standing very much in the condition that Kirkstall Abbey presents today. In more recent years, the curios dug up have been quietly appropriated by the digger whose cottage has the nucleus of a small museum. The pavement of the Augustinian Priory would in time have graced the rockeries of the town in company with maimed teapots and stucco statues'*. Another writer gave this account: *'A few weeks ago, the sexton whilst digging a grave unearthed an arched doorway, which he thought was a drain, and it would have been bricked up but for the intervention of a passer by. A few days later the base of a column was unearthed but this time the burial took place. The sexton dug into some crypts some years ago and turned them into a vault.'*

For the excavations, *'It is proposed to excavate the site of the church and the north cloister and a considerable part of the conventual buildings down to the floor level thus exposing the walls and pillars; to remove and preserve the tiles, to erect retaining walls to support the graves and parts of the churchyard already used for burials; to make good and cement the old walls and pillars; to spread the soil obtained by excavation over the lower part of the churchyard so as to make it on a proper level, and to construct an iron fence to preserve the ruins from depredation and the churchyard from trespass, with a gate to afford access to the churchyard'*. The scheme included the laying out of a road through the churchyard sufficiently wide to carry out funerals.

William Pears was appointed treasurer to handle subscriptions. A good start was made with the vicar promising £20, Pears and William Evans £10 each, and F Stanger-Leathes, F Wyer and Thomas Hawley £5 each. By June, the fund had reached £128, almost entirely from Kenilworth people, and soon reached £147. Smith announced he was to start work on Monday 16th June and he had taken on *'a large number of hands'*; the gravedigger confidently predicted they would have *'a very troublesome task'*.

Work began with the erection of notices warning against the theft of relics and, as expected, several were found very quickly. A stone head was amongst the first, as were several lettered tiles. By August the excavation was nearing completion. Now exposed were the entrance and porch, north and south transepts, part of the chapel and annex, part of the south cloisters and north cloister walk, the nave, and columns of the tower. It had proved necessary to dig at greater depths than expected. Many of the relics were locked in the Tantara Gatehouse but remained visible through the barred windows. The churchyard was being levelled, in particular the new extension, and old hollows filled in. The boundary wall with palisades was still under construction and some turf was being laid in completed areas. Smith was praised for the speedy and careful manner in which the work was done, there was not a single case of damage to the remains. Large numbers of visitors watched the excavations. (For a full account of these excavations, see *Victorian Kenilworth and its People*.)

With no sign of any **park-like developments**, in May 1891, Board member and nurseryman Richard Whateley asked if the Board had any *'definite ideas about the future of the estate'*; he assumed that as several of those responsible for purchasing the fields were still on the Board, they at least must have some ideas. Mr Wyer mentioned it would be 60 years until the purchase was complete, *'It will be ancient history by then'* replied Whateley. Thomas Hawley saw the fields as *'a costly toy'* and Whateley continued by saying he did not understand what benefit the estate was bringing to the town, but Henry Street re-affirmed the saving of £2-300 a year by the extension of the churchyard.

The following month, Richard Whateley again raised the question as to the future of the fields, asking what benefit there was to the ratepayers and saying they would not be satisfied until the estate was turned into a park. In February the Board had agreed to put in a floodgate to prevent the flooding of Mrs Draper's field, but despite that Whateley proposed a permanent lake should be formed on the fields rented by her and Joseph Roberts (numbers 38 and 43) and stocked with fish; the work he thought may not cost more than £200. Board Chairman William Evans pointed out that two schemes already existed including a lake for boating and fishing with walks around it. Dr Wynter, once opposed to the purchase, was now opposed to the lake *'on sanitary grounds'* but wondered when the promised cricket ground would appear. These and other ideas had all been outlined as reasons for purchasing the fields at the original inquiry, but although nothing positive had actually happened to the land since purchase, it was also noted that nothing detrimental to the plans had happened either and all were still possible.

Hoping at least to make a start on laying out the park, at the next meeting it was agreed that the Town Surveyor was to get estimates for creating a fenced pathway through the fields alongside the southern side of the brooks from Borrowell Lane to Bridge Street, and this he did reporting back at the September meeting. An 8ft wide path would cost £541 10s, 10ft wide £619 12s 6d and 12ft wide £697 15s. Needless to say, at that cost it was decided not to go ahead, and so five months of discussions about the development of the fields resulted in no action.

An early 1890s view of St Nicholas church, looking across the brook with (probably) the 1881 sewer pipe crossing in the foreground. A shelter is attached to the Barn and there are undulations where Abbey ruins are buried *(KL)*

Occasional alterations were made around the perimeter. In December 1891 the supposed former Abbey boundary wall alongside the High Street Plots 3 - 8 and part of 9 (see page 21) was removed, the boundary line staked out and a footpath created for the road. In March 1891 Mr Church agreed to block up the doorway from Sion House into the fields.

Just how much the fields in their existing state were appreciated by the inhabitants became clear in the summer of 1893 when three elderly 90ft beech trees alongside Abbey Hill were deemed to be dangerous due to age and the Local Board began the task of cutting them down. Opinion was divided as to the condition of the trees and the townsfolk were outraged, *'it would be a great stir in Kenilworth if these trees came down'*, and a quickly assembled petition was *'largely signed, and want of time prevented hundreds of others'* from adding their names. The trees were *'some of the most beautiful in Kenilworth and are a picturesque feature of the higher part of the Abbey Fields'*. The *Kenilworth Advertiser* joined the campaign, *'Let our Local Board pause before proceeding further with the cutting down of fine old trees in the People's Park, it is easier to remove them than replace them'*. A month after the furore began, the Board decided to keep the two remaining trees.

Later the same year, as the nights drew in, there was a plea for lighting in the fields as there was *'not a single lamp from one end of the fields to the other, although the path is used almost as much in the night-time as in the day'*. Of particular concern was the *'groping about in the dark'* trying to find the latch on the gate on the Iron Bridge, which was vital to stop livestock wandering.

This photograph is taken from a window of Kenilworth Hall in Bridge Street. Note the prominent hedgerow across the centre, and beyond it Finham Brook is difficult to spot due to its mostly bare banks. Grazing animals are in several locations. On Abbey Hill, Manor House / Belmont is prominent as are the beech trees mentioned in the text. A clue to dating this photograph is the 220ft tall tannery chimney in the top left hand corner; built in 1858, it fell in 1894 and was replaced by a much shorter structure *(WCRO, PH 77/36)*

Joseph Holland Burbery died at his home Montague House on 25th March 1892, aged 84; his wife died just 6 weeks later and they are buried in one of the graves now lost in front of the chapel on Rosemary Hill, now the Priory Theatre. The sale of Burbery's estate took place on 10th August 1892 at the Abbey Hotel by Grimley & Son of Birmingham, and included farms at Rowington and Meer End, and his remaining Abbey Fields, 19,260 sq yds (4 acres or so) in Area D, described as *'eligible freehold building land'*; this was the 17,000 sq yds on offer in 1888 plus the Plots 14-16 that were already in Burbery's name. This all sold to Henry Street, one report says for £400 and another £500, but either way it was a bargain at the cost per acre and the cheapest known price for any area of the fields.

The Conveyance to Henry Street is dated 14th November 1892 but his ownership was brief. Something of a 'wheeler-dealer' in Kenilworth property, Street sold the land for an unknown price on 24th December 1894 to Ada, the wife of Estate Agent James Whittindale; why in her name and not his is unestablished. On it they built a splendid new house, The Bungalow, designed by W De Lacey Aherne, and moved into it in 1896; James died there in November that year.

In the mid 1890s the **building plots** along High Street finally began to sell. Numbers 2 & 3 (originally in the name of William Evans), and 4 & 5 (George Turner) became combined (probably at the time of the 1888 agreement) and by 1895 a new house Abbotsfield was built more or less on the former Plot 2; the rest of the land becoming its gardens. The first person known to live in Abbotsfield was Dr Edmund Bourne, the Fire Brigade Captain and perhaps the leading doctor in the town, in the days when doctors were also surgeons. In the Autumn of 1896, Bourne put Abbotsfield up for sale; it was due to be auctioned at The King's Arms on 28th September but the advertisement was withdrawn from the local newspapers before that date and no sale result was published, perhaps it was sold privately. Surviving documents are incomplete but provide a conundrum; George Turner became sole owner of the land in the separation agreement of 15th October 1888 and he later sold it complete with Abbotsfield on 31st July 1897 to Enoch J West, and yet in the autumn of 1896 it was Edmund Bourne who had the house for sale. In July 1901 it was for sale again by its owner Mr West, but was withdrawn from auction at £3,300.

Enoch John West, a *'motor pioneer'*, lived at and owned Abbotsfield but on 25th March 1903, it was bought by Lincoln Chandler, who was moving to Kenilworth when a Director of the Amalgamated Carriage & Wagon Co, and later in 1912 replaced another Kenilworth resident, Frank Dudley Docker (known by his second Christian name), as a Director of BSA. In 1906, Chandler took over the tenancy of the Abbey field that his house overlooked. West moved to Priory Road.

George Turner managed to sell some of his land bordering Millbrook Lane. On 14th May and 18th July 1898, he sold two areas totalling 571 sq yds to Mr Lissman of Coventry; this was the very southern part of the plot adjacent to the Abbey Fields nearest the brook and on it Mr Lissman built Oakdale. Then on 22nd December 1905 Turner sold the prime corner plot of 550 sq yds directly adjacent to Little Virginia, to Coventry café proprietor Arthur Hampton for £137 10s. It came with covenants restricting the size and style of any building and on it Hampton built the well-known Garden Café, perfectly positioned to catch Castle-bound tourists. (Graham Gould, *Kenilworth History 2011.*) The area in between the two remained unsold.

The days of the Local Board were numbered. For reasons outlined in *Victorian Kenilworth and its People*, but mostly to do with gaining extra powers over the town's development, under the Local Government Act of 1894 the Board took the decision that year to abolish itself and form the **Kenilworth Urban District Council** (KUDC). An election needed to be held, at which some women could vote for the first time. Although the Board and its members had been successful in saving the Abbey Fields from developers, they had failed to provide a park, and the process to form the new Council gave new impetus to the growing clamour for opening up the fields and building a **swimming pool**. Political parties were prominent for the first time and in their manifesto the eight Liberal candidates proposed *'an early investigation into the question of the proposed Park and Pleasure Grounds... placing the case before the inhabitants... so they may decide if they are necessary. Money has been borrowed, the land has been purchased, the Park has not been laid out, and the public have little or no ground for healthy recreation'*. As regards to the swimming baths, *'Money is in hand for supplying the Baths, the ground is at the disposal of the town and little or no difficulty will arise with the supply of water. We consider it highly desirable that a scheme should be proceeded with straight away'*. It was calculated at this time that the loans for £6,000 and £425 taken out by the Board would result in repayments of almost £17,000, yet the townsfolk still had no legal right to walk upon them. Largely due to its Abbey Fields manifesto, all eight Liberals were elected to the inaugural KUDC in December 1894 and one of them, Henry Street, became its Chairman. William Evans who had led the Local Board for ten years did not stand for election; now 70 years old, he had been the driving force behind the fields' purchase, but had been unable to push through the expected subsequent developments.

In March 1895, on the back of the Liberals' election promises, and the coincidental issuing of a Local Government Board circular instructing work to be found for the unemployed, the KUDC took the first major step to look into the financial and practical aspects of building a swimming baths by forming a Bathing Committee consisting of Henry Street, Reverend G Field, Dr Edmund Bourne, E P Hodges, James E Jackson, George Church and William Riley. Within a week, four of the committee were seen near the Iron Bridge in the Abbey field rented from the council by Joseph Roberts, *'the one where the skating was'*.

Their eagerly-awaited report and designs were made public at the KUDC meeting in May 1895; it was unanimous that the best site for the baths was indeed at the spot the committeemen had been seen investigating. Baths at Leamington and Warwick had been inspected but copying either was discounted as they would cost £700 - £800, *'Far too much for Kenilworth to expend'*, and so Kenilworth's Surveyor Edward Purnell had drawn his own designs.

The plans revealed the swimming pool's water supply was to be *via* a sluice or weir built into the stream near the pool, and it would drain through a *'6 inch drainpipe running into a back-drain 7 yards away'* before finally discharging into the brook near to Townpool Bridge, the natural lie of the land providing the water flow. The pool itself was to be 75 to 80ft in length with a width of about half that, and vary in depth from 2ft 6ins to 5ft. The sides, varying in thickness from 14ins to 18ins, would be of hard-pressed bricks and topped with blue coping bricks. The bottom would be 9ins or 1ft thickness of concrete covered with an inch of asphalt. Around the pool would be a planted mound made from the excavation material that would act as a screen and perhaps also reduce the chances of flood waters entering. At one end of the baths, next to the brook, a dressing room was to be provided made from *'thin boards or corrugated iron'*. The pool would be excavated by council employees, after which contractors would be used for the brickwork and concrete. The cost was estimated at between £150 and £200.

Councillor Riley, an ironmonger and tobacconist of High Street, became a driving force behind the scheme and he built an ingenious model to demonstrate the operation of the water system: *'A tin trench is made to represent the river flowing, and in the real thing a weir is to be made of stone, which can and will be made to look very pretty. A pipe conveys the water into a receiving chamber, where it percolates through different meshed sieves, entering the baths proper at the shallow end. A pipe at the deep end takes the surplus water back into the brook. A pipe at the bottom of the deep end will take the sediment off into a dumb well, which will have to be pumped out occasionally. There will always be clear and fresh water in the baths. Of course in flood time measures will be taken to keep out the flood water'*. Despite Mr Welch suggesting at the 14th May Council meeting that work should not start until the money was raised, on 25th May it was reported that Councillor Riley had had the honour of cutting the first sod and that excavating was now under way.

Despite the indications that the construction of the bath would benefit the unemployed, the excavations were carried out by council employees under the watchful eye of Mr Evans the road surveyor, though it is probable that extra 'hands' were taken on. In early June, within weeks of the excavations starting, a quantity of sandstone 'very useful for making walls' was found, and advertisements were placed inviting tenders for the brickwork as it would be needed immediately if 'the baths is to be of any use this season'. Some artefacts were found including a canon ball and two ancient large posts; they were all taken to the council offices for safe keeping. Reverend Pennefather donated the money raised for an earlier abandoned swimming baths scheme. In mid-June the owner of the water mill at Mill End, William Thompson Pears, gave permission for the use of water from the brook over which he had rights of use, but only verbally to Councillor Edmund Bourne. Mr Welch again protested at work starting before sanction had been sought from the Local Government Board (LGB).

It was decided that only local builders should be allowed to tender for the building work and the three submitted were from E Lee for £103, E Marriott for £80, and the accepted bid from Joseph Smith of Ed Smith & Son for £72 19s which was signed by 25th June. By the beginning of July the brickwork laying had started even before the excavations were complete; there was a hurry to have the pool completed so it could be in use before the season ended. The *Kenilworth Advertiser* editorial on 13th July stated *'I very much pitied the men excavating the baths in the recent hot weather'* and the writer suggested they should be promised a meal upon the bath's opening by way of support and encouragement. On 3rd August it was lamented that the swimming pool would not be ready for the Bank Holiday just two days away; *'There was more work to do than was thought but it is hoped it will be ready before the end of the season'*. To make such statements, completion must have been close.

At the 13th August KUDC meeting it was proposed to make an application to the Local Government Board for a loan of £200 towards the cost of the baths, but only as a last resort; the resolution was passed, and Mr Welch's earlier pleas vindicated. Reporting the meeting and its discussions, the *Kenilworth Advertiser* quoted Obediah Woods as saying *'the baths was as a matter of fact completed'*. Town Surveyor Edward Purnell was paid £15 15s for 'making plans and estimates of the swimming baths'.

On 24th August it was reported that the contract for the *'shed'*, as the changing rooms were honestly described, was *'completed'*; the cost of construction was £39 18s. The 'shed', at the brook end of the pool, had a 4ft wide path in front with a step up to it, was 25ft long and 7ft 6ins wide and split into three compartments, one of which was 'private'; this may have been an office for the caretaker and paybox, but maps show a separate building close to the entrance by the Iron Bridge which could also have been the paybox. There was *'an entrance gate at the back and a hoarding'* which it was soon suggested could be used for advertisements to increase the Council's income.

With the swimming season's end rapidly approaching, it was said that it was *'improbable that the baths would be ready this year'*; the remaining difficulty was with the water supply. Water for the pool was to come from the brook and this involved building a weir. Despite promises to the contrary, the weir, not surprisingly, interfered with the water supply to the water mill at Mill End. Its operator J G Eagles was not pleased and complained to his landlord, William Pears of Kenilworth Hall who backed him. With Eagles and Pears prepared to take legal action, *'the law is very stringent in cases such as these'*, in early September the Council had no choice but to back down leaving the more or less complete swimming pool with no water supply, and thus ending any chance of it opening in the near future. Finishing work continued and by the end of September, with the swimming season practically over, boards were being erected around the church side of the baths, a contract won again by Joseph Smith. The fence was painted an unknown colour, 1cwt of leaded paint was ordered for the task.

Despite approaches, William Pears would not discuss the water supply with the Council until the weir was actually dismantled and this was agreed to at the 8th October KUDC meeting. The Road Surveyor Mr Evans, who appears to have been in charge of all construction of the baths, was instructed to remove the weir and Pears was then happy to visit and to discuss other ideas *'provided such schemes were properly prepared and submitted in detail and did not affect in any way the working of the mill.'*

With only the water system needed for completion, a decision was finally made to borrow £200 towards the costs, but this in turn meant that the Local Government Board (LGB) had to approve the construction at an inquiry, despite work being more or less finished. In preparation for this, Town Surveyor Mr Purnell had to prepare details of three water schemes to present to the LGB; Joseph Smith surveyed from the footbridge at Castle Ford for a scheme to fill the pool by gravitation and Edmund Bourne was to seek Mr Pears consent.

The inquiry was held by the Inspector Mr Tulloch on Thursday 12th December at the Council Offices on Upper Rosemary Hill. Henry Street outlined the three possible water schemes; by gravity from the brook, by an adjacent spring, or by town water. The last two would need to run in conjunction with each other; refreshing from the spring by 1,000 gallons daily and emptying and replacing with town water twice a year costing 25s each time. However, the construction of the baths was the first occasion that the Covenants included in the purchase of the fields could be tested; Mr Wyer suggested that the baths should not have been built as it was *'contrary to the terms upon which the land was purchased'* and in reply Mr Tulloch said that the inquiry would not have been granted by the LGB if those terms had been contravened; presumably the building of swimming baths was seen as acceptable under the term of using the fields as 'pleasure grounds'. Mr Jackson revealed the scheme prepared by the Local Board some years ago was for a baths just ten yards from the present scheme. Mr Tulloch visited the baths after the inquiry closed.

The LGB delayed their decision until the method of filling the pool had been finalised; the Council's choice was the gravity scheme surveyed by Joseph Smith and in early February 1896 the KUDC wished to make a start constructing it, again before the LGB had sanctioned the work, but this involved the laying of pipes parallel to the brook from near the Castle Ford and under the field (number 38) rented by Mrs Draper. In early April 1896 she asked the Council if the work could be delayed until after haymaking (indicating the use her field was put to) and later developments suggest her wishes were granted; the 6ins glazed pipes were ordered in readiness. At the same meeting a letter was received from William Pears confirming he was happy with this particular scheme and so the last obstacle to completing the baths had been removed. Mr Pears' agreement was sent to the LGB for approval.

However, in early May with the planned opening approaching, *'the operations among the hay are not sufficiently forward'* and so with the water system incomplete the 60,000 gallon pool was filled for the first time from a water company standpipe on Abbey Hill, an operation carried out by the Volunteer Fire Brigade; hopefully gravity did much of the work rather than the men operating their manual-pump engine. Starting on Wednesday 13th May, the process took 20 hours to complete and cost the KUDC 25s. The spectacle was *'a scene of considerable interest.'*

A *'young and active'* (in case he needed to perform a rescue) caretaker had to be employed and one of the council's workmen, Arthur Newey, was appointed at 18s a week. *'In the event of the baths being used by females, Mrs Newey be requested to act as attendant. The caretakers are at liberty to make a charge not exceeding 1d for the use of a clean towel or a pair of bathing drawers'* which they had to supply themselves. There was now an 'earth closet', and a blind had been fitted at the front of the female's dressing room; although this suggests there were separate facilities, no mixed bathing was allowed.

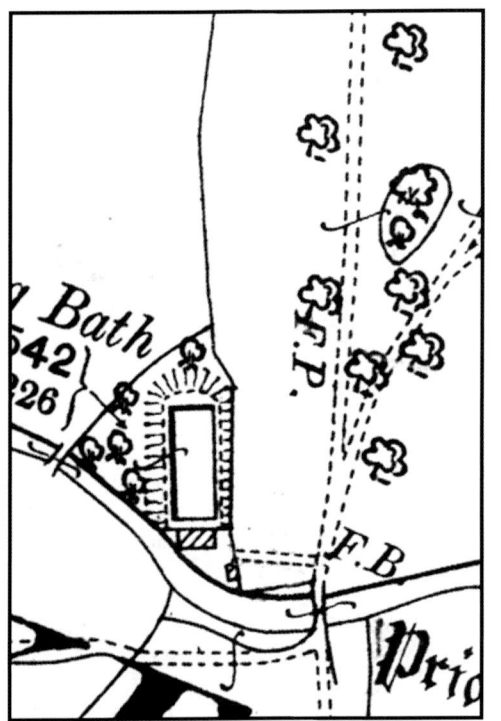

The pool's setting was bowl-like with steep slopes on three sides, partially created by excavated material and partially by its low position in the ground to get a favourable water flow. The east bank was of about 6ft in height above the water surface topped by the upper two feet or so of a pre-existing wall (that had originally formed the boundary to the plot) which proved a useful spectator vantage point; the new fence was erected outside it. The top of the slope on the western side was planted with shrubs, as was the northern end. There was a paved walkway, perhaps only 2ft 6ins wide, around these three sides at pool level. The southern end by the brook, where the entrance alongside the Iron Bridge and the changing room was sited, had a fence only for screening.

The bowl-like setting of the swimming pool with the changing rooms at the brook end and entrance near the Iron Bridge. The east wall of the enclosure, seen in the map on page 24, is its boundary; the other enclosure wall, seen in the photograph on page 32, was approximately in the centre of the swimming pool.

The antiquity symbol marking the site of the Priory Mill has been removed for clarity

(OS, 1905)

At last, the opening took place on a Monday afternoon, 1st June 1896, a week after Whit Monday, in delightful weather. The Town Crier, Mr Jeacocks (who lived at 39 High Street), with his bell announced the event and the ceremony was performed by KUDC Chairman Henry Street who after a brief speech was handed the key by Councillor Riley and he unlocked the door. The first in to the pool was Councillor William Holmes (hopefully dressed more decently than he had been in the incident 55 years previously!); there were about 60 bathers in the first two hours, and 128 bathers in the day, 119 men and 9 boys; participating ladies were absent. A dinner to mark the event was held in the picture gallery at the Queen & Castle and included as guests all those involved in the construction; their toil the previous hot summer was finally rewarded. The second day saw 131 bathers. Wednesday was Ladies' day; *'On Wednesday three ladies presented themselves but were too late for admission'*, and so an attendance of nil was recorded; the first occasion ladies braved the waters has passed unrecorded. On Thursday there were 128 male customers but on Friday the pool was much cooler, following rain, and only six braved the chilly water. Up to Sunday 7th June, 619 persons paid for admission. The pool's popularity continued; by the end of the second week 1,217 had swum and on the second Saturday the *'caretaker was severely taxed at times issuing tickets'*. Sunday saw 85 swimmers in the three hours it was open.

Until the gravitation scheme was complete, arrangements had been made to pump water from the brook into the pool and each Saturday after 6 p.m. a little water was run off and replenished. As much water as required could be pumped from the stream for 15s a week, payable to miller Mr Eagles; had this arrangement not been made, the baths would have had to close within days of opening due to stale water.

On 17th June the loan and construction were finally approved by the LGB. The gravitation filling system was completed and used for the first time on Friday 24th July, almost 8 weeks after the opening, giving an abundant supply of fresh stream water passing continually through the baths.

The pool's popularity was a considerable surprise and passed all expectations. The official figures published in the first week of September showed that since the baths opened 2,779 adults and 865 children, a total of 3,644, had paid for admission. With the season coming to an end, it was decided to keep the baths open for only three days a week. Males were allocated Saturday 9 a.m. till dusk, Tuesday from 2 p.m. till dusk, and Sundays 7 to 9.30 a.m.; females had use of the baths only on Tuesday from 8 a.m. until 1 p.m. although how many took advantage is unknown. The final cost of building the baths was £470 *(£57,000)*.

The opening of the swimming pool produced something of a paradox; the fields were supposedly not open to the public and yet the town's newest amenity was in the middle of them, increasing the pressure on the Council to deliver the rest of the Liberals' election promises. The Bathing Committee had the entire fields added to their responsibilities and, acting swiftly, on 17th June 1896 it declared, 'Your committee, having fully considered the questions of the tenancies of the Abbey Fields recommend that the Council take over on 29th September 1896 the part of the public lands numbered 46 and 47 upon the Abbey Fields estate plan (see map, page 17) and that they also give notice to the other tenants that after 29th September the public lands will be let by public tender'; it was adopted. The two fields in question, known as The Church Abbeys, were north of the brook alongside Bridge Street and became referred to as The Park. The choice of area to open was quite straightforward: to the west was the boundary wall built past the churchyard extension which was linked to the swimming baths by a fence, the northern side was bounded by the church, its yard, and High Street properties, to the east was the wall and fence separating the fields from Bridge Street, and southwards of course the boundary was the brook. Thus the 'park' area of the fields was enclosed and well-defined with three access points, over the Iron Bridge, from High Street and the path from Bridge Street to St Nicholas Church which joined it.

Perhaps not leaving themselves enough time to give suitable notice to its Church Abbeys tenant, the KUDC granted Joseph Roberts a further three months occupation; he paid £7 10s 1d to rent the fields from 29th September to 25th December and so perhaps it was Boxing Day 1896 that an area of the fields became the public park. Even then Roberts was reluctant to leave as in January 1897 he had to be reminded that his tenancy had ended at Christmas and he was to leave immediately.

Although the Park area was no longer to be used by grazing cattle, it was not to be without livestock. Mr Wringrose was allowed to keep sheep at a rent of £10 a year (compared to Mr Roberts paying £28), and the Council also 'turned out' into the field for retirement their elderly horse Merryman that was no longer fit for work, and their other horses in June, July and August, saving them £12 a year. With the area still being used for grazing, precisely what 'opening' the Park area amounted to is unclear; it may have just been the Council declaring their intention to at last carry out some development work there, or simply allowing unlimited public access. No reference to any grand opening declaration or public reaction can be found but an Abbey Fields Improvement Committee consisting of Councillors Bourne, Riley, Middleton, James and Jackson was appointed on 12th January 1897.

As access to the baths was only from the south over the Iron Bridge and north from the church path and High Street, a much-needed **footpath** was built eastwards to Bridge Street along the line of a hedge (see photograph, page 33) in readiness for the 1897 swimming season; work was well under way in February 1897, the hedge was *'grubbed up'* and the path surfaced with ashes. At the same time, a ditch running through the field was filled in and drainage pipes substituted.

Other improvements to the area were soon under way. In January 1897, the shed (not to be confused with the shelter) of unknown origin on the eastern side, and the short wall on the western side, of the Barn were removed; half the removed shed was re-erected in the *'upper corner of the field'*. *'The removal of these structures will open out the old building, the interior of which might be utilized at some future date for the preservation of objects of local interest'*. The Barn had a use until at least November 1897 when the sexton was requested to *'remove from the old barn, all graveyard tools and implements connected therewith'*, and it was locked to await a decision on its future. The area in front of the Barn was also tidied up, the work being done by the roadmen.

After further elections, a new Abbey Fields & Baths Committee was formed in April 1897 comprising Councillors Field, Jackson, Francis, Middleton, William Holmes and Henry Street. They were to *'prepare a scheme for the enjoyment of the public'* and in June reported that the fields needed no structural works to ensure public safety. Also in early 1897, two wych elms were planted in the public area and other **trees** were added, the first ornamental trees known to be planted in the fields since the sale by Clarendon. In September 1897, a further 21 trees - 9 beech, 2 wych elms, 3 copper beech, 1 ash, 3 elm and 3 oaks - were planted.

Queen Victoria's Jubilee in 1897 saw a parade terminating in the Abbey Fields. At one point the parade had halted in Warwick Road and the 2,000 or so assembled sang the first three verses of the National Anthem; a remarkable scene from a town of just 4,500. More than 1,200 meals were provided in marquees erected in the fields, and sports were held; the novelty 'race' section included Treacle Bun Eating open to all-comers. The money raised to celebrate Victoria's jubilee produced a surplus and £10 of this was used to provide some seating in the fields, probably the first; *'The seats are a great success, a permanent reminder of the Jubilee and the best way to have spent the small amount of money at the disposal of the committee.'*

There had been an excess of funds for the **swimming pool's** construction; the money from the loan had been spent first and £27 was left over from the earlier public collections and rather than being put to a specific use, the money was simply added to the KUDC General Account. The interest in the pool quickly waned. In the 1897 season, starting on 1st June, by the first week in September only £11 10s had been taken in ticket sales; for the next four weeks to the season end, takings dipped to as low as 11d a week. Expenditure for just the first three months was over £18 and so there was a notable loss on the season. Added to this was a drop in field renting, due to both opening the fields to the public and reducing the actual rents, from £153 to £111; had the KUDC miscalculated and the prudence of the Local Board been vindicated? However, it was pointed out that for years the Abbey Fields had been a cost with no benefit, and at least now the public were able to gain some use. The swimming baths however, was destined to never break even.

Towards the end of 1897 at the **Tantara Gatehouse**, the top rail of the *'movable style'* or 'clappergate' (seen in the photograph on page 11) was repaired, dangerous stone taken down, and rubbish removed *'from the enclosure'*; the key to the gatehouse was entrusted to the KUDC surveyor.

The **Barn** with its attached shelter (see page 32) was ideally placed in the park to have some alternative use. In 1898 it was suggested that if the *'rack and manger'* were removed, the floor paved and the walls whitewashed, the shelter would make a good retreat for children caught in a shower, in turn confirming the fields were established as a play area for children. *'It would not be such a shelter as one would like, but would be better than nothing'*. However, in early March the following year the shelter was removed. *'It was not an object of beauty by any means, and the removal will take away an objectionable feature'*.

With an area of the fields open to the public, **bye-laws** needed to be compiled for their use. A complete set does not survive but a *Kenilworth Advertiser* writer in early 1897 did not seem to be at all impressed with the copy he had: *'I cannot now digest all of them, some I never shall. I cannot conceive how they can be adopted in the face of the purpose for which the fields were bought'*. Rule 13 was particularly controversial: *'A person shall not play or take part in any game of football, golf, quoits, hockey or cricket or any other game the Council may prohibit'*; it was suggested that it should be amended to include the phrase *'nobody over the age of 14'*. This led to a heated discussion; getting children to stop playing in the streets was a priority, but allowing them to play *'dangerous and boisterous games'* in the fields could stop others from using them; unhelpfully, Mr Hodges observed *'they might just as well be killed in the streets as fatally struck by a cricket ball'*. The age amendment was included, but this led to the Kenilworth United Cricket Club, who had recently lost the use of their regular ground, to apply for use of an area of the park claiming it would be no more dangerous for them to play cricket than 14-year-olds, but they were turned down. It was hoped that better sporting facilities could be provided at a later date. Rule 4 stated, *'No wheeled vehicle such as a perambulator or cycle shall be taken onto the grass'*; although this suggests that cycling on the paths was established and permitted, taking a pram onto the grass for young children to have a picnic would have been frowned upon. It is likely that the healthy youth and young men of the town were cycling to the swimming baths. It is unclear if the new laws at this time applied only to the designated Park area or the entire fields.

Regular visitors to the fields were the **fire brigade**. The brook had always proved a useful water source for testing equipment and men, and the fields were also where the new steam fire engine, Queen Bess, was handed over and put through its paces for the first time in 1898; *'A hose was laid from the brook to the wych elm in the Park, a distance of about 200 yards, and the water was thrown above the elm to a height of about 135 feet'*. Mr Fancott allowed free use of his field for fire brigade practices. The regular demonstrations of the brigade's capabilities became annual in-house competitions, and others were held against visiting brigades.

In 1898 there was still no sign of the promised lake being made, and the absence of a **path** along an obvious route was lamented; a nicely made walk from the Townpool Bridge to the Castle Ford following the north bank of the brook was a regular suggestion and adding a few ornamental shrubs along its length would achieve a pleasing appearance. The condition of the replacement footpath from Borrowell Lane to the Iron Bridge was the subject of complaint in 1898; it saw a great deal of use as the most direct link from that area of the town to the church and Post Office in High Street, but it was impassable *'for the greater part of the year when the ground is soft'*. It was suggested that a path of cinders could be laid at minimal cost as a basis for something better, and that the stiles upon the path should be replaced by gates. A memorial was submitted by the residents of the area, and the KUDC did agree to re-level and improve the surface of the path and replace the stiles with clap gates; in April 1899 the path was 'made up'.

This path was not alone in causing problems as the poor surface of that from Abbey End to the Iron Bridge caused an accident in January 1899 when Mrs Robertson twisted her ankle and fell on her way to church; the rain had disturbed the gravel making ruts. *'On a very dark night one does not know if the next step will not land one in a ditch, or on one's nose in the field'*. Twenty yards from the bridge there was a depression which filled with water *'and ladies have either to go on the field or step in the water'*, suggesting gentlemen simply strode through. Making a channel to the brook to drain it was suggested. There was a similar depression on the other side of the bridge *'on the path leading to the tumble-down stile'*, presumably a reference to the stile within the Tantara Gatehouse.

The avenue to the church planted in 1902 with tree guards made by Kenilworth smiths *(HS)*

39

In January 1902, the Council took the decision to plant **trees** on both sides of the swimming pool path leading from Bridge Street. It was of course immediately suggested that this should be followed by trees along the paths from the Iron Bridge to the churchyard gate, and from there back to Bridge Street, creating a triangle of avenues. It seems the trigger for planting good quality trees in the park were the much-admired fine specimens in Priory Road. In April, 60 tree guards (to deter livestock) were ordered from four Kenilworth smiths, Shard, Sumner, Riley and White, in preparation, but the first trees from Bridge Street to St Nicholas church planted in the second week of April 1902 were described as *'rather stunted'*. The following week, workmen began digging them up to be replaced with larger more robust specimens provided by nurseryman Henry Whateley who oversaw the work. Those that were removed were replanted near the swimming baths with the expectation that once established they could be moved to a more suitable location. The cost was met from *'the Councillors'* own pocket, the first known occasion that improvements were made to the Abbey Fields from private funds.

Newly planted trees and their guards along the paths date this photograph to soon after 1902. Removed in 1897, cattle are again grazing in the 'park' area. The prominent tree is the wych elm referred to in the text *(HS)*

In celebration of **Edward VII's Coronation** in August 1902, delayed two months due to his illness, the Abbey Fields were put to good use. There was an extraordinary parade of townsfolk in all manner of costumes and guises that terminated in the park where prizes were handed out. This was followed by sports that had a collection of races for all-comers over a variety of distances, such as a 40 yard flat race for ladies over 40, and novelty events such as a *'blind-buff duck hunt'* won appropriately by a man named Lake. This was followed by an equestrian egg-and-spoon race. Over 2,000 cheered on the competitors. Just before 6.00 p.m. an oak, to be known as King Edward's Oak, was planted by KUDC Chairman Edmund Bourne whilst Mrs Joynson planted a copper beech nearby, to be known as the Queen Alexandra. Edmund Bourne made a speech and was given three hearty cheers. The tree names had been suggested by Councillor E Swann. There had however, been an obvious oversight; within hours, the leaves of the newly planted trees were eaten by the council's own horses that grazed in the field! The complete lack of protection for the trees was rightly criticised, but they were in any case likely to struggle to survive having been planted out of season, as was the case for the other recently planted trees; *'The absence of one here and there spoils the effect of the avenue'*. The coronation oak was then guarded, but in 1914 it was decided not to replace the guard around it; *'it is such a poor specimen it is doubtful that it would develop into a suitable memorial of the occasion.'*

In September 1902, it was decided that the eleven seats *'enjoyed by the public'* installed in the 'Pleasure Grounds' by Mr Keatley for the Coronation were to be taken by the Council for £2 15s; the *'Coronation benches are very useful but not very ornamental, and are at the mercy of anyone who wants to knock them about'*; one had disappeared altogether!

The KUDC administered the Public Pleasure Grounds (the Park), and Abbey Fields (for renting for grazing) quite separately; the annual accounts published in May 1903 saw expenditure on the former was £51 4s 5d, the latter £24 11s 10d, and for the baths, also separate, £14 9s 11d. It appears that The Public Pleasure Grounds now included all 57 acres of the fields owned or managed by the Council.

William Holmes had become Chairman of the Fields & Baths Committee and was leading the **tree** planting which included replacing older trees. In 1903, due to safety fears, the Council considered cutting down elm trees that bordered the fields at Rosemary Hill, *'the sooner they are down the better'*, and dangerous boughs were removed. At this time 100 trees were purchased, 25 each of elm, beech (mixed) silver birch and lime, and planting started on the diagonal Abbey Hill to Bridge Street path. Work was not confined to tree planting, the footpaths on the estate *'are very bad'* and received immediate attention.

Not everyone was in favour of the KUDC's management of the fields, especially as they expanded away from the original park area, and by January 1904 they were receiving letters complaining about the tree planting, leading to many discussions. It was decided by 6 votes to 3 to keep just ten trees in the Abbey Hill to Bridge Street avenue but at the same meeting the Council accepted a gift of 50 English oak trees from a Mr Gowers. There was also dissatisfaction about the trees being planted in the Cross Abbeys (alongside Abbey Hill) as when mature they would obstruct the view of the church and Castle from Abbey Hill. They *'could have been planted in clumps with shrubs to give a park-like appearance to the outer park'*. Over the next few months, there were whispers of a petition from the occupants along Abbey Hill to have them removed; the residents had bought the field from Clarendon to preserve their outlook, paying the highest price of any Abbey Fields acreage, and those still alive deserved to be heard. Councillor Jackson was one of those against the planting which would spoil *'one of the prettiest views in Warwickshire'*. Even though he was on the Abbey Fields Improvement Committee, Arthur Street was against those alongside Abbey Hill being planted so thickly; he would not have supported the resolution to plant trees had he known that there were to be so many. He suggested lifting some of the newly planted trees forming the avenue from Bridge Street and *'replanting them in promiscuous places'* in the fields. With a heated argument developing, William Holmes moved that the trees be left where they were and this was carried. It was then announced that Lord Clarendon had offered yet another 50 oak trees and despite objections, the offer was accepted.

The Abbey Hill properties that had enjoyable outlooks; George Turner's Montpelier House is prominent, Arthur Street, briefly, lived just beyond the church in his uncle Henry's house. From a postcard stamped 17th July 1907 *(HS)*

There was by now an unsightly 'clump' of trees in the park, presumably those replanted from elsewhere, the appearance of which, it was suggested, could be improved by the planting of rhododendron bushes. There continued to be much controversy over the tree planting; as examples, the cost of protective railings around them could be better spent upon asphalting the footpaths, whilst others thought that gas lighting the paths was preferable to planting trees. The *'forest of oaks'* was enclosed by a fence at a cost of £11.

The digging of pits for the trees in the park suddenly caused a stir when a quantity of bones were found, all, *'presumably human'*; one was clearly the upper part of an arm. It was supposed to be the remains of people buried at the Monastery but due to their location this was described as *'conjecture'*; the path being planted at the time was that diagonally from Abbey End to Bridge Street. This pathway had now become known as 'Holmes Avenue' from the fact that Councillor Holmes was *'the presiding spirit of the movement... and most enthusiastic in the planting of trees'*. In April 1904 Holmes announced his retirement from local politics, it was joked he was to become a forester.

The plantation of trees in the original Park known as *'the forest'*, which was the replanted stunted trees from the church footpath mixed with newly planted oaks, soon became more of a copse; in June 1904, it was observed that for every live tree there were two dead ones despite them being fenced off. *'The expensive guard is worthy of a better fate than to guard a dozen dead trees and shrubs with about six living ones'*. A 'circular enclosure' had been made near the baths, presumably for the 'forest', and Mr Whateley had promised trees for it which had yet to appear.

A horse grazes the Abbey Hill field in a photograph that has proved difficult to date (the sign on the Institute building is illegible) but is in a collection otherwise dated to the later Victorian and early Edwardian years *(WCRO, PH 77/37)*

The problems of **grazing** rights mixing with public access provided occasional incidents. One spring day in 1904, two ladies were sitting quietly in the park when *'a couple of horses, being frisky and delighted with having their quarters in so magnificent a place, came kicking up their heels to where the ladies were sitting, giving them a fright'*. It was suggested by one of them that a gate could be made in the fencing around the forest, *'wherein timid folk might take refuge by hiding among the trees'*, but the enclosure was an eyesore and destined to be removed in 1905.

In the summer of 1900, Mrs Draper gave up the occupation of the field she had held for some years, the western part of the **Oxpen Meadow** and site of the former Priory lake. This was seen as the ideal opportunity to make the lake that was shown on the grand plan of the 1880s still hanging on the KUDC chamber wall. It was seen as a money-making scheme, with fishing and boating in the summer and skating in the winter, and a great gain for the town. It was even suggested at this point that the lake could be leased to a private company that could be charged 50 times the rental provided by Mrs Draper. However, within a few weeks the Council were advertising the near 6 acres for letting on an annual tenancy.

In late November 1903, the then flooded part of the Oxpen Meadow of Joseph Roberts, had a visitor; *'Kenilworth is not often visited by wildfowl but a wild goose has taken up residence on an island in the pool. Several of our sportsmen have tried to get a shot at him, but cannot get close enough for a fair shot, so at the present he is an ornament in the landscape'*. In May 1904, Joseph Roberts received £3 compensation from the council due to the damage of his land from *'the overflow from a spring'* on the council's land in the park near to Abbotsfield; this may have been the spring which it was suggested could be used to fill the swimming pool. It is interesting to note that until comparatively recent times, the occasional skating area was known to some residents as 'Joe's overflow'.

The **brook** had an absence of trees and shrubs alongside and was a greater waterway than it is today; in 1902 Mr Hughes caught a 2¾ lb trout. As an indication of how much water was in the brook, in July

1904 a group of boys made a canoe and paddled it from Washbrook to the ford near the Castle; it appears that the brook was at its normal level at the time and not in flood as, if it was, the boys would then have had an impossible task propelling themselves against the flow. The brook provided a drinking place for grazing animals and depressions alongside for that purpose were provided and can still be seen. In early 1905 a *'very useful'* horse belonging to Mr Fancott, who rented the field on the Abbey Hill-Rosemary Hill corner, was found lying in the brook at a drinking spot apparently having become entangled in the fence installed to prevent livestock crossing. The horse was released but found to be so badly injured that it was put down. In the cold winter of January 1907 even the brook froze, enough for people to skate along it.

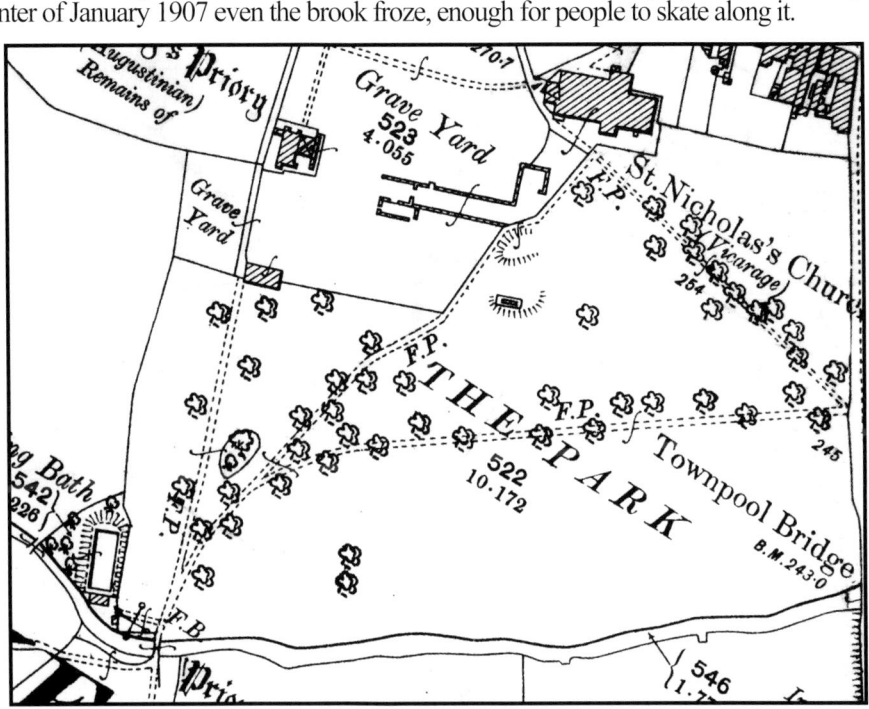

The Abbey ruins inside the churchyard have been uncovered, and the Chapter House wall is shown. In the junction of the paths appears to be the tree enclosure described as 'the forest'; other trees include the new avenue to St Nicholas Church, and other planting along the pathways *(OS, 1905)*

A regular park entertainment was the performance of **bands**. Kenilworth had a string band formed and conducted by Louis Schneider, a musical instrument seller and contractor. Louis Schneider's band performances prompted calls in 1901 for a bandstand to be built in the Abbey Fields, with Schneider himself willing to contribute to and organise the collecting of donations towards it; as he was also a building contractor, perhaps he was also willing to construct it. However, Charles Stringer was amongst those councillors who thought it would set a dangerous precedent if the council became involved in such an enterprise, and the bandstand never came to fruition.

Each May, the KUDC discussed the **swimming pool** in preparation for the new season. The bath was left full of water throughout the winter to protect the brickwork and was emptied, cleaned and refilled each spring. In the whole of 1900 the bath took only £6 yet the expenses were £37 10s; such was the lack of customers, for 1901 Mr Gee calculated it would be worthwhile dispensing with the caretaker and not collecting money! The bath was to be open from 6.30 a.m. to 8 p.m. on weekdays, and 6 to 9 a.m. on Sundays. *'There will be no day for ladies as they take no interest in the baths; only two went last year.'*

Perhaps one reason that ladies were not very enthusiastic was because the water looked yellowy. It was said that this was because the baths had a cement bottom and it was suggested that glazed white tiles would give a truer indication of the water colour. In July 1901, the bath's attendant Mr Thomas showed a *Kenilworth Advertiser* correspondent a water sample from the baths, it was clear with no sediment. It was claimed, *'The bath is well patronised, and would be more so if people would go and see the water'*. Thomas filled his time by looking after all the field's paths, which were weed free, and keeping the hedges smart and trim; he was clearly little occupied at the baths. He was being paid just 10s a week, almost half the wages of the first attendant who was paid 18s in 1896; *'His pay is not much, most people will agree that an extra 2s a week would be money well-bestowed.'*

The fields were of course a magnet for children to make their own entertainment, the brook being the focal point for many. A group of boys larking about alongside the Iron Bridge in the summer of 1901 almost had serious consequences. Young Arthur Satchwell, just 4 years old and from High Street, was standing by the brook when another boy ran down the bank and pushed him in. The other boys cried out for help, alerting the swimming pool attendant Mr Thomas who was some 200 yards away cutting down thistles. He collected the 'drag' from the pool and rescued the boy, who had by now floated under the bridge. Other than being extremely frightened, he seemed none the worse for his immersion. Mr Thomas said that boys regularly played near the spot and he often sent them away due to the dangers, but the water was *'only about 3 to 4 feet deep'*. As an aside, when 78-year-old builder George Satchwell died at his High Street home in 1916, it was reported that 5 generations of his family, of which Arthur was one, were living in the house.

For 1902, James Aitken of Castle Green was appointed baths caretaker at 16s a week, receiving the pay rise deserved by his predecessor, and he too had to keep the footpaths of the fields in order; what Mr Thomas thought of losing his job to someone who received a 60 per cent pay increase can be imagined. Again, there was no provision for ladies. The baths closed on 13th September after its 16 or so week season, and the weather was blamed for falling attendances with less than 2s a week being taken; even if entrance was just a penny that would be just four swimmers a day. *'People* (do) *not seem to take advantage of the baths.'*

Cleaning the pool would normally take 2 or 3 men several days, but in preparation for the 1903 season, the fire brigade used it as practice and emptied it in 3 hours with their steam fire engine, but they left the mud at the bottom for workmen to get out by hand. This perhaps suggests that the drain from the baths back into the brook had a shallow angle and draining took a long time. In 1903 ladies were once more welcomed, perhaps any attempt to attract a few extra customers was considered worthwhile; the baths opened on 1st June with Tuesdays and Fridays, 2 to 6 p.m. for ladies. James Aitken remained as attendant and caretaker on 16s a week, and his wife was paid 2s a week to attend to the ladies for their 8 hours.

On the **path** leading from Abbey End to the Iron Bridge was an elderly barn. Put upon it since at least the 1870s, were posters mostly advertising coming events; it was an ideal spot as so many people passed by. In the attempts to improve the appearance of the park, in April 1904, Town Crier and Bill Poster Mr Jeacocks was surprised to be told to remove all the posters and to refrain from putting any more up. The park was being tidied; it was suggested that the barn could do with painting, perhaps in the black and white style of a cottage.

There were to be more problems with **trees**. The Abbey Fields Committee met on 18th March 1905 and, perhaps in response to protests, suggested moving alternate trees alongside the diagonal Abbey End to Bridge Street path and to replant them in place of the young trees that had died in the Park. Only two attended the Abbey Fields Committee meeting on 9th October when the formal decision was made to buy new trees, 3 dozen at about 2s 6d each, as replacements and for new locations. Mr Jackson said they should take all the trees from the Cross Abbeys as they would not grow there and use those as replacements. Arthur Street agreed, adding that the trees would block the view from Abbey Hill and it was wrong to plant them there. *'Seeing as so many are now dead, I think they ought to be removed, and the live ones planted in convenient places in the park'.* The matter was referred to the General Purposes Committee. Listening to the complaints, on 18th November 1905, the Highways Committee recommended that all ten trees should be removed from the Abbey Hill to Bridge Street path and be planted to replace dead trees elsewhere in the pleasure grounds; Mr Gee however said it would be wrong to undo the work of others after all the trouble and expense, but there was still a feeling that when mature they would hide the view across the fields. Mr Margetts said he would like them all gone; they were there due to a small committee and he had not heard any favourable comments about them. Mr Bostock, one of the committee, said they had been thinned once and did not think they would interfere with the view. Another said *'The residents of Abbey Hill and Rosemary Hill were unanimously of the opinion that it was a mistake to plant the trees there, it would obstruct their view for which they had to pay very heavily'.* The counter argument was that if they were to make the pleasure grounds attractive they must plant trees; the discussion was sent back to the committee but the ten trees remained on the diagonal path.

In 1906, an application was made to connect the telegraph system to the Post Office in High Street by erecting a series of poles across the Abbey Fields down to the Iron Bridge then either continuing to The Square or by following the brook; although poles went up in other parts of the town, it seems this part of the scheme failed to materialise.

Despite the disappointing use of the swimming pool, it had a collection of regulars and on 20th July 1904 a meeting to form a **swimming club** was held just outside the baths. Behind the move were 35-year-old schoolteacher Richard Taylor (of Kenilworth Boys College, Priory Road), and tannery foreman John James

Ward of Barrow Road, whose son attended the college. Taylor expressed the hope that the council could help the club without mentioning specifics, and said there was an intention to hold a sports day at the end of the season. Councillor Jackson said how pleased he was that the pool would be used for the teaching of youngsters, and another of the councillors present, Arthur Street, was elected to preside; he extolled the virtues of swimming and the necessity of a club. Councillor Riley, the man behind the building of the swimming pool, proposed the official motion to form a club and his resolution was carried unanimously.

Arthur Street was elected its President, and the committee was formed of James Everitt Jackson (master cabinet maker and Deputy Captain of the fire brigade), W Riley (ironmonger, High Street), W Riley (newsagent and newspaper publisher, The Square), J J Ward (tannery foreman), E Adkins (tannery clerk), Sholto Douglas (Town Surveyor), S Hiscock (schoolteacher), R Barwell, and R B Coleman. Mr W Cooper (of the tannery) was the secretary. A committee meeting was immediately held at which it was decided to split the club into senior and junior divisions, the seniors to pay 1s a year membership and the juniors 6d; this would not include entrance to the baths. The secretary was asked to write to the council asking if the club could have the exclusive use of the baths one evening a week, Thursday, from half an hour before sunset until dusk. No ladies, or girls, were mentioned.

Councillor James E Jackson, right, in 1907 when he was deputy to the fire brigade's Captain E K Bourne, left. For interest, the other fireman is C J Penn *(KFB)*

The *Kenilworth Advertiser* noted that the club committee were all good swimmers except one, Councillor Riley. Riley had been instrumental in having the pool built and had taken his first swim the day it was opened, but it seems he was not one to take advantage of the opportunities it provided. Richard Taylor was the club captain, and Mr Adkins vice-captain, and the newspaper stated Mr Hiscock was the secretary, contradicting the earlier report. Arthur Street being elected President of course provided a connection to the pool's opening, a ceremony performed by his uncle Henry when KUDC Chairman.

The following week it was announced that the club had over 50 members with the prospect of reaching 100. On Saturday 3rd September 1904, the club held its first sports, Arthur Street presented a trophy, the Presidents Cup. There was a large attendance and Dr Edmund Bourne, now Chairman of the KUDC, officiated as starter. A variety of races was held including team races and the trophies were presented by Arthur Street's *'little daughter'*, either ten-year-old Florence or five-year-old Ethel. A minimum charge was made for entry and this raised over £3. One great attraction were the performances of John Arthur Jarvis and Mr Wright who gave a display of diving. *'Their superb performances created great astonishment and admiration, ringing applause testifying to their signal merit'*. The performance by Leicester-born Jarvis was something of a coup; he was the self styled 'Swimming Champion of the World' and had won three gold medals at the 1900 Paris Olympics, the first ever triple-gold Olympian. He was known as 'The Professor' and 'The Wonder of Swimming' at a time when the sport itself was seen as 'wondrous'. He introduced a new style, and was a leading exponent of life-saving, it is said that he saved hundreds of lives by teaching his methods. How he came to be in Kenilworth that day is unknown.

The swimming pool was a target late at night for those on their way home from public houses. On 30th July 1905 there was a particularly bad incident caused by *'fellows in a beastly state of intoxication'*. Having climbed over the fence to get in, they trampled on bathing costumes and towels covering them with dirt and threw them into the pool, pulling up *'stakes'* and causing other damage; it was *'a riotous affair'*. The police knew the culprits and the council was awaiting their report. It was not the first time but was perhaps the worst incident. One of those responsible wrote a letter of apology and offered to pay all costs for *'putting things in order again'*; he added that the offence was committed on the spur of the moment and there was no intention to cause damage.

In 1905 the swimming club had 60-70 members and held another Sports & Gala that was attended by over 600 spectators. It included *'trick swimming'*. The club seems to have boosted swimming in the town as when the baths closed for the year 5,784 persons had used them, boosting income by £6 6s 11d on the previous year to total receipts £18 11s 4d. This interest was however, short-lived. In 1906 the club had only 14s in its accounts and the gala that year had fewer spectators, only 377, and the pool made a loss of £28; 1907 was even worse with 300 for the gala and only 2,038 used the baths in the entire 4 months it was open; takings were down by half.

Initially, the club held its AGM at the Lecture Hall, Rosemary Hill (today it is the Priory Theatre), but by 1908, the club meetings were at Kenilworth Boys College in Priory Road; headmaster Mr Taylor was still heavily involved in the club, as were his boys, but that year only 150 spectators attended the 5th annual swimming gala. It was an improved year for the public swimming as 2,460 adults and 1,310 juniors used the baths giving £13 9s in takings against £33 13s 2d expenses. The available figures for this time suggest an entrance fee of just 1d for adults and ½d for children. It was suggested that the pool should be cleaned more often, but for this it needed to be closed for four days, and it took 24-36 hours to fill.

Although the pool had good arrangements for schoolboys, schoolgirls were not so fortunate. Miss Blatchcox who ran a school for young ladies, and had sympathies with the suffrage movement, pointed out that having only two opportunities for ladies to use the pool each week was no basis on which girls could learn to swim; she suggested a short daily allowance would suffice. The response reveals the attitudes of the day; *'Last year they were allowed from 2 till 6 o'clock two afternoons a week, now they want 3 till 6 o'clock each day; it is the usual way if we give ladies a bit of encouragement'*, and the comment was greeted with laughter. Bravely, Charles Randall suggested some hours of mixed bathing; the response, *'We cannot countenance that at all!'* was greeted with more laughter. In trying to explain the poor attendance record of girls at the pool, Mr Weetman said that it was a very cold summer, but added that he did not think extending the hours was *'worth considering'*. Against the prevailing views, Miss Blatchcox did have some success; the ladies were granted an extra afternoon a week, 2-6 p.m. on Monday, Wednesdays and Fridays.

The *Kenilworth Advertiser* thoughtfully published a description of the latest *'extremely fascinating'* lady's swimwear: *'Woollen materials are best, dark colours and black relieved with white or coloured trimmings seem to be in favour. The designs are simple of cut, consisting in most cases of a skirt and blouse joined at the waist and opening the whole way down the side, over knickers slightly longer than the tunic.'*

An early 20th century view of field 41 (see map, page 17), the photographer having an elevated position presumably in Borrowell Lane. The Luzley Brook is a barely discernible ditch running through a gap in the hedge and is acting as a barrier to the livestock. Towards top right can be seen the fence separating the park from land owned by William Evans, and the path created alongside it in 1885. The park boundary with Area D is just out of view to the left *(HS)*

In early 1908, Colonel Nelson was at the head of a movement to start a Kenilworth *'miniature rifle club'*; central to the plans was a **rifle range** with one suggestion being that the Abbey Fields was the ideal location. Clarendon had already approved a site at the back of the golf club (in the moat at the rear of The Brays), but a more central site was sought for the club that already had 135 members. Nelson was invited to outline the proposals to the KUDC; the object of the club, in which Lord Ernest Seymour was also involved, was to *'instruct young men and lads in the use of a service rifle, and to provide recreation for older inhabitants'* and *'only'* service rifles would be used, *'unless private members wished to have match rifles'*. Already in operation was St John's shooting club, though it is thought that they restricted their weaponry to air rifles.

In the Abbey Fields it was proposed to build a corrugated iron structure 48yds long, 20ft wide and 9ft high at a cost of £60-£70. Immediately Councillor Jackson raised the question of the covenants covering the fields that prevented such structures from being put up; *'A great many people paid a considerable sum to prevent any building being put up on any part of the estate'*. Although the council were favourable towards the establishing of the club, the *'terms and conditions upon which the Abbey Fields were vested in the Council precluded...'* the building being anywhere in the park. Colonel Nelson's proposed club did come to fruition, it evolved into the Kenilworth Volunteers and had its open range built to the west of the Echo Meadow *c*1912 about 400 yards from the Castle.

It had been suggested that steps should be taken to lower the gradient of the **path** from Abbey Hill to the Iron Bridge, however in February 1908 with estimated costs for the two proposed ways to achieve this being £58 and £66, the idea was set aside. Months later, it was decided to make a path from the Iron Bridge to the Castle Ford by simply fencing off part of the meadow. The cost did not exceed £10 and included a contribution of £1 from the (unnamed) new tenant. The fence was of 'iron and wire', no surfacing was added but a clap gate was provided at each end. The route was described as *'very pretty'* and did, of course, provide a short cut to and from the Castle; in the vicinity of the swimming baths it passed around the end furthest from the brook. At some unknown time, an oil lamp was installed near the Iron Bridge; in 1910 it was decided to replace it with a Petrolite lamp at a cost of £3 15s and Ironmonger William Riley supplied the petrol at 1s 4½d a gallon.

The Iron Bridge, of unknown antiquity but specifically mentioned in the 1860s, is a focal point at the centre of the Abbey Fields *(8th March 2017)*

The position of **swimming pool** attendant was for only four months a year and not being full time was generally taken by a council employee and his wife; Mr & Mrs Aitken for 16s a week were appointed in 1905. The next was former soldier and one-time road labourer Henry Trunkfield in 1907 who held the position until the end of the summer in 1908 when, aged 73, he received an old age pension of 5s a week but still worked occasionally for the council at the sewer works pumping station. Henry, a popular man who had served in the Crimea and was at the Indian Mutiny in 1852, was strong, healthy and vigorous for his age and lived at Millbrook Cottages at Washbrook with his wife Sarah, who attended to the female swimmers in their allotted few hours; she too was a council employee, cleaning the offices for 3s a week. Although the wages were low, the attendants were still allowed to increase their income by the hiring out of swimming costumes and towels but for this they had to provide their own, an arrangement existing from the bath's earliest days.

For the start of the 1909 season on Monday 31st May, Trunkfield sold his towels and swimwear to the new attendant, Irish-born 55-year-old Robert Howie McQuilkin, for 5s; he had been in Kenilworth as a 17-year-old in 1871 but spent time in the army and navy and was receiving an army pension. In 1881 he married Lilly Summerskill in Liverpool but it appears they divorced, a rare occurrence for the era, as Lilly McQuilkin remarried in Liverpool in 1900, and Robert remarried in 1908. His new bride was Kenilworth-born Mary Naomi Watson; in 1881 Mary was a dressmaker aged 22 living at 6 Odibourne Terrace with her grandparents William and Mary Simpson, and in 1885 she had married Henry Cooper; it is not known if they divorced or he died. The McQuilkins lived at 73 Henry Street, next door to Mary's parents at number 75. McQuilkin was of medium height, stiff build, his hair tinged with grey, and he had a slight brown moustache.

On Thursday 5th August, Henry Trunkfield informed Sholto Douglas, the Council Surveyor whose responsibilities included the swimming pool, that McQuilkin was drunk at Mill End and had left someone else in charge of the pool; Douglas immediately set off for the pool where he found a man named Watson in charge, presumably a relative of McQuilkin's wife. McQuilkin was sacked, and Douglas gave the attendant's job back to Henry Trunkfield as from Saturday 7th. McQuilkin went to Trunkfield's house at 11 a.m. on Monday 9th and asked Sarah Trunkfield to buy back the swimwear available for hire, also claiming that some was torn and that others were missing and it was not worth the 5s he had paid, but Sarah informed him that they had no need as Sholto Douglas was to supply new swimwear and she and her husband were to pay for them at a rate of 2s a week until the cost was paid off. In addition to getting him the sack, Robert McQuilkin now had a second grievance against Henry Trunkfield.

On Friday 13th, Henry Trunkfield arrived at the pool just before 6 p.m. to replace his wife who had been attending to the ladies for their two-hour session. As they sat together outside waiting for the last lady to leave, Henry told his wife that for supper he would like two eggs and some bread and butter, and he would be home soon after 8 p.m.; with that Sarah, *'a diminutive old lady with a very weak voice'*, set off for home.

Auguste Schneider, the 14-year-old son of bandsman and contractor Louis who lived at 16 Warwick Road, and two of his friends were the last at the pool, arriving at about 7 p.m. and ready to leave by 8. Trunkfield was *'cheerful and sober'* but seemed in a hurry, Auguste was the last to leave and was asked to do up his boots outside. Auguste and his friends made their way up the path towards Abbey Hill leaving Henry Trunkfield on his own to lock up. Although the pool closed at 8.00 p.m., Henry was in the habit of letting the last boys stay as long as they liked, sometimes past 9.00, but when he hadn't returned home by 10.00, Sarah became concerned. She went to his usual drinking place The Coventry Cross, and later tried The Wyandotte without success. By now nearly midnight, she met the lamplighter extinguishing the gas street lights and decided to return home due to being wary of the dark. After hardly sleeping, early next morning soon after 5 a.m., she made her way to the swimming pool, found the outer gate had not been locked and, being unable to get further inside the baths, found a ladder; she leaned it against the fence surrounding the pool, looked over, and saw her husband lying face down in the water, quite lifeless. *'His white head told me it was him. He was quite quiet'*. She raised the alarm with a council foreman she knew, Harry Newey, who went to the pool as *'the gentlemen would be arriving soon'* for their early morning swim. Sarah went to the police station to report her husband's death at 5.55 a.m.; Inspector Parkinson and PC Hall left for the pool and without entering the water they removed the body which was about 7ft from the edge at the shallow end. Trunkfield had injuries about his head, there were markings and a pool of blood on the pool's surrounds; his body was taken to the police station.

The night before, Robert McQuilkin had been seen drunk in the Abbey Fields and heading for the baths; 13-year-old George Sheepy was by the Tantara Gatehouse with some friends when McQuilkin went past muttering to himself. The next sighting was by Harry Skelsher of Bridge Street Cottages who saw McQuilkin at about 8.25 p.m. coming from the direction of the baths, he was soaking wet and his boots were *'squelchy'*. He was then seen just before 9 p.m. in The Albion Tavern where landlady Charlotte Brewer served him with two pints of ale and ½ ounce of tobacco. In the tavern, Ellen Shelswell of 75 Albion Street asked McQuilkin about scratches on his face and he said he had been through some brambles; the scratches were bleeding, more blood than scratches, but Ellen thought that as he had *'been on the beer, he had been catching it at home'* and told him *'it looks as if your missus has been giving you a milling.'*

Francis Watson, McQuilkin's brother in law living at 75 Henry Street, heard Robert's confession at about 9.00 that night: *'I have done the old **** in'*. Inspector Parkinson arrested Robert McQuilkin on suspicion of murder at his house at 1.00 p.m. on Saturday. He found a soaked set of clothes hanging to dry, and a pair of saturated boots under a chair; he charged him with murder later that day.

At 6.45 on the Saturday evening, Sholto Douglas returned to the pool with Inspector Parkinson. The pool had been drained enough to uncover the shallow end and at the bottom was found Trunkfield's purse, cap, and loose change scattered about *'in the mud'*. There were also boot prints that matched exactly those of McQulkin's with a distinctive nail pattern on the soles; they also matched scratches on the side of the pool where he had climbed out. At 1.30 p.m. on Monday, McQuilkin made a confessionary statement.

'The residents of Kenilworth have been suddenly thrown into a state of excitement', but the funeral had to be held; it was on Tuesday 17th at St Nicholas Church and a large number of people gathered including many council workmen. *'An effecting scene took place at the graveside, the widow showing great distress and other women also wept'*; mourners of course had a direct view of the swimming pool. Floral tributes included one from *'his little friend Ada'*.

The trial was held in Warwick on Tuesday 16th November 1909, but McQuilkin pleaded not guilty to murder. The medical evidence was given by Dr Growse; injuries to Trunkfield's head could have been by a fist or bottle and were sufficient to knock him unconscious; when Trunkfield hit the water he may have been unconscious rather than dead, his postmortem could not conclude with certainty either way. Under his fingernails were scrapings of skin, similar to what would be expected from scratching a face.

There was little doubt that McQuilkin was involved in Trunkfield's death but what actually happened could only be told by the accused man. Taking the witness stand, McQuilkin said he went to the baths to see Henry Trunkfield about buying the towels and costumes back, arriving at the pool just as he was about to close up. Trunkfield said he did not want them back and told him to get out as he wanted to close. McQuilkin replied *'Can you put me out?'*, and Trunkfield *'rushed the prisoner and knocked him down'*; he got up, *'rushed'* at Trunkfield, and they fell locked together with Trunkfield underneath, explaining how he sustained the serious wound to the back of his head. Trunkfield had hold of McQuilkin's throat, so he retaliated by butting him in his face a couple of times, saying *'let me go'*; the two rolled into the bath's shallow end, separated, and McQuilkin climbed out *'and went off as hard as I could'*. He did not know Trunkfield had died until the next day; he had not gone to the pool with the intention of hurting Trunkfield and had not touched him before Trunkfield attacked him. After deliberations of just 15 minutes, during which time McQuilkin stayed in the dock, the jury returned a verdict of manslaughter, and the judge sentenced him to 15 years penal servitude.

A fund was raised for Sarah Trunkfield to give her 5s a week until she was eligible for old age pension at the age of 70. This was done successfully but as her 70th birthday approached in November 1911, she discovered that she had miscalculated her age by a year, and that she was actually soon to be only 69. Another appeal was made and Lord Leigh was the first to donate, £3, and this was matched by Dora Schintz of Thickthorn, and Gertrude Evans donated £2; £15 15s 6d was raised within a week. Sarah later left her home at Washbrook and moved into one of the Almshouses in High Street, number 20, where she saw out her days just a short walk away from where her husband died, and was buried. She died in 1926 aged 83 and was presumably buried with Henry; sadly, the grave of Henry and Sarah Trunkfield cannot be found in St Nicholas graveyard, any stone that may have been in place is missing.

McQuilkin's wife reverted to using her previous married name Mary Cooper; she continued to live at 73 Henry Street until 1937 when she moved to 27 Stoneleigh Road. Her death is recorded as Mary Naomi McQuilkin in 1946 at the age of 87. Robert Howie McQuilkin can be found in the records of Parkhurst Prison on the Isle of Wight; it is thought he died in Islington aged 72 in 1927, two years after his jail term was due to end.

William Ingram was the new attendant for 1910; that year just 1,862 people used the pool. From 1910-1914, the annual Swimming Gala crowd varied between 200 and 400, except for 1912 when due to appalling weather there were very few spectators. The swimming pool was struggling to attract customers; the income for the entire year of 1913 was only £7 17s 4d. The ladies days reverted to just Tuesday and Friday afternoons, suggesting low attendances. However, hot weather in June 1914 created a claimed new monthly record for the baths since they opened, and increased use was recorded following the managers of the New Council School and St Nicholas National School sending the boys to learn swimming, sometimes twice a week; St Nicholas had several *'capital'* swimmers. The girls too attended with their teachers. A new springboard had to be ordered as the original was becoming worn out.

The Bungalow, and much of the undeveloped **Area D**, became owned by Frank Randolph Mullings Phelps on 29th September 1906. At the 12th November 1907 KUDC meeting, a letter from Phelps was read asking if the Council would be interested in an exchange of lands around his property, an area of his grounds swapped for an area of the original 40 acres of the Abbey Fields purchased by the Local Board. The land in question was staked out so that an on-site meeting could take place. Quite obviously, there was a covenant for the Abbey Fields land inserted by the seller Clarendon prohibiting its sale or use for any purpose other than as pleasure grounds; however, at the KUDC meeting the following February the town clerk announced that he had conferred with Clarendon's solicitors and they expressed their opinion that 'there would be no difficulty in obtaining a release from the limiting covenant entered into with his Lordship when the Abbey Fields estate was purchased'. As he had inserted the clause, it seems Clarendon's approval for the swap was mandatory. The town clerk had also had a series of correspondence with the Local Government Board in London and 'was definitely assured that the Board will raise no objection to the proposed exchange'. It was unanimously resolved by the council that an agreement should be entered into provided no expense was incurred by them.

For reasons undiscovered, it would be another five years until, with a conveyance dated 29th November 1912, Phelps and the KUDC exchanged the areas of land with 1473 sq yds from the plot becoming part of the Abbey Fields, whilst 986 sq yds was lost giving a net gain of 487 sq yds (about 16p), and thus allowed Mr Phelps to improve the shape of his garden. The Abbey Fields under KUDC control was now 57a 1273 sq yds, or about 57¼ acres. Somewhat ironically, the same wording used that failed to protect the 'lost' piece of land appeared in the conveyance protecting the new:

> ... forever hereafter be solely used for public walks and pleasure grounds under the control of the council and the same shall not nor shall any part thereof at any time hereafter be sold leased or disposed of for any other purpose inconsistent with the same being solely used as aforesaid.

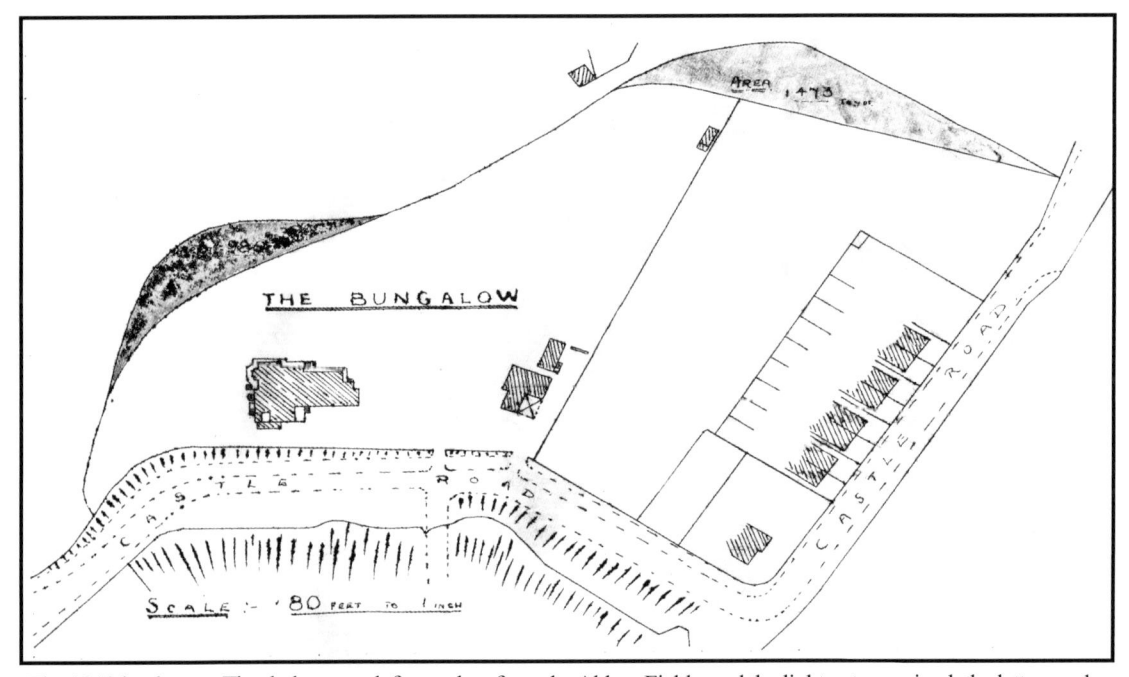

The 1912 land swap. The darker area, left, was lost from the Abbey Fields, and the lighter, top, gained; the latter can be seen fenced whilst still in private ownership in the photograph on page 30 *(WDC 36)*

Whilst the above was in progress, before committing to building a cemetery in early 1909 the KUDC again investigated a further extension of the **churchyard** into the Abbey Fields, despite the earlier discovery that such an extension was illegal. They examined all title deeds they held for the Abbey Fields, and also visited the churchwardens to look at their title deeds and to get their views. They then contacted Clarendon to see if he would consider waiving the conditions of the covenants for the reduced Area F; the outcome of the discussions is unrecorded. In the event, even the 1885 two acre extension of the churchyard was excessive and it was predicted that as interments encroached upon the ruins, problems would include: burials may unknowingly be on top of stone thus preventing drainage, the ground is 'made up' and liable to subsidence and as graves were liable to fall in so brick-lined graves would be necessary, and graves made in the vicinity of the ruins would be detrimental to the stonework *'which has been exposed at considerable cost in the past, and much of its beauty and attractiveness would be spoiled'*. The decision of course was in favour of a cemetery. *'Lovers of the picturesque heaved a sigh of relief with the news that the churchyard will not be extended, for the view of the ancient place of worship from Abbey Hill was rapidly being spoilt by a vista of tombstones'*. And so, with enough churchyard space for three more years of burials, a new cemetery was opened in 1913 leaving almost an acre of the churchyard extension unused.

As far as is known, this was the last time the 5th Earl was involved with the land he had sold to become a park; he died on 2nd October 1914 aged 68 and was succeeded by his only son from his first marriage, 37-year-old George Herbert Hyde Villiers.

An undated but pre-1913 photograph showing a Kenilworth Fire Brigade demonstration or competition in the park. The original manual pump engine from 1863 is to the left, the steam Queen Bess of 1898 is alongside the brook *(HS)*

The **Coronation of King George V** in June 1911 was to provide similar entertainment to that for his father; the parade, which was *'of larger dimensions than any previous occasions'*, again dispersed in the Abbey Fields. A dinner was provided in tents and over 1,000 sat down in batches of 500. Sports were again held, including a *'needle threading race'*, and a tug-of-war tournament won by a team from the tannery. There was to be a schoolchildren sports and all the pupils marched to the fields, with St Nicholas at the front and St Austin's at the rear; they sung two verses of the National Anthem in a marquee before moving to another where Lincoln Chandler had arranged a Punch & Judy show. Their sports were cancelled due to dampness underfoot after rain and were held later at one of the schools. As the weather improved, a tug-of-war was held between councillors and the organising committee, and Lady Seymour planted a commemorative oak tree. There was an evening concert in the park, and a bonfire was lit at 9.30 p.m.

In September 1910, Joseph Roberts asked for permission to allow the land he rented in the Abbey Fields to be used as a **football** field; permission was granted and this is the first known occasion that organised football was played in the fields.

In almost 30 years of public ownership, the only new facilities provided in the Abbey Fields by the council were the largely disappointingly attended baths, a couple of footpaths and the unpopular planting of numerous trees. In the early 20th century, **bowling** was a popular pastime but few bowling greens had existed in Kenilworth by this time. For public use, the Bowling Green Hotel obviously had one and its successor built in the 1880s, the Abbey Hotel, is thought to have initially retained it. The King's Arms & Castle Hotel also had a green, but this is not mentioned after *c*1890 and so it may have gone. The Queen & Castle boasted both a bowling green and tennis courts in an 1887 sale advert. In 1912 there is a report of the Coventry Cross having a bowling club but it seems unlikely to have had its own green due to its situation; where the club played is therefore unknown. There was a good number of large houses with grounds in Kenilworth at the time but only one is known to have had a bowling green; that was Montague House on Upper Rosemary Hill. (It became the Working Men's Club in 1919 and the green survives in use today as part of the Sports & Social Club facilities.)

On Tuesday 27th August 1912, a meeting was held in the Lecture Room of the Parochial Hall to *'consider the desirability of establishing a bowling green'* in Kenilworth. Councillor Lincoln Chandler, who lived at Abbotsfield, took the chair and explained that he called the meeting as he thought there was a great desire for a green, particularly amongst the working men. Architect Joseph Crouch suggested applying to use a portion of the Abbey Fields near the baths; others suggested staying independent of the council. A show of hands showed a great majority in favour of forming a club, and upon the suggestion of National School headmaster Andrew Hacking, a committee was elected to ascertain the likely number of members and to go into other details; Chandler, Crouch, Hacking, Sholto Douglas, Hughes, Ridsdale, A E Dencer, Shelswell, Jarrard and Blakeman were elected, and Thomas Sherwin was appointed secretary.

The construction of its own green was paramount and having chosen a preferred site in the Abbey Fields, a deputation from the committee of Crouch, Jarrard and Sherwin, attended the next KUDC meeting to outline the proposals. Crouch did most of the talking and the site suggested was described as *'where the path comes down to the baths, where there are two big trees at the end. It is above flood level and some of the prettiest views could be obtained from the site'*. A fifty-yard square was required.

Clearly having made detailed considerations, Crouch stated that as the cost would be in the region of £100, they appreciated that it could not be met by the council and so the club intended to raise its own finances; all that was required was the council's consent. Crouch continued by saying that the man employed by the council who had charge of the swimming pool could cut and roll the green, and hand out the woods and take money from players. Thoughtfully, *'This would not cost the Council anything, as the club would give him a present at the end of the season'*; the bath attendant was clearly still underemployed. Storage space for equipment was also required, it was suggested this could be at the pool. The club proposed to fence the green *'sufficient to keep out the cattle'* at their own expense and be responsible for it. In return, the club would keep the green open for public use at all times for a suggested 2d a game. Crouch continued by saying it would attract visitors, and that in other towns it was the council who had the expense. Such was the movement to have the green, the club already had over 60 members. The council promised an early decision, and when it arrived, it was in favour.

This instigated the formal creation of the bowls club at a meeting held at the Parochial Hall on Friday evening, 20th September 1912. Lincoln Chandler was in the chair and announced that £100 would be needed to construct the green, and that the council had agreed to charge only a nominal rent for the ground. With subscriptions set at 2s 6d for artisans and 5s for all others, it was soon realised that it would take years to pay the cost of construction. Chandler then announced that Dudley Docker, who lived at The Gables, was contributing £50 towards the construction, provided the other £50 could also be raised; Lincoln Chandler, Joseph Crouch, Andrew Hacking, Thomas Sherwin and A E Dencer all stated that they would contribute £5 each; three quarters of the cost had been promised at this first meeting. The Kenilworth Bowling Club was then officially formed with Chandler as its committee chairman, and the first rules, game fees, were agreed; free to all members on Saturdays, 1d a game on all other days, and 2d a game for non-members.

The construction of the green by club members was quickly underway; it was described as *'making headway'* in the first week of December 1912. The choice of location near to the swimming pool had advantages by being centrally placed on the existing pathway system and also the area was slightly raised above the level of land to the east which was prone to flooding. The swimming pool end of the green needed a little excavating whilst at the other end the land had to be raised due to the slope in the ground. At the February 1913 KUDC meeting, Lincoln Chandler officially proposed that the club should be entitled to use the area of the fields until 29th September 1916, provided the public were not excluded from it. There were however doubts about the fence that had been erected around the green; the council had been led to believe it was to have been of iron, but it was in fact of wood. Mr Jackson said, *'I think it is a very ugly fence, I think it is against the wishes of the council that such a fence should have been put up'*. Chandler contested that it was an oak fence and was in keeping with the general appearance of the area. When it was suggested that a decision should be deferred as many of the councillors had not seen it, Chandler said, *'It is apparent the Council walk around and see nothing; this has been erected 8 weeks and no one has seen it!'* The councillors met at the green to inspect it, and found the fence to be acceptable.

The bowling green was officially opened on Saturday 26th April 1913. Unfortunately, the club's president, Dudley Docker, was unable to attend and his place was taken by Lincoln Chandler. After a short speech, Chandler joined a team of club members who took on a team of councillors in the opening match that was won by the club by just one point. The unfavourable weather kept the spectator numbers down to about 40. One of the club's first matches was against the well-established Kenilworth Working Men's Club team, whom they beat comfortably 212-143. The Bowls Club team members that day were Alty, Salkeld, Gabb, Dencer, Burton, Bennett, Tibbatts, Hiorns, Aitken, Mansell and G Dymond.

At a committee meeting held at the end of April 1914, it was announced that Miss Schultz (*sic*, likely to be Miss Schulte or Miss Schintz) had sent a cheque of £30 towards the deficit of making the green, thus allowing the club to consider the building of a small pavilion and a few seats. The green was closed for the winter months and re-opened in early April 1914 and was soon reported as doing brisk business. An attendant was present every day from 2 o'clock. The green was described as being in excellent condition. Patients from the nearby Convalescent Home were allowed a weekly ticket for 1s.

On 29th August 1912, three girls, Kathleen Waites (a week short of her 9th birthday) of 21 New Row, Doris Wallis (aged 9) and Edith Tarver (11), were playing alongside the **brook** in the Oxpen Meadow at a favourite spot for paddling. Recent heavy rain and some flooding had given the brook a strong current in addition to extra depth, but failed to deter Kathleen from having a paddle. Her two friends told her not to, but Kathleen took off her shoes and stockings; as she took her first few steps in the water, the current took her legs from under her. She cried out *'Mother!'* as she was swept along and was soon lost from the view of Doris and Edith. The alarm was raised; her mother had to be prevented from entering the stream, her lodger Mr Hetherington attempted to find Kathleen but he in turn needed help to leave the brook. The police were alerted and a search began. A team of helpers searched the brook, including the millstream to Mill End, until dark with no success. It was not until two days after the accident that the body of Kathleen was found by lamplighter Arthur Ellis; he spotted her in the now calmer brook just 80 yards on the Bridge Street side of the Iron Bridge, retrieved her and carried her to Clarke's the wheelwrights in Bridge Street. Kathleen was an only child; her mother Amy was too ill to attend the inquest and her place was taken by her brother, builder Joseph Hubert Lawrence. Kathleen's father was a one-time licensed victualler but his whereabouts was unknown. The verdict was as expected, accidental death.

Letters appeared in the local press suggesting that a 5ft high fence ought to be erected along the waterways of not only the Abbey Fields but also other dangerous spots such as alongside the School Lane mill race. Indeed, just six months later a man named Edward Harris fell and drowned in the mill race by The Close; it was remarked that children *'often'* fell in the local waterways. There were also concerns as regards to the bridge at the Castle Ford, which had become submerged during the flooding.

The contradictory nature of discussions regarding the oft proposed Abbey Fields lake were summed up by Councillor Jackson in February 1913; it was he that had proposed fencing off the brook as it was dangerous but incongruously was in favour of constructing an unfenced lake, which, it was observed by another, *'would give further facilities for drowning accidents'*. These incidents, and probably many unreported others, ensured that a permanent lake in the Abbey Fields was not likely to come to fruition.

Kathleen Waites' grave with its fallen cross, is within sight of where she was found by Arthur Ellis

(12th January 2017)

A mild winter meant the trout in the brook were in *'quite good condition'*; however *'through over attention from anglers the very limited water in the public pleasure grounds has become sadly depleted of fish, and a catch is quite an exception. A visitor on Easter Monday* (1914) *got only one 'run' for a day's fishing but landed a two and a half pounder.'*

Soon after the 1895 death of her husband Aaron (a watch manufacturer often called 'the father of the American watch industry'), Charlotte Dennison bought High Street building **Plot 11** of 3,330 sq yds, which George Turner had increased from its original size of 2,750 sq yds to accommodate Charlotte's plans.

On it was built a new house, The Wantage, designed by Arts & Crafts architects Buckland & Farmer of Birmingham. As the house was nearing completion, on 4th January 1901 Charlotte in any case bought the adjacent **Plot 12** of 2,230 sq yds which had been reduced from 2,774 sq yds, presumably to increase the size of her garden; thus altering the plot sizes was in the end unnecessary, and the purchase of Plot 12 was obviously an afterthought. Charlotte and her daughter Ethie were resident by 1901, the year that Charlotte died aged 89; unmarried Ethie inherited and her sister Charlotte Terry and her husband came to live with her. In May 1904, Ethie Dennison was allowed to remove 2 or 3 loads of sandstone rubble from the Abbey Fields, presumably for some building project, possibly the landscaping of her garden, at a cost of 3s 6d a load.

In a short space of time, three members of the Evans family died; daughter Beatrice died aged 39 on 6th May 1906, her father William Evans died on 22nd July 1907, and mother Sarah on 1st February 1909. This left daughter Gertrude living on her own at The Spring, and son Percy, who like his father was a lawyer and had a business address of 4 Paper Buildings, Temple. Percy had been educated at Eton and Christ Church, Oxford, and became a Barrister being called to the Inner Temple in 1889.

> **Beatrice Hope Evans** died on Sunday 6th May 1906 aged 39. She had suffered for some time from an internal complaint caused, it was said, by a fall from a horse several years before. She was for many years a teacher at the St Nicholas Sunday School and was of gentle manner and *'shared the great general esteem in which her family is regarded'*. She was buried at St Nicholas churchyard the following Wednesday. On the next Sunday, the Vicar made particular reference to Beatrice in his sermon; *'She combined in a remarkable manner a great tenderness joined with a great power of will.'*
>
> **William Evans** served on the committee responsible for the Bill in 1888 regarding the Constitution of the County Council, and was elected a County Alderman in 1889, a position he held until his health began to fail. In Kenilworth he was responsible, as chairman of the Local Education Committee, for starting technical classes. Kenilworth was *'chiefly indebted'* to Evans for the St Barnabas Mission Church, and he was a trustee and administrator of the Parish Church Charities. In addition to his 25 years public work after his retirement, he was also at the forefront of personal donations to numerous local causes. After an illness of nearly two years, William Evans died at noon on 22nd July 1907 at his home The Spring in his 82nd year. He left almost £100,000 nett *(£11 million)*. His widow **Sarah** died on 1st February 1909 aged 68; no life-details were reported in the *Kenilworth Advertiser*.

In April 1909 Mary Draper died and on 21st June at The King's Arms her property was put up for auction, including Clinton House and its 2 acres, and the Abbey Fields building **Plots 7 & 8** totalling 4,458 sq yds and described as *'a fine building site'*. House and fields were sold together as one lot and were bought by Percy Evans for £3,000, his funds doubtless swollen by recent family legacies; Percy had moved away and so his only surviving family member, sister Gertrude, moved in to Clinton House from the family home The Spring, which was later sold. One surviving document records that despite it being Percy that paid for them, Plots 7 & 8 were conveyed directly to Gertrude from E H & E D Draper (Mary's sons) on 26th July 1909. It was now Gertrude Evans' turn to enjoy the uninterrupted view from Clinton House created by Mary Draper, across her land and the rest of the Abbey Fields.

Included in William Evans' will was of course **Area E** comprising 27,739 sq yds (about 5¾ acres), fronting onto Forrest Road. This was held in trust while his widow Sarah was alive but upon her death in February 1909 clauses were activated that conveyed the land to their surviving children, Percy and Gertrude: *'... one half thereof for the said Percy Bagnall Evans absolutely and as to the other half thereof upon certain trusts for the benefit of the testator's daughter the said Gertrude Emily Evans.'*

However, on successive days, the 17th and 18th January 1910, all the land became 36-year-old Gertrude's outright. *'Percy Bagnall Evans in consideration of the natural love and affection which he has for his sister... hereby conveys and confirms unto the said Gertrude Emily Evans one undivided and equal half part or share of and in all those pieces of land... fronting to a road called Forrest Road... formerly part of The Abbey Fields'*. With one half-share gifted to her by her brother, Gertrude released the other that was in trust for her, with brother Percy and Phillip Evans (a cousin) being the land's trustees: *'In consideration of the sum of one thousand seven hundred pounds now paid by the said Gertrude Emily Evans to the said Percy Bagnall Evans and Phillip Herbert Lee Evans the... trustees hereby convey unto the said Gertrude Emily Evans one undivided equal half part or share of and in... all those pieces of land... fronting to a road called Forrest Road... formerly part of the Abbey Fields.'*

Even allowing for the twenty and more years that had passed since the original transactions, £1,700 *(£185,000)* seems an extraordinary amount to pay for a half-share in less than 6 acres of land; is this in some way tied into her father's original acquisitions of the land and the 1888 separation agreement? It is also an indication of the cash that Gertrude Evans had at her disposal.

On 24th February 1913, Gertrude Evans bought from George Turner the High Street plot adjacent to those she owned, **Plot 9** that included the cottages numbers 81 & 83. On the same day, Ethie Dennison bought **Plot 10** of 1,724 sq yds from Turner that included the cottage 85 High Street, for £174. There was clearly collusion between the two ladies as the boundary between Plots 9 & 10 had been redrawn so as to pass directly down the common wall of the cottages; Ethie's Plot 10 had been narrowed from 87ft to 53ft, increasing the size of Gertrude's Plot 9 area by about 500 sq yds. Turner presumably redrew plot boundaries to provide areas more agreeable for sale; they were no longer building plots, the two ladies wanted the cottages. Gertrude fenced a piece of her land to provide small gardens for numbers 81 & 83, and then she and Ethie set about renovating all three cottages that, as mentioned earlier, were in a poor condition; Gertrude's alterations plans for numbers 81 & 83 were deposited on 22nd August 1913, passed on 9th September and had amendments passed on 10th February 1914, whilst Ethie's plans for number 85 were deposited on 30th October 1913 and passed on 4th November.

Ethie Dennison died in April 1915 aged 65, her sister Charlotte Terry inherited her Kenilworth home The Wantage, and Ethie left her *'cottage adjoining and £200 for the upkeep thereof as an old fashioned English cottage for the use of poor ladies'*. The residents, Alice Ellis and her daughter, were to remain if they wished, and they did. Had they left, the cottage would have been offered to Nettie Danks, Ethie's old servant, and in either case Ethie would pay for an education of Nettie's son, and others. Number 85 became a charitable cottage on 4th January 1916 and its garden was formed from plot 10 the same year.

It seems the elderly George Turner, the last of the Syndicate members, was looking to sell all his remaining portion of the Abbey Fields estate, **Area C** that included Little Virginia, ensuring his pledge for the public cause was honoured in his lifetime. In February 1914, the KUDC wrote to Turner to *'endeavour to secure an option for the purchase of the land between the Café and Mr Polley's house'*; Polley lived at Oakdale Villa, on the edge of the plot not far from the brook, and the café was that built by Mr Lissman on the corner alongside Little Virginia. Why the Council was interested in this land is unrecorded but it was most likely to prevent further development by adding it to the Abbey Fields; there seems to be no other reason.

The future of the fourteen **Little Virginia** cottages had been causing concern; they were *'dilapidated'* and suitable for demolition and redevelopment as they had been almost 30 years previously when first offered for sale by the original Syndicate. However, doubtless inspired by the restoration of 81-85 High Street, there were those who thought the Little Virginia cottages were worth preserving to the extent that a *'private Syndicate of Kenilworth gentlemen'* was formed specifically to look after their future. With George Turner disposing of his Abbey Fields property, by 1st August 1914 Lincoln Chandler of Abbotsfield had stepped in and bought Little Virginia and the land behind *'with a view of gaining time for a few influential residents to consider the position and the possibility of maintaining Little Virginia in its present character'*; the purchase kept the cottages *'from the hands of the speculative builder'* and it was Chandler's intention to later sell them to the proposed private syndicate. Interestingly, a reference to an Indenture dated 31st December 1914 indicates the involvement of Chandler's daughter Marjorie (born 1894). It was hoped that the cottages would be restored in a way similar to those nearby (81, 83 & 85 High Street) that were renovated by the Misses Dennison and Evans which retained the thatch. It is probable that building **Plot 13** alongside was acquired by Chandler at this time too, although no evidence has yet been found.

In January 1913, part of the wall retaining the Abbey Fields on the **Rosemary Hill** corner collapsed and this led to a significant widening and reducing of the gradient at the top of Rosemary Hill, starting in November 1913. This included an incursion into the Abbey Fields; as has been seen on page 19, the covenant included in the conveyance for this area allowed for such a road widening. The cost was £200, raised by a loan, and the two trees that were felled were sold for £2. It seems the work was re-assessed as in March 1914 'the surveyors were instructed to remove to a further depth indicated by certain trial trenches the soil in the Abbey Fields on the top of Rosemary Hill at an estimated cost of £290'. It was decided not to fence the new corner of the fields but a pavement was constructed; its extent along Abbey Hill was probably only to about opposite the Congregational Church. The spoil from the road widening was moved on a wagonway, bought second-hand by the council, descending into the field alongside Bridge Street on the northern side of the brook and used to raise and level the area to help relieve the flooding and dampness; there were numerous depressions, some probably the remnants of ponds associated with the Abbey. The bowling green had rekindled the original intentions of the fields by providing sporting facilities and it was suggested that the newly levelled area would be suitable for the construction of tennis courts, and perhaps even the cricket pitch promised 30 years previously.

The boundary hedge by the Abbey Hotel dates this photograph to before the 1913 widening scheme; newly planted trees on the diagonal path suggest about 1904 *(HS)*

Mrs Rebecca Hughes died on 23rd December 1914 at 48 years of age. Her funeral and burial took place at St Nicholas Church; despite the cemetery now being open, the closure of the town's churchyards had yet to take place and Mrs Hughes was buried at the western end of an avenue of lime trees which her husband Leonard, a solicitor, had planted through the 1885 churchyard extension just a few years before. They lived at Hill House on Upper Rosemary Hill. Leonard joined her in 1944.

July 1914 saw the last gala by the **swimming club** due to the outbreak of war. Three hundred attended and there was a greater number of competitors too, especially amongst youngsters some of whom competed in the senior events. It was a notable month for another reason, the last payment for the swimming pool loan was made.

It is possible to make out the newly planted avenue of lime trees donated by Leonard Hughes in about 1910. The lime avenue planted westwards from the church door after 1883 is beginning to mature. The fenced Tantara Gatehouse is more or less covered in foliage

Chapter 2: *To benefit the community*

The Great War of course changed all aspects of life particularly after volunteers joined the forces in droves. It was stated (in 1919) that there were over 800 ex-servicemen in Kenilworth from a population of between 5,810 (1911) and 6,751 (1921); a large proportion of course were the young men of the town. During the course of the conflict, the Abbey Fields continued to be a focal point.

The 1915 annual meeting of the **Bowls Club** was held in March at The Virgins Inn. This time it was said that it was Miss Schintz whom the club had to thank for the £30 donation towards the debt of building the green, but the overall debt, steadily increasing due to paying the KUDC rent, still stood at over £106. Receipts did not cover expenses for the year, and so subscriptions were raised from 5s to 7s 6d in a bid to improve the finances. Dudley Docker was president, Lincoln Chandler was chairman and treasurer. Many of the club's members had volunteered, as of course had regular non-member players, but the club did what they could to keep the green open despite the struggle to financially break even. Even so, they generously allowed recuperating soldiers at the Kenilworth Red Cross Hospital set up at the Parochial Hall to use the green for free.

The **Swimming Club** disbanded during the war but the pool remained open. From June 1915 the scholars of all four of Kenilworth's public schools could swim for free when in the charge of a teacher; fine weather resulted in *'a record attendance'* in the first three weeks of the month. The 1916 season had problems at the start, this mid-August report perhaps suggesting that the pool opened late: *'It was only a few weeks previously that an attendant's services could be obtained, perhaps as well as there would not have been many bathers under the early season weather'*. The newly appointed attendant was a disabled and recently discharged soldier, Austin Martin; no female attendant was appointed as female swimmers could be covered voluntarily, and Mrs Sholto Douglas and Miss Nora Crouch stepped forward. The appointments were quickly followed by a spell of hot weather leading to *'an unprecedented run of attendance'* with 800 bathers noted in one week. It was claimed as *'the heaviest week during the last 17 years.'*

The attendant, Austin Martin of Spring Lane, had been a professional soldier with 5 years service and 7 in reserve at the outbreak of war. At the Aisne advance he was badly injured in his right arm, and also received a bayonet wound to his leg on 6th October 1914. Although his arm was not amputated it had no use and he was discharged from service in March 1916. This was to be his only summer of work at the baths; his health failed, he was eventually admitted to hospital and died of sceptic poisoning in June 1920 aged 33.

The growth of Mr Hughes' avenue of trees dates this to the time of the Great War. The mound in use by picnickers is covering the part of the Abbey ruins that caused the dog-leg in the churchyard extension boundary and pathway *(HS)*

The war did not stop vandalism. In June 1915 it was decided to set the seats in concrete beds because *'of the unfair way in which they have been badly treated at night, being turned over, knocked about and broken up in the quickest manner possible'*; the cost was 6s or 7s for each of the dozen or so seats.

In *'fine weather'* in August 1915, the fields were chosen as the venue for a public speech raising the awareness of the necessity of War Savings Certificates. After introductions from Dr Growse, the speaker, Mr Bartley-Dennis the MP from Oldham, spoke at length to the *'large gathering'* about the wartime finances of spending £3 million daily on men and munitions, and an annual wartime budget of over £1,100 million compared to the peacetime level of £200 million.

In September 1915, the Kenilworth and Leamington Volunteer Training Corps had an exercise in Kenilworth; the Leamington lads in uniform carried out a 'sham attack' on Kenilworth Castle which was defended by the *'workmanlike'* and ununiformed Kenilworth Volunteers Training Corps (KVTC). The first part of the assault was across the Abbey Fields with shots being fired by both sides. As the attack developed it came more from the direction of the golf club (then at Castle Farm). Blanks were used, obviously, and rattles were used to simulate machine guns, but the attackers got a little carried away at one point by charging with fixed bayonets. After two hours of manoeuvres the opinion was that the defenders from Kenilworth had won the day.

Heavy snow at the end of February 1916 allowed five days of tobogganing on the north-facing slope of the fields; this was a more regular, but less reported, pastime than ice skating.

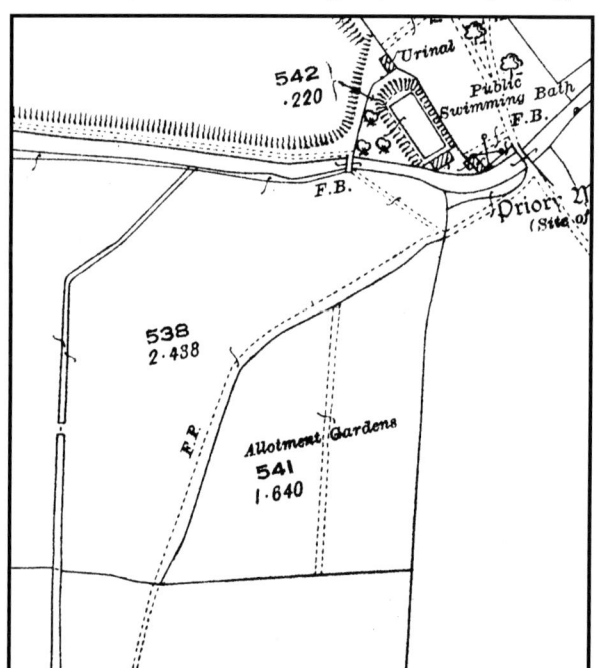

Although details are scarce, during the Great War parts of the Abbey Fields were put to use for the **growing of food**. On 12th December 1916 Lincoln Chandler asked to dig up an unnamed area of the fields for the planting of potatoes by the Volunteer Training Corps. A War Allotment Committee was formed with Andrew Hacking and Joseph Crouch at its head and the land between the Luzley Brook and The Bungalow was cultivated. In January 1917, the War Allotments Committee allocated an area 'in the centre of the Abbey Fields' as an allotment, one of a dozen or more places in the town being newly converted; the 1925 OS map shows an area south of the swimming pool but east of the path to Borrowell Lane as 'allotments'; a path is shown through the plot.

The wartime allotments south of Finham Brook. Note also the cattle bridge over Luzley Brook, linking two fields for grazing
(OS, 1925)

After his father's death, Percy Bagnall Evans, being passionately fond of the Lake District, made his home in Keswick but being a keen historian and archaeologist he spent his holidays visiting Italy, Greece and Egypt. *'He was of a particularly kindly disposition and did a deal of Philanthropy in an unostentatious manner'*. Percy died quite suddenly in Ilfracombe on 13th April 1916 at the age of just 46. He had been ill only a week and had been recovering when his condition worsened and he died before his sister Gertrude arrived. Percy was buried with his parents and sister in St Nicholas churchyard; his funeral included flowers from Gertrude's maids at Clinton House; Mrs Plumber, Lizzie, Alice and Florence.

Gertrude Evans was now 42 years old, had no close family, and being unmarried had no heirs, but she was the owner of extensive property, including her 27,739 sq yds of Abbey Fields **Area E** alongside Forrest Road. She was in possession of legal documents that included the Abbey Fields covenant signed by her father stating, 'It is not the intention of any of the parties to derive any personal benefit from the property'; perhaps she could also recall his words that he had *'no interest in the property except... to benefit the community'* and that *'any residue'* would be donated to the town. And so in a time of war, once Percy's probate and affairs were settled she followed her father's wish for the land to benefit the people of Kenilworth; in January 1917 Gertrude wrote to the KUDC formally proposing to gift the Forrest Road land to add to the park. It was perhaps also in tribute to her brother, who had after all gifted her half the land 'in consideration of the natural love and affection which he has for his sister.'

The letter included the desire that the land was not to be made into *'ornamental gardens, and may be kept as open fields'*. The offer was accepted on 9th January 1917 and councillors were quick to recall the debt the town owed to her father. On behalf of the town, the council 'accepted with gratitude this magnificent gift' whilst Councillor Crouch added that 'this noble gift has forever removed the dangers of buildings destroying that view of the Abbey Fields'. The council sent this letter of thanks to Gertrude signed by every member:

> The District Council of Kenilworth desires to convey to you our sincere thanks and appreciation of your most munificent gift of land to the town of Kenilworth.
>
> It was to a large extent due to the exertions of your late father that the Abbey Fields estate was purchased by the then Local Board and dedicated to the public on perpetuity and we cannot but feel that your magnificent gift today has set the coping stone to his endeavour to reserve for future generations the amenities of the town.
>
> It is therefore with deepest gratitude and in the name of the whole of the district which we have the honour to represent that we accept this important addition to the estate and in token of our appreciation and of the high esteem on which we hold both your father's memory and yourself, we subscribe our names and affix our common seal to these present.

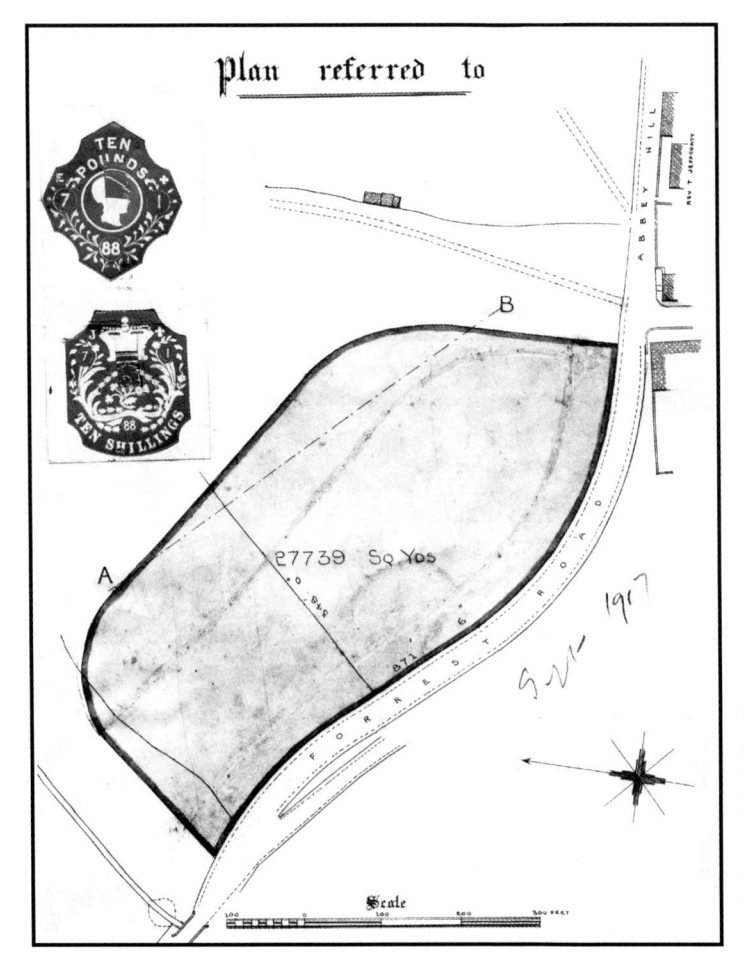

The plan included in the conveyance of the Forrest Road land donated by Gertrude Evans; the relevance of the rubbed-out inner line is unknown. Note Reverend Jeffcoat's house on Abbey Hill and the building line A-B designed to preserve his view of the Castle

(WDC 132)

The conveyance was dated 15th February 1917, and with covenants Gertrude ensured the land's future as an open space:

> ... and whereas it would be of great benefit to the inhabitants of Kenilworth that the public grounds dedicated to their use should be a greater extent than the lands so vested in the Council and that the heriditaments hereafter described should forever remain unbuilt

59

upon... Gertrude Emily Evans... hereby conveys unto the Council and their successors as Trustees for public grounds in Kenilworth... all that piece of land fronting to a road called Forrest Road formerly part of the Abbey Fields... to the use of the Council... to be held by them as public grounds for the purposes of the Recreation Grounds Act 1859 subject to the reservations restrictions and conditions hereinafter contained... the same may be managed in connection with the public grounds vested in the Council... and is hereby also declared that no building or erection shall at any time hereafter be built upon any part of the land hereby conveyed except for boundary walls or fences as may be considered desirable for separating the said premises from the adjoining road and except such gates and gatehouse that may be considered for the purposes of providing access thereto and subject as aforesaid the said land shall forever remain an open space for the purposes of the said act.

Although Gertrude's intentions for the land to be for recreational purposes are clear, there are no restrictions placed upon grazing and this allowed the council to gain an income from the extra 6 acres they were given for free. Despite the clear legal restrictions, Sholto Douglas remarked that it would make an excellent site in the future for *'municipal offices'*, but he was quickly reminded of the terms of the conveyance that prevented such a development. Presumably soon after, the fences around the land came down and the park was increased to almost 63 acres (62a 4812 sq yds).

As the war progressed, the situation at the **bowls club** deteriorated with three quarters of its members then in the forces. A whist drive was held in early March 1917, Mrs Randall provided prizes, and without such events to raise funds it was likely the club would have closed down, but for now the committee was happy to just cover its running costs. Keeping the green open was seen as *'valuable'* particularly for the Red Cross Hospital patients who had free use, and it was mainly for their benefit the club members made the effort. The wounded soldiers also played cricket on the levelled area alongside Bridge Street.

The green closed at the end of September 1917 on what was described as a disappointing season as the members had been busy on *'work of importance'*. The green had been used all summer not only by Red Cross Hospital patients, but also by the Army Service Corps based at the Cherry Orchard Brickworks. The club were sent a letter, reproduced in the *Kenilworth Advertiser*, thanking the club for providing the facilities and wishing them well for the future; it was signed by 20 successfully recuperated soldiers on behalf of many others.

On 11th October 1917 a whist drive and dance was held in the drill hall of the Abbey Hotel; it was attended by 148, and brought a profit of £8 10s. In the speeches it was again stressed how grateful all were that the club kept the green open for the benefit of the wounded soldiers; the club secretary Mr Pigeon (manager of W H Smiths in Priory Road) and club captain G P Dymond were singled out for praise.

The AGM in January 1918 was held at the Virgins Inn with E Nixon in the chair. The club had shown a loss of just £2 8s 2d over the year, but an effort had been made to reduce the club's overall debt to just over £84. It was reduced further to a little over £40 by whist drives and donations made by Percy Martin and Kevitt Rotherham, and the Red Cross Society giving £10 in appreciation of the free use by convalescing soldiers; *'I can assure you that the privilege has... benefitted our wounded men.'*

The club was now down to just 16 members, suggesting that about 45 or 50 were in the services and this no doubt contributed to the efforts to benefit of the injured servicemen. Mr L W Pratt offered the club a pavilion at a nominal figure; it was accepted and the KUDC had no objections to its installation, sending a letter of permission in mid-March. It is not known what form the building took, but its location may be the building later described as 'near the bridge'. It cost £5 to put up and was insured for 20 times that amount and provided a choice of lockers or strongboxes in which to keep equipment. Lancelot Wilfred Pratt was a partner in the coach and motor body manufacturers Hollick & Pratt, specialising in windscreens and hoods mostly for the Morris Motor Company. He also donated a cup to be played for in an internal competition.

The last part of the club debt was finally cleared by a generous cheque of £43 from Dudley Docker in April 1918. The members had not sought to obtain donations as they firmly believed that those who played should pay for the privilege, but with member numbers so low this had become impossible; it was the effort in keeping the green open for servicemen that had prompted donations by individuals. Docker believed that a game of bowls was a particularly useful form of exercise for those with a sedentary occupation, and was necessary for *'maintaining their fitness of mind and body, and dispelling their gloom'*; he thought it deserved every support for being the only publicly available recreation in the town (he had obviously overlooked the swimming pool). With the debt cleared, once more the bowling green opened for the new season in May 1918; *'The wounded soldiers and convalescents are making good use of it'*.

In August 1916, the **National Union of Railwaymen** paraded through town collecting for their orphans fund, set up to help the children of its members who had died at work. Kenilworth had its own members of the union, but not its own branch, who assisted in the organisation of what became an annual event. Members arrived from Coventry and Birmingham on the 2.45 p.m. train and paraded through the town; they were joined by 15 members of Kenilworth's VTC, and various Oddfellow lodges dressed in full regalia. The procession became a large crowd and ended with an open air meeting in Mr Fancott's Abbey field alongside Abbey Hill. As an indication of the dangers of working on the railways, in 35 years the NUR had catered for 2,800 orphaned children, paying money directly to each child's family. The 1918 event was very similar to those previous, members again arrived by train from Coventry and Birmingham and were once more joined by Kenilworth institutions such as the Caledonian Corks and local Oddfellows in full regalia, and paraded down *'most'* of Kenilworth's streets before again assembling in Mr Fancott's Abbey field. A Birmingham band that had accompanied many of them played for a couple of hours until they all headed back to the station having collected £20. The annual event is recorded in the *Kenilworth Advertiser* for the last time in 1929, its 14th parade.

Patriotism was obviously to the fore and in May 1917 **Empire Day** was celebrated by a 1,000 Kenilworth schoolchildren parading and assembling in the Abbey Fields and singing the National Anthem. They were probably not prepared for the speech made by Council Chairman Charles Randall calling for them to be frugal in the consumption of food due to shortages, in particular bread as the growing of grain was much reduced and grain-laden ships were being sunk. He also urged the children to stop buying sweets as sugar was scarce; *'Save your pennies and put them in war savings'* he suggested as their contribution to defeat the enemy. The children were also asked to sign a pledge of allegiance to the king, and wear a purple ribbon to demonstrate that they had.

As part of the war effort, waste paper was collected throughout the town, mostly by children, and the place chosen to store it was the Abbey Barn; in July 1918 it was sold and raised £20 which was donated to the Red Cross. In August 1918, a 1lb trout was caught in the brook; it was said that there were now very few fish, perhaps the introduction of food rationing late in the war was to blame.

On 7th June 1917 a site was approved for a *'sanitary convenience in the shrubbery at the northern end of the baths'*, but it was decided not to proceed until *'normal times'*. The **swimming pool** was an easy target for vandals. The outer fence had been damaged in places allowing access, and some of the floorboards of the dressing rooms had been torn up and thrown in the pool. One June day in 1918 whilst the baths were closed, two boys, Ben Kimberley aged 10 and his brother Sam, just 6, left their home in Lower Ladies Hill at about 4 o'clock to go and play in the Abbey Fields. There they met up with other boys, some Sam's age but many were younger, and they made their way into the bath through the hole in the fence. Sam was trying to reach and push some of the planks in the water when he lost his balance and fell in. Most of the boys ran off, but Ben jumped in, despite the fact that he could not swim, in an attempt to reach his brother who was beneath the surface of the 4ft deep water. He could not reach him and after a struggle managed to get himself out of the pool and go for help. Two men were on the bowling green and others were around; Joseph Chambull from Coventry was the first into the bath and walked around the whole pool trying to find Sam. Two ladies walked to Mr Woodisse's chemists shop in High Street to telephone the police. By the time they arrived, Chambull was out of the pool having made a thorough search and said he did not think a boy was in the pool, the water must have been very murky, but PC Baines brought a drag and found the body of Sam about 45 minutes after he had fallen in. Artificial respiration was continually tried until Dr Asplen arrived but he announced the boy was dead. The pool had claimed its second victim.

Surprisingly, no one representing the council appeared as a witness at the inquest. The verdict was *'accident'* but the jury foreman Mr Nixon added a rider saying that the council should drain the pool when not in use for long periods, suggesting the accident happened before they had opened for the season, but this was impractical due to the likely damage it would cause to the brickwork.

Despite the war, in 1915 Lincoln Chandler began renovation work on the Little Virginia cottages; the deposited plans for the alterations were in the name of *Miss* Chandler, presumably Marjorie, and were approved on 13th July. In February 1918, Chandler left the town due to *'pressing business'* and moved to Derbyshire, putting his Kenilworth property up for sale. The earlier hoped-for syndicate failed to materialise and it was KUDC Chairman Charles Randall who stepped in and privately bought Little Virginia and the field behind it, ensuring its future and *'relieving its tenants of needless worry'*; the conveyance is dated 10th October 1918. Randall also bought Chandler's home Abbotsfield in High Street overlooking the Abbey Fields (moving in on the 29th September 1918) and probably also at this time building Plot 13.

Soon after moving in, at the bottom of his land near his boundary with the park, Randall built a 50ft by 15ft combined piggery and cow-house, which included a calf pen. This was in contravention of the covenant preventing any structure both south of a building line, or other than a dwelling (see pages 20 & 21). The pigs wandered around the house-grounds (they were not allowed in the Abbey Fields) but the location of the cow-house and its south-facing doors suggests the cows would have been let out into the fields, and Randall is known to have rented the adjacent field plots after the war.

Early post-WW1; cattle graze amongst the maturing trees planted in the park in the previous 20 years or so, including some along the 1897 swimming pool path *(HS)*

The ending of the war obviously brought great jubilation and captured **German machinery** was much sought after. Around Christmas 1918, there was a parade through Kenilworth of captured enemy cannons; this was before many Kenilworth combatants had returned home. While the newspapers reported almost weekly upon Kenilworth's soldiers (from those that died, were seriously ill or in one case walked out on his wife, an action attributed to his experiences) in February 1919, the council received a German machine gun, but minus its tripod; *'A real war trophy, showing the effects of wear and tear in the field. No one seems very pleased with the award'*. The accompanying letter stated that there would be another distribution of spoils and it was hoped a more fitting trophy would come Kenilworth's way. Rather than put the machine gun on display, the council locked it away; its fate is undiscovered.

On Saturday 17th May 1919, Charles Randall called what became a well-attended meeting at the Abbey Hotel drill hall to discuss what form a **memorial** to the townsmen who had fallen in the war should take. Randall said it should be of *'a lasting character, to be handed down from generation to generation'*, and suggested that somewhere in the Abbey Fields would provide *'a lovely site'*. The first idea was from Arthur Spicer, whose son of the same name had died of pneumonia in May 1918 whilst serving with the Royal Warwickshire Regiment; he suggested a monument inscribed with the names of the fallen. Lord Seymour proposed a cottage hospital, E H Jeacock proposed a combined gymnasium, public hall and reading room, but his suggestion that it should be in the Abbey Fields was not so well received. Joseph Crouch suggested the restoration of *'the southern side of the cloister garth of St Mary's monastery... to become a garden of peace for meditation'*. The discussions returned to a monument, and J E Jackson added that a suitable location in the Abbey Fields would be *'at the top of Abbey End'*. A large committee numbering over two dozen was appointed including ex-servicemen and family members of the fallen.

After likely costs had been investigated, further meetings were held and other proposals discussed. A public hall for £3-4,000 was a popular choice, Joseph Crouch's idea for a Garden of Peace would cost £2,500 and was well received, but less so was a suggestion for playing fields costing over £2,000. As unlikely as it may seem today, the least popular idea was the first suggested and the cheapest, the simple building of a monument. As the cost was to be met largely by public donations, one would think that the cheapest option would have found more favour.

An extensive programme was planned for the **peace celebrations** on Saturday 19th July 1919, organised by Sholto Douglas, and the Abbey Fields were to be the focal point. Soldiers and sailors assembled outside the council offices and about 200 marched through town led by the Town Band for a united religious service in the park at noon. There was a crowd of several thousand and they cheered heartily as each serviceman was individuality presented with a token of the town's gratitude. A stirring speech of thanks by Charles Randall received rousing cheers. The discharged soldiers and sailors, now 400 of them, sat down to a meal served by the Kenilworth Volunteer Corps and several ladies in a highly decorated marquee. Mrs Randall planted a 'Peace Oak' at an unknown location in the park.

Schoolchildren in a combined procession, many in fancy dress, arrived at the park after 2.00 p.m. and had their own sports until about 4 p.m.; their events included three legged races and running backwards. They then adjourned to the marquee for a tea in two batches of 500, but heavy rain fell and the second batch were severely cramped trying to eat whilst the first also sheltered in the marquee. Later, others had their tea at the Parochial Hall. After the children's sports was a variety of adult's sports, ranging from a mile steeplechase for soldiers to a *'pillow fight on a pole'*, and a less energetic hat trimming contest; heavy rain at 5.30 p.m. put an end to the events.

A dance band provided music for 200 at the Abbey Hotel drill hall, and a bonfire was lit on Castle Hill at 11.00 p.m., the still falling rain had failed to put a damper on the occasion and many had left the dance early to be sure of witnessing the last event of the day. The rain and mud underfoot coupled with the flames must have rekindled many memories for the soldiers.

In October 1919, the KUDC was allocated three further machine guns as trophies but declined the offer. However, within weeks they accepted the prize of a **field gun** and several smaller trophies. In January 1920, the KUDC received a letter from the Lord Lieutenant of Warwickshire saying that the field gun would be sent from the War Office to Kenilworth in due course, and that the smaller trophies, such as rifles and bayonets, could be obtained from the Coventry Town Clerk into whose custody they had been placed. The town did not have to wait long for its prize; in early February 1920, it was announced that the 6-inch German howitzer had been placed in the park on the site of the wych elm that had been taken down in 1906. All the movable parts were removed or *'chained down'*.

The German field gun, type sFH-02 from 1902, on display in the park in the early 1920s

Each winter, the **Oxpen Meadow** was still flooded to provide skating for all if it froze. In February 1919, *'several hundred people have thoroughly enjoyed the rare opportunity, in recent years, of a week's skating, and the prospects seem to favour the skates for the next few days'*. The *'shallow overflow of the public pleasure grounds'* was the only suitable skating place in the town, but due to *'the lack of protection when the ice was forming there are several dangerously rough patches where the ice is broken and many falls* *naturally result'*. There was a conflict however in that the tenant of the field wished to make a little money out of the skaters, but some objected to having to pay to use what was public ground. The solution, suggested the *Kenilworth Advertiser*, was for the council to take over the field and then install a *'suitable secure retaining valve'*; the money then raised from skating in the winter would offset the loss of grazing income from the summer.

Inevitably the question of it becoming a lake again appeared in the local press; *'A sheet of shallow water, safe for boating and skating, would be a good source of attraction for Kenilworth people and outsiders. The field in question is so naturally adapted for the purpose that it will be a surprise if it is not converted into a lake, and thus complete another step in the direction of converting the Abbey Fields into a real Public pleasure ground'*. After the seasonal flooding, in March 1920 the field was once more drained and the absence of the lake lamented. The *Kenilworth Advertiser* pointed out that there was a big difference in flooding the field to a depth of a foot for skating than what was required to create a lake of depth; if it was just left in its winter state, *'the weed covered mud pit would not long maintain its look which it had before being drained.'*

The history of Charles Wicksteed & Co, the **children's playground** equipment manufacturer, states that its first items made were swings from old heating pipes to celebrate the ending of the Great War. Just eight months later in July 1919, Kenilworth Town Surveyor Sholto Douglas submitted an estimate of £85 to buy *'swings, trapeze bar, giant stride, etc,'*, from Wicksteed's and it was decided to start preparation work at once; thus Kenilworth was to be one of the earlier locations to benefit from Wicksteed's creations. (A 'giant stride' had a high central pole with chains from the top and handles on the end, similar to a maypole.) It was not until the following March that work got underway in the area between the swimming pool and the Barn; the excavations for the equipment uncovered nothing of archaeological interest. A sandpit was also planned but it is not known if it was constructed. The play area was opened in late May/early June 1920; *'The swings, etc, erected for juvenile recreation are in great demand and have been found very satisfactory'*. The surveyor had been instructed to lay down tar around them and to *'lock them up on Sundays as their proximity to the Parish Church was liable to interfere with devotion'*. The creation of the play area prompted calls for the council to *'improve the appearance of the 60 acre site'*, particularly for the winter, by the steady introduction of fir trees and shrubs.

In July 1919, a scheme to widen School Lane and the construction of new housing on the Noah's Ark allotments, that became Hyde Road, was begun. It created a lot of spoil and one obvious nearby place for its disposal was the uneven, low-lying, and prone to flooding area of the Abbey Fields between the Townpool Bridge and the bowling green, partially levelled during the earlier Rosemary Hill widening. Turf was lifted for spoil to be placed before levelling and the relaying the turf. As work progressed at Noah's Ark, in March to May 1920 the area levelled in the fields increased and it was soon being suggested that the area would become suitable for a second bowling green, or tennis courts. It is difficult to quantify the amount of spoil moved and by how much the land level was being raised, or whether it was just hollows being filled, but in March 1921 the process was continuing and the material being moved was described as *'a very large amount of soil'*. The quality was not always the best, it was said it would have to receive a top covering of decent soil to be suitable for tennis and bowls turf.

In January 1919, the KUDC received a letter from the Vicar of St Nicholas Church, 'relative to the preservation of the **Abbey ruins**'. This led to a major discussion based upon the future of burials in the nave of the Abbey. Arthur Street said that everyone thought it would be impossible to carry out burials in that part of the churchyard, 'It was never in the mind of any man when the ruins were taken in, that the ruins would be used for burials.'

As stated, in May 1920 the small excavations made whilst installing the children's playground equipment had disclosed nothing of interest, but known to pass beneath it was a subterranean passage 4ft by 5ft discovered when a sewer pipe was laid. Near the site the passage had a branch leading towards the swimming pool; it was concluded that this was a *'secret connection'* between the Abbey and Abbey Mill which was on the site of the pool. *'Most people in Kenilworth are quite familiar with the passage which is open near to St Nicholas Church, and which the gravediggers have several times broken into'*. The gardener at Mr Randall's house Abbotsfield had broken into a passage there some years previously.

An interesting discovery, apparently in the nave of the Abbey Church, was made at the end of September 1920. Whilst the *'supposed tomb of Prior John Warmyngton'*, the Prior in 1313, was being *'repaired'*, it was found the grave was only 4ft deep and had only 2ft of soil. This was removed and below it was a slab covering the entire grave. *'At the head was a stone pillow upon which rested the remains of a skull with about two inches of vertebrae attached. Immediately below were two leg bones crossed; there were no other bones'*. There was a foliated cross on each side of the tomb, the carved pillow was mortised into the bedstone, and there was no sign that the grave had previously been disturbed. Under the guidance of the vicar, the grave was cleaned and all put back into the original positions and the tomb once again closed. The discovery gave rise to suggestions that the skull and vertebrae were part of the remains of Simon de Montfort whose dismembered body was spread far and wide, and that his head and legs were sent to his wife Eleanor, who perhaps had yet to leave Kenilworth, and could have had them buried privately in the church of the Priory away from his public tomb at Evesham.

After the 1890 excavations, a plan of the discovered and supposed layout of the Abbey and its immediate surrounds was drawn by Coventry Architect and Archaeologist Thomas Whitley; it was now thought that the tomb marked 'B' on his plan was possibly the concrete pit used for casting the pig of lead, which when it was found still had some *'bits of concrete'* attached.

As the response to the appeal for funds was far from what was expected, on 22nd January 1920 the **War Memorial** Committee decided after all to build the cheapest option, a cenotaph just inside the Abbey Fields opposite Abbey End. At the 10th February meeting, on the proposition of Councillor J E Jackson it was resolved 'that the council widen the highway at the top of Abbey End including a strip of land now being part of the Abbey Fields estate to such an extent as to permit the erection of a War Memorial at that point'. An open competition was held to design the memorial and was won by Francis William Doyle-Jones, a man who was primarily a painter and sculptor but had designed a number of Boer War memorials including a particularly splendid one at Penrith; he was to create many for commemorating the fallen of the Great War, one pleasing design being on the seafront at Weymouth. Amongst his best-known earlier works are the Captain Webb memorial at Dover, and the Robert Burns memorial at Galashiels; Kenilworth had chosen well.

Despite the design being circulated in 1,500 letters of appeal for funds, donations were in short supply; by the autumn of 1920 Charles Randall had contributed £100, and two others £50, out of a total of £350 raised of the required £1,000 or so. Doyle was approached to modify his design, he reduced it in height by a quarter, and the cost came down to £600, later reported to be £500 *(£22,500)*.

The fields were to become the focal point of further war commemorations; in October 1921 a Drumhead Service was held, attended by 1,500 including the Boy Scouts and Girl Guides.

In the post-war years, a combination of returning servicemen and the re-adjustment from wartime conditions and factory production took unemployment to nationally high levels. There were a number of government initiatives to provide work on a local level and one, in 1921, was the clearing of waterways that had been neglected for years, and work on the brooks through the Abbey Fields was authorised in December. Another idea designed to help give work to Kenilworth's unemployed, was to create a toboggan run for youngsters by making an excavation and using the soil to provide a varied course. The youngsters currently used the paths for their runs and were doubtless grateful that at the same October 1921 meeting it was decided not to ease the gradient of that from Abbey End to the Iron Bridge.

On Monday 18th October 1921, a meeting was convened by the council with representatives of Kenilworth's unemployed in a bid to find opportunities for work. As road repairs were subject to subsidies it was decided to hire a second road roller and take on an extra ten men to help with the repairs; providing pavements at the sides of several roads was also suggested, as was a bandstand and pavilion in the Abbey Fields, and of course the provision of a lake. Another idea met with great approval; it isn't known who suggested it but many favoured the excavation of the **Abbey ruins** within the park, but not the churchyard, continuing the work of about 30 years previously and it was expected to be taken in hand very quickly. A sub-committee of Councillors Crouch, Hacking and Nixon, along with the town clerk was appointed to confer with the vicar and churchwardens with a view to co-operation. There were over *'100 receiving out of work relief in the town and nearly half as many whose benefits are exhausted'* and eight extra men were taken on to help improve the ford at the Castle, but the suggested ruins excavation stalled due to lack of funds; it was thought that subscribed money would be needed.

In April 1921, Charles Randall was replaced as Council Chairman by James Everitt Jackson, now in his 27th year as a councillor (his extra work load saw him resign from the fire brigade after 40 years service), but in November it was Randall who found a possible solution to the shortfall in the **War Memorial** funds: 'In view of the local lack of employment and the distress which must inevitably arise therefrom, the council considered the possibility of inducing the committee of the defunct Prince of Wales fund to expand the balance on their hands upon the object for which it was collected, the Chairman of the Council and the Clerk were asked to find from the Chairman of the Committee, Arthur Street, if the sum balance thought to be about £150 could be made immediately available and to ask him to convene a meeting of such Committee to obtain the sanction necessary'. The fund was part of a national scheme set up in 1914 to alleviate 'civilian distress' caused by the war; it was agreed that the building of a monument to the fallen, particularly if the unemployed worked on its construction, would satisfy the cause of the fund, although it seems the rules had been stretched on previous occasions; *'the money was collected for one purpose, and expended on a dozen different things'*. A meeting was arranged with the fund's trustee, Arthur Street, but within a couple of weeks Street communicated that the fund was not available for civil matters but he would contact higher authorities for clarification.

No confirmation that the fund was used to finance the memorial has been discovered, but at about this time extra funds were found, almost certainly by private donation, and the construction was authorised.

When came the time to drain the **Oxpen Meadow** at the end of the winter in 1921, the question of a lake inevitably rose again, particularly with the high unemployment levels. The Abbey Fields Committee were in favour of forming a permanent lake but one obvious flaw in the plan was pointed out by the Council Chairman Charles Randall; the brook water did not belong to the town, the mill at Mill End had the legal claim to it. In winter, flooding the meadow with plenty of water available was not a problem but maintaining a deep lake during the drier months would inevitably cause problems with the flow of water downstream. Randall did not however mention his vested interest; since 1918 he had been the mill owner. Randall was sure the time would come when a lake could be formed but it would have to be *'in a fair manner'* without causing problems to the mill. J E Jackson was hoping the eventual lake would be a *'good one, with boats upon it'*. However the necessary excavation would need to be huge and was another problem to overcome.

In 1919, a diving board was added at the **swimming pool**. The summer of 1921 saw what was claimed to be the busiest time ever at the pool; at a time of a *'drought'* with *'everywhere parched'*, in a single week more than 600 paid for admittance in addition to which was the free use by schools on four afternoons a week for boys and girls. This was followed by a two day closure for regular cleaning, the shallow end was described as slippery. The following year another group, the Boy Scouts, were given free use of the bath for one evening a week, later increased to two, and allowed to use the fields for *'a drill'*. In 1923 another disabled soldier was hired as bath attendant, Mr Porter of School Lane at £2 a week.

At the December 1921 council meeting, 'the committee having charge of the erection of the **War Memorial** asked permission of the full council to set back their memorial 6ft from the public footpath at the top of Abbey End, this was readily granted and the surveyor advised to widen the highway at that point by the 6ft suggested'. The agreement to 'widen the highway' neatly sidesteps the covenant for this area of the Abbey Fields that prohibits the building of any structure but allows for road widening schemes; thus the War Memorial was built on the widened highway and not in the Abbey Fields. To ensure it was built in the prime location, the top part of the footpath from the swimming pool was moved eastwards towards the field boundary.

By the end of 1921, the construction of the twelve Portland Stone blocks began and was completed by 11th February 1922; the unveiling was set for Sunday 26th February. Between 2 and 3,000 (from a population of 6,700) braved the continuous rain to watch as the official procession left the council offices at 2.45 p.m.; more than 400 were in the procession including the Band of the Royal Warwickshire Regiment, the British Legion, Red Cross, Girl Guides and Boy Scouts, various Oddfellow lodges, Working Men's Club, railwaymen and Post Office workers. Many were to get nowhere near the memorial due to the crowds, and such was the rain on umbrellas that only a few could hear the blessings and prayers. How poignant for the servicemen that both the peace celebrations and memorial unveiling should be in weather for them so reminiscent of the worst times in the trenches.

In the week the War Memorial was unveiled, the council received another deputation representing the unemployed, and they were heard with much sympathy; some of the men were getting desperate. Mr Adams, one of those representing the unemployed, asked if anything was happening about excavating the **Abbey ruins**; he was told that the proposed meeting with the vicar had yet to take place. There were now 233 unemployed signing on in Kenilworth, but when the seasonal agricultural workers and gardeners were added it was over 300; this was from a population of approaching 7,000.

Within weeks, thanks to the efforts of Charles Randall, the last obstacle to release the Prince of Wales fund had been removed. On Monday 13th March 1922, the War Relief Committee met at the Council House

The War Memorial, soon after its unveiling *(HS)*

with Arthur Street in the chair; the committee had a larger than expected £299 in hand, the surplus collected locally for the fund. It was confirmed that the money could be used to relieve any situation caused by the war, and it was agreed the current underlying unemployment situation was; excavating the Abbey ruins was thus an option, provided otherwise unemployed men were used. A *'prominent gentleman'* had promised to add £20 to the fund should it be used for excavating the ruins, and many thought it a worthwhile project.

The next day the council granted permission for the Abbey Ruins Committee, *'composed of interested residents'*, to excavate the ruins on the council's land in the Abbey Fields and appointed a sub-committee comprising Eustace Carey-Hill, Joseph Crouch, Arthur Street, Sholto Douglas, Charles Randall and Harry Quick, 'to watch the council's interests during the operations. The work is entirely of a pick and shovel and, or, unskilled nature and therefore suitable for all classes of unemployed.'

Eustace Carey-Hill is another case of the right man being elected to the KUDC at just the right time. Born in 1882, he fought in the Boer War as a teenager, and then worked in Coventry, first at a firm of aluminium founders and then at Dartmouth Auto Castings, rising to be Deputy Chairman and Director in Charge. But it was his 'hobby' of local history for which he will be remembered, researching and writing many papers about local antiquities, and becoming involved in a wide range of groups and societies. He lived at The Hollies in New Street. (For a fuller account of his life, see *Kenilworth: The Story of the Abbey*, Harry Sunley & Norman Stevens.)

Days after the sub-committee was formed, the War Relief Committee decided to donate £250 *(£13,000)* from the available funds to the excavations *'on behalf of the town and country'*, and the rest was split with £25 each to the relief of distress in Kenilworth, and the Soldiers & Sailors Families Association. The council committee were to work in conjunction with the excavation committee. It was agreed that to do the job thoroughly more funds would be needed and so a public appeal was suggested; Randall, likely to be the *'prominent gentleman'* mentioned above, started a subscription list with a £20 donation, Hodges and Crouch added another £30 making £300 available. It was thought that £500 would be enough. There would be no expense except that of labour.

The excavations began on about the 22nd March; observations and suggestions were plentiful. *'A lot of soil will have to be moved and it should be put down to make the place look attractive'*; 'The Excavation Committee should put things back as they found them'. Crouch said that any interesting finds should be put in the Barn, he had always thought it would make an ideal museum for the town, and once exposed the lines of the Abbey should be kept so they could be seen.

In the first week of April it was reported that remarkable progress had been made in uncovering the ruins and every day had produced fresh finds of great interest. *'The immensity of the great pillars and extent of the foundations show the Parish Church to be puny by comparison'*. The disposal of the soil and loose stones was already a problem and caused concern that some parts of the ruins may become reburied by spoil. The discovery of tiles near the high altar was the *'chief interest'*, more so than the discovery of a *'perfect'* skeleton found in a shallow stone tomb in the choir. Copper coins too had been found.

The excavations quickly attracted archaeologists from far and wide. A London expert said the tiles were made in the London area in about 1250 and were probably the first known use of such tiles outside that city; the recovered glass he thought dated from about 1220. Particularly fine tiles had been stolen within days of discovery and a reward was offered for the capture of the thief. The expected overall length of the site had already been exceeded. A wagonway, probably that bought second hand by the council for widening Rosemary Hill, was used to move spoil away from the excavation.

Ongoing Abbey excavations in the early 1920s. Spoil is piled near St Nicholas Church, a wagonway turn-plate is to the left
(WCRO, CR 2134/11)

The excavations of the Abbey site started just at the time the spoil coming from the Noah's Ark development was at an end. As well as providing more earth for levelling low lying areas should it be required, it also produced so much stone rubble that almost immediately it was separated and sold at 7s 6d 'a load'; 'All amounts realised by the sale of stone from the Abbey ruins be kept separate and credited to the Urban District Council'. However, the tenants of the newly built council houses on the Hyde Road estate had half a load free per house, of which there were 112; this stone is still prominent on the estate.

By the beginning of May the main point of interest was the exposure of the Chapter House with *'a range of stone seating around it'* and a large collection of carved stonework. Much was buried under about 6ft of soil and yet *'the most remarkable feature is the preservation of the red paint'*. By the end of the month, the earth dug out of trenches that revealed the lines of walls and their foundations was being removed, as was *'the debris, which to the depth of several feet, has buried the whole site'*. The ruins of the chapel, choir, high altar and south aisle were being laid open to ground level; the exposed site was already 240ft across. It had been decided that enough had been used on levelling the area near the brook and so spoil was used to create terracing. One concern was that all the excavations were low-lying and thus rubbish easily accumulated in them, it was hoped that a solution to this could be discovered, but already funds were running low and a new appeal started. Some discoveries had been sent to the British Museum.

There was great excitement in early June when two tombs were found side by side lying east to west under a 7ft long slab of slate in the south chapel. One was in good condition and inscribed *'Brother John of Hockley'*; the other was not so well preserved. Joseph Crouch had made a large copy of the plan drawn by Thomas Whitley, and put it up on the site. All the initial funds set up for the investigation had now been used and the dig was relying on new donations; Charles Randall led the way with another £20, and others included a Miss Evans, probably Gertrude, with £5, adding to the available total of over £80.

At the beginning of July a new trial hole was dug south of the Chapter House and this revealed a doorway and steps of great craftsmanship which served to increase the desire to reveal the whole range of buildings, but with the continuous problem of low funds and only half the contemplated work completed, later that month the KUDC changed the destination of cash raised from the sale of loose stone; the excavation committee were empowered to 'dispose of surplus stone from the Abbey ruins to provide funds for further excavations'. Private donations continued to come in and now totalled £150.

A newly revealed passageway between the main building and Chapter House revealed hundreds of tiles which were then stored in the Barn, and a fireplace with still blackened walls above. Messrs Crouch and Carey-Hill discovered fragments of oolitic limestone, unique in the location and from some distance away, which they reconstructed into a coffin. *'No human remains were near, and its date is at least as old as the Abbey's inception'*. Another coffin was found nearby in the centre of the Chapter House and about a foot below floor level; made of local sandstone its lid was missing and it held only soil. There were still many visitors, especially from out of town. The work was seen as *'being a great help in lessening the unemployment in Kenilworth'*, although how many were at work on the site is undiscovered. However, work was *'within sight of being stopped.'*

The ruins in the vicinity of the Chapter House wall give an indication of the extent of the work involved. The depth of the excavation, often unappreciated, is clear *(WCRO, DR 598/5)*

The earliest known reference to **tennis** in Kenilworth is of a mid-1870s club started by a clergyman, using 'strangely shaped racquets and balls covered with a woolly cloth'; sadly, no more details are available. In the later Victorian years, tennis rapidly grew in popularity. The 1883 sale notice of Spring Cottage, the home of H A Farwig, includes a reference to the house having a tennis lawn, the first known reference to one in Kenilworth. Thickthorn, Kenilworth Hall, and The Yews are other houses known to have tennis lawns by the later 1880s. Not surprisingly, an established sporting club soon provided facilities and in 1886 a tennis tournament was held at the Kenilworth Cricket Club ground, today the site of Queens Close and Faircroft. This eventually led to the formation of a tennis club with four courts (five from 1921) at the ground. Crackley Hall, The Cedars, Thornby House and Hill Crest followed with their own courts, each first known in the early 20th century.

In June 1921, it was lamented that the ever-increasing popularity of tennis did not have the same chance of expansion in Kenilworth that it had in other towns because there were no public courts. At the time, Harold Winstanley, formerly of Crackley Hall, was regaining his pre-war success on the tennis courts by representing Warwickshire in competition with Northamptonshire and winning, giving added interest to the game in Kenilworth. It was again suggested that the levelled area of the park between the swimming pool and the Townpool Bridge could be laid out for tennis, and thanks chiefly to the chairman of the Abbey Fields Committee, Mr Nixon, by April 1922 a start was made on two grass tennis courts by laying turf alongside the bowling green. Although the choice of location was straightforward, the lie of the land was still a little lower than the green despite the infilling; Mr Lawrence built an enclosing fence for £21. Thus the summer of 1922 saw the tennis courts construction and Abbey ruins excavation simultaneously create a great scene in this part of the fields.

The Bowling Club volunteered to take on the operation of the tennis courts with an arrangement similar to that for the bowling green, and in November 1922 the club suggested a little more ground should be laid out for a third court, to which the council agreed; the council were to pay an extra £10 to fence it in but the club had to pay this back out of its profits. James E Jackson was one of several councillors who had reservations about a private club having part of the fields and making a profit; *'I think it is an injustice and a great shame to take the land off the public and give it to the few. It was opened out for a public park and it was taking away the best part of the ground and enclosing it for a special few'*. He found others backed his view but all agreed that the provision of recreational facilities was behind the purchase of the fields and the KUDC had a duty to provide them; the arrangements that were made cost the town nothing and ensured the public had access to some facilities.

The club were concerned that the cost of maintenance and equipment would leave them short of funds and so asked the council to indemnify the club against loss in the first season. The club stressed that the cost incurred in laying out the bowling green was met entirely by members, and added that they were in favour of the efforts of the council in providing sporting facilities and were willing to help in any way.

In August 1922 the funds were so low that the termination of the **Abbey excavations** was expected but new theories about the ruins evolved; the long held belief that the Barn was the Abbey infirmary was now beginning to be disproved as its size and location suggested another use was more likely, and footings discovered well away to the south-east of the supposed extremities of the Abbey were a more likely infirmary. The last week of August was spent mostly clearing the foundations already exposed and following the line of a *'subterranean passage'*; this was now found to open into a channel, 7ft deep and 5ft wide with a fall to the east and was thought to be an overflow channel from the upper lake to the lower, the bank in between being in line with the swimming pool. The lower lake water was retained by a bank midway between Townpool and Washbrook bridges, on which stood Noah's Ark.

Work slowed by mid-October due not only to low funds but also the problem of spoil disposal. Much had been used to create a terrace around the south-eastern end of the Abbey, but it was now realised that the Abbey extended underneath it and thus the spoil was hampering the extending of excavations. The solution was moving thousands of loads on top of the area between the Abbey and the brook despite it burying the good turf already growing there, but that was a problem to be faced later. The big find of the week were pillars supporting cellaring which extended the southern extreme of the buildings beyond the swimming pool path. Also at the southern extremity was found a wall some 30yds long running east to west with a 4ft wide stone culvert on the inside, thought to be a substantial boundary wall. The remains of the buildings to the west and north remained untouched as the estimated cost to excavate was hundreds of pounds.

In November, funds remained very low and work was slowing but focussed upon clearing the exposed ruins rather than extending the digging; only in one location was it thought that the full extent of the buildings had been realised and that was the south-running domestic buildings that stopped after about 250 feet. It was already feared that the bulk of these buildings, underneath adjacent uneven ground, were likely to remain unexcavated. In December it was reported, *'Work has been concentrated on finishing off the exposed buildings, lying south and south-east of the Chapter House, and as will be seen by the portions finished off by being battered down and turf re-laid, the effect when completed will be quite artistic'*. The best view was from the terrace of displaced spoil. Even at this stage more walls were being found; 50yds east of the Chapter House were walls being traced towards Bridge Street. Into January 1923, the work concentrated upon clearing up the debris created, and in levelling the terrace formed by spoil tipping. Where walls were exposed to ground level, the ground was cut back so they could be seen and then the turf was neatly re-laid. The indications were that work had for now been brought to a conclusion due to the exhausting of funds, with only about two-thirds of the known or suspected buildings uncovered.

A pile of loose excavated Abbey stone, perhaps set aside for sale. A tipper wagon used on the tramway is on a spoil heap. In the background is the avenue from Bridge Street to St Nicholas Church, and beyond are the taller trees at Kenilworth Hall

(WCRO, DR 598/5)

The disposal of spoil continued to be a problem, but where possible it was put to good use. On 13th February 1923, at a special meeting it was decided that 'when the tipping of excavated material in the Oxpen Meadow at the back of the bath has been completed, the depression in the ground to the north of the bowling green be filled up'. Through April, work continued on clearing the foundations and levelling the soil tipped on the lower portion of the park. *'When the soil between the wall foundations has become overgrown with grass, and also the various tips that are now incongruous amid the green surrounds, the expenditure will be deemed better justified than it is today'*. There was an *'immense quantity of building unexposed'*, including the north chapel, but wisely the committee decided to clear up the accumulated mess whilst funds were still available, and saying that perhaps more could be done if there was a resuscitation of interest.

The site was still being explored. A small building had been found abutting the supposed boundary wall to the east, and in the north-east direction a trial hole had found building foundations far from where any were predicted. To the south-west, more buildings were expected and the contours of the land confirmed this but now with funds so low they were to be left undisclosed. By the end of July, 16 months after the excavations began, the levelling and seeding down of the excavated area was the work of just two men; work around the ruins was progressing well and with most of the loose stone and rubbish removed, *'the ruins no longer present so objectionable an appearance'*. It was said that some of the patterned tiles found, including some with coats of arms, were very valuable and could fetch good prices and it was suggested that by selling one or two duplicates, funds could be raised to continue the excavation. About 2,000 tiles and fragments, and 680 pieces of glass were retrieved from the excavations. At the beginning of August, Joseph Crouch gave a conducted tour of the ruins to a party of 200 Canadians.

On 25th August 1923, the *Kenilworth Advertiser* reported that the KUDC had received *'a letter dated August 10th from HM Office of Works stating that it had been decided to include Kenilworth Abbey gateway and domestic buildings to the south thereof, and the remains of the church and monastic buildings of which the council are said to be the owner, in the list of ancient monuments and formally declare the same to be a monument, the preservation of which was of national importance'*. There appeared to be an obvious oversight as this did not include all the ruins and the return letter from the council acknowledging the listing also included the hope that *'similar steps have been taken in regards to the portion of the ruins in the churchyard'*. It was later reported that the Abbey remains within the churchyard were not listed until 1935. (English Heritage no longer have their records relating to the original listings, so this cannot be verified.) Surprisingly, the KUDC minutes of the day make no mention of the letter or listing.

The **Bowling Club** organised fund-raising events for itself. Particularly popular were the whist drives usually held at the Parochial Hall; one such event in February 1923 saw no fewer than 37 tables occupied and it was at this event that it was publicly announced that agreement had been reached with the council to extend the club's activities in the Abbey Fields by taking on the newly built grass **tennis courts**. This was outlined at the March KUDC meeting: 1) The club be granted security of tenure of the courts for five years; 2) The Council to be responsible for the netting around the courts and the fencing; 3) That all the courts be open to the general public when not in use by the club members but one court always be available to the general public (the three courts to be taken in weekly rotation); 4) The charge to the general public to be 1s per court per hour; 5) The courts to be open to the public for the same time as members, such hours to be agreed from time to time with the council; 6) That the council have two representatives on the committee of management.

The tennis courts were not ready when the bowling green, *'one of the best three crown greens in the Midlands'*, re-opened on Easter Monday 1923. Several hundredweight of worm killer had been put on, and ten loads of sand and finally fertiliser spread over the green. *'With the additional attraction afforded by the tennis courts this corner of the park should afford a considerable attraction to the public'*. The membership fee for the now renamed Bowling & Tennis Club was 15s, Mr Pemberton was the club's honorary secretary and the bowling committee was augmented by Miss Tandy, Miss Lynn, Mr A Barnett, Mr E Hopkins and Mr W G Griffiths for the tennis section; Councillors Carter and Parkinson were the council's representatives on the committee.

The day the tennis courts were due to open, Saturday 5th May, the club was also due to play its first bowls match of the season; *'Kenilworth's green has no superior in the district, it is perfect'*. It fell to Councillor C Barwell to open the new tennis courts; two were in playing condition, the third was a few days from completion due to its later seeding, but the event was witnessed by just a score of people due to the persistent rain and unfortunately no play was possible due to the weather. By Monday 7th, the weather had improved and the two courts were opened, and play was watched by a good crowd of spectators. Nearby, soil was still being tipped from the Abbey excavations to the low lying area of the park.

Such was the interest in tennis that summer, the club thought it would fully justify further courts and by the end of September 1923 they requested that another three courts be laid; the club would reserve three courts for the public who could also use the others when they were not in use by the club. The council agreed and the matter was put in hand immediately with the council to make the courts and fence them, and the club to have them on the same terms as the others. At the club's AGM, held at The Virgins Inn in December, it was said that the tennis courts had *'provided very many with healthful and pleasurable recreation'* and *'entertainment to a far greater number of onlookers'*. The bowling green had been *'fully occupied'* at all times of favourable weather. Three successful whist drives enabled the club to employ labour to maintain the courts and green.

An undated but inter-war view of the Oxpen Meadow *(HS)*

Torrential rain for a few days in August 1922 caused the **Oxpen Meadow** 'lake' to appear in the form of flooding. Youths were quick to take advantage of the *'nut-brown colour of flood water... but the following day when its muddy contents had precipitated'* no fewer than 50 bathers at a time went for a swim! About six acres were under water to a depth of 4ft and the spectacle *'converted the usually deserted and rustic scene into Kenilworth-by-the-sea'*. It was seen as *'a full dress rehearsal of the attractions of a lake, maybe the council will reconsider the 30-year-old scheme of Councillor Jackson'*. It perhaps also indicated the limitations of the swimming pool, and the adventurous and hardy nature of the day's youths. Despite the yearly winter flooding, skating was not an annual event; it was not until December 1925 that skating returned for the first time since February 1919, hundreds at a time took advantage of the conditions.

In March 1921, chestnut and copper beech **trees** were planted, and gaps were made in the hedges that abutted the south side of the brook, in which stiles were inserted to give a walkway. Also, a clap gate was installed in the fence opposite the end of Southbank Road; this had first been requested by residents in 1917. The following year it was proposed to make a **footpath** from the Iron Bridge *'across Charles Randall's land'*; there are no further details but it may have skirted the churchyard and joined High Street alongside Randall's house using the Earl of Clarendon's 1867 'spur' that was specifically saved to create just such an access to High Street. However, it does not appear to have been pursued; there was already a right of way between that access point and 39 High Street.

In late 1923 the *Kenilworth Advertiser* reported that the council were about to look into the planting of the *'pleasure grounds'*. It was said that in 40 years of ownership nothing had been done save for the occasional planting of trees in the central 10 acres, and *'attempting the similar wholesale blotting of the landscape along the course of the footpath from Bridge Street to Abbey End'*; that earlier effort was, it was said, stopped by somebody *'breaking down 19 out of every 20 trees'* which after 20 years it appeared that they *'did the town a service'*. Despite the comments, more trees were planted as just a few months later Mr Phelps of The Bungalow offered twelve beech trees for planting in the fields near the ford, the offer was accepted, and £30 was allocated for the purchase of more trees with the type and location to be decided; one would replace the Peace Oak planted by Mrs Randall which had died. In September 1924, the fences around the now established George, Edward, and Alexandra commemoration trees were removed and tablets placed alongside to record their significance.

First discussed in June 1919, and probably instigated by the additional land donated by Gertrude Evans being accessible, new divisions were created in the fields so they could be let for **grazing** in simple plots numbered 1 to 10 rather than the dividing of fields numbered 36 to 49 in use since Clarendon's ownership. In mid-November 1919 it was recorded that *'Fencing alterations in the Abbey Fields are practically completed'*. The numbering started with Plot 1 in the field alongside Rosemary Hill, and continued clockwise. In 1921 Joseph Roberts jnr, continuing his father's High Street butcher's business, rented Plot 1 and Plot 8 for just over £61 a year. Roberts had actually emigrated to Canada to take up cattle ranching in 1919, using skills no doubt honed in the Abbey Fields, but seems to have returned; in 1925 he and Mrs Roberts, it is unclear if that is his wife or mother, had a very public argument about selling the High Street family business which she claimed had existed for about 200 years. That same year the trustees of Mr Roberts snr's estate refused to pay the rent on the Abbey Fields plot because the horses on it belonged to Mrs Roberts; she too refused to pay and the horses were removed. Plot 2 was rented to J H Lawrence, a builder, and Plots 9 & 10 were offered to Charles Randall; in theory these numbers should be the original Park area but Randall is known to have rented the plots immediately behind his house Abbotsfield so perhaps the numbering system still had complexities.

In March 1922, Councillor Dencer voiced his opposition to the letting of the *'park area'* for grazing in the summer; *'The few acres should be kept solely as a pleasure ground. Children get plastered with dirt, the seats are* (damaged)*, the Bowling Club at their own expense had to pay for their fences damaged by cattle; the bowling green costs the town not one halfpenny'*; cattle had previously been banned from the original park area. It was pointed out that losing the cattle would entail a cost of cutting the grass, but Dencer replied that the cut grass could be sold to raise an income. The matter was not even put to a vote.

As the **brook** cleaning by the unemployed progressed in 1923, there were complaints that perhaps the workmen were being a little too enthusiastic, *'the brook is not being left like a brook, it is being converted into a canal'*, suggesting that it was not being just cleared but maybe excavated too. It was decided to make it more attractive by the addition of trees and shrubs along its banks in the next round of planting. Despite the *'temporary prosperity'* in the motor industry, there was still much unemployment in the town and queues at the labour exchange; a couple of extra men were taken on for the brook work. The positive effect of the clearing was reported in early 1924 when despite heavy snow and rain falls there were no Abbey Fields floods *'when there may have been'*; it was said that the straightening of the brook was not the main aim, and once the trees had become established *'the aspect would be much more picturesque and pleasing'*. Hundreds of locals tobogganing was reported.

In December 1923, work started on building the first **public conveniences** in Kenilworth, alongside the end of the **swimming pool**, but it required the laying of 300 yards of pipe to reach it and so at the same time, a gas pipe was laid for a gas lamp at the Iron Bridge in the middle of the park. The conveniences were ideal for summer months when the park was well used, but it was remarked that they would be of little use the rest of the year. However, with a second convenience planned to be built near the Castle, and those at the Abbey Hotel to be taken over for public use, it was seen as a move in the right direction.

At the end of 1924, some 40 years after the fields were purchased, the KUDC minutes record the outstanding balance of the purchase loans; loan 5 for the central 40 acres of the fields, originally £6,000 was down to £3,604 5s 8d, and Loan 6 for the area around the churchyard, originally £425 was now down to £214 6s 1d.

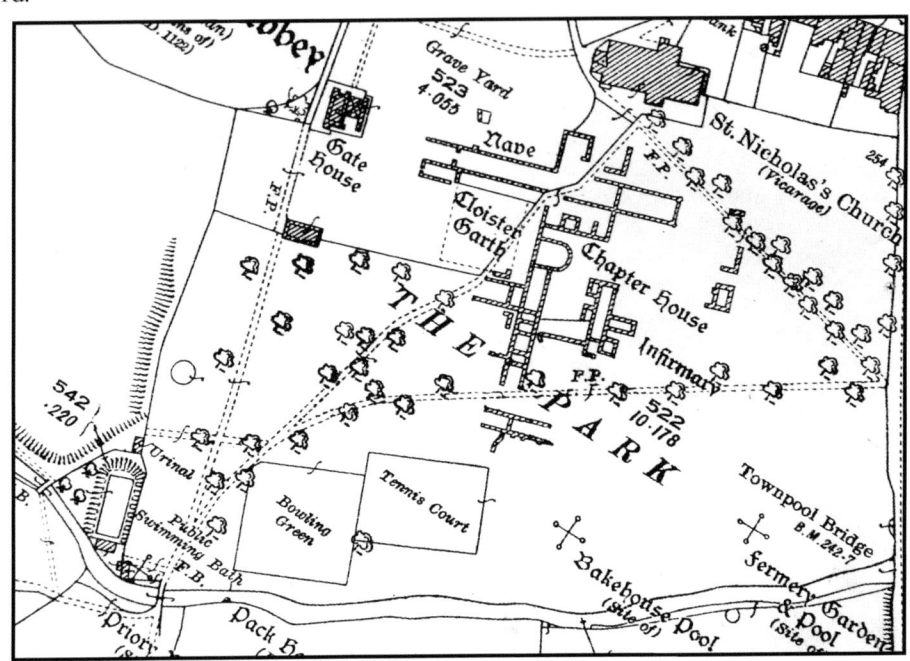

1925 Ordnance Survey map showing the extent of the exposed ruins including south of the swimming pool path; likely sites of further antiquities are marked. The new public conveniences are behind the swimming pool, and the bowling green and three tennis courts are evident

At the first annual dinner of the now named **Kenilworth Bowling & Tennis Club** in February 1924, its president, Councillor Barwell, was quick to point out that the provision of these park amenities was down to the club members and not the council, but the support from the council was vital for *'this semi-public club'*. The *'broad minded views'* of the council were subsequently appreciated in a toast, as was *'the long-sighted policy that led the council to acquire the large and naturally beautiful expanse of land at the centre of the town'*, and not far away as ever was the hope that a permanent lake would one day arrive; the current presence of a pair of swans on the flooded Oxpen Meadow was mentioned.

The club began the annual task of putting the first three tennis courts in order for the coming season; to do this they applied to the council for 50yds of turf to which they agreed. Rent and terms were discussed for the three new courts, but with them not likely to be ready until late in the season, they were to be left until the following year. The original three were constantly in use; on 14th June 1924 it was reported that they were fully occupied from 10 a.m. until dusk on the Bank Holiday Monday.

The popularity had produced another problem with club members and visitors cycling to the facilities across the fields and the club were asked to put notices up. At least one man was successfully prosecuted for driving a motorcycle across the park that summer and this led to calls for a parking area, but the Bath Committee was adamant: 'This committee does not see any necessity whatsoever for providing a parking place in the Abbey Fields for motorcycles and cars.'

In early 1925, agreements were reached for the Bowling & Tennis Club to take over the three new courts once the council had completed the final preparations of cutting the grass and had 'thoroughly rolled' them. Water was to be laid on for use on the bowling green with the club to pay its cost. Due to the tennis courts, the pavilion donated by Mr Pratt was now insufficient and the club submitted a design for a custom built pavilion; in May, Town Surveyor Sholto Douglas produced a design that would cost about £110 for the council to build and suggested the club could commit to renting it for five years at £10 a year. The site chosen was *'on the south side'* of the three tennis courts and bowling green, alongside the brook. Councillor Dencer thought that more details were needed before the council could commit itself.

However, the popularity of the courts also demonstrated the pavilion design to be inadequate and after a rethink, in September 1925 a larger pavilion was planned provided the club agreed to pay the interest on the loan, set at £300, necessary to build it. Agreement was reached for the club to pay the interest as their annual rent, and to also pay rates and keep the building in good repair. The council agreed to have the pavilion ready for the 1926 season, Douglas drew up new plans and the location was changed to being convenient for the bowling green and tennis courts but near the path to Bridge Street. The formal letter from the club accepting the council's terms was received in October 1925. The earlier pavilion donated by Mr Pratt was kept for storage purposes.

On 5th January 1926 the tender from J H Lawrence of £299 for building the pavilion was accepted, and a sub-committee of councillors Grindrod, Parkinson and Barwell, and Bowls & Tennis Club representatives met to decide the precise location. The loan of £300 for the pavilion was to 'for as long a term as the Minister will allow', which was 15 years. On 11th May 1926, the final payment was made to Lawrence, suggesting the pavilion had been successfully completed.

The club played competitive matches of both sports against other clubs and generally did well.

Taken between May 1926 and the summer of 1928 showing the new thatched Pavilion, and grass tennis courts with a laid picnic table, a roller, and spectator benches. Note the court's alignment with the bowling green which is also on higher ground. Trees, several of which survive, unfortunately block the view of the swimming pool. The exposed ruins are part of the 13th century dorter *(WCRO, DR 598/5)*

After the war, the **fire brigade** continued to be regular users of the fields, and each summer arranged a competition inviting brigades from other towns and, notably, factories. Typically, 10 or more brigades would take part in a variety of competitions for trophies donated by the Kenilworth Brigade and its supporters. In August 1925 competitors included Rover 'A', Daimler, Triumph, and B T-H (who entered 3 teams; Rugby, Blackheath and Coventry). These events were normally followed the next week by the brigade's competitions for its own members. There were generally very large spectator numbers.

On 6th May 1924, the KUDC issued instructions: 'With a view to eliminating vegetable growth on the bottom of the **swimming pool** the surveyor to have the water treated with chloros'. Hopefully the problem was solved by the time the pool opened to the public weeks later. The pool attendant now earned £2 a week; the wages had more than doubled in 10 years largely due to the effects of wartime induced inflation. At its May 1925 meeting, the Abbey Fields & Bath Committee approved swimming pool repairs, a new springboard, and a fence to avoid the pool being overlooked; Councillor Dencer lamented, *'there were a few Peeping Toms, even in Kenilworth'*. The pool opened on Whit Monday 1st June.

A public meeting was held in the Lecture Hall on 22nd May 1925 with the intention of reviving the old **Swimming Club** that had expired due to the Great War. Town Clerk Mr E F Hadow was in the chair and some 40 others were present; a Mr Kimberley, the Chairman of the Coventry Amateur Swimming Club, was present and invited the new club to become affiliated with his own and in return he would provide an instructor of great experience. Not surprisingly, all voted in favour of resuscitating the club and Hadow was elected president, with Stuart Carter its secretary and D Dencer, F Faxon, L Edmund, W Parkinson and Harris as its committee.

The following month, the club wrote a letter to the Abbey Fields & Bath Committee as regards to the changing accommodation at the baths. A joint conference took place and the council decided to obtain the necessary materials of wood and corrugated iron so the club could erect at the rear of the conveniences a building 18ft by 8ft for changing, provided the club would build it to the satisfaction of the town surveyor. The reason for the request became clear; at this same 12th June meeting, the committee agreed to the club's request to allow mixed bathing for club members on Wednesdays from 4.00 p.m. *'on condition a male person being accompanied by a lady'* and of course, this was not to come into effect until the suitable additional dressing accommodation was completed. Just how the new changing area was accommodated in the cramped pool area is unknown. It is remarkable that the club that had existed for only a few weeks could influence the council to such a degree. One likely result of the new mixed bathing was discussed at the next meeting: 'Proceedings are to be taken against any persons infringing the privacy of bathers at the open air baths'. It was also agreed to let the club have exclusive use of the bath from 1.00 p.m. on Saturday afternoon 25th July to hold a swimming gala. It was the first since 1914 and attracted 250 spectators, and included a novelty race for which the competitors had to wear a fireman's helmet and carry a bucket; it was won by H Newey, who also won *'the pillow fight'*.

1926-28: Kenilworth's first public conveniences, built in December 1923 adjacent to the just visible northern end of the swimming pool; a temporary fence surrounds the convenience and swimming pool site. A pathway, appearing to be inclined, passes through a gate; this is the start of the path to the Castle Ford. Trees planted in the Edwardian years are maturing, several survive today, including that in the centre foreground. The corner of the churchyard wall can be seen below the conveniences. The exposed ruins include the Chapter House wall extreme left *(WCRO, DR 598/5)*

The activity in constructing the tennis courts revived calls for other **sporting facilities**. In January 1924 the council made arrangements with the tenants of the Abbey Fields wartime allotments for them to leave so the space could be utilised for sports. The tenancies expired in June but were extended to September free of extra rent so that produce could be gathered. That autumn a field, it is not clear which, was ploughed up, cleared, levelled and seeded at a cost of £50; Edwin Gee was not opposed to the spending but thought £50 could be better spent on the roads and was concerned about losing rent on the field. Council Chairman Charles Randall stated that as 75 per cent of the expenditure could be reclaimed in a grant for using unemployed workers, the cost to the town would be little.

It was not until the summer of 1926 that the sports field 'opposite The Bungalow' was ready for use by schoolchildren. Quickly off the mark, St Nicholas School headmaster Andrew Hacking asked if his school could use the playing field for sports and if goalposts could be erected. They were granted permission for *'athletic games'* but the council did not put up goal posts. The school was in School Lane and had no playing field of its own.

In June 1925 a roll of tickets numbered 8561 to 9,000 was stolen from the swimming pool; Coventry youths were suspected. In August 1925, the swimming club suggested mixed bathing on Sunday from 7 to 10 a.m., apparently for the public, but this was declined as the same hours were already allocated to gentlemen only and it would exclude unaccompanied gentlemen bathers. The club's formation induced increased attendances generally at the pool; by the close of the season, it was said that it had regained its immediate pre-war popularity, *'easily proved by a visit to the swimming bath, especially on a Wednesday evening when mixed bathing is allowed'*. It was now *'one of the best kept open baths in the district'* and the club had passed the 100 membership mark.

In early 1926, as part of a proposed Town Plan, it was suggested that the vacant plot on the corner of School Lane, bought by the council for the road widening scheme, would be suitable for the building of an indoor swimming baths, but there was little support for it.

In July 1926, canvas screens were erected in the new dressing rooms to ensure a greater privacy for bathers; after a further request from the club it was resolved to split the dressing rooms into two or more parts, and extra barbed wire was added around the fence to prevent trespass. The second Wednesday club evening of July 1926 saw over 200 at the baths, another supposed record. The 1926 gala in August coincided with a fire brigade competition in the Abbey Fields but still attracted a crowd of 300. Also in 1926, St John's School held their own swimming gala.

The same year saw *'thoughtless and wilful damage'* to the pool and children's play equipment; the police were *'requested to provide stricter supervision'* of the council's property with a view to prosecute. In January 1927 there was malicious damage to the conveniences and proceedings were taken.

Just prior to the opening of the 1927 season, the swimming club held a concert at the Abbey Hill school, at which was sung the newly penned club anthem that included the chorus, *'The more we go a'swimming, the healthier we'll be'*, based upon a popular song of the time. The 1927 season also saw the repeated request for Sunday morning mixed bathing, a *'public petition in favour'* was sent to the KUDC with an additional suggestion of mixed bathing at all times over the Whitsun holiday weekend. This year the club membership rose from 65 to 135; the number of members fluctuates noticeably, perhaps varying with the weather, but there were likely to be many exploiting the discounted use of the facilities, particularly as the 16 club nights averaged an attendance of only 26, with 35 being present on the final evening in September. Andrew Hacking was awarded a life membership certificate for his brave efforts at Bude in August 1927 in rescuing a youth in distress in the sea, in an incident that saw a woman lose her life.

Despite the **tennis courts** location, carefully chosen for its attractiveness, there was one obvious flaw; despite the attempts to raise the ground, they were on land that regularly flooded and 1926 was a particularly bad year for flooding. In January, 10 acres of the Abbey fields were under water including the tennis courts; 'This had its advantages however, for it effectively disposes of the worms which are so troublesome'. Then in May the tennis courts were under six inches of water, *'The new pavilion is rising out of the watery waste like a Noah's Ark'*. The bowling green flooded less frequently due to being on slightly higher ground. The club played matches against others on a regular basis, results being published every couple of weeks or so; in 1927 they joined a league.

Behind the courts was a piece of 'waste ground' that had been suggested for the pavilion but was ideally suited for the laying out of a *'golf putting green or greens'*, putting being described as *'a big source of attraction'*. In the summer of 1926, two new **putting greens** were proving a great attraction and there were many entries for a putting competition, in full swing by early August. The description of two putting greens suggests that this was not the familiar 9 or 18 hole putting course. Some youngsters, rather than find *'the few coppers'* needed to play on the greens, had constructed a putting course of their own in the park that provided them with as much enjoyment as the official greens. Details are scarce but presumably the Bowls & Tennis Club were also responsible for the putting green and equipment.

In March 1927 the club were told not to store petroleum in the Pavilion, suggesting that they had been, and were informed that although they were responsible for cutting the grass in its immediate vicinity, they were not to dump the cuttings in the fields. The Pavilion provided an attraction in itself as in September 1927 it was broken into using tools stolen from an earlier break-in at Hickman's Nursery; cigarettes and other goods belonging to the caterer were stolen. On 21st June 1929 it was robbed for the third time in three years; tobacco, canned goods and cutlery were taken on this occasion. Frances Elizabeth Dilworth provided the catering at her own expense and this time the club helped to meet her loss of £11. It is thought that the catering was provided for members only and not the public. Two men were arrested and in court it was stated they had stolen 30 boxes of matches, 94 packs of cigarettes, chocolates and other articles, all the property of Mrs Dilworth. They were released on bail. After the burglary, Mrs Dilworth had been given £5 compensation by the club, but many of the goods were recovered and she paid it back. In June 1928, bowls club member G P Dymond won the Warwickshire & Worcestershire Championship at Hall Green, from an entry of over 700.

Due to the continual problems with flooding in the tennis court area, a decision was taken in January 1928 to straighten one part of the course of the brook, *'at the foot of the weir near the Townpool Bridge'*.

The **bye-laws** and their implementation sometimes caused discussion; one was the prohibiting of the playing of games on Sundays and in March 1927 several petitions organised by the local churches supported the continuation of the ban. At the Bowls & Tennis Club AGM in March 1929, a proposition was put forward to ask the KUDC for permission to use the bowling green and tennis courts on Sundays at hours not clashing with church services; it was narrowly defeated after a strong speech by Parks Committee member, Reverend David Smith. After complaints, in October 1928 it was decided not to enforce the bye-law preventing carriages from being driven in the fields in the cases of the infirm or elderly going to church for Sunday services.

The interest in the **ruins** had spread far and wide and *'a gentleman who took considerable interest in the stonework'* took a collection to a Birmingham exhibition and reconstructed them into an arch. Some artefacts were given away to interested parties; for example the Duke of Rutland was given some duplicate Abbey floor tiles. In April 1925, new Council Chairman Charles Barwell said that a lot of money had been spent on the ruins only for them to become *'more or less a playground'*, and perhaps they should consider handing them over to the Ministry of Works. The following month a new unclimbable fence was proposed to safeguard *'the most important part of the ruins'*.

In May 1925 the decision was made to move the German **field gun**; this was probably due to landscaping the large spoil heaps in the Abbey excavations area where gun was located. The new location was controversial - alongside the War Memorial. Councillor Dencer was against the move: *'They are going to move it to a place as sacred as the old Abbey. Instead of an implement of torture, children should be looking at the memorial and thinking of the men who fell in the war'*. Councillor Grindrod took the opposite view saying it was a *'trophy of devotion, achievement and victory, and is equally sacred with the memorial'*. Dencer's motion was lost and the weapon was moved alongside the memorial. In November 1929 it was decided to enclose the gun in its new location with an 'unclimbable fence', but there was still opposition to its very existence; it was suggested it should be melted down and *'made into implements of husbandry'*.

Four of the six tennis courts and the soon to be covered Abbey ruins; 1926-28 *(WCRO, DR 598/5)*

In 1926, as part of continuing interest in preserving the **Abbey ruins**, the roof of the Barn was re-tiled by Mr Joyce for £43. In May 1927, the council discussed whether the ruins should be re-covered to save them from the effects of weather *'and other destructive influences'*. A small committee was formed to look into the matter and in September £250 was allocated by the KUDC to *'fence in the most important features and cover other parts'* of the ruins. By May 1928, the covering and levelling of the ruins had reached the buildings to the south. About a third of an acre had been covered using soil displaced by the excavations, a move described as *'sad'* but *'unless the council are prepared to safeguard the ruins, this is the only alternative'*. Eventually, south and east of the chapter house wall, the dorter, or dormitory, and infirmary were covered, so too the few ruins uncovered south of the path to the swimming pool and adjacent to the Bridge Street to St Nicholas Church path; south of the church path a terrace was created from remaining soil. In August, work commenced in putting up a 4ft high iron fence around the chapter house and eastern end of the Abbey church, which were to be left exposed.

On 1st March 1927, Thomas Tipson asked the council for use of the Abbey Fields, to charge an entrance fee and hold events as part of Kenilworth's second **Hospital Carnival**, a great expansion on the first. Tipson, the man who had instigated the carnival the previous year, further requested permission to allow 'steam merry-go-rounds' in the park; this was declined but all other suggested attractions were allowed. With the ongoing exposed Abbey ruins work and its spoil heaps restricting space, Town Surveyor Sholto Douglas decided upon the layout of the tents and stalls; the carnival date was set for 2nd July.

Judging of the participants took place in the Abbey Fields before the procession around the town but perhaps as many as 500 non-participants were in fancy dress for the occasion. *'There was a cavalcade of wondrously attired riders, and the originally decorated motor cars and horse drawn vehicles were so charming or alternatively so funny that the judges must have been in a quandary when awarding the prizes'.* Pedal cycles and motor cycles, the fire brigade and Boy Scouts, and visiting participants from Coventry combined to make a show *'so large, so fine and so utterly unexpected that Kenilworth was amazed at the magnificence and magnitude of this its second effort on behalf of the Warneford Hospital.'*

The park saw a crowd of 5,000, *'a supposed record'*. There were 20 gate attendants, mainly members of the British Legion, and Lloyds Bank staff were responsible for looking after the cash. There were many locally organised sideshows - coconut shies, hoop-la, shooting and darts - and others by showmen, such as the *'Alpine Glide'* (helter-skelter) and swing boats. Dr Cregan was in charge of the *'ambulance tent'* and had a serious accident to deal with when a Canadian visitor broke her leg *'on the alpine glide, striking the buffer at the end at too great a speed'*. Entertainment was provided by *Daily Mail* push-ball matches between local teams. In the evening The Sparks Concert Party from Leamington gave a concert, with the bowl-like swimming pool being cleverly utilised as an outdoor auditorium. Schoolchildren gave a demonstration of dancing and there was a torchlight tattoo with marching and counter-marching. The proceedings were brought to an end with the singing of Abide With Me.

As the annual carnival developed, then so too did its use of the fields. From 1929 the swimming club provided a gala at the bath as an added attraction. This was mainly for entertainment and included demonstrations of the latest strokes, diving and life saving; the club's own gala for prizes continued to be held at a later date. Also in 1929, at the start of the week's carnival events an open-air service was held in the Memorial Field (the flat area alongside the War Memorial, donated by Gertrude Evans in 1917), attended by over 300 including scouts, guides and the British Legion. In the Abbey Fields for the carnival on the first weekend of July 1930, tug-of-war and Morris dancing provided entertainment, as did Pat Collins' funfair with steam-powered roundabouts and 'scenic railways' now allowed. Handbills had suggested a two-day stay but in the event they stayed for just one; the explanation given was that the carnival organisers could not afford to put a temporary bridge over the brook, suggesting a living area would have been needed on the opposite side of the brook to that on which the fair was placed. Discussions between Pat Collins and the KUDC failed to find a solution. The carnival parade always concluded at the Abbey Fields for its dispersal.

The next year the fair stayed for four days, perhaps a temporary bridge had been installed for the first time. Hoardings were erected alongside Bridge Street to discourage the free view. This year there was a problem with later flooding in the park caused by damage from the heavy traffic of the fair. (For a full account of the first 25 years of the carnival, see *Kenilworth People and Places, Volume 2*.)

As a climax to the season, in September 1928 the **swimming club** staged an evening 'Carnival' at the pool in which most of their 105 members took part. Kenilworth's *'star comedian'* Mr Trangmar kept all entertained dressed in a nightgown and nightcap. The pool was decorated with fairy lights and Chinese lanterns, music was provided by a gramophone, and fireworks ended the event. A club dance was held in December.

There had been many complaints about the changing facilities at the swimming pool and in February 1929 it was agreed to build an extra 12 *'single dressing boxes'* on the east side of the pool, the cost being seen as a necessary expenditure. The chairman of the Fields & Bath Committee, Mr Parkinson, said he felt *'they could not do better than support the swimming club'*. The surveyor submitted the cost of building an extra 12 changing boxes but was then asked to submit another scheme with the boxes being built more simply of a wooden frame and corrugated iron; this scheme costing £75 went ahead immediately. It was suggested that a partition should be placed centrally in the new changing area to provide accommodation for ladies, but as it would not make 'the boxes suitable for the use of females' it did not go ahead. The east side of the pool was a very steep embankment so it is not clear how the new changing facilities were incorporated. A good deal of painting was carried out too.

The annual swimming club meeting in May 1929 was held at the Parochial Hall. The secretary Mr W H Ward announced an increase in membership for the year from 135 to 192 with 10 new members being taught to swim from scratch. They had a cash balance of just over £12 and assets of £34. Again trying to influence the council, the club suggested that the pool should be opened from 18th May (the opening was delayed due to the work being carried out), and that Sundays from 7 to 8 a.m. should be allocated to male bathers, and from 8 to 10 a.m. for mixed bathing; this was presumably for the public and not just club members and is the first recorded certain occurrence of allocated times for public mixed bathing. One particularly warm May evening saw 36 members make use of the cooling waters, and they played water polo. There had been only a small attendance for the mixed bathing on the previous Sunday due to a thunderstorm, but mixed bathing for the public was subsequently allowed throughout the Whitsun Bank Holiday weekend. J D Siddeley was now the club president and there were 28 (unnamed) vice presidents. The committee included four ladies in its 16 members.

The swimming club was prominent enough to have its notes posted weekly in the *Kenilworth Advertiser*; perhaps the proprietor was a member. Those on the 15th June 1929 announced some were training for a half-mile race at the Carnival Gala on 4th July, despite the water being rather cold; *'after feeling it with one foot, it took a lot of courage to brave the plunge'*. The 29th June notes reported 20 new members and a good attendance on mixed bathing night; *'Some jolly snapshots could be got, for the baths were one long round of gaiety'*. The instructor was teaching a dozen children from 6 to 9 years of age.

The 5th annual gala of the new club in July brought *'nearly a thousand people sitting on the grass slopes surrounding the open air swimming bath... sitting in the boiling sun and endeavouring to keep themselves normal by fanning their faces, drinking lemonade or water, and eating ice cream'*. It had attracted swimmers from Coventry, Leamington and other towns, and in addition to various races there was a demonstration of *'fancy strokes and floating'*, a polo match, and an escapologist thrown into the water in a tied sack. In August it was reported that the weather had resulted in crowded baths, and on mixed bathing nights they were *'full to overcrowding'*. The new cabins had greatly improved the baths. The club had had a fine year, *'the instructor is overwhelmed with pupils.'*

The Royal Warwickshire Regiment **band** offered to play in the park for a fee in the summer of 1929; the Kenilworth Town Band's offer to play for free was accepted instead. A new pedestrian **entrance** to the fields was created in 1929; the fencing alongside Abbey Hill 'midway between the two seats be set back and a 'V' shaped stile be erected.'

A most notable addition to the council staff in 1929 was the new **Parks & Cemetery Superintendant**, 25-year-old John Drew, who preferred to be known as Jack. He was born in Solihull but had lived in Kenilworth since he was four when his father came to work as the gardener at The Gables for Dudley Docker, and thus he was perhaps involved in the making of the park's bowling green. Jack's responsibilities also included the cemetery, all council owned allotments, and (from 1932) the common and Crackley Woods. He moved into the house alongside the cemetery.

In 1930, Mr Phelps of The Bungalow was allowed a gateway from his home into the fields at a cost of 5s per annum. There was concern that one boundary fence with an unnamed property was not strong enough to stop cattle. In 1930 it was necessary to repair the worn 'tarpaving' under the swings in the **children's playground**.

The later 1920s saw an expansion in the provision of sports facilities. In November 1929 the Kenilworth Working Men's Club were allowed to use the **football** pitch 'in the park', presumably goal posts had now been provided, at cost of £2 10s for the season. The next season the club were to have the 'Forrest Road pitch' for the season for £3 14s, and the Kenilworth Early Closers club had it on Thursday afternoons for 25s for the season. It is not known if the 'Forrest Road pitch' is the same as that 'near The Bungalow' mentioned previously. Percy Fox complained that as grazing Plot 4 (the flat area south of Finham Brook and either side of Luzley Brook, that also included the former allotment site) had been made a 'permanent football pitch' after he had agreed the grazing lease, he was entitled to some allowance, but was turned down.

A photograph dated '1930s', showing goalposts erected alongside Bridge Street, either those for the football pitch 'in the Park' used by the Working Men's Club, or put up later in the decade for use by children. Two worn patches suggest other, regular, sporting use. Of note is the fence and absence of vegetation along the brook *(WCRO, PH 352/101/121)*

By March 1930, there were concerns that the **Abbey ruins** were not being properly protected, the Tantara Gatehouse in particular was in urgent need of attention. It had been two years since the council covered the least interesting parts and fenced the remainder, but some other form of preservation was thought to be necessary and the time had come to discuss it. Eustace Carey-Hill's motion along these lines was agreed and the Bath & Playground Committee were to look into protecting all the remnants from vegetation and weather. In December 1930 a letter was received from the Ministry of Works (following a site visit after a request from Carey-Hill), reminding the KUDC of their obligation to preserve the ruins, after which a subcommittee was formed of Councillors Carey-Hill, Hodges, Wilson and Gee.

It was of course the lack of money to pay for conservation work that was causing consternation. It was agreed that no charge should fall on the rates, and so in February 1931 an appeal was launched to raise £191 for work on the Barn and £385 for the Gatehouse; the excavated ruins were to be looked into later. This was described as a *'world appeal'* and Carey-Hill hoped to *'touch springs of sympathy in Ireland and America'*; Councillor Wilson suggested Scotland too! The first donation was from *'A lady on the south coast for £5'*; this was probably Gertrude Evans (see later). An appeal committee was proposed and it was argued that as there would be no contribution from the council through the rates, only those interested in the ruins should be on it. When the Abbey Ruins Appeal Committee was formed in May, Councillor Hodges proposed Charles Randall as a suitable committeeman, but he replied *'No, I am not much in favour of these ruins'*. Work started in March 1932 with the removal of ivy from the Gatehouse.

The early 1920s Abbey excavations in the council-owned park had of course raised much interest in the ruins, their history and preservation, but by being outside their jurisdiction the remains within the churchyard had not on that occasion been touched. A meeting of parties wishing to correct the imbalance took place at Crackley Hall, the home of, soon to be Sir, John Siddeley on 20th May 1932. The group named themselves **The Friends of Kenilworth Abbey and its Surroundings** (which for convenience will hereafter be shortened to The Friends).

An Executive Committee was appointed and they met for the first time at The Vicarage on Monday 18th July 1932. Churchwarden H R Hands presided, and also present were E S G Wickham and Major B H Thomas (representing the Parochial Church Council of St Nicholas), G Tisdale and T G Jackson (representing the Kenilworth Urban District Council), and E Carey-Hill who had been appointed Honorary Secretary. (It is not thought that Councillor T G Jackson was related to former Councillor J E Jackson, who stepped down in 1925 and died in his 80th year in 1931.)

The society's aims were to raise £250 a year to help with the preservation of the Abbey ruins within the churchyard, and to undertake the care of the churchyard itself. It was also hoped to extend this work to the parts of the Abbey outside of the churchyard and for this aim to work in conjunction with the Abbey Ruins Committee of the KUDC. They also wished to collect up all the bits of carved masonry that were scattered over the site, and to investigate the foundations of the St Nicholas Church Norman doorway. The start was to be the *'laying out, with trees, grass and flowerbeds'* of the churchyard, beginning with the wedge-shaped area between the footpaths north of the church, the oldest part of the churchyard.

The Friends first annual meeting was held on 26th September 1932 at the Parochial Hall following a Service of Dedication of their work; by now they had a membership of over 200. Dudley Docker and Sir John Siddeley were amongst those present, and Secretary E Carey-Hill outlined the group's aims and progress. Subscriptions had raised £60 and he suggested that a membership of one in ten of a population of 8,000 was not unreasonable (they were currently 600 short of that figure) which would help raise their target of £250 a year income. The object of the association was *'to unite on common fellowship all who had at heart the worthy preservation of their Kenilworth Heritage; the ancient graveyard, the Abbey ruins and the St Nicholas Church west doorway'*. First they were going to get the churchyard in order to make it a *'gracious garden of remembrance'*; he hoped that eventually they could *'unite the two halves of the ruins, now half within and half without the churchyard wall, by acting as a means of co-operation between the Urban District Council and the Parochial Church Council...'* to remove the churchyard wall and enclose the ruins with one fence. The Dean of Norwich, Dr Cranage, then gave a talk on various aspects of the Abbey; he too lamented that the wall *'goes so cruelly across the remains of the Abbey.'*

Membership peaked in 1933 at 237. For three years the Friends tidied the churchyard, collecting Abbey masonry as they went. A lot of coarse vegetation had to be uprooted at the beginning as the ground had been neglected for so many years. Some of the work was paid for from the group's funds, a workman was employed at £2 a week, but much was done by volunteers. In March 1933 the KUDC allowed the Friends to build a retaining wall of Abbey stone within the churchyard. A shortage of funds was a constant problem; George Tisdale was the first to voluntarily double his subscription.

In the spring of 1934, a man named Vincent Bailey of Kenilworth, New Jersey, a town named by its Literacy Society after reading Scott's novels, wrote a letter to the KUDC; he claimed he had recently visited the town yet addressed his letter to 'Kenilworth, Scotland'! He asked if the council had a crest or Coat of Arms that could be copied in some way to be included in their new public library. Councillor, and builder, Henry Wells Lawrence suggested that perhaps a piece of Abbey stone could be sent, and this was agreed to. Although it was initially intended to incorporate the stone in the fabric of the building, the piece chosen was unsuitable for such a purpose; instead it was put prominently on display for many years, and today it is in the hands of their local History Society.

The summer of 1930 saw an increasing problem for the KUDC, the parking of cars on the fields by visitors. Notices had to be put up in several places to stop the practice. However, it was the playing of games on **Sundays**, in particular the afternoons, which caused most debate with tennis being singled out as likely to be a *'particularly offensive'* sight to people coming out of church. This led in September 1931 to a memorable quote from Councillor T G Jackson, well-known for his *'outspoken utterances'*, who said, *'Can it be offensive to the eye to see beautiful and graceful ladies playing tennis? When that is offensive to the eye I hope that my day of exit is at hand!!'* He was in favour of allowing bowls and tennis on Sunday afternoons and noted there were *'thousands at a cricket match in Leamington on Sunday last week'*. His campaign found particular favour amongst the young. However in December it was decided to not alter the existing rules, largely due to the proximity of St Nicholas Church. Jackson commented *'It is a narrow minded policy, and inconsistent with several members approval of Sunday golf. The members should be willing to exercise the same right to people playing in the park as they themselves exercised in regards to golf'*. Jackson however *'bowed to the committee's findings'*. It is worth noting that the swimming bath was open on Sunday afternoons from 2 until 5 p.m.

In March 1933, four youths were prosecuted for their infringement of **bye-law** 26; they were caught using the swings at the age of 15! In January 1934 a man was seen shooting birds in the fields; he was apprehended and was asked for an explanation but no action was taken. In November 1934 it was suggested that a new bye-law should be introduced that restricted horses to walking pace, in turn suggesting that horses being ridden at a faster pace was becoming a nuisance.

Organisations other than from Kenilworth often used the fields for their **events**, proving their attraction from outside the town; Vine Street School, Foleshill Baptists Church and other Coventry organisations received permission to hold their annual picnics or gatherings in the park. In May 1930, Rodney 'Gypsy'

Smith, a renowned Evangelist, was allowed to erect a marquee in the field near the War Memorial. Kenilworth organisations too had regular use of the fields; the fire brigade still held its annual competition in July, and often additional displays in connection with the carnival.

In May 1932 the Girl Guides were allowed to plant 'two double red hawthorn **trees**' between the Pavilion and the path; they were 'commemorative' for the *'coming of age'* of the Girl Guide movement. Many local worthies were present including Mrs Cay, Mr & Mrs Siddeley, Sir John and Lady Higgins, and District Commissioners of the Guide movement. A few months later a *'commemoration tree'* needed to be replaced, but further details were not recorded. Later that year additional beech trees were planted alongside Abbey Hill in line with existing ones, and the following year an ash tree near the Bridge Street entrance was cut down and replaced by a copper beech.

The annual tenders for the **grazing** rights in March 1927 were: P Fox Plots 2 & 4 for £57, F S Fancott 1 & 3 for £36 10s, C Randall 9 for £30, E Gee 5 for £12, and P A Eykyn 8 for £13. It seems Plots 6 & 7 were not let but despite this the income of £148 10s was well above the original need of paying off the Abbey Fields purchase loans and helped the council to offset the regular losses at the swimming pool, and gave an amount to allow for repairs and other costs in the park. Although grazing contributed to keeping the grass short, mowing was taking place in at least some areas particularly for events to take place.

In March 1932, the grazing plots were let as follows: P Fox Plots 1, 2, 4 & 5 for £50, Fancott 3 for £14, J Hubbard 8 for £14, and C Randall 9 for £25; Plots 6 & 7 still appear to be unlet as in 1927. Presumably at least partly due to the unletting of Plots 6 & 7, for the next season the plots were once more rearranged, this time into 7, and rather than inviting tenders they were let by public auction with the results as follows: H V Booth Plot 1 for £12, P Fox 2 for £20, H V Booth 3 for £15, E Gee 4 for £15, E Gee 5 for £9, J Hubbard 6 for £23 10s, J Hubbard 7 for £8 10s; an income of only £103.

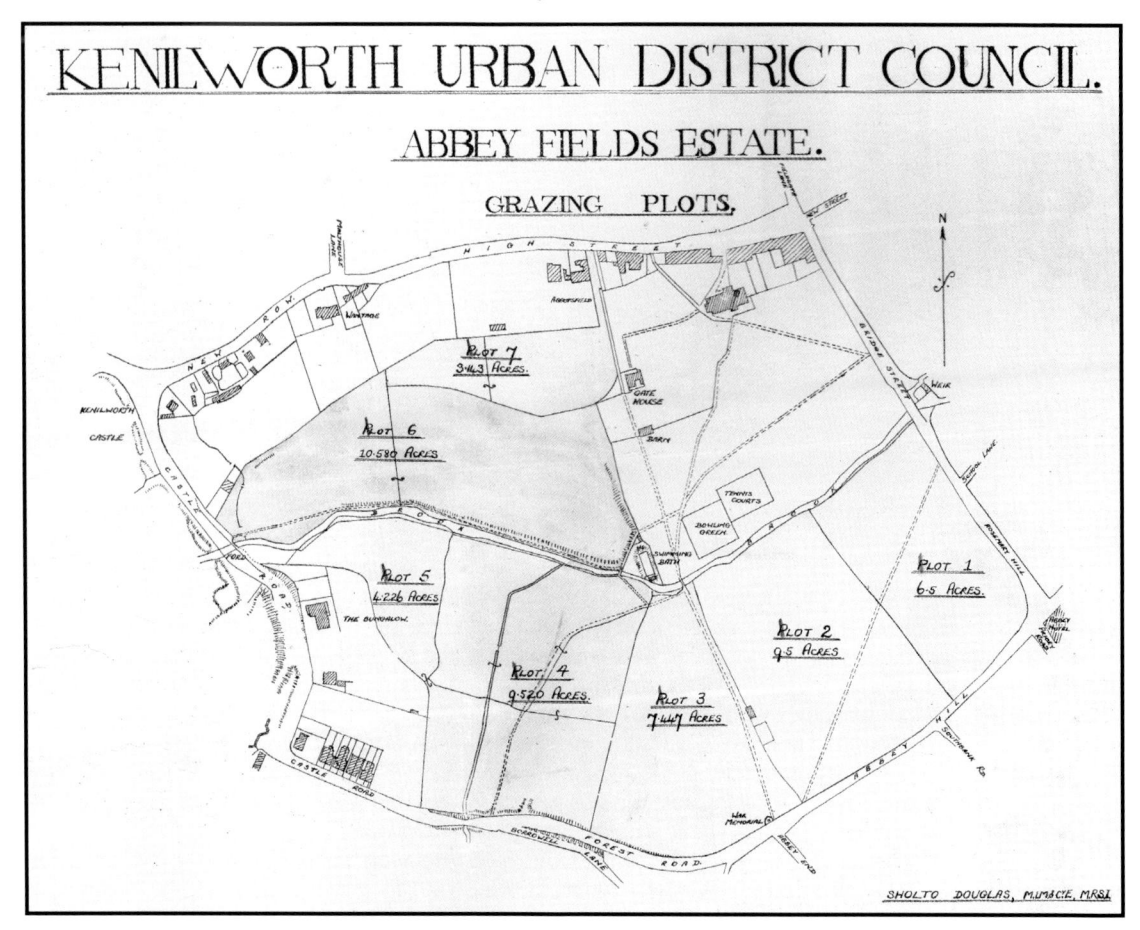

The rearranged Abbey Fields Grazing Plots dated March 1933. Plot 4 includes the area west of Luzley Brook connected by the cattle bridge, and Plot 5 includes the area southwards connected by a gate *(KHAS, FoAF)*

The **Bowls & Tennis Club** takings from subscriptions and fees had risen from £19 in 1919 when it was still only bowls, to £140 in 1930, giving a total of £1,181 in 12 seasons, but the summers of 1931 and 1932 were very wet making the grass courts almost unplayable; the fields flooded again in May 1932.

At about this time, there was a major development in the tennis courts; two hard surface courts were added, squeezed in lengthways between the existing grass courts and the footpath, the regular flooding and subsequent drying out period is likely to have influenced the decision. Surprisingly, this cannot be found reported in the newspapers, nor is it mentioned directly anywhere in the KUDC minutes, although in 1932 there are mentions of a new agreement between the club and KUDC, and a new fence being put up around the courts; it is thus likely that the new hard courts opened in time for the 1933 season. All the grass courts seem to have been retained at this time, giving a total of 8, though perhaps not all were maintained for continual use.

Before the start of the 1933 season the club asked the KUDC if they could do something to relieve the regular tennis court flooding; the surveyor was subsequently asked to *'endeavour to locate the old stone drain which it is understood is blocked'*; later in the year (September) it was decided to clear the brook and other water courses and a suggestion that the brook to Bridge Street should be widened was discussed. However, the summer the same year created the opposite problem, it was so hot and dry that the tennis hard courts became unplayable; the three successive summers created a substantial drop in takings for the club and it now had a rent debt to the council. The Oxpen Meadow had remained flooded until May that year so grazing had started late, leading the rights holder Mr Hubbard to ask for a refund.

The two tennis hard courts squeezed in lengthways between the neatly-mowed grass courts and the footpath. Uncovered Abbey ruins can be made out *(HS)*

As usual in the build up to the new season, in 1931 the **Swimming Club** made a number of requests to the council. This time they asked for more dressing room for ladies, the replacement of a damaged diving board with a springboard, and, important for warming the water, the lopping of some trees around the pool to let the sun in. The council replied that the dressing accommodation was adequate, the board would be removed but not replaced, but they would lop the trees. A further request saw the pool open for mixed bathing during all public hours from Saturday to Tuesday over the Whitsun Bank Holiday weekend. The mixed bathing was a success; it was reported that the sunshine *'drew many to the mixed bathing, the number of Coventry people present was noticeable'*, and perhaps inevitably *'the new terraces were well patronised by the men'*. What form the *'new terraces'* took is unknown.

One issue did not go away; in June the Bathing Committee met with the Swimming Club Committee 'to go into the Ladies changing accommodation matter', the outcome of which was to divide the most recent 12 'boxes' by a wooden partition 'to enable one half to be used by ladies and that the dressing boxes be numbered'. This led to the next great innovation, following on from the Whitsun experiment, by July mixed bathing was allowed every day except Tuesdays (females) and Thursdays (males), and the club still had use of the pool on Thursday evenings. The club itself had few ladies in its 49 members but those few did create problems when having matches against other clubs; Leamington's pool for instance had still to allow any mixed bathing, thus excluding Kenilworth as match opponents.

As mentioned, in May 1932 much of the Abbey Fields had been underwater and the pool had to be closed due to flooding; it took several days to empty, clean and refill it. This was followed by a spell of hot weather reaching 85 degrees Fahrenheit and in mid-June the cutting back of trees allowed the sun to shine directly on the water and its temperature rose to 60 degrees (15.5 C). In July, despite the ongoing arguments about Sunday games in the Abbey Fields, public Sunday opening for the pool was agreed to be from 7 to 10 a.m. and 2 to 5 p.m. until end of August. However, the price of admission on Sunday afternoon was to be doubled.

In 1933 the cost of a season ticket, presumably still for 12 visits, was 3s for adults and 1s 6d for a child. The Central School was allowed exclusive use of the pool on Tuesdays and Thursdays from 9 a.m. until noon, Warwick County Council paying their fees of £2 2s a season. The club had exclusive use on Thursday evenings for £2 a year, and now the pool was open for 'mixed bathing only' during Whitsun week and August Bank Holiday. It was a successful season with regular overcrowding problems, and late in the year a new discussion was begun; did the increasing popularity of the 37-year-old pool require it to be enlarged?

In the summer of 1931, junior **football** clubs applied to use the 'pitches' in the park; evidence as to the precise locations is conflicting. The fields were however still in use for grazing (the arrangements, if any, for removing livestock to allow matches is not known) and that September the grazing tenant asked the football clubs for £1 a season for the loss of his grass. The council as landowner ensured that no such payment was made. The St Austin's club had one of the pitches in 1932.

In April 1933 St Barnabas Cricket Club asked for exclusive use of the **cricket pitch** 'in the War Memorial field'; the exclusivity was not permitted. This is a rare mention of cricket in the Abbey Fields, the original prime sporting reason behind the fields' acquisition and intended site for a permanent pitch. As far as is known, references to the 'War Memorial Field' at this time refers to the flatter area alongside the memorial.

In 1934 Kenilworth Juniors was amongst the football clubs asking for pitches, such was the demand that another council pitch was being prepared in Dalehouse Lane.

The annual flooding of the **Oxpen Meadow** with the hope of providing skating was not without its problems. In January 1931 a 'communication' suggested that the council had 'exceeded their rights in this matter' and permission ought to be obtained from the Mill End cake mill owner and operator before taking the water; the council in reply said that they hadn't broken any agreements. At the beginning of the next December, flooding the meadow was imminent, 'the water for this purpose to be taken from the drain which supplies the bath with water'; it isn't known if this was the usual arrangement or the problems of the previous winter had caused a rethink, but the following spring the cake mill operator complained of a water shortage all winter, since the very day the meadow had been flooded.

Each deliberate flooding and draining of the Oxpen Meadow re-ignited the question of a permanent lake, but many inhabitants believed the *'Natural beauty and the amenities of the fields will be completely spoilt'* if one was created. Residents and tradesmen urged the townsfolk to protest and by January 1933 up to 200 had signed a petition against; A J Cooke, Edgar Whittindale, A J Berkeley, and Major Watling were amongst those who signed. However, within a week a counter petition in favour had been set up in pubs and other places claiming *'the lake will be in keeping with the natural beauty of the fields, its provision will bring extra trade to the town and the local unemployed will find work'*, and in two days had been signed by 500! It was organised by Councillor T G Jackson who was continuing the work of J E Jackson who had been advocating the lake since the Victorian years.

Despite the numbers, it was the petition against what it called the *'alleged improvement'* that carried the argument. *'We protest in the strongest manner against any steps being taken which will have the effect, or risk, of altering the present character of the Abbey Fields whether by intention or otherwise. We feel the amenity shall suffer from any such alteration and will lead to expense without any compensating advantage to the ratepayers'*. The KUDC had not in any case chosen a particular lake scheme from the several proposed, and as the subject was not on the agenda they could not discuss it; this caused arguments about being honest and open with the public, but the decision to send it back to the committee stood.

In response to a number of requests from the public to allow **horse riding** other than at walking pace to be permitted, in September 1932, Councillor George Tisdale suggested the creation of a 'rotten row' in the fields. Tisdale said that as some loans for the purchase of the fields were almost repaid, saving a rate of over a 1s, new schemes could be planned and would give work to the unemployed in the winter months. It was to be discussed by the Parks Committee. Another *'well received'* scheme the same year was the making of a promenade alongside Abbey Hill with flowerbeds and shrubs on the inside. However, this could not yet be started due to embryonic plans to build an extra road creating two-way traffic on Abbey Hill, which would isolate the beech trees on an island between them. Another proposal was again for proper toboggan runs to be created.

On 20th January 1933, the Parks Committee listed its fourteen **proposals** for the Abbey Fields: 1) A lake in the Oxpen Meadow and improving the path to the baths; 2) Clearing the brook course from the bath to Castle Road; 3) Provision of a lamp halfway from Bridge Street to the baths; 4) Provision of suitable accommodation for horse riding; 5) Provision of a mini golf course or putting green; 6) Removal of the boundary fence; 7) Removal of hedges on the south side of the brook; 8) Provision of a bandstand; 9) Laying out of a cricket pitch; 10) Provision of shelters; 11) Laying out of a piece of land between the new lake and Castle Road with ornamental roads and shrubs; 12) Provision of a promenade along Abbey Hill; 13) Provision of a toboggan run; 14) Improvement of the path to Forrest Road. Of these, the committee suggested the council should seriously consider the lake, clearing the brook to Castle Road to prevent flooding, the lamp, and additional beech trees along Abbey Hill (as a start of the promenade). All of these were approved, except the lake for which the cost and how it could benefit the unemployed needed to be investigated. Councillor Gee said that the expected cost of £3,000 for the lake would be better spent on helping to purchase the Castle, and a lake around the Castle would then be more beneficial.

The following month the decision was made that there was to be no lake, but the idea would 'lie on the table'. Councillor Jackson was not impressed saying the council was initially unanimously in favour, the surveyor was told to prepare plans, but the petition against changed everything; the council had been guided by it although the subject had not been properly debated. There were 750 signatures on the petitions but Jackson described the council's 'abject failure' to properly gauge opinions.

In November 1932 it had been proposed to have a **drinking fountain** in the park and work started in January 1934. It was located halfway along the path from Bridge Street to the centre of the fields; the stone work was 2ft square and 10ft high and it was surmounted by a gas lamp, number 3 of the 14 proposals of January 1933. The structure was located so as to tap in to the water and gas supplies laid for the new conveniences in 1923.

In 1935, there was a complaint of standing water from the fountain on the path.

The gas lamp on top of the water fountain, date unknown

(This photograph was copied some years ago from the Abbey Fields file in the Kenilworth Library collection, but is now missing.)

In February 1933 it was finally decided that the **path** from the Castle Ford to the *'clap gate on south side of the swimming pool'* was to be made up for the first time with gravel, and was to be 4ft wide and cost £100; that from Forrest Road was repaired at the same time. In 1935 the path from Bridge Street to Abbey Hill was tarred, probably for the first time. In May 1933 a seat in the fields was broken by one of the council's grazing horses; the following year a seat was provided for the first time in an obvious location, halfway up the steep path alongside the Memorial Field.

In February 1934, the Kenilworth Town Band were given permission to play in the Abbey Fields on Sunday evenings provided they did not start until after the conclusion of the evening service at St Nicholas Church. In July the same year the fire brigade took on that from Rover in one and two man competitions, which the visitors won; refreshments and entertainments were provided. A few weeks later the brigade had their own sports and internal competitions in the park, there were about half a dozen different events, each with their own trophy. In June 1935 Kenilworth Baptist Church held one of several outdoor services.

In October 1935 there was a solitary report of a growing problem in the fields; its resident rabbits were burrowing into neighbouring gardens! The Park Superintendant Jack Drew was instructed to take unspecified action.

In February 1934, the **Bowls & Tennis Club** asked the council for a reduction of £45 in the balance owed in respect of renting; poor weather over several seasons had caused financial difficulties. It was argued that the club could sell its assets to pay their debt but then the KUDC would have to fund the amenities, and so George Tisdale's suggestion that the £53 19s 3d debt was cleared and the club pays only half rent for the next year but then give half its profits to the council, was carried. This however brought counter arguments: the holders of the council-owned allotments owed £60, would they let them off as well? How about owed housing rents?

With growing disquiet, in May 1934 club secretary H Prince wrote to the *Leamington Courier* defending the club, and the council's decision. His argument was one of cost, and how the club had saved the town a large sum. He began by saying that Leamington's bowling green was at a cost of a 2d rate, Coventry's a 4d rate, and that Kenilworth's was void of all costs to the town. The club was set up 1912/13 at its own expense including £120 for the green, provided all woods, mower, roller, storage shed, *etc*. When the tennis courts were opened, the club were asked to take them over, which they did, again providing all the equipment. *'Such a large number of the youth of this town took advantage of the courts'* that another three were opened and the club again paid for the equipment. The *'absolutely necessary'* pavilion was built by the KUDC but paid for by the club at £15 a year plus rates, and furnished it out themselves for £25. A motor mower was needed, it cost the club £33; the hard courts were put down, the club agreed to pay an extra £30 a year for them. The club not only provided all the equipment but also paid a groundsman to look after the grounds, whilst for all that time the KUDC stipulated that the public should be allowed to play bowls at 3d an hour and tennis at 1s an hour. *'Thus the club agreed to pay the Council £45 a year for the privilege of doing the work that should have been done by the Council'*. The losses from the last three summers had the club in financial difficulties for the first time and the KUDC were asked to make a payment. With the situation so well explained, the council's decision was accepted.

In an attempt to reduce flooding in the area, in November 1935 the brook through this part of the fields was cleaned out to improve the water flow. The following month a 150yd chain fence was put around the tennis courts, and also in 1935, the Pavilion had a gas line and hotplate installed.

The tide was turning on the **Sunday** games debate and in November 1934 it was officially proposed that the **bye-laws** be altered to allow organised games, except for football, in the Abbey Fields between 1 and 6 p.m. on Sundays. Also, it was confirmed that riders on horseback would be required to pass at walking pace only. The proposals had to go through various procedures to be verified; by May 1935, the KUDC had approved the new bye-laws and lodged them with the Minister of Health. Church leaders were *'aghast'* and the Kenilworth Council for Free Churches organised a petition to send to the Ministry, asking not to sanction the allowance of Sunday games. The Reverend E S G Wickham writing in the St Nicholas parish magazine asked, *'Everyone will sympathise with those Councillors who have the opportunity of playing games on Sunday on private grounds; it is only natural for them to wish to give the same opportunity to the general public, but does the general public desire it?'* Perhaps giving the Reverend Wickham his answer, in May 1935 the tennis club voted 31-3 in favour of playing hours on Sundays being the same as weekdays, and finally as from 1st August 1935 the council allowed all games to be played on Sundays. The bowling green and tennis courts were open to the public from 2 until 6 p.m., the children's play area also, with the equipment being locked outside these hours.

The bye-laws were also amended to include, 'A person shall not bring into the pleasure ground any barrow, truck, machine or vehicle, unless used for the conveyance of a child or children or an invalid. This bye-law shall not be bedeemed to prohibit the wheeling of any bicycle, tricycle or other similar machine to or from any part of the pleasure ground'. This was the first (known) attempt to prohibit cycling, but the inclusion of the phrase 'conveyance of a child' either deliberately or accidentally allowed children to continue riding their bicycles. The KUDC were not done with altering bye-laws; in February 1936 they started the process for a new law to prevent dogs fouling on the footpaths.

Starting work on 25th September 1933 was a new town Surveyor, Eli Shaw, a Lancastrian who moved from his position as Kearsley Sanitary Inspector that he had held since 1921. The April 1934 KUDC election saw a number of new councillors, and a new chairman in George Tisdale.

In readiness for the new **swimming pool** season, at the March 1934 KUDC meeting it was agreed that the 'bank near the entrance of the baths' was 'levelled' to provide better sunbathing facilities (the 'bank' in question presumably being one of those constructed from spoil at the bath construction), a wider path around the pool was to be considered, as was the introduction of turnstiles. The matter was left in the hands of Messrs Hiorns, Tisdale and Bennett with power to act. By the following meeting, the work had been started; in the early spring the sun bathing bank was under construction, and a wall was built *'skirting the main footpath, and from this the bank will slope down to the water. It will provide ample space for local sun worshippers to tan themselves.'*

Due to continual problems with overcrowding the previous season, in May 1934 the newly elected Council decided to seriously consider the question of either increasing the size of the existing pool or constructing a new one on another site, and at the July 1934 meeting Surveyor Eli Shaw submitted plans and costs for both. Either way it was agreed that doubling the size of the swimming bath was needed and perhaps not surprisingly it was the extension of the existing pool that was approved on cost alone; the comparative figures and possible alternative sites were not recorded.

At the same meeting, at which Councillor Gee was congratulated on reaching his 80th year and starting his 38th on the council, problems with the water supply in general due to an ongoing drought were highlighted; the public were asked to show *'the greatest economy for some time to come'* in a situation described as *'alarming'*. It is likely that water supply difficulties were at least partly responsible for the next problem at the pool as a couple of weeks later, the Medical Officer Dr Gibbons-Ward visited and was *'rather perturbed'* at the apparent condition of the pool's water. He took samples to the county analysts who then stated the water was not fit for use; the matter was reported to the Abbey Fields Committee who decided an adequate filtration plant was needed; as far as is known the *'meshed sieves'* mentioned in the planning stage was the only filtration the pool had. It is not known when the water test results were available and the bath stayed open until the normal season's end in mid-September, but it was later stated that *'In the interests of public health, the bath was closed in September (1934)'*; perhaps that infers a permanent closure until problems were sorted. Users of the pool at this time still recalled in the later 20th century years how they swam with frogs, and there was mud on the bottom of the pool.

A sub-committee was formed of W Bostock (as chairman) and Councillors J Leaver, Dr L Smalley, G Tisdale and H R Watling, to look into all matters concerning the pool but in particular public health and the costs of improvements, and in January 1935 the committee unanimously recommended 'that if anything is done in the matter, the present bath be extended to double the size and a filtration plant installed'. The proposed extended pool would be 88ft by 60ft with a depth from 2ft 6ins to 7ft, and at a suggested cost, to be raised by a loan, at £700 for the pool extension, £870 for the filtration plant, £130 for the plant's new building and £40 for the installation of electricity; a total of £1,740. The suggested filtration plant would provide complete filtration, aeration and chlorination of the water once every eight hours.

The committee's findings were discussed at a full council meeting on Tuesday 15th January 1935, and immediately concerns were raised. Councillor Griffiths said the committee was supposed to report on filtration plant investigations but had not, and he was concerned at the extra expense for all ratepayers; he continued, *'I do not feel the question of the water supply has been sufficiently investigated. It is said that after two dry summers the water from the brook has been curtailed, and as a result the water from the brook is not fit to bathe in. We could supplement it from the town water supply'*. Councillor Jackson was disappointed that the subject had not been communicated to the press; *'We are proposing to spend nearly £2,000 and the public have no knowledge of it.'*

The committee members were persuasive; Councillor Bostock said that *'Kenilworth without its swimming bath would be a very funny place, what are the children to do if there is no swimming bath?'*, and J Leaver said that if they did not go ahead with the scheme there would be no swimming in Kenilworth and thought that a *'Kenilworth Lido'* would be close to making a profit. Dr Smalley thought that if the pool was to be increased in size it must be brought up to date as well; he reminded the council that they were responsible for any infection in the water and *'unless there is a chlorination plant, the only way to deal with infection, the size of the bath should not be increased'*. Every other town was putting in a filtration plant and Kenilworth should not be left behind.

Councillor Jackson then made a new suggestion; he claimed the falling use of the pool in the last two years had been *'terrific'* (in 1933 visitors had numbered 15,669) and he thought they should go for a closed-in pool open all year with heated water as it would be financially viable due to all other local pools being open-air. Jackson said he was in favour of progress but believed that outdoor pools would be obsolete in a few years time. *'We have calculated that only one person in 75 uses the bath, but the cost will have to be borne by the other 74'*. The possible cost of a closed-in pool had not been estimated by the committee, but all thought it would be far too expensive. With two dissentients, presumably Jackson and Griffiths, the voting was in favour to go ahead with the enlargement of the pool.

With work to begin as soon as it was possible, the project was set in motion by deciding to examine the filtration systems at other local baths, and Eli Shaw revisited his plans; in a report dated 12th February 1935 he recommended that the best way to carry out the development was to raise the whole pool by 3ft due to the 'considerable amount of upward water pressure' at the present depth. This would put the bottom of the new shallow end just above the level of the top of the old baths, and allow a good width walkway to be made around the pool yet retain the existing hedgerow boundary on the western side. The Baths, Playground & Cemetery Committee recommended the report's acceptance.

Work was rapid. On 15th March it was reported that the excavation had been completed, work on concreting the surface was to begin shortly, and by early May the pool itself was almost finished. Electricity could now be laid and a wooden structure near the bridge used by the bowls and tennis club (probably the earlier pavilion supplied by Mr Pratt in 1918), needed to be moved. Much of the work was carried out by the formerly unemployed under the supervision of the council workmen, notably T Gundy (soon to be leaving for a position at Crewe), C Bricknell and Mr Woodward.

By June 1935, the cost of equipment for the new bath began to be recorded in the KUDC Minutes. E O Shanks & Co, a Coventry wood dealer, supplied the ladies dressing cubicles (£75 10s) and turnstile office (£20); Messrs Tuck & Blakemore (Coventry) supplied galvanised handrails and 286ft of galvanised tubing (£70); Charles Wicksteed & Co supplied the diving stage *etc* (£94 1s 9d). The filtration and cleansing unit was obtained from Thomas Piggott (£457 12s) and chlorine for it cost £6 15s. The Premiere Artificial Stove Co built the aerator (£47 15s 4d), and Alfred Williamson's company supplied the tickets (£2 12s 3d). Thatching for the dressing boxes and 'engine house' cost £27 10s.

The 'Lido' prior to filling; the surface of the original pool was about 3ft lower than the surrounds of this. Dressing accommodation, right, was built in the style of the tennis pavilion; the bushes to the left, with the filtration plant behind, were those on the top of the banking around the original pool; the cascade aerator is extreme left *(LC, 12th July 1935)*

The opening of the enlarged pool took place on Monday 15th July 1935, and hearty congratulations went the way of its architect, Eli Shaw. The pool held 160,000 gallons, was 81ft by 62ft, with a depth from 2ft 6ins to 7ft. The new *'dressing accommodation'* was built thoughtfully in *'conformity'* with the tennis and bowls pavilion with elm side boards and thatched roofs; there were two buildings, one at each end of the pool, with 66 lockers for ladies, and 36 for men. There was a wide space on the eastern, bowling green, side on which was built a several-stage terracing for sunbathing and spectators; the northern end had a five-stage 'diving pedestal', three metre springboard and chute for adults, and the shallow end the children's chute, all provided by Wicksteed & Co. The aerator, effectively a several stage water fall, had coloured lights behind giving *'a pleasing effect as the water cascades.'*

Council Chairman George Tisdale presided at the opening, but as head of the committee responsible it was Mr Bostock that made the major speech saying, *'they had taken a step in the right direction, taken a step that was a credit to the town. They had no option but to provide a bath with clean water, or lose the bath altogether'*. Overlooking the major consideration of building costs he continued, *'For several reasons it was decided to construct the bath on the original site, the chief reason was the beauty of the position and the fact that brook water could be used more economically than town water'*. Despite this, in a reflection of the pool's first filling in 1896, the pool had been filled by the fire brigade using its steam fire engine and the water left to circulate through the new filtration system. The fire engine had been decommissioned in February 1934 and was uninsured so this was a rare outing; it allowed the new fire engine (delivered on 28th June 1932) to remain available for emergencies. Tisdale implored the local swimmers to return to their own pool rather than go out of town, as *'their bath, I can honestly say, is unsurpassed by any in the county. The equipment is guaranteed to fill the bath with water fit to drink'*. He declared the bath open and swimmers dived in from all sides and slid down the chutes.

The ceremony was followed later by the annual gala organised by the swimming club in aid of funds for the carnival. Mr A R Woods, the Warwickshire 100 yds champion set a record for the pool of 4 lengths (107 yds 1 ft) in 66 seconds. The cost for swimming was 6d for adults (or 4s for a book of 12 tickets), 2d for children, the hire of a towel or costume cost 2d, and spectators could enter for 3d. The bath was open from 7 a.m. until dusk with mixed bathing allowed at all hours except for periods allocated to schools (Monday to Friday 9.00 a.m. until noon), ladies only (Friday 2.00 to 6.00 p.m.), the swimming club (Wednesday 7.00 to 8.00 p.m.), and closed for lunch (Monday to Friday, noon to 2.00 p.m.).

As a point of interest, the use of the word 'lido' in January 1935 to describe Kenilworth's new outdoor pool was before the first British pool that included the term in its title, that at Edmonton, North London, had opened on 27th July 1935; had it been officially named the 'Kenilworth Lido', it would have been the first in the country, by twelve days. As it was, Kenilworth's was one of 169 outdoor pools built by local Council's in the 1930s.

The quality of water in the bath was analysed at Manchester University (at a cost of £4 17s 9d) and the tests showed that the 'water is practically sterile' with 'B Coli absent in samples up to 100cc' but the new pool's popularity caused difficulties. Within weeks, extra dressing accommodation was being contemplated, and those arriving by car were causing problems; it was decided to allocate a car-parking area specifically for 'lido' users, the place designated was Forrest Road.

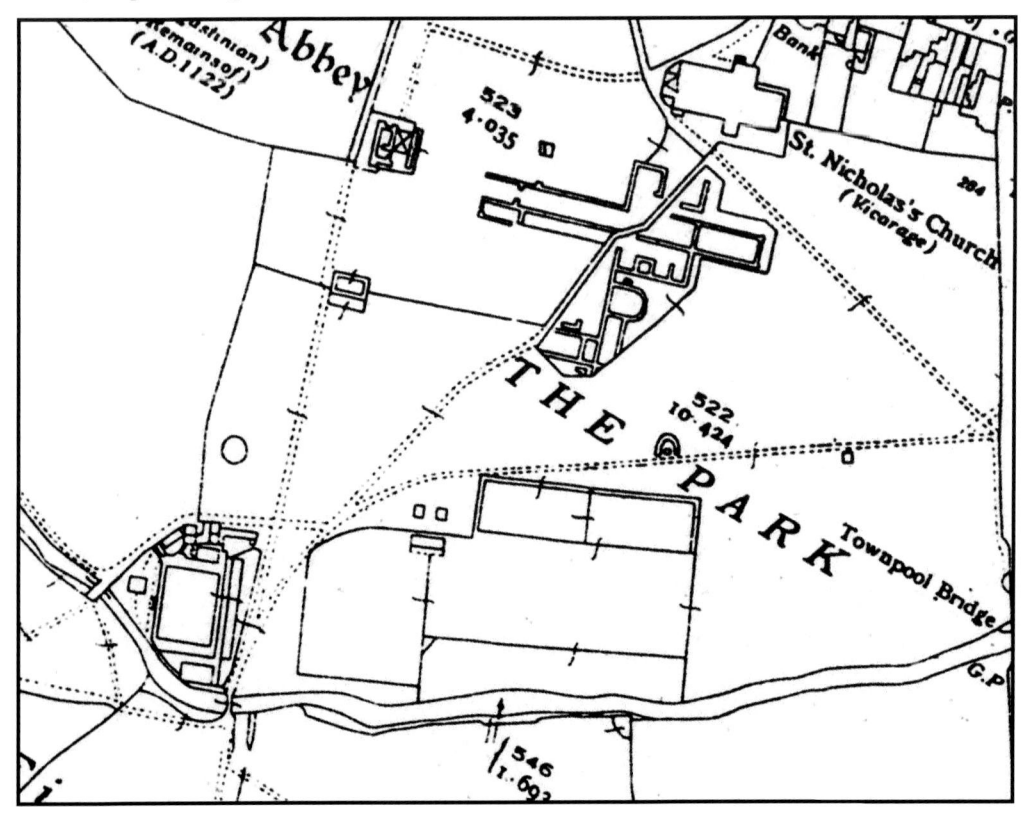

The rebuilt swimming pool extended eastwards to the north-south path. Some of the Abbey ruins remain uncovered, the two new hard-surface tennis courts are squeezed in lengthways covering the ruins between the six grass courts and the path, and a fence encloses the bowling green and tennis courts. The water fountain has been built *(OS, 1938)*

In 1910, 1,862 people had used the baths, in 1933 15,669, and in the first nine weeks after the rebuilt bath opened, 12,670. In addition 117 season tickets had been sold. The population was now 8,100.

However, in another reflection of when the pool was first built, the KUDC had failed to notify the Ministry of Health of its intentions and did not apply for a loan for the construction until after the pool was complete. The inquiry was held on Wednesday 18th December 1935 at the council offices and, due to applying retrospectively, the KUDC were immediately on the back foot once the Ministry of Health Inspector said the action of the council was *'unsatisfactory'* and set *'an undesirable precedent'*. The inquiry was not just about approving the loan but also the plans; *'by the procedure adopted, the Ministry have been given no chance of offering any criticism'*. Mr Tisdale said it was *'impossible for him to justify the procedure of the council in making the application.'*

The loan requested was for £2,752 to cover all costs of the bath; as it had cost £1,000 more than the original estimate, it was perhaps just as well the loan had not been applied for prior to construction. The loan was for 15 years with charges of £233, and working expenses £123 (totalling £356); the estimated revenue was £20 a week for 18 weeks (a remarkably similar £360). A total of £2,565 had been paid out of the Council's general account, wages were £4 10s a week, and chemicals £2 6s 6d a week. Receipts so far were £227, expenditure to date £2,564, and the extra dressing room being considered had an estimate of £187.

In February 1936, the loan for the rebuild was sanctioned provided extra men's lavatory accommodation was built. A suitable location for them, near existing drains, meant that the footbath had to be moved. The extras increased the requested loan to £3,026 for 12 years but in June the Ministry of Health initially only approved the major alterations and not this addition; after discussions, in September the swimming pool loan application for £3,034 *(£197,000)* over 12 years was finally agreed.

The alignment of the new pool exactly overlaid the western side and two ends of the original, suggesting three original pool walls were used as the foundation for the new. Also, as the new pool was set 3ft higher than the old, and judging by the speed the excavating was completed (less than a month), it seems likely that the concrete floor of the original pool was left and simply filled in by newly excavated material; this leads to the probability that much of the original pool still lies buried beneath the current one. Also, a wall along the brook from the Iron Bridge, was extended to support the plinth of the changing rooms and help protect the newly raised surface from flowing brook water, particularly in time of flood (the new changing and office accommodation at that end is shown on maps as abutting it). It has been suggested that part of the wall was perhaps originally associated with the mediaeval mill that is marked at this site on OS maps. In January 1936 part of the wall fell into the brook; it was quickly repaired.

Following its performance in filling the bath, the 40 year-old steam fire engine continued to be maintained for use; still in full working order, its boiler (there is no record of the original having been replaced) was certified for use in February 1937.

Edward H Draper's original **Plot 6** in High Street was conveyed from his son Warwick Herbert Draper to Charles Randall on 13th February 1922, and was absorbed into the land of his home Abbotsfield. At some time, perhaps when buying Plot 6 or in his dealings with Lincoln Chandler, Randall also had acquired Plot 13 alongside Little Virginia. Sometime in the late 1920s on it was built a new house Virginia into which moved Charles Randall jnr.

In October 1932, Charles Randall 'intimated' that he was willing to sell 'for a reasonable price' the field now numbered 381 in Castle Road behind **Little Virginia** (part of the field originally numbered 36 that the KUDC had tried to obtain a purchase option on from the then owner George Turner in 1914), so it could 'be preserved as an open space in conjunction with the Abbey Fields'. By 13th December, an offer of £500 from the council had been accepted and an application was to be made to the Ministry of Health for a loan to buy the field, 'adjoining the Abbey Fields estate, for the purposes of Public Walks and Pleasure Grounds'. However, on 2nd February 1933 Charles Randall died at Abbotsfield, his illness likely to have been delaying the completion of the purchase. On 27th February, the KUDC passed a resolution that 'the field adjoining the Abbey Fields fronting onto Castle Road and numbered 381 on the Ordnance Survey be purchased from the executors of the late Charles Randall for the sum of £500'. Thanks were given to the council chairman, solicitor Edward Spaven, for his services in this matter.

However, despite the apparent advanced stage of negotiations, nothing more happened in the matter until November 1935 when the executors of Randall's estate, his sons Charles jnr and George who were also of course beneficiaries, offered to sell the field to the council but with a *proviso* that they had to purchase Abbotsfield too. This was not refused as the council had been looking for a suitable location to move their offices from Upper Rosemary Hill, and so they investigated whether Abbotsfield would suffice. It seems the house was unsuitable, but in June 1936 after Abbotsfield had been sold to Sydney Robert Holbrook, the council made a renewed attempt to purchase just the field, but for now the priorities had changed; they were looking for a site to have a car park in the vicinity of, and for, the Castle; field 381 was ideal. Land at the Queen & Castle was also investigated, as was land at the rear of The Square for parking in the town centre, but, fortunately as it turns out, Charles Randall's executors refused to sell field 381 on its own.

In addition to Abbotsfield, in 1936 the council had also been offered for use as offices the Abbey Hotel, and investigated two other properties then on the market, Zion House and Wilton House; the latter being their eventual choice (in 1946).

The **Friends of the Abbey** membership stagnated and the group's efforts do not seem to have been appreciated as widely as expected. At the annual meeting in May 1935, the association's president Sir John Siddeley said that the people of Kenilworth had shown *'a certain lack of patriotism'* in not supporting the society, and claimed it was *'the duty of most of the inhabitants to help in this good cause'*. Subscriptions for the year ending the previous August amounted to just £54, the payment of wages for improving the churchyard was over £120, and there was then a debt at the bank of £12. Since then there had been an improvement and there was now a balance of £12 at the bank largely due to Sir John's donation of £20.

The Friends had done a *'tremendous amount of work'* in the graveyard and bought a motor-mower *'through the help of Sir John'*. The work to date included levelling the churchyard, keeping the grass down and laying new turf where needed, planting bulbs and flowers, and building one wall and lowering another *'to give a better view'*. However, some of that work was already being undone by neglect and they needed the support of the whole community, but Sir John thought much of the work in the graveyard ought now to be done by the church members. It was Major B H Thomas that was overseeing the work.

Over the following winter and into the next spring, the Friends created a scheme to put some of their, and earlier, finds on display to the public. The idea was to utilise the Barn as a store and museum and charge a small entrance fee that could be put towards the cost of more work. The Barn would need much effort to prepare and so the KUDC were coerced into helping out; they had to be impressed by the group's work, 'the immense improvement in the state of the churchyard must be apparent to all'. Electricity was needed for lighting but the council deferred a decision; in May 1936 an agreement was reached, provided the Friends dropped the request for the expensive electricity installation (£14 10s), which they did. Towards the end of May, Eustace Carey-Hill assembled a group of young volunteers and together they began further clearing in the churchyard which quickly revealed part of the undercroft of the western cloister range; this was used to promote the need for more funds which in turn promoted the Barn museum scheme. The Ministry of Works had by now approved of the Friends efforts.

The following month the Friends submitted to the KUDC a list of work required in the Barn and it included the removal of cow stalls, windows to be opened up and glazed and guarded for security, a bench to be built on which to display the relics, and a supply of labour to clean the relics. Workmen's tools also had to be rehoused. However, as the Friends moved in to the Barn, an alarming discovery was made; a stone coffin that had been found in the ruins, supposedly that of Geoffrey de Clinton, had been placed within for safe keeping along with much other loose stone, but when council workmen were told to break up the loose stone they broke it all, including the coffin. The smashing was kept quiet by the council when they found out, until its discovery by the Friends. Carey-Hill pieced it back together again, but it was quite possible that further relics had been destroyed. *'The lack of foresight by the KUDC in providing a proper accommodation for the relics is nothing short of deplorable. On the other hand the work done by the Friends is of the highest commendation.'*

Improved access to the Barn took place over the winter of 1936-37; a path was made to the doorway branching from that nearby to the churchyard, and the step into it was raised. The roof needed attention as loose mortar fell on the relics. The KUDC carried out many of the Friends' requests including the removal of the derelict cow stalls and of tools and equipment, patching the floor and putting in some new windows. By the end of April 1937 the relics were displayed and labelled, with much of the preparation work achieved by the younger volunteers, and donations for display included a sketch book of the ruins drawn by a Colonel Digby in 1821; although loaned to the society it was to remain the property of the council.

The museum was officially opened on 1st May 1937 by Sir John Siddeley, the Friends' president. T G Jackson suggested that visitors knew more about Kenilworth's history than its residents, and that the Education Authority ought to ensure the history of their own town is taught in the schools. Admission for the public was 6d, and it was to open on Thursdays and Saturdays, and later possibly also Sundays. Carey-Hill also published a booklet, *The Abbey of St Mary, Kenilworth* to boost the group's income.

Sir John Siddeley resigned as president in November 1938; his son declined the invitation to replace him. Work in the churchyard was continuing but total funds in July 1939 stood at 6s 1d. Income from the

Barn museum was negligible.

Before the start of the 1936 **swimming** season, the club protested at the cost of 6d for adults to swim. It was argued that swimmers were 'likely to swim twice for 4d but only once for 6d'. The council did drop the entrance to 4d, but only for club members. It cost £20 a week to operate the pool.

Such had been the pool's popularity and the increasing use of **motor cars**, in April 1936 the council began seeking an area for parking for swimming bath users. The bye-law banning the parking of cars in the fields had recently been consolidated but as a temporary measure, the field in front of Abbotsfield was used specifically as a swimming pool car park, the access being through the gate between numbers 39 & 41 High Street, but the surveyor was to find out if the field near the ford was still available.

The opening hours were the same as the previous year and mixed bathing at all times was now accepted as the norm, but after poor attendances due to wet weather, in June 1936 the council put up boards around the Abbey Fields advertising the pool; one was next to the War Memorial which led to protesters claiming they degraded the fields, and they were quickly removed. The 1936 Carnival Gala saw the Midlands District Champion H Daniels set a new record for four lengths (now stated as 108yds) of 65 and 2/5 seconds. A water test found that 'organically the water is completely pure.'

Due to workloads, the responsibility for the swimming pool was transferred from the Parks Superintendent Jack Drew to the Town Surveyor in May 1937. In July 1937 a wringer-mangle was bought to help dry the costumes and towels at the baths. Over the four days of the August Bank Holiday weekend 2,365 people used the pool, but despite this boost and fine weather the annual takings were low. It was agreed at a council meeting that they could do no more to encourage the use of the pool; it cost a 1½d rate to maintain it. There was a suggestion that the old pool still held the attendance record, but it was stated that the first week of the 'lido' was the busiest week ever.

In 1936 there were 5 applicants for the one available Abbey Fields **football pitch** alongside Forrest Road and other sites were investigated; the only other suitable spot was said to be *'at the side of the brook leading from Forrest Road to the Oxpen Meadow, which is the field next to the one with the existing football pitch'*, although it needed a thorough draining.

The **Bowls & Tennis Club** was still struggling financially, and the bye-law change to allow Sunday playing didn't help as the members were having difficulties in providing personnel to cover all public opening times. A new arrangement, agreed in February 1936, was for the club rent to stay at £22 10s for a year, the council to forgo the agreement of taking one half of profits and to provide labour to let bowls and tennis be played on Sundays but using club equipment. As a show of goodwill, on 30th July the council played the club in a friendly bowls match.

In January 1936 the grass **tennis courts** flooded again, and generally poor drainage of the two tennis hard courts resulted in them needing to be resurfaced; somewhat ironically, they needed to be watered in dry weather. In 1937, the council continued to pay the wages of the Sunday attendants at the Tennis & Bowls Club facilities, but once again, early in the season the courts were flooded, the grass courts were described as *'waterlogged'*. The council agreed to carry out more drainage work provided the club paid half the costs; the club agreed to pay a maximum of £6, and then reported that the Pavilion's thatched roof was leaking. The following year, the tennis posts were concreted in to the ground.

In December 1937, the club asked the KUDC if they could again set up a ***'mini golf course'*** between the tennis courts and the brook; the council agreed and the course, actually a putting green of probably 9 holes, was ready for the start of the next season. But no sooner had it been made than there was a complaint of the club's use of a public park; Councillor Faxon, the only councillor opposed to the idea, said, 'You have already fenced in a large portion of the People's Playground for them', but the club stressed the putting green would not be enclosed and it went ahead. It seems that putting greens were at this time not a permanent feature.

When discussions began in November 1936 for the next round of letting the fields for **grazing**, Councillor Naylor suggested fencing an area of the fields where cattle would not be allowed so that mothers with children could have a quiet place. *'It is a great regret that mothers with children have to go to Leamington to have quiet fields, a thing they cannot do here. It is time all year round grazing ended'*. There was a suggestion that cattle should be kept off all the grass until April, but again it was the extra cost of cutting the grass that was highlighted; 'after careful consideration with special regard for the expense' it was decided to let the fields as before but to take on additional labour to 'keep the fields as clean as possible'.

In 1937 the grazing was let by tender rather than auction and Plot 1, that which bordered Rosemary Hill and Abbey Hill nearest the Abbey Hotel, was let to F Newcombe; Freda Newcombe operated a riding stables from the Abbey Hotel and in a six week journey in 1939 became the first lady known to ride from Lands End to John O'Groats. She passed through Kenilworth on her journey, one of two stops made for a horse-change; no doubt the Abbey Fields provided welcome relief for the retiring horse. She arrived in Scotland on her 9-year-old Starling; they returned to Kenilworth by train.

The following year the tenant of Plots 6 & 7, that included the **Oxpen Meadow**, claimed a rent refund as for much of the year the field was flooded and unusable, and that he also gave up 'the use of the other field for a car park for the swimming baths'. A regular renter of several fields was now Phillip Hubbard of Malthouse Farm.

In June 1937 the grass was cut in readiness for the carnival; the amount of mowing was on the increase and the council decided to purchase a one-horse mowing machine. Councillor Smalley donated a horse solely for use with the machine, on the condition the council would not at some later time sell it! A float was bought so the horse could take the grass cuttings from the field to the local tip.

In January 1938 the grazing areas were to be let as before with the exception of Plot 1 which was to be reserved as a 'playing field' and for the grazing of the council's horses. To give access to it from the original park area, it was planned to build a **footbridge** across the brook. This was given the go ahead the following month when George Tisdale said he would pay any costs over £25. The wooden bridge, later described as a 'rustic bridge', was completed by December not far from the Townpool Bridge; the council were so pleased with it that they seriously discussed giving it a name! In May 1939, gates were installed at each end to stop any livestock wandering across. Despite the grazing horses, the area was mowed to keep it in good condition as a 'playground'.

The turnover in **trees** continued. In 1937 £60 was set aside for new trees alongside Forrest Road and the path from the War Memorial to the Iron Bridge, but a beech tree was removed from the Abbey Hill boundary and others were causing concern. A dead pine tree was also cut down. Mr Hiorns donated a tree from his garden at 13 Barrow Road; it was moved to the park in November 1938, but no further details were recorded.

At the KUDC meeting in July 1937 it was said that *'several influential residents have claimed the KUDC are turning the park into a wood'*; it was now impossible to see the church clock from Abbey Hill. Despite this, the Parks Superintendent Jack Drew was authorised to spend another £60 on trees, but it was claimed the intention was to only replace dead trees in Abbey Fields, the rest were to be used in the streets.

The weight of the traction engines entering the fields for the carnival caused a concern; in the spring of 1937 it was decided to concrete over the main sewer that was just 15 inches below the surface to prevent potential damage. In May 1937 the Royal Warwickshire Regiment band was given permission to perform in the park; a remarkable audience of 2,000 spectators attended.

Exactly when **Gertrude Evans** left Kenilworth is not known. She continued to be recorded in Directories at Clinton House until 1925 and it was put up for auction in London and sold in 1927, but Gertrude kept her pieces of Abbey Fields land opposite. Clinton House had 9 bedrooms, 4 reception rooms, stabling for 4 horses, lean-to greenhouse, walled-in kitchen garden, a 6 room cottage, thatched summer house, and electric lighting. However, as early as 1921, when aged 47, she was recorded as living at The Bungalow in Charmouth as she appears on the Electoral Register at that address. Nearby was a large house Hammonds Mead with 7 acres of land, at the end of a long drive off Lower Sea Lane, that Gertrude bought in which to spend the rest of her life.

Hammonds Mead, just 100 yards or so from the beach, was owned and probably built by Alfred Barrow; coincidentally or not, Alfred's father Samuel had bought Kenilworth's tannery in 1888, and his son Samuel jnr, Alfred's brother who was knighted during the Great War, was involved in the company until about 1926; Samuel snr was the man after whom Barrow Road is named. Possibly coming with the house, but in any case purchased by Gertrude, was a good deal of land along the sea front between Hammonds Mead and the sea, and in 1935 she leased the area to the west of the River Char to the local council for a nominal rent, and in 1938 sold it to them, ensuring an undeveloped future for that part of the coast.

The following is recorded ten years after Clinton House was sold, in the KUDC minutes for 14th September 1937:

> A letter was read from Miss Evans' agent intimating that she is willing to consider transferring her property in the Abbey Fields to the council in her lifetime, subject to the council being responsible for the cost of the transfer and to certain restrictions being embodied in the

conveyance to ensure that no buildings or games of any description shall be allowed on the ground, and after a short discussion it was recommended that the offer on behalf of Miss Evans be accepted with thanks, and the cost of the conveyance be borne by the council.

Under the Local Government Act of 1933, the KUDC were entitled to receive any gift of property. At the meeting the following March, Gertrude Evans, now 60 years old, confirmed that the two cottages 81 & 83 High Street would be included in the offer on one condition; 'After a discussion it was recommended that the council will be pleased to accept the two cottages and observe the condition that the present occupants are not disturbed'. However, for undiscovered reasons the cottages remained Gertrude's, but the transfer of land went ahead. The draft conveyance for the land from Gertrude Evans included the covenant, 'no games involving an artificial layout should be allowed upon the land and that no buildings or erections of any kind be erected thereon', and at the April 1938 KUDC meeting it was recorded that the 'Covenant now drawn would not prevent the playing of simple or unorganised games, or the laying out of paths and the placing of seats upon the land'. The second draft of the conveyance was then approved and adopted, and at the September meeting it was recorded that it had been completed and Gertrude's legal costs had been submitted. The legal process was finished in September and the 'voluntary conveyance' to the KUDC dated 22nd October 1938 has these restrictions in addition to the existing Covenants:

> The grantor as settler hereby freely and voluntarily and without valuable consideration conveys unto the Council all that piece or parcel of land formerly part of the Abbey Fields.
>
> It is hereby declared and agreed that the land hereby conveyed shall forever hereafter be preserved and kept as nearly as it may be in its natural condition as open grass land and that no buildings or erections of any kind shall at any time be built or erected thereon and that no games of any kind shall be allowed to be played thereon nor shall any artificial means of entertainment be permitted thereon.

By insisting it remained as open grassland, the covenant ensured that all subsequent occupiers of Clinton House would not have their view of the Abbey Fields obscured (the reason that Mary Draper bought the area in 1884) by the planting of trees, and she also prevented the tree-planting arguments seen at Abbey Hill. The area of the land was 1.55 acres (1a 2662 sq yds) bringing the total for the Abbey Fields to 64 acres 2634 sq yds. There was an unnamed tenant of the land whose agreement expired on 25th March 1940. Soon after, the fence separating the area from the Abbey Fields came down and a new foot-worn path was established from near 81 High Street. The 'feet' in question were hooves belonging to the cows of Mr Hubbard of Malthouse Lane; after morning milking they were led to the High Street field gate from where they found their own way nose-to-tail down the slope to the Oxpen Meadow gate, creating a narrow cow-path, its diagonal course ensured as gentle a gradient as possible. Pedestrians created a path extension to the children's playground.

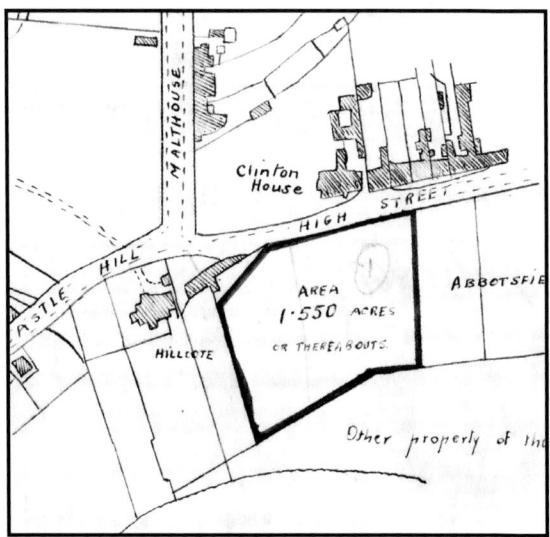

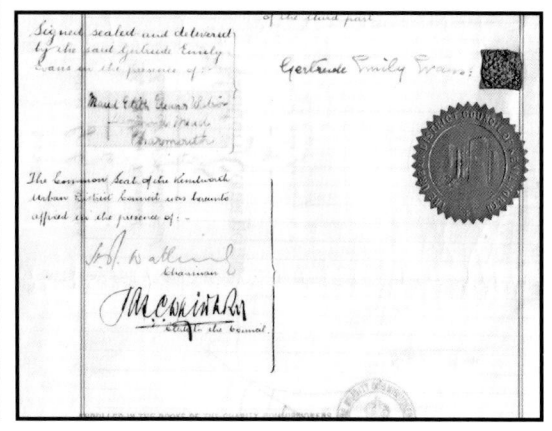

The area of land, formerly Plots 7, 8 and most of the enlarged Plot 9, donated by Gertrude Evans in 1938; Wantage has been renamed Hillcote. The signatures transferring the land are those of Gertrude Evans, Maud Watson as a witness, KUDC Chairman Major Watling and Town Clerk Mr Whittaker. Also prominent is the KUDC seal *(both, WDC 133)*

Victoria Park in Leamington had a paddling pool, digging began in December 1935, and a fund was started for a similar pool in Jephson Gardens. Not wishing to be left behind, on 10th May 1938, the KUDC approved a plan for a **paddling pool** with an adjacent **shelter** in the Abbey Fields *'near the Abbey Ruins'*. It was suggested that a loan of £550 would be needed. The plan was quickly amended with seats to be built into the pool's surrounding wall and a separate shelter to be provided near the Abbey ruins; the projected pool location was now described as *'in the park'*.

Discussions in June put the cost of the pool and shelter at £700, but the pool was classed as an *'unproductive luxury expenditure'* and would only be used for several months a year, but cost about £60 a year to run and maintain. The town was now facing many extra costs with Air Raid Precaution (ARP) and associated work, but Mr Bostock thought it would be money well spent; he had seen children enjoying themselves in such pools in many places but Kenilworth parents had to take their children to Leamington to use its paddling pool. George Tisdale observed, *'we want to encourage the youth of the town to use the Abbey Fields; we don't use them 5 per cent of what we ought to.'*

However, the Ratepayers Association opposed the suggestions and the shelter was dropped in favour of more seating to be at various locations throughout the park. Eventually the paddling pool only was agreed, subject to the cost of £550 being accepted, but upon the application for the loan in September 1938, the Ministry of Health asked for more details; they were sent but no more about the idea was recorded.

In January 1937, Council Chairman T G Jackson again raised the question of the **lake**, pointing out that the last vote on the subject was 5-5 and thus it did not even appear in the minutes. He still felt there should be a lake with a footpath and seats around it; once filled, the stream could keep it healthy and fresh. This time there was a just a discussion and no vote.

Despite its hopefully annual use for skating, the **Oxpen Meadow** was still divided but in 1936 it was decided to remove the iron hurdles that split the field; presumably they were not in the skating area. Starting the previous winter, the field was provided with floodlighting for evening skating, although details are not mentioned, and this continued at least until the winter of 1938-39; it would obviously not have continued during the war. It cost a guinea a year for insurance for providing skating.

In March 1939 it was decided once more to investigate the possibilities of keeping the meadow permanently flooded to form a lake; 'After a useful discussion about costs, it was decided to drain the meadow'. Then in April it was George Tisdale's turn to suggest that the customary early-spring draining of the Oxpen Meadow should not take place so that a permanent lake could be formed, perhaps initially for a trial 12 month period. He thought a lake would be an *'advantage'* to townspeople and Councillor Jackson agreed saying it was *'better to have a lake than a useless piece of land'*. Mr Griffiths was in favour too but noted at least some of the water in the winter-time flooding became stagnant around the edges; as there was no direct outlet, water did not flow through the site as claimed. On the suggestion that the lake could replace the proposed paddling pool scheme it was remarked that *'the meadow was not a proper place for children to paddle'*. Over £600 would be needed to create a weir at each end, but Dr Smalley observed that the present state of affairs could not continue. A suggestion the proposal should be referred back to committee was lost.

April 1938 saw the first attempts by the KUDC at providing **refreshments** for the public in the park; they had been provided at the tennis pavilion by Mrs Dilworth in at least the late 1920s but this was probably for club members only. Tenders were invited for a machine to sell cigarettes, yet to be seen as injurious to health, and for a tricycle to sell ice cream. Perhaps due to the absence of suitable applicants it was decided the following month not to proceed, but in June the KUDC began to investigate the possibilities of themselves installing cigarette and chocolate machines at the baths, but again it led to nothing. In June 1939 tenders were again invited for the selling of ice cream from a tricycle and this time F J Fancott of Warwick Road won the tender and thus became the first person to sell refreshments to the public in the park (other than on carnival and special event days).

In 1938, it was reported that children were 'annoying' the adults at the **swimming pool**; stricter supervision was required. The number of school users was falling, swimming instruction of pupils at St John's School for example had ceased altogether, and in February 1939 the Education Director asked for a reduction in the payment of £10 for schools using the pool, but this was declined as it was already a reduced rate. In March 1939 the latest floods to hit the Abbey Fields resulted in part of the swimming pool retaining wall alongside the brook being partially washed away, and repaired, for a second time.

In 1939 there was still a shortage of football pitches; this led to a number of sites the council had purchased for future housing schemes being used temporarily including the rear of Roseland Road and the area that became Scott Road. For the Kenilworth Pageant staged at the Castle in July 1939, unspecified areas of the Abbey Fields were used as a temporary car park. The pageant organisers had to make good the damage.

A photograph of unknown date showing the closeness of the Abbey Fields boundary to the houses on Abbey Hill *(HS)*

In 1936, buses stopping at the Rosemary Hill junction with **Abbey Hill** began causing congestion. At the end of the year the KUDC Roads Committee again considered the 1932 idea 'for a double carriageway on Abbey Hill from the War Memorial to the Abbey Hotel, and to discuss it with the County Surveyor with a view to prepare a scheme'. This would involve an incursion into the Abbey Fields and the existing row of trees along the boundary would form an island between the two rows of traffic. Two years later, the financial estimates were approved, but this prompted a full revision of the scheme; in January 1939 a new proposal was submitted to the County Council to widen Abbey Hill from 22ft to 40ft and improve the junction with Rosemary Hill, and provide a footpath on the Abbey Fields side of the road. Councillor Griffiths remarked that the scheme would mean that several beech trees would have to come down *'which I think will be against the wishes of the average resident'*. However the chairman said that the trees were not *'under a sentence of death yet.'*

It was eventually decided not to widen the whole road as it was only categorised as a 'second class' road but to just improve the corner at a cost of £750, and provide the footpath for £336 but only in the vicinity of the junction and along Abbey Hill to a point approximately opposite the Congregational Church, to where the retaining wall and footpath would be extended. The scheme would involve removing a few trees and an incursion into the Abbey Fields, but as seen in the covenant reproduced on page 19, this had been allowed for. The work was approved in April 1939. As far as is known, it went ahead the same year.

As the political situation in Europe deteriorated in 1938, the council of course became heavily involved in preparations for the possibility of air raids and other aspects of the growing likelihood of another major conflict. The first involvement of the Abbey Fields was in April 1938 when recruitment notices appeared at all entrances to the park. Air Raid Precaution Committee meetings were already regularly held and at one in June 1938, it was mentioned that the Abbey Fields was a suitable location for an **air raid shelter**; this was to be investigated. The following month the idea had escalated and it was suggested that a structure more like an underground bunker could be built to be used as the ARP Headquarters; although outside both the government and district guidelines of the time, and thus would not qualify for financial grants, it was said that army engineers in town could help with designs and volunteers asked to assist with construction.

By the autumn of 1938, a series of air raid trenches had been dug across the town including in the park; in November it was decided to dig extra ones in the park and on the common. Enough were to be dug to hold ten per cent of the town's population.

In the January 1939 discussions for the provision of a first aid post at St John's and a decontamination centre somewhere on council property, Councillor Griffiths suggested that some of the available money would be better spent on creating a *'tunnel under the park'* in preference to more trenches; Councillor Faxon agreed saying that trenches were *'useless, and we may as well fill them in'*. Chairman Major Watling said they were only allowed to spend money on the trenches that had already been dug and the *'whole question of trenches against tunnels, dug-outs and the like was under consideration'*. The surveyor did however have a scheme that he was to present at a later meeting and the ARP officer present said that he was *'now in a position to complete the trenches in the Abbey Fields and at the Common in accordance with the Home Office specification.'*

The way in which the ARP and other organisations were being controlled gave rise to a heated discussion at the council meeting in February 1939; Councillor Jackson said, *'officialdom will sink this grand old country of ours'*. Of the preparations needed to defend the area and its citizens Mr Faxon said, *'We have two things, the trenches which are an eyesore, and gas masks which are useless'*. There were no gas masks at all for children; *'What parent would put his mask on if his child did not have one?'*

On the subject of the trenches Mr Griffiths said, *'The trenches were dug at a minute's notice. The park has been marked out with small pegs, and I suppose that it had been done by the County Surveyor with a view to the construction of some form of underground shelters'*, but the town surveyor said that he marked them out *'as a preliminary measure and the purpose of surveying only'*.

Then in May 1939, contracts were signed for 'the concreting and otherwise making permanent the trenches in Kenilworth'; in August those in the Abbey Fields had still to be completed, but were soon after. In a time of such crisis, the covenants preventing the building of structures were necessarily disregarded.

Despite the worsening situation in Europe, the carnival managed to hold its usual attractions in the Abbey Fields in 1939; it had moved its date forward to the beginning of June due to the Kenilworth Pageant taking place in early July. The swimming club still intended to put on its annual gala, although fixing a suitable date proved difficult.

On 29th September 1939, three weeks after war had been declared, what turned out to be the last AGM of Friends of the Abbey and its Surroundings was held; work in the churchyard stopped in November and the meeting on 8th March 1940 was the last record; there was a debt of £27 19s and the KUDC were asked to take over the care of the churchyard.

The Abbey Fields air raid shelters on Rosemary Hill *(right)* and Forrest Road *(below, both)*

(21st November 2010)

Chapter 3: *Privileges of the Abbey Fields*

The troops stationed in town needed recreational facilities and in April 1940 were given permission to use the Abbey Fields for football, basketball, badminton, physical training, *etc,* and after consultation could also use the **swimming pool** at the same prices as adults. The pool's takings for June were double those of the equivalent period the previous year, and the soldiers were even allowed use of the pool when it was closed to the public. In October 1940 the troops' commanding officer asked and was allowed to put up six tents in the field in front of Abbotsfield for unknown reasons or duration. The ATC were also allowed use of the football pitch.

In October 1940 the fire chief requested that the **Oxpen Meadow** was kept flooded to provide a ready large water supply in case it was needed, and a month later an additional suggestion was made to dam the brook; two landmines fell in the town the next night. It seems the damming at least was done and the deepest parts were identified with yellow posts. The Victorian steam fire engine had already been placed alongside the brook at the bottom of the Memorial Field so it was immediately available as a pump should it be necessary. To avoid vandalism, railings were placed around it; these were taken from around the World War 1 German cannon still on display alongside the War Memorial.

The Coventry Blitz in early November 1940 caused some concern for one historic Kenilworth relic: 'The wooden structure in the roof of the Barn in the park has moved again through the vibration from the air raids. This most valuable article should be removed to a safer place'. This was the item known as 'the ducking stool' and concerns were raised again the night before Kenilworth's landmine explosions; that night several tiles on the barn roof were displaced but there was no report of the 'ducking stool' moving.

The carnival organisers were hopeful of putting on a full fundraising event for Warneford Hospital in 1940 but the parade and funfair in the Abbey Fields were cancelled. However providing some light relief on 12th September was **Sanger's Circus** who rented an area for £5 to put on a performance.

Despite the war, at least until the time the landmines fell, Parks Superintendent Jack Drew had managed to keep all the hedges in the Abbey Fields trimmed.

In March 1940 the field plots were let as usual for **grazing**, but Plot 1's short time as a playing field was over. For £36 10s, Freda Newcombe again had Plots 1 & 2 in which was a barn where she was keeping three pigs; despite her claim that they were helping the government's plea for extra food production, the KUDC rules forbade pigs in the park and they had to be removed. Ironically, in January 1941, one of her fields was indeed used for food production; Plot 2 was ploughed and immediately planted for oats and her horses removed. Part of Plot 4 that included the Forrest Road football pitch was also to be ploughed ready for oats; 100 yards of fencing to keep the cattle out was required and this was made from wire, and posts cut from old trees recently felled. Existing hedging and fences helped enclose the area, and there was a *'fine crop of oats'* in the fields in July. In September 1941 Lieutenant Payne of 134 Pioneer Company based at 9 Abbey Hill, was granted permission for his men to use the Forrest Road football pitch, thus not all the plot was being sown. In all, eleven Abbey Fields acres were 'under the plough'. The remaining fields were let for grazing but this only brought in £119; it is thought that farmers H Gee and P Hubbard were the major field renters. The oats were harvested in September from the fields including the 'Forrest Road triangle' but they were of poor quality due to storm damage a few weeks before.

In 1941, the Wartime Horticultural Society that had been involved with establishing dozens of extra allotments throughout the town on many small areas of land, asked for 300 sq yds to be made available for an 'experimental plot' near the War Memorial alongside Abbey Hill; experimental plots were essentially for training and demonstration purposes so its location was perfect for easy access for the townspeople. Permission was granted and the plot was fenced. There was some private enterprise too; Frank Phelps at Ford House, which he renamed from The Bungalow just before the war, successfully asked to cultivate a small area of the Abbey Fields alongside his garden, provided it was fenced.

In 1941, wheat was planted in the fields; after oats, wheat and straw had been thrashed the following year and the fields tidied, Jack Drew was complimented on the fine job he was doing in growing crops and looking after the ground.

The **swimming pool** remained in full use throughout the war. Youths between 14 and 18 years of age could buy a book of 12 tickets for 4 shillings, but in July 1941 there were complaints of too many young children using the baths late into the evening; under 14's were subsequently banned after 7 o'clock leaving three hours of comparative quiet for the adults. The locker system was proving to be 'quite unsatisfactory' and so a system using canvas bags replaced it the same month. The takings for 1941 were £357 but fell back to £235 the following year. In January 1941 the swimming pool retaining wall alongside the brook collapsed for a third time and was repaired, and in early 1942 a dozen broken glass panes in the men's changing rooms roof were replaced; it isn't known if this was left-over damage caused by the Abbey End landmine explosion.

The **Bowls & Tennis Club** suffered during the early days of the war. Personnel and paying customer shortages resulted in a dramatic reduction in the annual rent they paid to the KUDC to just £5 as early as January 1940; had the club been unable to continue, the KUDC would have faced additional costs of its own, or had to close the facilities. At the club's April 1941 AGM, H Prince was in the chair, E Shrimpton was secretary, George Dymond captain of bowling, and Miss Rita Tibbits captain of the tennis section. The balance in hand was only £13 8s 4d. The tennis hard courts opened at Easter weekend and the grass courts a little later; subscriptions were 15s for tennis with grass fees up 4d to 1s 4d, and for bowls it was a 10s subscription and 4d a session. On Sundays both sports were still restricted to between 1 and 6 p.m.

In 1942 there was nobody available to carry out the usual procedures of cutting the tennis courts' grass and so Jack Drew did it with the one-horse mower. One grass court was kept in condition for the public, but in general they were in a very bad state. Perhaps as an indication of their reduced use, beginning in July 1942 open air dancing was allowed on one, presumably hard surface, tennis court on Saturday evenings with electricity for the music laid on for free, provided the organisers donated the takings to charity. The putting green behind the courts was still in use.

Despite the war taking a grip on all aspects of everyday life, standards had to be maintained; after a series of complaints, in August 1942 the police were asked to take action over numerous cyclists that were using the Abbey Fields paths.

Bowling Club members outside the Pavilion. Back row: E Shrimpton, M Robbins, B Lowe, Matthews, A Summers, H Prince; Front Row: Megainey, J Lees, ?, G P Dymond, Rollason, Nason. Dymond and Shrimpton were founder-members; the former had played in the very first match and was now Captain, the latter was now the Secretary *(SaT)*

With the tide of the war turned, the threat of invasion all but gone and the allied invasion of occupied Europe expected, efforts to raise actual cash and 'loans' in the shape of bonds and savings to aid the war effort were prominent across the country.

In May 1943, **Wings for Victory** week in Kenilworth raised an astonishing £80,000, enough for six Mosquito aircraft; the target had been four. The focal point had been an extraordinary parade through the town with the salute taken at the clock tower and a destination of the Abbey Fields where speeches were made on the plateau near the church. The parade was headed by the band of the Royal Warwickshire Regiment followed by *'a good assembly of tanks and motor cycle despatch riders'*, the police, a naval drum

& bugle band, a detachment of sailors and infantrymen, the local Home Guard, ATS, men and women and cadets of the RAF, the fire service, local ARP Wardens, St John's Ambulance, VAD nurses, the messenger service and finally the land girls. In total there were 400 uniformed members of the Civil Defence and armed services. In the park Lord Willoughby de Brooke made the major speech. The new equipment of the local Home Guard was laid out on the grass for inspection, and two 500lb bomb cases were placed in the park and in *'the selling centre at the gas showrooms'* convenient for *'patriotic citizens to stick saving stamps thereon'*. A bomber made a low flypast in the afternoon.

In August 1943 a week-long gala for the **Merchant Navy Comfort Fund**, that included a parade and had 17-year-old Jean Davies of Southbank Road as Queen of the Seas, was held in the Holiday at Home week. Although there was no procession as such, led by the Leamington Civil Defence Band Jean Davies rode through town in a Victorian coach from St John's to the Abbey Fields to perform the opening ceremony. The fields hosted a fashion show with outfits chosen by Jean, a flower show, a rabbit exhibition, a pony display, a *'comic dog show'*, tennis finals and other sports; a swimming gala was held another day. A boxing display featured the Leamington Boys Club and included 15-year-old Randolph Turpin, then the 8-stone Junior Champion of Great Britain. Fifty *'money making contrivances'* helped swell the takings to over £1,500.

The **Salute the Soldier** event in April 1944 saw another parade of armed services through the town, a particular attraction being three platoons of American servicemen. The salute was taken at the clock tower, and again the assembly ended in the Abbey Fields where speeches were made.

In November 1943, the KUDC received a letter from Warneford Hospital saying they were launching an appeal for £60,000 for numerous improvements, including a new operating theatre, children's ward, an extension to the maternity facilities, an administrative extension, *etc,* and asked if Kenilworth, whose fundraising events for Warneford started in the 1880s and had evolved in to Kenilworth's **carnival**, would play its part. A meeting was held and George Tisdale, the pre-war carnival committee chairman, was elected as president. A week long list of events was held including in the Abbey Fields a swimming gala, garden fete, cricket and baseball matches, and the park was also the terminal point of a parade through the town by Miss Kenilworth and her Maids on a float; it was in effect a carnival and referred to as such in the local press. On the day itself, August Bank Holiday Monday 1944 and about two months after D-Day, also in the Abbey Fields were *'all the fun of the fair'*, *'bowling for a pig'*, a miniature railway, concerts, fancy dress, a tennis tournament and *'dancing on the plateau'* (presumably the 1928 terrace) in the evening. The bowls and tennis club members alone raised over £20 for the Red Cross, Wings for Victory and Merchant Navy funds.

The chains on **the swings** had become worn but despite the wartime scarcity of materials new ones were found and installed in early 1944, although they had taken over a year to arrive; extra swings were provided at the same time.

The 1944 **swimming pool** season opened on 13th May. The availability for schools was: Roseland Road jnr School, Monday 11 a.m. to midday; Priory Road Seniors, Tuesday and Wednesdays 9.30 a.m. to midday; School Lane School, Thursdays 10 a.m. to midday; and Abbotsford School, Fridays 11 a.m. to midday. The pool takings for 1944 was £322, the same as the previous year's total which in turn was a great improvement on 1942. The storage of clothes was still a problem and this resulted in the council in June 1944 deciding to purchase 200 clothing bags and a shed in which to keep them for a total cost of £70. The timber was ordered for the shed which would adjoin the pay box, but 'it has been impossible to obtain a permit for clothing bags so I have acquired a number of string bags which were previously the property of WCC for decontamination purposes.'

Youngsters were continuing to cause problems with reckless cycling in the swimming pool area, and in May 1944 this resulted in a review of the most recent edition of the bye-laws, those from 1935, but it was not until 1st July 1947 that 'No Cycling' notices were put up all around the fields for the first time.

The beech trees alongside Abbey Hill were again causing concern and two needed to come down in 1943 but Jack Drew did not have the manpower to do it; George Tisdale stepped in and arranged for two of his workmen to carry out the task at a weekend.

The fields were more or less being used as a farm and in April 1943 there was *'an official order that the fields must be let for grazing young dairy stock'* and it was decided not to auction the grazing rights but to simply let them to the sitting tenants 'in the interests of milk production'. The fields were let at 45s an acre but it was suggested they were worth £5 an acre. The growing of crops continued; in June 1943 25 tons of lime was added to the 'ploughed field', and in August the barley in the field alongside Forrest Road had been scythed, and in the next month barley ricks with a thatch top had been built. In October the field opposite the

Abbey Hotel had been ploughed ready for sowing and 'the other two fields' had been scuffled. In November the ploughed field was sown with wheat.

The War Memorial field, Plot 3, was kept for grazing the council's horses, for public recreation, and military and NFS drills, *etc,* whilst the Rosemary Hill corner, Plot 1, was ploughed ready for sowing with barley. A problem was encountered with 'the wooden bridge out of the park into the field we have just ploughed. The public are walking from this bridge across the field that has been planted with corn; this must stop'. Another problem was rats; 4 or 5 dozen were killed in the planted field alongside Abbey Hill.

The wartime uses of the Abbey Fields, along with an increased demand from various Civil Defence units, created a shortage of football pitches; Councillor Weetman helped by providing one temporarily at his Chase Farm.

The salvage of scrap metal also caused problems. The railings on top of the **churchyard** wall had been taken down but this allowed Mr Hubbard's cows from the Oxpen Meadow to get over the wall into the churchyard, particularly where children had created gaps by continually taking the wall stones down. These were filled with any material that could be found by the council workmen even though the wall was deemed to be the property of the church. The WW1 German cannon, Victorian steam fire engine and associated railings almost certainly also went in the drive for scrap metal; there is no further mention of them after this time.

May 1944 should have seen the final payment of the original **loan** of £6,000 for the purchase of the central 40 acres of the fields but there is no mention of it in KUDC minutes. This should perhaps have led to the end of **grazing** as the income was no longer needed to pay off the loan, but for some years inflation had seen the rents well above the comparatively modest loan repayments, and the fields were producing a clear profit; this helped to 'balance the books' for other Abbey Fields amenities and expenditure. In any case, in a time of war the fields had become vital for food production.

In the spring of 1944, two 5-barred gates were built into the fence of the Memorial Field to provide easy access for machinery, previously a length of fence had to be removed. That same month oats were sown, and the following month Jack Drew reported 'the three rick of barley in the Forrest Road field have been thrashed. The clover seeds have been sown in the Abbey Fields, the docks have been weeded out of the corn and the oats rolled'. The year's crops of oats and wheat were harvested in the autumn and after ploughing, the field in front of the Abbey Hotel was planted with wheat. In 1945, the Forrest Road field was planted with potatoes; weeds were hand-hoed in July.

The war effort had seen literally hundreds, perhaps thousands, of trees cut down locally for use as timber but now there were local shortages. In July 1944 it was intended to provide six new seats for the Abbey Fields; the iron work supplied by J C Clarke in Bridge Street was perhaps surprisingly not a problem but the supply restrictions allowed only £1 of timber a month so the seat manufacturing had to be spread over 6 months. Pessimistically, such was the design of the seats, 'they will be simple to repair when damaged by cattle.'

By the autumn of 1944, the grass **tennis courts** were in a 'dilapidated' condition due to neglect. The grass needed to be scythed and hand weeded, and then given a dressing of lawn sand; they would then need worming, and aerating with a spiked roller, after which about 40 tons of sharp sand with 5 tons of charcoal had to be evenly spread and brushed into the turf. A suggested but not pursued alternative was to raise the courts about 18ins above the brook level which would also cure the bogginess.

In January 1945 the bowls and tennis club, struggling with a reduced manpower and subscriptions, suggested that the council should immediately take over the running of the bowling green, tennis courts and all the equipment valued at £120, but with the concession that the same playing facilities were granted to the club members that they had enjoyed in the past. The club also generously offered to pay back the £53 19s 3d that the KUDC paid on 23rd February 1934 to keep the club going. The club also asked the council to pay some compensation for the green they had made at some cost and made great efforts to maintain. The outcome was that the council took over the administration of the tennis and bowls facilities, but the bowling green remained in the care of the club, a situation to be reviewed at the season's end.

On the day the agreement was made at the end of March 1945, the condition of the grass courts forced a decision on their future. It was agreed that only one grass court was to be readied for the new playing season along with the two hard courts, and a scheme was to be proceeded with as soon as circumstances permitted to reduce the number of grass courts from six to two and to add two more hard courts. A month later the surveyor G A J Edmundson reported that the two existing hard courts were ready for play after 8 tons of Griselda gravel had been applied, screeded and rolled but the new lead tapes needed for the markings could not be sourced; the nets were repaired, the fencing painted, and the grass courts scythed, harrowed and rolled, and cutting was proceeding. In September 1945, the club agreed to look after the green for two more years. Councillor Jackson remarked that only 5 per cent of the townsfolk used these facilities and more should be done to provide football and cricket pitches; W Bostock agreed.

At the end of the war, the population of Kenilworth was 10,010.

In the autumn of 1945, Friar H J Fynes-Clinton, a descendant of Geoffrey de Clinton, asked for a few **Abbey** tiles from the museum to place at the front of the altar recently erected at Walsingham in Norfolk. An extension to the church in 1938 included several memorial chapels, one of which was to Fr Fynes-Clinton's ancestors which included an effigy of Geoffrey de Clinton that had a model of Kenilworth Priory at his feet. A dozen or so tiles were sent and they were set around the effigy in its base and survive today.

The following February the Barn needed re-roofing and it was said that the walls had moved outwards sufficiently for a tie bar to be needed.

The victory celebrations of 8th June 1946 took place in heavy rain that lasted much of the day. In the Abbey fields, an open air thanksgiving service was moved to the Parochial Hall, but the sports arranged for children went ahead despite the continual downpour; the ground was sodden and muddy and some children ran in macintoshes and overcoats! Two Punch & Judy shows went ahead in a tent. A stage had been created in the park for an outdoor variety show but this too was transferred to the Parochial Hall. The day concluded with a fireworks display in the fields.

With the war over, the process of returning the park to its pre-war status began. In May 1945 the government was encouraging local authorities to plant **trees** to replace the millions used for the war effort and the KUDC asked Jack Drew to prepare a report for the planting of 1,000 trees locally. His estimates were £375 for the trees, £192 for stakes and £165 for labour; the scheme was specifically 'planting trees for timber' and would include 'filling any odd corner on the Abbey Fields estate' and planting alongside the brook and in hedgerows; the locations were designed to not interfere with any future development of the park. In October 1945 the tree planting was approved, the first arrived in January 1946 and planting progressed as the weather allowed. In March, flowering trees were planted alongside the brook from the ford to the swimming pool, and also 'along the top of the field at High Street'.

After the potatoes were dug up in November 1945, the Forrest Road field was levelled and seeded to become a grass field once more. Yarrow was becoming a problem at the 'top part of the Memorial Field' and was killing the grass, and in January 1946 a local farmer asked if he could take over and seed the fields on Rosemary Hill and Abbey Hill, but for unrecorded reasons he was turned down.

In early 1946 with wartime crop-growing at an end, **grazing** rights, including those at the cemetery, were awarded to the sitting tenants but the area alongside Bridge Street was now 'reserved for the use of the public' and its days for grazing were at last over. In the spring of 1947, the main path from Bridge Street to the swimming pool was kerbed and resurfaced. The 1947 grass cutting in the fields included work by two German Prisoners of War who were used on the scything. In December 1948 the plot of land alongside Ford House let as garden ground, initially to Mr Phelps but now to George Leonard Loasby, was reclaimed as part of the park, as was the former demonstration plot near the War Memorial; this had become an allotment used by the Horticultural Society but was re-seeded to become part of the park once more.

In June 1945 the Kenilworth Rugby Club unsuccessfully applied to the council for using the Abbey Fields as a temporary ground; this was necessitated by their pre-war pitch owned by farmer Mr Gee now being 'under the plough'. In 1946, Jack Drew repaired the old pre-war **goalposts** and put them up in an unknown location in the park for children to use.

In early 1946 another of the 1935 **bye-laws**, that prohibiting the playing of football between 1 and 6 p.m. on Sundays, was amended to allow organised games after 1 p.m. but only in certain areas: 'A person shall not on a Sunday play or take part in any game of football, cricket, quoits, bowls, hockey, or other like games in the Abbey Fields except between the hours of 1 in the afternoon and 6 in the afternoon, and a person shall not play any organised game of football between those hours except in that part of the pleasure ground set up by the Council and described on a notice board.'

Kenilworth Baptists had use of the Abbey Fields **football pitch** in 1946, presumably on Saturdays, and due to the lack of other facilities were allowed to use the Forrest Road air raid shelter as changing rooms. But within a month, the council had received replies to an advertisement, tendering for the demolition of the air raid shelters; it was suggested that the Forrest Road one should be kept for its new use as changing rooms, and this was agreed. The surveyor was asked to prepare a plan for small changing rooms to replace the shelter but this did not come to fruition. In fact all the town's main shelters were retained at this time.

Just which area was in use as a football pitch is unclear. In the summer of 1947 both the Kenilworth Baptists and British Legion asked to use 'the swamp football ground'; this could either be a pitch set up on part of the Oxpen Meadow, or on the often marshy area between the Luzley Brook and Ford House. The Parks Committee discussed whether the Forrest Road ground should be used that year, but Jack Drew advised against it as it was still recovering from its wartime sowing, so clubs had to use 'either the ground in the Abbey Fields or one on the Bulkington estate'. That same month the headmistress of Abbotsford School asked for the use of a hockey pitch and the use of a pitch for netball; they were offered the football field known as the swamp on the same terms as the previous year, and given permission to erect netball posts. The swamp pitch was also used during the week by the Secondary Modern school.

The following year (1948), four clubs, Kenilworth Baptists, British Legion, Kenilworth United FC and Kenilworth Rangers, all requested pitches despite the poor amenities. Half way through the season residents Albion FC asked for new changing rooms as the air raid shelter in Forrest Road was streaming with water and not fit to use, and as a result repairs were made to the old barn alongside the Memorial Field, halfway down the steep path from the War Memorial, as replacement facilities. It was intended to lay on water to the barn but initially the only water supply was from a spring near the brook. A standpipe was soon installed by the council but this became regularly broken by vandals. It had also been suggested that perhaps the changing accommodation at the swimming pool could be used.

A group of young ex-servicemen were trying to start a cricket club and asked if they could use the vacated Forrest Road shelter for changing and play on the adjacent field, keeping both in good repair themselves; there appears to have been no successful outcome, but cricket did return that year with the Secondary Modern School given permission to play on an unknown area.

Attendances at the **swimming pool** are always difficult to assess as they were dependent upon the weather, but takings in 1945 were 20 per cent down on those of 1944. At the end of the season there was a discussion, with details unrecorded, about heating and roofing the pool. The 1947 charges were for adults 9d, spectators 6d, children 3d, 1s on Sunday for all classes but after 1 p.m. adults only, with Wednesday 1 to 4 p.m. reserved for ladies only. Closing time was extended to 10 p.m. with the wartime 'double summer time' still in operation. The pool was open in time for Whitsun and provision was made for bathers to wash their feet and the attendant was to insist they did so before entering baths. The chlorination plant had been repaired by the manufacturers only just in time for the season, but the pool was closed on 5th and 6th June 1947 as the water was turning green; this was due to an infestation of *euglena*, the baths were emptied and refilled. Swimming galas returned on 21st June as part of the 1947 re-launched carnival; there appears to have been no swimming club at this time so it is not known who organised it.

In June 1947 it was decided that 'more hygienic types of containers are required for storing bathers' clothing' and until they arrived the former decontamination unit bags in use since 1944 were to be washed and disinfected regularly. The following month, 200 new string bags were on order and if found to be suitable then another 300 were to be ordered, allowing for up to 500 to be in the pool at any one time.

At the end of 1947, the loan repayments for the 1935 pool rebuild ended.

In readiness for the 1948 season, Mr Hoggins of Leamington repaired the thatch of the toilets and pay box with 'first class wheat straw', and several trees near the baths were taken down, including one rotting oak that was leaning ominously over the men's changing rooms. In 1949 the Girl Guides were allowed the same use of the pool as the Boy Scouts, and repairs were made to the 'boy's cubicles'; this was becoming more difficult due to the flimsy nature of the construction. Illegal access to the pool after closing was both easy and commonplace; although there are no reports of damage, legal proceedings were planned against anyone caught. Bye-laws specifically for the use of the baths were drawn up for the first time.

The 1949 takings at the baths up to 25th September were £931 *(£30,000)*.

The fields were soon once more being used for **large events**. On 2nd May 1946 Sanger's Circus hired a field for a day for £10 (the cost of providing a water supply) and that July saw a field day for the Forces Home Fund, and The National Fire Service once more began public competitions. In 1947 Pat Collins asked if he could bring his funfair to the town and was allocated a date on the St John's playing field, but in March the council re-contacted Collins and asked if instead he would like to be in the Abbey Fields as part of the revived **Kenilworth Carnival**, and this he did. Also, as part of the carnival, the trades union NALGO received permission to stage a tennis tournament partly on the Abbey Fields courts, and also on the lawn they had levelled and created at the rear of the council offices at Wilton House to provide another court. (This became the lawn of the Old Folks Club in 1951.)

The carnival was no longer for the benefit of Warneford Hospital, due to the creation of the National

Health Service, but was re-started by the Kenilworth branch of the British Legion to raise funds for new premises, its pre-war base of The Globe Hotel having been destroyed. The week-long list of carnival events in the Abbey Fields were a swimming gala that included a life saving display, a variety of races and a water polo match, and perhaps the most popular early event was a ladies football match *'between two specially trained teams'*; the Rovers beat the Bumpers 5-2 and the standard of play *'surprised 95 per cent of the spectators who had come along to laugh'*. This was staged in the field alongside Bridge Street with tarpaulins raised to block the view from the road.

The coronation of Carnival Queen Patsy Wheeler, took place at Castle Green on 28th June at 2.15 p.m., immediately prior to the parade which culminated in speeches made in the Abbey Fields on the 1928 terrace that gave a raised position. The following day there was an open air service in the park. The popularity of the ladies football match was such that it was played again but at the Forrest Road ground, due to the funfair now being on the Bridge Street field. The crowd included German Prisoners of War and spectators from as far away as Walsall, this time the Bumpers won 3-0.

Although many carnival attractions were held away from them, including an extraordinary military show at the St John's cricket ground, the Abbey Fields was once more the focal point for major town events.

In April 1946, there was a rearrangement of the tennis facilities. The hard courts were enlarged and four were laid in the place of two, and two grass courts which fell into disuse during the war were brought back into use. The layout of the six courts is not known for certain, but perhaps it was at this time the two original hard courts were dug up and the four new ones were on the site of the grass courts.

In March 1947, the **bowling & tennis** club agreed to look after the bowling green at least until the autumn of 1949. At the end of the 1947 season, the KUDC Finance Committee asked the cost of getting the two grass courts in order, or as an alternative how much it would cost to convert the courts to a 9-hole **putting green**. By May 1948 the council had its answer, the putting green would cost £50 including the provision of all equipment; this was agreed to and put in hand, thus ending the life of the grass courts after 25 years. Such was the success of the putting in its first year, it was extended to 18 holes in readiness for its second.

School use of the **tennis** courts continued: in 1947 Abbotsford School was granted use of two hard surface courts for 2 hours on Wednesdays, whilst the Secondary Modern School had them for an hour on Fridays at a cost of 1s 6d per hour per court. They were allowed use of the other courts if they were vacant. In 1948 the Secondary Modern School had three hard courts on Wednesdays for an hour but Abbotsford School were denied use of the courts for netball as it would be 'injurious' to the surface. The tennis court playing times for Sundays were amended to 8 to 10.30 a.m. and 2 to 9 p.m., and the hard courts allowed the playing season to be extended to the end of October, or later if conditions were favourable.

In 1948 the Working Men's Club arranged a bowls competition in the Abbey Fields as part of the Carnival fundraising. In July 1948, the Pavilion had a telephone installed which for the following season enabled the booking of tennis courts a day in advance. There were four courts in use but perhaps inevitably there were problems with all the courts being booked and those turning up on the day having nowhere to play, a situation exacerbated when some booked players failed to appear. The solution was to allow only two courts to be booked in advance. The charges in 1949 were 2s per hour per court, but 1s for juveniles. They were open from 9 a.m. to 1 p.m., and 2 till 9 p.m. on weekdays, and on Sundays from 8 to 10.30 a.m. and 2 to 9 p.m.; juveniles were allowed on courts from Monday to Friday from 9 a.m. to 1 p.m. and 5 to 6 p.m. According to the annual receipts, the new arrangements for tennis seemed to have been a success; takings were £92 in 1947, £96 in 1948, and £141 in 1949. From 13th June to 30th September 1949, putting took £38.

The Kenilworth Town Band re-formed in December 1948 and was allowed free use of the Pavilion in winter months for its practices; the next May they left never to return being in need of somewhere larger.

Kenilworth's Agricultural Society had formed in the war years and held its first shows at Thickthorn before moving to Stoneleigh, but they wished to return to Kenilworth and applied to hold their 1948 show in the Abbey Fields on the **Oxpen Meadow** in August. They argued the show would be an asset to the town and the council agreed to their request, provided the organisers left the fields in an acceptable condition. Probably due to that successful application, the Kenilworth Horse & Pony Club asked if they could hold a gymkhana at the same place on Whit Monday and they too were successful. The Agricultural Society set about preparing the meadow for its show; after its customary early-year draining, the ground was levelled, seeded with grass and clover, and in arrangement with the grazing rights holder (thought to still be Phillip Hubbard, likely to be a society member) the proposed ring area was fenced off to keep the incumbent grazing cattle out. No damage by the gymkhana was reported. The Agricultural Show was a great success, and so was its setting described as *'an amphitheatre'*, the slopes on two sides aiding the viewing.

Two views from the temporary grandstand near Finham Brook at the Agricultural Show in the Oxpen Meadow in 1949. *Upper:* A parade of horses and cattle in the ring, the churchyard with canvas screens is in the background. *Lower:* Showjumping, with cars parked on the land leading up to High Street *(both, HS)*

Following its new-found use as a showground, in early 1949 plans were put in hand to further drain the Oxpen Meadow. Three existing drainpipes had been found just 12 inches below the surface and they were connected to a new main drain that was being laid. About '1,000 land drainpipes' were used to take the water away, and on the north side of the field were found two springs that had not been connected to any drains and were part of the reason areas of the field remained boggy; these were piped into the new system.

Provision was made with connections to main sewers for temporary toilets during shows; these were capped and slabbed over when not in use. The remaining parts of a hedge across the meadow were also due to be removed, although it appears in the photograph, opposite, top left.

Such was the success of the draining, a football pitch was made on the meadow; not, it was said, for the use of clubs but only for 'special occasions', perhaps suggesting a quality playing surface was expected. It is uncertain as to how this relates to the existing football pitch referred to as 'the swamp', but a photograph in the *Leamington Courier* of the 1953 Agricultural Show does seem to show a set of goalposts in the middle of the showground. At this time, all talk of conversion to a lake was absent.

Another event to take place in the fields was the annual tea party of the Old Folks Club, held in a marquee in the Memorial Field.

In March 1947, the town clerk was asked to compile a report as regards to the provision of **refreshments** in the Abbey Fields, an improvement on the pre-war ice cream tricycle was obviously intended. A year later the council requested suggestions as to how the amenities in the park could be improved and those received included investigating the behaviour of children in the male changing cubicles, a tree planting programme to be prepared, the grass to be mowed as early as possible each year, the replacement of the 'rustic bridge', and that the provision of refreshments at the swimming pool by the council or a contractor should be considered. A month later, a letter was read from the proprietors of the White House Café in Warwick Road, Mr & Mrs Postins, seeking to provide catering in the park. A long discussion followed covering a variety of details such as whether to allow a mobile canteen in the grounds, the provision of gas and water, or providing a room at either the Pavilion or swimming pool. It was decided to take no immediate action for the current season but to arrange for catering by the start of the next.

By April 1949, the surveyor had calculated it would cost £95 to convert part of a building at the baths and to supply all necessary equipment to provide the catering; its previous use is unknown but it was in the north-east corner. Mr & Mrs Postins offered a rent of £70 plus 10 per cent of their gross takings and this was accepted with the caterer providing all utensils and equipment. The White House Café would be the sole provider of refreshments and ice creams in the fields (except on special days such as the Carnival) for seven days a week, on the only conditions set that prices must be 'reasonable' and a cup of tea no more than 3d. By mid-June the café kiosk was opened, with a server both inside to the pool and outside to the park; by September there had been several break-ins. The kiosk was a success, in its first year the takings were £1,379, about 25 per cent more than the £1,108 taken by the swimming pool, tennis courts, and putting green combined. The following year, Mr & Mrs Postins submitted the only tender for the kiosk, now increased to £130 for the year due to their success.

There continued to be requests and suggestions for further development of the Abbey Fields. In 1948 a letter suggested they were the perfect place to build the proposed youth centre, however the covenants prohibited any such building as it had to remain as open pleasure grounds. Councillor Jackson tried to revive the pre-war idea of a **paddling pool** and even offered to pay for it.

The fields increasing use, however, was leading to a problem and the Parks & Cemetery Committee were in agreement in principal that **car parking** facilities for the tennis and swimming seasons within the fields should be made, and they were to look into it further. Despite requests, they would not sanction the use of the triangular piece of land near the church off Bridge Street; the proposal was 'not entertained' and the bye-law excluding cars from all areas of the fields remained. In early 1949, a High Street resident wrote to the council asking for part of the Abbey Fields to be set aside for car parking, but the council replied that it was not necessary.

In 1949 the hedge between the two fields known as the **Memorial Field** and The Triangle, thought to be the field used for WW1 allotments (see map, page 58), was taken out and burned, as were the thorn bushes nearby on the brook from Forrest Road to the swimming pool, again altering the plot layout for grazing. This tidying up led to calls from the Parks Committee chairman, E B Smith, to ask for the **brook** to be cleared of glass and other accumulated debris; contractors were employed to carry out the improvements including flattening the bottom and regrading the brook to give a continuous fall to improve the flow from the tennis courts to Townpool Bridge. Now the mill at Mill End had ceased operations and no longer needed the water, the mill race from Townpool to Mill End was closed off and later filled in, and a curved wall built directing the brook away from and protecting the end Bridge Street cottage. This contracted work was completed in August 1949. Jack Drew suggested that once the work was complete, all the thorn bushes alongside the brook from the Castle Ford to Bridge Street should be removed, and replaced with trees and shrubs, saying it would 'make a great improvement to the Abbey Fields.'

In December 1949, stone from the 'old tumbled down wall' from the **Oxpen Meadow** to the Abbotsfield boundary was taken down and the stone used to make an ornamental garden with a lily pond as part of the works alongside Bridge Street. There was a proposal to edge the High Street boundary of the plot given by Gertrude Evans, with an elaborate wall of iron railings on brick pillars, but in the event a more economical wooden fence was installed.

In February 1949, Councillor E B Smith attempted to improve the park for visitors by saying *'the absence of cattle would be appreciated by the people and result in a net loss of only £10 to the Council'*. It was instantly opposed; Councillor Weetman said the true figure was nearer £200, and Councillor Bostock, another farmer, explained *'Grazing in the Abbey Fields brings 10 to 15 beasts to maturity each year, I do not think we should monkey with people's food in the present critical situation. If everyone did the same, the country would be in an even more sticky situation'*, and he also mentioned the extra cost of mowing. Dr Smalley said that *'while every beast counted, it had to be set against the health benefits the children would receive'*. Councillor Huckvale thought there was *'not a person in Kenilworth who would object to a 1d rate to maintain the fields'*, whilst Councillor Watling thought the loss would be about £45-£50 a year without the grass cutting. With extra costs inevitable and the rates in any case about to go up 10d in the pound to 17s, not surprisingly E B Smith's motion to end grazing was defeated purely on financial reasons.

Grazing plots were let in March 1950. Plot 1 of 6.5 acres was let at £6 per acre, Plot 2 of 9.5 acres at £6, Plot 3 (now including 3 acres from Plot 4) of 10.457 acres at £3 10s, the reduced Plot 4 of 6.510 acres at £3 10s, Plot 6 (which now incorporated the former Plot 7 and the High Street land donated by Gertrude Evans) of 15.273 acres at £4, all these were to E Hubbard; Plot 5 of 4.226 acres was let to D S Fancott at £5 2s 6d, the Fancott family had now been renting a field for at least 120 years. The area used as a wartime experimental plot next to the War Memorial was levelled ready for seeding with grass. Land at the cemetery was also used for grazing; in 1951 the 3½ acres was let to T Pritchard & Son at £3 5s per acre.

The Oxpen Meadow as it appeared in the 1952 Town Guide *(CG)*

The 1950 Gymkhana and Agricultural Show passed off leaving the **Oxpen Meadow** showground in acceptable condition. In the autumn the old sheds in the meadow (on the slope on the northern side), presumably part of the Oxpen itself, were removed and the materials used to construct a tractor and equipment 'house' at the cemetery. In preparation for the 1951 season, trees and bushes alongside the brook in the meadow were trimmed back and a permanent water supply to the showground installed, but this year there were to be problems. At the end of the agricultural show the wet state of the meadow caused the ground to be 'heavily churned up' by the leaving vehicles. The cause was water in low lying areas that could not be drained off with pipes. Jack Drew suggested that about 80 to 100 loads of clinker should be tipped into the low areas, and 'the high bank of soil pushed over', then reseeded to solve the problem. The council was not convinced and were to have discussions with local farmers that had similar problems.

In early 1952 the whole question of the meadow was to be looked into again, but the Agricultural Society said they were willing to improve the drainage if the council would contribute £50 to the work, which they did. For undiscovered reasons, for their August 1952 show *'a last minute appeal to the authorities allowed the Agricultural Society to include a few local cattle in their Monday show'*, but the main attractions for the 8,000 spectators were the gymkhana organised by the Horse & Pony club, and the Horticultural Society display and competition. Ted Edgar won one of the jumping competitions on his horse Come Closer, as well as several awards for his Leek Wootton farm and livestock.

The gymkhana held in the Oxpen Meadow two weekends after the Coronation in 1953, saw a disappointing turnout of support from the public; the expected rainstorm arrived at the approximate middle of the event but the programme was completed. The Agricultural Show of August Bank Holiday 1953 drew a record crowd and the *'elaborate programme was carried out without a hitch'*, and provided a *'high standard'* of *'first class entertainment'* for the 13,000 that paid at the gates. Ted Edgar of Leek Wootton for the third time won the cup for the highest aggregate points, and amongst the other local winners were farmers Major Hibbert and George Bostock, in competitions entered from all over Warwickshire and beyond.

A parade of Shire horses at the August Bank Holiday 1953 Agricultural Show. Part of the 13,000 crowd are on the north bank of the Oxpen Meadow with cars parked behind. Canvas screens are erected on High Street to prevent a free view. Clinton House is just visible behind the tree *(LC, 7th August 1953)*

The effort and money spent on improving the drainage of the Oxpen Meadow did have one drawback; it was decided that it would not be flooded to provide skating in the 1953-54 winter as this would damage the turf that had been laid down. However, due to a very wet summer, on 22nd June 1954 some six weeks before its show was due, the Agricultural Society asked if it could use an area of the fields other than the Oxpen Meadow, and permission was granted. The clearing of hedgerows around The Triangle field in 1949 had created a large open space on the south side of Finham Brook and east of Luzley Brook, and the slope of the land up to Forrest Road made *'a perfect natural grandstand'*. The *'usual'* 1,000 seat temporary grandstand would still be constructed. The new layout also provided for better parking facilities and all entrances were from the *'clock tower side of the fields.'*

The show of 1954 set a record number of livestock entries, 417, but the move to the new location was hardly the resounding success expected due to the continued bad weather. Torrential rain the night before caused the committee tent to be flooded and even before the arrival of participants, *'the ground at the centre of operations resembled a quagmire. The mud was in better supply than ever before. Many vehicles were bogged down as soon as they entered the Abbey Fields necessitating the employment of straw, grit, sacks, and boards. Even the tractors flailed deep into the mud, cattle trucks were in the worst plight'*. Despite this, *'10,000 people braved the sludge'* and the show itself was described as successful, but problems continued afterwards in other parts of the fields used for parking; *'A private car hitched to a caravan completely failed to negotiate the gradient to the Abbey Hill exit'*. For some time afterwards, the *'churned up pastureland is still testimony to the appalling conditions'* and roads leading from the ground were still covered in mud. The reports were written by legendary *KWN* editor Charles Porter whose flowery use of words embellished the local newspaper until 1977.

Despite the problems underfoot, the new site for the show was seen as preferential to the old and the society quickly asked if they could use the same field the following year; the council wisely decided to discuss it at a later date once the ground had been 'put back into condition'. Once more they investigated options for the Oxpen Meadow: lay a large drain to near Townpool Bridge so it drained quicker, make a lake, or infill for use as sports pitches. The first would be a waste of money, but the second two were to be looked into and costed. The Oxpen Meadow was still said to be the *'most natural arena for holding events'* but the council had finally begun to realise how costly it would be to provide and maintain proper drainage.

During discussions, the Agricultural Society offered to level the area at the bottom of the Memorial Field and remove a length of hedge adjoining the footpath from Forrest Road at their expense to improve the field for their show. The council gave it careful consideration before, in December 1954, saying that prior to any agreement the society must put back into good repair the path from Forrest Road to the swimming pool so it 'can again be used by residents without inconvenience'; presumably it was still unrepaired since the August show. Once done, the Parks Committee would recommend the acceptance of the use of 'the Memorial Field and the area known as the Triangle' provided the society carried out works which would improve the site as a showground including the removal of three chains of hedge, the levelling of the ground at the bottom of the bank, dredging the brook and the repair of the existing cattle bridge over it to the football pitch. The council were adamant that they were not going to spend any sum whatsoever but if the society carried out the works satisfactorily they could expect the granting for annual shows for the next few years. This however brought complaints from residents and ratepayers saying the council should not commit themselves to longer term use, but the Parks Committee were agreed that the works would improve the facilities and amenities, and as they would cover only a small area it was unlikely to alter the general character and appearance of the fields. The council was also justified as the work granted facilities to 'provide entertainment and relaxation to the people of Kenilworth and visitors.'

It was not until June 1955 that an agreement was finally reached; the society had provided the cost of the path repair and also agreed to move 15 yards of fence 'below the hovel', 'fill in and pipe the ditch', put ashes on the bad patch in the middle of the ground, and cut and lay the hedge. The show went ahead with no problems, and Kenilworth now had a proper **showground** with sloping land alongside for spectators that remains in use to this day. It is quite probable that the society vacating the Oxpen Meadow also bought to an end any use of that field as a football pitch.

In March 1951 the Kenilworth Town Band asked the council if they wished to engage them to perform in the park on Sunday afternoons for a fee; the council refused to pay them but said they could make a collection if they wished, and their performances were not to clash with church services.

In September 1951, due to the condition of the **air raid shelters** in Rosemary Hill and Bridge Street, the council wrote to the Ministry of Works asking if all the shelters could be closed up. In the spring of 1952, Mr Castle won a £90 contract to brick up the entrances to the shelters, including those in the Abbey Fields; consent had been received from the Home Office. The work started immediately.

In early 1951, much work was carried out along the **brook**. In February, the ground softened by thawing snow caused an oak tree to fall across the stream and this instigated a general tidy up of the banks, including willows being planted 'where necessary'. The old wooden fence along the brook from Bridge Street to the Iron Bridge that prevented livestock from crossing was replaced by a wire fence.

The **bowls club** licence continued to be renewed every two years. In 1951 they asked if an ash tree alongside the green could be removed as its seeds played havoc with the green; it was kept due to being a healthy specimen but an elderly and hollow ash tree near the tennis courts was removed.

Eight new **seats**, including two on the diagonal path to Bridge Street, were installed in May 1951. In November 1952 a Miss Cramp of Fieldgate Lane asked if she could purchase a **seat** to be placed in the Abbey Fields in memory of her brother; the council agreed and this may have been the first such private memorial. In 1953 another oak tree fell across the brook near the bowling green; it was cut up and used by the council for repairs to the seats and similar work.

In 1952 problems were caused by the playing of games in the fields during church services, and the following year the police were again asked to take action against **cyclists** using the Abbey Fields paths; there were no reports of prosecutions.

Following earlier attempts to widen **Abbey Hill** to ease the problem created by buses stopping, in February 1950 the KUDC considered a proposal to make a recess into the Abbey Fields along Abbey Hill to enable buses to pull off of the highway. After 'careful perusal' of the plan it was agreed to go ahead; the location was near the end of the wall from the 1939 scheme that eased the corner, and part of the wall needed to be removed; this again of course did not contravene this area's covenants as the widening of the adjacent roads was allowed for. At the same time, the provision of **shelters** in the park was discussed and agreed; after considering designs, 'a double type be approved and erected near Abbey Hill and that provision be made in the estimates for another to be erected in the park in the vicinity of the Bridge Street entrance'. By the end of the month only one shelter had been approved, that near Abbey Hill.

The bus lay-by was brought into use on 25th August 1950. The previous month, 'the walling stone demolished at Abbey Hill' was used for repairs of the sewer-crossing over the brook near the swimming pool. That November, tenders were invited for the construction of the 'park shelter'; it is interesting to note that at no time was the structure referred to as a bus shelter, but dual use for park-goers and bus passengers was clearly intended with its two-sided design and location. After tenders were received, the surveyor decided the council could do the work cheaper, for £333, and this they did in the autumn of 1951 putting up what is thought to be a prefabricated structure. However the shelter clearly contravened the area's covenant which states 'no building or erection shall at any time hereafter be built or erected upon any part of the premises'; perhaps the same side-step was used as for the War Memorial and it was considered to be on a widening of the highway and thus a contributory reason to locate the 'park shelter' alongside the road.

The Abbey Hill shelter being assembled

(LC, 19th October 1951)

As preparations were in hand for building the shelter, in December 1950 Jack Drew submitted an idea to move the boundary fence along Abbey Hill some 30 yards into the fields to enable the planting of 'an avenue of stately trees' and adding beds of flowers and shrubs each subsequent year; later, this 30 yard corridor could be extended around the edge down to Bridge Street, 'and so help beautify this section of the town'. The Baths, Playgrounds & Cemetery Committee were in favour of the scheme in general but objections were raised to the flower beds and shrubs; however in December 1951, work began to plant ornamental evergreen shrubs around the new shelter, and at this time it was the only part of the scheme that came to fruition. It was not to be until 1963 that steps were built leading from the shelter allowing easier access into the fields; the seat facing the park had become *'a favourite resort of old folk'*. The new wall around it and the lay-by was of brick; redundant Abbey stone was no longer in plentiful supply.

The provision of the lay-by was the cheapest solution to increasing traffic problems along Abbey Hill but such was the congestion and narrowness of the road that still no pedestrian footway existed between the new shelter westwards to the top of the Abbey Field's diagonal path. By the summer of 1952 it was again being proposed that the road should become a dual carriageway but initially, in March 1953, traffic control was to be improved by creating islands at the Abbey Hill crossroads by the Abbey Hotel, but, 'It is hoped that in the very near future serious consideration will be given to the question of dual carriageways in Abbey Hill and Rosemary Hill'. By September, 'we now have before us a map showing the road development that may take place along the Abbey Hill area'; due to this, planned tree planting inside the park in the vicinity was restricted to only 5 trees, and a 'few' along the Forrest Road frontage.

The provision of the 'park shelter' alongside the bus lay-by led to bus shelters costing £172 each being provided at certain popular stops in 1954. They were smaller but also prefabricated with a cedar-clad wooden frame, and were installed at Crackley, St John's and in Bridge Street; the latter backed on to the Abbey Fields but was almost all contained within the road's boundary. At this time it was reported that the Abbey Hill shelter was already suffering from woodworm.

In December 1950, the Carnival Committee informed the council that it intended to put the proceeds of the following year's carnival towards children's play equipment in the park. However, they later changed this to helping the scouts and guides fund for new premises and donated over £600.

In 1950, **bye-laws** specific to the use of the **swimming pool** were submitted to and approved by the Ministry of Health. The pool's sides were coated in 'Snowcem' to help protect them from the effects of chlorinated water, and a new brick wall, of unknown use and precise location, was put up between the cascade and men's changing facilities. That June, pilfering in the 'boy's cubicles' became a problem and was reported to the police, and as glass bottles were occasionally broken within the pool area they were to be banned. Schoolchildren who won races at the Carnival Swimming Gala were given free passes for the rest of the season. A Mr A Morris and Mr Blood were allowed to use the pool for giving lessons for an hour from midday on Sundays starting in 1951.

On the last Thursday of June 1951, Councillor E B Smith, the *'sponsor'* of the scheme, arranged a meeting with the intent to start a new **Swimming Club**. The meeting had been called after a Mrs Norris had heard of a promising young Kenilworth swimmer who travelled to Coventry weekly to be a member of the city's club as there was none in his home town. Fifty, mostly youngsters, attended and provisional arrangements were made; subscriptions were to be 5s for adults and 2s 6d for children. Officials were appointed, Mrs Norris herself became secretary, and G Franklin of Coventry agreed to act as a swimming teacher. All those interested were asked to attend the baths between 7 and 9 p.m. on Thursdays; if there was enough interest then exclusive use of the baths at that time would be requested. In July the club, now with 100 or so members, was indeed granted permission to have exclusive use of the baths at its preferred time for the rest of the season, and also to hold a gala between 2 and 5 p.m. on Saturday 8th September; the event was opened by Council Chairman Alan Huckvale and 300 spectators turned up.

The swimming pool as seen in the 1952 Town Guide. The shrubbery on the west side and partially the northern end, which appears to be on a slightly raised mound, is a remnant of that surrounding the original pool which was the same length but half this pool's width. The thatching and style of the changing room and filtration house complements that of the tennis pavilion. See the photograph on page 89 *(CG)*

One great difficulty of this and previous incarnations of the swimming club, was that the pool was not available for 7 or 8 months of the year, and so Mrs Norris arranged for the swimmers to continue their meetings at the indoor pool in Leamington, hosted by that town's club. By the time of the annual meeting in March 1952, the club had amassed 176 members ranging from young children to *'seasoned experts'*, all of whom could swim, and the club had made a profit of £2.

In 1952, there was to be no swimming gala directly associated with the carnival, but the club's own swimming event was to make a donation to the carnival funds; lanes had been painted on the bottom of the pool for the first time. One new carnival event, arranged by the St Nicholas Boys Club, was a **putting** tournament; there were 42 entrants and it was played on a knock-out basis over 18 holes and the winner was Mr C Reader beating Miss Woodward 47-50 in the final. The contest added £4 to the carnival funds.

For 1954, the **swimming club** once more had exclusive use of the baths one evening a week; adult members had to pay 6d and children 3d. The second hour of their allotted time was occupied by water polo matches for which the public could watch for a small fee. Knowle Hill School was the latest to have time at the pool allocated to them. The 1954 carnival again included a putting competition on the Abbey Fields course, and after the 1955 carnival Jack Drew said that the 'Fair people were the tidiest and quietest he has had to deal with during holding fairs in the park.'

In early 1953, a Coronation Committee was established and given funds to spend on worthwhile projects for the town. Some of this was allocated for new **play equipment** in the Abbey Fields; purchased from Wicksteed's and installed in time for **Coronation Day** was a 30ft Safety Slide number BD471 for £118 *(£3,023)*, a 10ft 6ins swing frame BD455 for £54, and a 10ft climbing apparatus with a tower number BD480 for £66. A shelter near to the children's play area was allocated £350 but was not built.

Also in connection with the coronation, an unnamed 'street' was allowed to give donkey rides in the Memorial Field to raise funds to stage its street party. According to the *KWN*, Kenilworth's celebrations for the coronation on 2nd June 1953 *'will be recorded by historians as a magnificent occasion'*. There were 20 or so street parties, *'scarcely a house in town failed to display a token of loyalty'*, and events planned for the Abbey Fields: *'For the first time the children's equipment in the park which forms part of the permanent memorial scheme, was made available'*, but unfortunately due to the *'unremitting rain, very little of the scheduled park programme was found possible to present'*. The Concert Party and Punch & Judy Show did make *'valiant efforts'* and Councillor Huckvale *'defied the elements in order to plant a memorial oak tree'* alongside Abbey Hill to commemorate the occasion, but due to the weather the old-time and modern dancing were transferred to the Parochial Hall, and the bonfire and firework display were postponed until the following Saturday.

One notable part of the coronation was its live showing on television; it is said the event can be blamed as the start of the new era of television culture. A *KWN* reporter wandered the deserted town randomly knocking on doors to talk to the gatherings inside watching televisions, *'The sight of a TV aerial was a sure sign of a communal looking-in'*, but one aspect was particularly fascinating; thanks to an anonymous donor, old folks gathered at the Parochial Hall to watch the live pictures projected onto a screen, a remarkable innovation of the time repeated in cinemas and theatres across the country.

For the 1951 season, Mr Postins provided the Abbey Fields **catering** on the same terms as for 1950, however, this was to be his last year. The following April tenders were invited and advertised twice but there was only one taker, Greyhound Catering, who agreed to pay only £35 for the whole season. It would seem that although takings were high, profits were low and this induced the lowered rent, but even this appears to have been too much for Greyhound; in March 1953 the proprietor had still not paid his rent for the previous year and legal proceedings were in hand. Mr P Lloyd of New Street tendered for the 1953 season, initially asking if he could also set up an ice cream stall at the Bridge Street entrance, which was denied, and wisely the council asked for his rent in advance. With trust established, the following year he was asked for only half his rent at the start of the season, the rest of the increased £50 for the season was to be paid later; presumably acceptable profits had returned.

In the summer of 1951, the question of providing a **car park** for Abbey Fields visitors was again discussed. It was thought that somewhere within the fields was the only plausible option and so the first hurdle to overcome was the council's January 1930 **bye-law** number 8 which prevented any cars entering the fields. The suggested new version was:

> A person shall not bring or cause to be brought into the open space any barrow or truck, machine or vehicle other than: a) a wheeled bicycle or other similar machine, b) a wheelchair or perambulator or chaise used solely for the conveyance of a child or children or an invalid; provided that where the Council by notice conspicuously exhibited on the pleasure grounds set a part of the open space for the use of bicycles, motorcycles motor cars constructed solely for the carriage of passengers and their affects and other passenger conveying vehicles, this bye-law shall not be deemed to prohibit the driving or wheeling in on to that part (of the pleasure grounds) of a machine or vehicle of the class for which it is a part.

It was expected that the Secretary of State would permit the bye-law change, subject to any objections by the public; there was only one but the details of the letter from the occupant of 9 High Street are not recorded and the council said that the lady had in any case misunderstood their intentions; 'This bye-law (change) was made in order that the council can legally permit the parking of passenger carrying vehicles in the Abbey Fields and it never was the intention of the committee to create a permanent car park which would be of some nuisance to adjoining property owners. Steps will be taken to prevent it becoming a nuisance to the amenities of the surrounding properties'. The *KWN* reported that the bye-law change was so that the *'Abbey Fields may be used on specific occasions as a car park'* adding that the council *'did not intend to establish a permanent car park with an attendant.'*

No specific location was mentioned during the revision of the bye-law, nor needed to be, but the previously mentioned triangle off Bridge Street was chosen, not for a *'specific occasion'* as claimed but for a semi-permanent arrangement; the car park was opened to the public on 30th May 1952 and the users quickly expressed their appreciation of the facility. Most of the parking area was in the original Area B conveyed by the Preservationists to the Churchwardens; it is thought that by now it had been transferred to the KUDC (see later). The question of an attendant at weekends was discussed as an experiment and the clerk was to arrange for a suitable person on a voluntary basis; thoughtfully, 'the committee are willing to issue an armband'. In June 1953, arrangements were made to keep the car park open until 10 p.m. at which time the park entrance gates were locked.

A post-war view of the area off Bridge Street before any discernible damage by car parking

One suggestion for the fields in January 1950 that came to nothing was the provision of a 'prefabricated cricket pitch'; the provision of a **cricket pitch** was one of the original aims when the fields were acquired. In late summer 1951, the County Council agreed to pay £10 a year for the use of three **football pitches** for the local schools, but the headmistress at Abbotsford School, Miss Higginson, requested the use of a hockey pitch. Despite an earlier use as such, this now involved the purchase of goals and the laying out of a new pitch and the school contributed £5 to the costs as did the County Council; its location is unknown. In August 1952, the school was again granted use of the Abbey Fields hockey pitch, the swimming pool (at 1d a child) and tennis courts (at 1s 6d an hour). For the 1953-54 season the allocation of the three football pitches were the Memorial Field to the British Legion for £2, the Forrest Road pitch to Albion FC for £2, and the poorer quality pitch known as The Swamp to RNA for £1. The Youth Centre was granted a sports day where the competitors were in teams designated by the voting wards.

Such was the demand for sports pitches, and an absence of locations to provide them, in May 1950 the KUDC had been actively seeking to purchase some land in Queen's Road; this may have been the tennis club and/or some adjacent land that had become the agricultural camp set up for the wartime Land Army girls. The owners said that the 'situation is extremely complicated so (they) can't consider a sale to the council at the moment'. The council seemed determined to acquire the site and were in negotiations in 1952, at one time pursuing a Compulsory Purchase Order. It was to remain an agricultural camp until 1954 but the Queen's Road land became set aside for housing and the council were later offered one of the wooden buildings described as a 'pavilion' but declined the offer. The Queens Road tennis club, losing its ground in stages, moved in 1963 to Crackley Lane.

In June 1953, the parks department was authorised to purchase a new tractor and tipping trailer, and post-hole digger, for a total £631; the old tractor was sold for £50. In 1954 the Kenilworth Caged Bird Society suggested that if the council would construct and maintain an **aviary** in the park, they would provide the birds. This was discussed several times and designs were sought, but it was eventually declined.

After long negotiations by Reverend A O Griffiths with the Ministry of Works, in May 1954 agreement was reached whereby the north transept of the **Abbey** could be used as a Garden of Remembrance wherein ashes could be deposited. This area had become part of the Ancient Monument listing in 1935 (some twelve years after the remains outside the churchyard were listed) which forbade any disturbance of the ground, hence the involvement of the Ministry. Decisions still had to be made as to the layout and type of stone memorial that could be used, but it was seen as a long overdue necessity.

In 1954 the four hard **tennis** courts were resurfaced at a cost of £180 and consideration was given to a further court; the work was contracted to the firm En-tout-Cas. The new Waverley Road Tennis Club was denied exclusive use of the courts one evening a week. The start of the 1956 season was delayed until after Easter as the courts were so wet. The **carnival** of course had annual usage of the Abbey Fields and each year a British Legion Drumhead Service was included as part of the events. Not all requests to use the fields were granted; in 1955 the Young Conservatives asked to hold a meeting but were turned down, the council would not agree to political meetings in the park.

The council's income from its Abbey Fields facilities in 1950 saw a large drop from the swimming pool, £931 to £548, and tennis, £141 to £134; putting however was on the up, from £38 to £50. All three fell in 1951. The 1955 incomes were from the swimming pool £1,200, tennis £80, and putting £67.

Continuing her generosity in Charmouth, in 1945 **Gertrude Evans** donated her remaining land between her house and the sea, which included the river estuary, to the local council. The conveyance included a familiar covenant; there was 'nothing to be done to or on the land that would alter its present natural state... no buildings or erections of any kind to be allowed' with the exception of bathing huts in a designated position, and a bridge across the river. One of the fields was on the top of a cliff, which to this day is known as Evans Cliff; it is that immediately east of the mouth of the River Char and has in recent years become subject to a sizable land slip.

Gertrude Evans never married but she had a close friend for much of her life; she was Maud Watson, a Berkswell girl she had known from childhood. Maud was born in 1864 (the year before her family moved to Berkswell) ten years before Gertrude so she was perhaps initially friends with Gertrude's older sister by seven years, Beatrice. Maud was a noted tennis player in her teens and at the age of 16 won the singles competition at the Edgbaston club (beating her sister in the final); the Evans family lived at Edgbaston at this time, is this how and when they met? In July 1884, just months after Clarendon sold the Abbey Fields, Maud, still undefeated in competitive tennis, became the first winner of the Wimbledon Ladies tennis title; Gertrude was a tennis enthusiast, perhaps she and her sister were there to see it. She retained the title in 1885. Maud, who also never married, lived at Berkswell until 1932 when in her mid-60s she moved to live with Gertrude at Hammonds Mead; she took with her the Wimbledon trophy, a delightful silver flower basket, but two years later she donated it to the Edgbaston Priory club, where today it is still presented to their ladies champion and is the oldest tennis trophy in the world. Maud's signature can be seen as a witness on the 1938 conveyance of Gertrude's High Street land (see page 95).

Living near to Charmouth was a regular opponent from Maud's playing days, May Langrishe, and she often visited; when May became ill she moved in to Hammonds Mead with Gertrude and Maud, and died there in January 1939. Maud Watson too died at Hammonds Mead, on 5th June 1946 aged 81 and was buried at Berkswell a few days later. Gertrude attended the funeral; whilst in the area she is likely to have taken the opportunity to see her part of the Abbey Fields and her cottages. She could be proud of her father and his efforts to provide the town with a park 62 years earlier when she was just ten years old.

Gertrude sold Hammonds Mead in 1948, it became a 13-bedroom hotel, and she moved into the adjacent The Poplars which she also owned and had been lived in by her chauffeur. From The Poplars, in February 1953 Gertrude Evans, now aged 79, for a third time contacted the KUDC with an offer of a gift; this time it was of her cottages 81 & 83 High Street, 'in view of their historic interest and that they should be let to old deserving residents of Kenilworth'. It was on the condition that Mrs Tipson in number 83 should remain for her life at the current rent of 4s 6d a week; the occupant of 81 was a carer for a former resident and could be evicted. 'It was unanimously resolved to accept the gift and to extend to Miss Evans every sincere and grateful thanks for her generosity and continued interest in Kenilworth.'

It was not until June that number 81's tenant left and the council finally had the keys. The cottages needed modernisation and decorating; Gertrude was in full agreement that electricity should be installed. Once the work was completed, number 81 was let to Mr F Faxon of Hyde Road for 5s a week. Gertrude observed, 'I think it is nice that Kenilworth receives cottages from the time of Queen Elizabeth I in this coronation year of Queen Elizabeth II'. The donation brought two probably late 16th century cottages into improbable council ownership, where they remained until about the mid 1980s.

As far as is known, Gertrude lived out the rest of her life alone. She died at 17 Ashbourne Road, Bournemouth, on 1st March 1966 aged 92, but the notice of her death says she was still of The Poplars. She had no close family so her executors are of interest. One was George Corbyn Barrow, who was part of the Cadbury family, a one-time Lord Mayor of Birmingham and by profession a lawyer; he was a partner in, and had written the history of, the firm of solicitors Wragge & Co of which Gertrude's father William had been a partner more than 80 years before. The other executor was Sir Arthur Ramsey Hogg; he was married to Mary Aileen Hester Lee Evans, the daughter of Phillip Herbert Lee Evans, Gertrude's cousin. The Hogg family were probably Gertrude's closest relatives and lived in Bournemouth, probably explaining how she came to be there when she died. She left over £71,000 nett *(£1.2 million)*.

Gertrude is buried in St Nicholas churchyard with her entire family: sister Beatrice, brother Percy, mother Sarah and father William, in part of the 1885 churchyard extension onto land sold to the church by William Evans and his Syndicate. The three siblings were childless; Gertrude had been without close family for the last 50 years of her life.

The grave of the entire Evans family is in the 1885 graveyard extension, land sold to the church by William Evans and the Syndicate. Beyond are Area C Plots 7, 8, and much of 9 donated to the park by Gertrude Evans in 1938, and her former cottages 81 & 83 High Street *(8th March 2017)*

There is no doubt that amongst the livestock grazing in the Abbey Fields there was one particularly popular animal; this was Punch, a council cart-horse. In May 1942, council employee Charlie Paxton, a life-long horseman, was given a lift to a farm in Shipston to collect Punch and walk him back to his new Kenilworth home; he arrived on Saturday 14th May. Punch, the name was given to him by his first owners, was a five-year-old strawberry roan Clydesdale gelding of 17 hands, and had spent his working life alongside his mother; he had at one time won a first prize at a Shipston show. Charlie Paxton 'broke' him in for working on the roads of Kenilworth; his first job was *'to transport 25cwt of basic slag from the station to the park'*. Charlie was his regular handler, but George Butcher also had spells with him, and it was of course a seven days a week job looking after horses whether working or not. In the winter Punch was stabled at night, but the rest of the year when not working he was turned out into the Abbey Fields alongside Abbey Hill, where he became a firm favourite with the townsfolk due to his temperament and friendliness. When at work he always carried Charlie's own collection of brasses, and occasionally his mane was plaited. In November 1950, Punch was the featured 'Personality of the Week' in the KWN at a time he shared his Abbey Field pasture with two other council horses, one was called Blackbird, but it was Punch that did the heaviest work. By October 1957, Punch was the last council horse but he had a break from work when his cart was out of order and there was a long delay in repairs due to the difficulty in finding a wright with the necessary skills; the age of horse-drawn vehicles was coming to an end.

Despite mechanised personal transport being banned from the Abbey Fields, the **bye-laws** allowed for 'animals of burden... to be led, or ridden at walking pace' through the fields but this was regularly broken with ponies and horses being ridden in a manner dangerous to walkers, and in particular children. The apparent main point of entry for the ridden animals into the fields was from High Street; this was to be locked up and a stile installed for pedestrians. By September 1957 the bye-law was being amended to ban animals of burden altogether, and so by the spring of 1960, Punch was the only horse allowed in the Abbey Fields. *'A cart horse... allowed the privileges of the Abbey Fields denied to the pride of numerous equine aristocrats so noticeable in the Kenilworth district'.* He had many friends and would follow them around the fields. Although now available only for light work, weaving in and out of the modern traffic and parked cars was seen as too much to ask and so he was effectively retired. At the age of 23 *'his future is something the council will have to think about'.* It was to be hoped that Punch had no future *'beyond honourable retirement in the Abbey Fields, and some suitable shelter during inclement weather.'*

An aerial photograph taken in April 1953 shows three football pitches; alongside the War Memorial, at the bottom of the hill on the showground, and one on the Ford House side of the Luzley Brook, probably that now referred to as the swamp. With the chances of **playing fields** being provided in Queen's Road fading, those in the Abbey Fields took on a new significance, but there were many problems. The RNA had the rights to play for the 1954-55 season but due to flooding were unable to and received a full refund; this seems likely to have been the pitch known as the swamp. The provision of alternative and new sports pitches was again being investigated, as was the rights to grazing on the park pitches. There were also regular spells of **vandalism** to contend with; in January 1956, the goals were pulled down and a crossbar broken on the Memorial Field pitch, and the fence around the tennis hard courts was damaged, and an attempt was made to remove the lead tapes that marked the courts.

At the start of the 1956-57 season, the *'top pitch'*, presumably that alongside the War Memorial, came in for severe criticism. *'Worthwhile football was impossible, the grass had been neither rolled nor cut. Where it was short where cows had found it appetising, cattle had left trademarks all over the pitch. In other places there were rangy tufts where the ball halted'.* The *'bottom pitch'* was perhaps better as it *'was not so tufty but the going was uncomfortable, the aftermath of the Bank Holiday Monday* (agricultural*) show, bovine influence was markedly obvious'.* The dressing rooms in the barn too had their less than endearing features: *'One is dark dirty and smelly, so smelly it drove out players sheltering from the rain, the other has plenty of light – it has holes in the roof'.* This second changing room had eight rusty nails for hanging clothes, a solitary bench for 22 players, and an old horseshoe hanging the wrong way up, doubtless reflecting what the players thought of their luck to be in such a place.

The second week of the season the hosts apologised to their visitors for having nothing better to play on than a *'tufty camber covered in cow manure'*; there were over 100 cowpats on the upper pitch alone. Visiting players, covered in *'the filth'* deposited by cattle included one player who landed in a cowpat face-first; all had to travel home in their coach in the state they left the field as there were no showering facilities. Some coach owners were simply refusing to carry players to the Kenilworth pitches. It was *'a shocking state of affairs and an affront to all visitors'*. The ever-present problem with cowpats on the football pitches was unintentionally amusingly described by one councillor as *'extensive fouling by cattle.'*

The village team from Bishops Tachbrook had to play on the top pitch twice in a fortnight and claimed it was the worst they had played on and local villages had far superior pitches. At the first visit two of their players stumbled on the uneven surface, causing injuries that made them miss the second. *'The ground ought to be called Hillside, we've never seen a ground with a hump like this one. Much time is lost retrieving the ball when it rolls down the bank'.* Another problem were the pitch markings of sawdust; *'We couldn't see the lines half the time.'*

In January 1957, Mr Hugh Eyton, a referee for 25 years and a member of the Scottish Referee Association, the Birmingham Senior League, *etc,* refereed a match in the Abbey Fields and used the old barn allocated to him for changing. It was the *'worst accommodation he has ever experienced'*; there was dirty loose lime on the damp walls, an inadequacy of seating accommodation, holes in the roof, and no toilet. He sent a letter of protest to the Leamington & District Referees Association. His complaints echoed those of many visiting clubs and, consequently, the council began planning improvements. Hooligans didn't help, bricks had been put through the roof, which was retiled only for it to happen again, and doors were seriously damaged as were padlocks, and an outside water tap was stolen.

Rather than the council, it was the clubs themselves that made improvements to the facilities of the *'cattle stall cum dressing room'* for their opponents in the summer of 1957; after the complaints and *'spicy comments'* the previous season about clothes hung on pegs getting dirtied from damp peeling white-washed walls, the Kenilworth British Legion and RNA football teams at their own cost improved the changing rooms by adding plaster board to the walls, and reinforcing the door to deter hooligans.

The barn changing rooms with holes in the roof, *c*1950. A cow can be seen grazing in the field beyond. The seat with the distinctive ironwork survives; its age is uncertain but is possibly 19th century; see also the seats on pages 3 and 57

With attempts to permanently cure the drainage problems of the **Oxpen Meadow** seemingly ended when the agricultural show opened up a new area as a **showground**, somebody visited the *KWN* office and suggested a solution to the problem. The council were in January 1957 looking for a new rubbish tip site; why not fill the Oxpen Meadow to a suitable level with tip rubbish, and then resurface it? The man continued that in the summer it was never better than a *'boggy, evil smelling, unsightly and useless tract of ground'*. By compacting and raising the level a few feet, within three years it could be grassed and be more useful for grazing, and be suitable for sports; a cricket pitch, several football pitches with a running track around the outside could be built, thereby solving one of Kenilworth's dire needs for sports facilities. It would also allow for the *'grossly unsatisfactory soccer pitches'* in the fields to be disposed of or improved, and give the council time to arrange for a permanent tipping site. It must be remembered that at the time the Abbey Fields was the only place the council had to provide sporting facilities; the earlier temporary pitches elsewhere were now being built upon.

This brought an alternative suggestion the following week for the area where the football pitch was visible from the bridge near the bottom of Forrest Road, still referred to as 'the swamp pitch'. Much of the time it was too boggy to play on, and the surface was always deeply punctured from the hooves of cattle. If this area was used as a tip, the level could be raised and then topped with good turf, giving enough space for two pitches. With its access from Forrest Road alongside the air raid shelter, it would then be the perfect site for the carnival. Then of course rather than fill in the Oxpen Meadow area known as 'Joey's field', it could be made into a lake which it was suggested would prevent flooding downstream.

At this time only Plots 1 to 5 were being let for grazing, all of them to Phillip Hubbard of Malthouse Lane for £250. Mr Hubbard should be singled out for praise as it was with his permission, and he having the expense and inconvenience of making alternative arrangements for his animals, that shows and football matches could take place; he had been the major rights-holder since the war years. The advantages of cattle grazing the fields were keeping the grass down, adding to the rural effect, providing valuable manure, and now contributing £250 *(£7,861)* a year to the Council 'coffers'; one suspects the latter was the most relevant as it was now 17 years since the purchase loans were paid off, the reason that grazing was retained in 1884.

For a period of several months, unattested animals had to be kept away from the showground area prior to the **agricultural show** on August Bank Holiday Monday 1957; it was said to be the best and largest to date, enticing no fewer than 14,000 paying customers through the gates. (The population in 1951 was 10,576, and in 1961 it was 14,427.) Despite the crowds, the profits did not wipe out the £1,200 loss from the previous year that was almost entirely washed out by rain.

There were many attractions. 'Bucking Broncos', actually 15 unbroken Welsh ponies, provided a challenge for anyone to have a ride without a harness and many tried to tame the *'wily nags'*. An *'outsize marquee'* displayed entries for the Kenilworth Horticultural Society show; many of the trophies were taken by entrants from outside the area, but Abbey Fields renter Phillip Hubbard did well in the flower classes. Altogether there were 98 individual classes, including some specifically for children. The Kenilworth Caged Bird Society held its show in a tent, attracting over 398 entries, including 42 different species in the Foreign Bird section. The same tent, with a central partition, had 21 tanks containing 600 tropical fish.

Of the 425 livestock entries, Guernseys and Herefords numbers were up, but Aberdeen Angus numbers were down, and sheep were down *'by a few pens'*. Amongst the locals coming first or second in the many classes were again Ted Edgar of Leek Wootton, Thomas Bates of Thickthorn, Helen Martin of The Spring, and C J Forsyth of Gibbet Hill Farm.

The Civil Defence HQ at Montpelier House did not have large enough grounds to hold an exhibition and so the council suggested the Abbey Fields. Their show on 19th October 1957 included a demonstration of rescue and other apparatus, and a BBQ showing emergency feeding equipment; it was one of the biggest such events in the Midlands for October's Civil Defence Month operations. The Civil Defence Band performed for the less serious pastime of dancing. Reassuringly, *'Civil defence is no longer just a wartime affair, but is available for day to day accidents and disasters.'*

The **carnival's** drumhead service on Sunday 8th July 1958 at 8 p.m., was organised by Number 11 British Legion Group comprising the branches at Kenilworth, Stoneleigh, Baginton and Leek Wootton. The parade included the Red Cross, St John's Ambulance, Civil Defence, and Boy Scouts and Girl Guides, and all assembled in Station Road; the salute was taken by Brigadier H E Collett-White DSO, near the Abbey Hill bus stop with KUDC Chairman Major Watling alongside. The Birmingham County British Legion Silver Band provided accompaniment. Where in the fields the service was held is not reported, but also in attendance were the Carnival Queen and her attendants, and members of the Carnival Committee. The collection was for the tuberculosis fund. For the following year's event the British Legion asked to use 'the lawn in front of the bus shelter as a saluting base as in former years.'

As usual, the **swimming pool** was reserved for a date in July 1954 for the club gala, but the club also received permission to reserve one hour each Thursday evening to stage water-polo matches. The thatch on the men's changing rooms had been badly damaged by gales in the winter and was to be replaced by 'tiles or wood shingles'. The following year a group of German Scouts visited the town, they and their hosts were allowed free passes at the pool.

The original chlorination plant from 1935 was beginning to wear out and Town Surveyor G A J Edmundson arranged for its replacement in 1957 at a cost of £393. As a result, swimming *'will be a more pleasant experience in the future than it has on some occasions in the past'*. The summer was to prove a difficult time that year as first an exceptionally heavy storm caused the baths to flood and they were closed for almost a week for cleaning up and refilling with clean water, and then just a week later they were closed again due to a pump motor failure. Pilfering had become a problem and notices were posted warning swimmers not to leave valuables in the changing rooms. An extra lady attendant was employed.

Despite the problems, income was up in 1957; the figures to 31st August showed the pool took £793 9s 3d against £541 in 1956. Over the same period, tennis increased to £82 4s 6d from £78 4s, and putting took more than tennis at £82 7s 6d up from £68 5s. The cost of playing **bowls** for the public was, in 1958,

9d an hour, or club membership for 25s giving unlimited play. Now in its 45th year, the one remaining original member was A E Dencer, who had become the club's chairman. 'The existence of the bowling club is not so well known as it should be, and the influx of new residents is unaware of the bowling facilities that exist for anyone.'

Founding member Albert Edward Dencer, left, and John Hurst, September 1952. The putting green is behind *(SaT)*

In March 1955, the rights for the **catering** service at the kiosk were granted to S W Palmer of Leamington subject to the payment of £54 of the £100 annual rent before the season started. In March 1956, Rheads Catering had the rights for £100 and a percentage payment above the £100 at the rate of ordinary refreshments 7½ per cent, ice cream 10 per cent, sweets and tobacco 2½ per cent, fruit 2½ per cent, and crisps and biscuits 7½ per cent; the details of prices had to be seen by the council before accepting the tender.

However, in 1956 there was an absence of the percentage from the profits; Parks Superintendent Jack Drew and Financial Officer H Newell were instructed to report upon the pros and cons of the KUDC running the kiosk themselves, and on 15th March 1957, after estimating the cost of equipment, wages, staff requirements, *etc,* the Baths & Parks Committee recommended that the council took over the kiosk, and this they voted to do. In April 1957, Mrs Warner was appointed as the catering manageress and a sink, water heater, *etc,* was installed and the building divided.

In September, at the end of the first council-run season, the kiosk was declared a success; a profit of £70 18s 6d on takings of £1,575 had been made. *'We never set out to compete with private enterprise but provide a service. The kiosk provided a good service, there were no complaints, we owe much to the lady in charge'*. Purchases for resale were ice cream £398, cigarettes and matches £293, sweets £275, drinks £145, milk, tea and sugar £24, sundries £15, and Oxo £10. Wages were £269, equipment 30s a week, and breakages £4 16s 8d.

It was already being suggested that larger premises were needed and it was thought that perhaps part of the Pavilion could be used, but since a position as near the swimming pool as possible was preferred, the question was deferred. Mrs Warner continued as Catering Manager and in 1960 her efforts were rewarded with a wage rise; for her 8-hour day, 7-day week she would now be paid £9 12s. In 1960 the takings were £1,752, and the profit £139.

In early 1957, the local Boy Scouts planted two **scarlet oaks** near the swimming baths to commemorate the 50th anniversary of the movement's origins. Assisting in the ceremony was Councillor Major Watling who knew Robert, later Lord, Baden-Powell. The planting was he said, *'Doing a good turn as it would give pleasure to future generations'*. In 1963, the Abbey Scout pack placed bronze plaques to commemorate the planting. In May 1960, a new fence was put up alongside Rosemary Hill, including two 5-barred gates for access, so that a length of fence did not have to be removed when shows were on.

In early 1960 there was a growing feeling that the **Oxpen Meadow** ought not to be drained to its *'summer hangover of a smelly bogland of little practical use'*. With a maximum depth of 4ft, and a water inlet to avoid stagnation, it was argued there was no reason not to have the lake.

By November 1960, the Parks Committee began to consider alterations to the sports pitches in the fields; *'We can seriously consider opening the park out more than it is at present'*. Councillor J Watts said he would like to see hedges removed, ground levelled and extra facilities for playing games provided. *'We should consider having* **grazing cattle removed** *from the park in order to put it to the fullest use for the public'*. Parks Committee Chairman, Mrs Alford, replied *'We want to keep the Abbey Fields for the use of the general public, not one section; a lot of elderly people use the park, they do not play football!'* Removing one particular hedge would provide one more pitch and that was thought sufficient.

Now settled in their new **showground**, in October 1960 the Agricultural Society pointed out that the hedge alongside the Forrest Road football pitch that overhung the path was 'outgrown and no longer stock proof' and suggested it was removed. Jack Drew further suggested the removal of a hedge at the rear of Ford House (between the house and existing football pitch, and more or less in line with the mound), and of an old rotting oak tree nearby; with a bit of levelling another football pitch could be provided. In January 1961 the work suggested by Jack Drew to provide the pitch went ahead but was delayed due to the ground being sodden. When felled, the 30ft oak tree was found to have hollows in which were discovered several honeycombs, and an estimated 10,000 bees. Despite being sent crashing to the ground, the honeycombs stayed more or less attached to their branches and were rescued by volunteers who took them to local keen beekeeper Stan Alsop, the manager of and who lived at the cottage alongside the Cherry Orchard Brickworks. The bees had been in a section some 20ft off the ground and had an entrance thought to have been created by woodpeckers. The four combs were in a 5ft length of branch . Stan Alsop 'planted' the branch vertically in his garden and covered the top with an industrial lampshade to keep the rain out.

Jack Drew also suggested the making of a **sports pitch** on the southern side of the brook opposite the library in Bridge Street, it would require the removal of a hedge but would be suitable for junior football and hockey, the current hockey pitch in the park (on an unknown location, but possibly near the tennis courts) was too wet for most of the season. The Agricultural Society again asked to remove or re-layer the hedge alongside the path from the baths to Forrest Road, but Jack Drew recommended no work and his was the prevailing view.

A one-off use of an Abbey Fields football pitch was by Common Lane firm M H Hurst & Co, who played a friendly match against a team from London. At last in November 1961, a new water supply was piped to the War Memorial path barn used as changing rooms.

From 1st October 1955, a 99-year lease was granted for an electricity sub-station to be built at the rear of High Street properties, near to the car-parking triangle.

With the **car park** established, the next logical step was investigated in the spring of 1958, the introduction of a charge. This was to be on Sundays only and without employing additional staff; payment would be purely to allow entrance and the council was to have no responsibility for the cars parked. It was agreed that there would be 'no loss to the council to give it a trial', and the newly appointed Park Keeper was to collect the money, 1s for cars and 6d for motorcycles whatever the length of stay. The vicar of St Nicholas, Reverend John Thomson, asked if his worshippers could still park for free on production of a pass that he would issue and this was agreed to, but the precise workings of the system the Vicar introduced were unrecorded. Despite the car park being created specifically for the benefit of Abbey Fields visitors, it was predictably being used by others.

The introduction of charges was delayed until the 20th July 1958 so as not to interfere with the British Legion's drumhead service in connection with the carnival the previous weekend. The council announced that the charge for parking was 'a new departure and is experimental' and that the parking area 'flanks the drive from Bridge Street to the church'; *'Hundreds of vehicles are parked in the Abbey Fields at the weekends and it is being increasingly visited by motorists on weekdays'*, the numbers suggesting that the grass on both sides of the path were being used. The *Kenilworth Weekly News* opinion was that over a period the fees would produce a considerable sum for the council coffers.

It seems that the seasonal collection of charges for a trial period was deemed a success as in May 1959 the council decided to reintroduce the charge for Sunday parking 'in the allotted area in the Abbey Fields' and the Park Keeper, perhaps following complaints, was to ensure that no nuisance was caused during church services. The next step was taken the following summer when the same charge was introduced for the August Bank Holiday Monday; the parking area was described as 'on the side of the entrance from Bridge Street', suggesting that for certain just the triangular area was in use. In 1959 the car park fees collected amounted to

£81; the following year it was a remarkably similar £80, equivalent to about 1,600 cars.

By the end of the 1960 parking season, the wooden entrance gates from Bridge Street were beyond repair and were replaced with tubular ones, the width was increased by 18ins to 10ft 6ins. Not surprisingly, attracting cars to the Abbey Fields caused problems, such as parking in other places either to avoid the charge or when the attendant was not around. By July 1961, the parking of cars in places *'other than on the triangular piece of land... has become a nuisance and injurious to the amenities. They venture well away from the triangle into parts of the park where all forms of transport, including bicycles and horses, are banned'*. A further problem was that it had been found 'impossible to engage an attendant to be there at weekends to control parking and collect fees', and so fees were dropped for the remainder of the season. The situation was reviewed in September, the first outcome being the construction of a gate and fence to stop indiscriminate parking, but the wider questions of car parking were producing a debate.

At this time the question of parking at the Castle was also being discussed; the preferred area there at the Brays was opposed by many as it would require the felling of 14 trees and produce a dangerous junction, *'the* (Castle Road) *sharp bend is known locally as crash corner'*, and so alternative sites were being sought and the Abbey Fields was the prime choice, particularly when combined with its own parking needs. Three suggestions were put forward in September 1961: a car park in the Oxpen Meadow with an entrance from near the ford that would provide a space for 100 cars specifically for the Castle; fronting onto the 'quiet and unclassified' Forrest Road for Abbey Fields users only; and alongside the swimming pool with a new access road being built from Abbey Hill. The Oxpen Meadow option for the Castle was immediately dismissed, *'the council are not in favour of losing any part of the Abbey Fields to a car park'*, particularly as the Ministry of Works who had the responsibility for the Castle should provide their own parking (and who did open a car park at the Brays by 1963) but the suggestions were to be considered at a later date along with other proposals for the fields.

As was usual, the **tennis** courts and **putting** green opened to the public towards the end of April in 1958, but the opening in 1959 was again delayed by the dampness of the area. In January 1960 it was decided that the four hard tennis courts were in need of resurfacing and again En-tout-Cas were contracted. They pointed out that the four courts took up the space of five and with a little rearrangement the extra court could be fitted in, and indeed that is what happened in time for the season's opening, giving the layout that exists today. Later in the year 240yds of 9ft high chain-link fencing was put around the courts; the fencing used was the modern plastic coated variety, and came with the recommendation that it had been in use at Stoke on Trent for several years, with apparently, 'Stoke being the best district for trying out anything of this nature'. Tennis courts were available on weekdays from 9 a.m. to 1 p.m. and 2 to 9 p.m., Sundays from 8 to 10.30 a.m. and 2 to 9 p.m. The cost was 3s an hour for doubles, 2s an hour for singles, and 1s an hour for children up to 16 years old. A new telephone system for booking was introduced and although this initially caused problems they were soon eradicated. In May 1961, after a particularly wet spell that left the area boggy, paving slabs were laid to the Pavilion from the nearby path. That same wet spell in early April had flooded the putting green, now between the courts and the brook, to a depth of four inches and it was some weeks until it was again playable. A round cost 6d.

The receipts for 1961 to the end of September were: swimming £1,810 (up from £1,746 in 1960), tennis £136 (£122), and putting £74 (£96).

The pre-war 'rustic bridge' across the brook near to Bridge Street was noted in 1947 to 'need replacing'; there is no record that it was, and no further reference to it can be found, and so the allowance of the **carnival** fair providers to park on the field alongside Rosemary Hill, created an annual problem as they were on the opposite bank of Finham Brook to their fair. In the late 1950s a temporary wooden **bridge** was built by the 'Carnival amusement providers' over the brook near to the Bridge Street bridge; it is likely that this was always the case after the demise of the 'rustic bridge' but just not recorded. In 1959 the temporary fair bridge was again installed and removed afterwards. In June 1960 the council again allowed the bridge to be installed but this time, after the fair was concluded, the operators gave the bridge to the Carnival Committee who in turn donated it to the council who agreed to take it on and maintain it. For public use, satisfactory side fences were required and gates to stop livestock crossing, and in September a gate was installed 'at the end of the little wooden bridge' with a stile at its side for pedestrians.

It was customary for the carnival procession to form up in Clinton Lane but the police were becoming concerned about the disruption and dangers to traffic along the main road, and so for the 1961 carnival, organisers asked the council if they could form up in the Oxpen Meadow; this they did but only for two years, in 1963 they moved to the new Brays car park at the Castle.

Swimming pool charges had stayed the same price for a decade since 1947. In good weather the pool was self-supporting, but in 'normal' or bad weather it ran at a loss and were thus chargeable on the rates; that was the council's view to justify price increases for 1958 despite an increase in takings the year before. The adults charge went up from 9d to 1s, children 3d to 6d, and on Sunday all swimmers prices rose from 1s to 1s 6d. There was a new charge of 1s for all swimmers after 7 p.m., and spectators remained at 6d. The club had the baths for £1 a session from 6.30 to 8.30 p.m. on Thursdays. With increased income, in readiness for the 1959 season the pool was painted throughout.

A probably early 1950s view of the swimming pool. To the left is the filtration house and original pool hedging from 1896; above the chute is the roof of the 1923 conveniences, and to the right is the flat roof of the refreshment kiosk. The changing rooms and entrance are built right up to the brook's edge, likely to be the reason for the still surviving wall along the brook. Note also the hedges and gates for the control of livestock (lower left), the remnant of the hedge across the centre, Clinton House top left, and the extensive grounds, Area C Plots 2 - 6, of Abbotsfield, itself top right

The swimming pool showing the terracing on the eastern side and a collection of buildings, including the 1923 conveniences, at the northern end. April 1953 *(HE, A53408)*

'They had a dip, while he had a swim' was a typically whimsical headline written by the *KWN* editor Charles Porter about the theft from a swimmer in June 1959, before continuing, *'A versatile place is Kenilworth's baths, it offers two sorts of easy dip, one into water and the other into people's pockets'*. The victim had returned to his cubical to find clothes and belongings had been strewn around, and the stolen items included a leather cigarette case of sentimental value. There were swarms of swimmers that Sunday

afternoon which had meant up to half a dozen sharing a cubicle. Overcrowding of the cubicles was regular but the string bags provided for clothes allowed the bathers to put them where they could keep an eye on them, and valuables could be left with the attendant who locked them in a drawer; however, cases of theft at the pool were reported but being minor *'were usually forgotten'*.

The problems in the changing areas instigated a review of the conditions at the pool and towards the end of 1959, the Parks Committee were preparing to submit proposals for improvements, and for new attractions elsewhere in the park; one likely addition was that of a clock, *'Children often stayed later than their parents instructed them to, because they did not know the time.'*

The proposed substantial improvements and developments, and their likely costs, were recorded at the 27th October 1959 council meeting. At the pool they were: resiting the main entrance away from the Iron Bridge, enlarging the terraces and changing facilities, £7,800; new public conveniences, £2,500; resiting and reconstructing the kiosk, £1,500; a sun terrace in conjunction with kiosk, £300; and a paddling pool to be constructed near to the terrace and connected to the filtration system, £900. Away from the pool plans were: forming a small lake by excavating to the required depth, £5,000; a footpath around the lake with seats and shelters, £4,000; constructing a carriageway approach from Abbey Hill with parking around the pool, £6,500; clean out the brook, and construct flower beds and a rockery, £500; and a miniature golf course between Abbey Hill and the brook (no costing listed).

The first five, the major work at the pool, were considered to be the first phase and rather optimistically it was hoped they could be ready for the start of the next season. The building work for the new kiosk and changing facilities had been designed to be outside the current pool's boundaries; this allowed for a future intended expansion of the pool itself and the possibility of the pool remaining open whilst some of the work was in progress. Footpaths needed to be rearranged and four trees felled, but these were to be replaced. The other developments were to happen when finances permitted. By March 1960, £10,000 *(£211,000)* had been allocated for the bath improvements; added to the list was tiling the sides and floor of the pool.

In September 1960, council surveyor and architect of the improvements, G A J Edmundson, submitted a detailed report to the council. The existing timber frame dressing accommodation at both ends was to be removed and the vacated plinths would provide extra terracing. The new cubicle block was to be on the eastern, bowling green, side and protrude into the fields an extra 30ft beyond the current pool boundary requiring the removal of the terracing; the building was to be 126ft by 23ft, incorporating a 34ft wide central hall with pay boxes and turnstiles, and included 24 cubicles each for men and women with 176 lockers, with an additional 96 lockers in an area without cubicles; its roof was to be used as a replacement for the terrace sun bathing area. All bathers would be provided with a locker key which was then returned to the attendant, the bathers were then given a numbered disc on a string; the lockers were positioned so as to be visible to the key attendant. Space was allowed for a further 12 cubicles each for men and women in the future.

The improved refreshment kiosk would be a matching brick building 38ft by 24ft including the shop, store and kitchen, and to cost £2,300 in addition to the above. The kiosk was at the churchyard end, near the corner with the new changing facilities, and was to project 14ft beyond current buildings. It was to be arranged to give separate counters for the swimming pool and park. There was however no financial plan in place; the rebuilding work was not to appear in the council budget until the financial year of 1963-64.

Occasional necessary work in the fields often revealed aspects of its past such as the excavations for a new sewer *'in the proximity of the **ruins** that are still visible'* in June 1961: 'During the excavations for the new sewer through the park the contractors came across an old culvert belonging to the Priory that emptied into the old brook course underneath the tennis courts. This has caused all the flooding in the Pavilion. The culvert has now been broken open and a six inch drain has been laid and connected up with the main land drain that runs through the park. We hope this will solve the flooding problem.'

Another report said that the old culvert, *'oval in shape'*, was at an approximate right-angle to the new work at a depth of about 7ft and headed in the direction of the public conveniences; E Carey-Hill suspected it may have been a drain from the Abbey kitchens to the brook, the course of which at the time of the Priory passed through what was now the swimming pool. At a depth of about 11ft, a brick structure was broken into; its shape and blackening suggested it was a domestic oven. Unfortunately after being disturbed, and the end removed as it was on the course of the new sewer, it collapsed. A stone slab of about 2ft square was found and was thought to be the top of a column; it was put into storage.

There was by now a fence around the Tantara Gatehouse and the council tried again to convince the Ministry of Works that they should take over the ruins and restore them, but still the reply was that they had a vast financial commitment and could not take them on, even though they hoped one day they could. The area was instead given a thorough tidy.

In June 1960 and 1961, the Leamington Spa Dog Training Club held a 2-hour show in the field off Forrest Road. 1961 was a particularly bad year for **vandalism**; in March the goalposts were damaged, and in April six panes of glass were smashed in the Pavilion but after repairs, in September some were broken again along with several frames. There was trouble with 40 youths at the carnival, and the night before the agricultural show a tarpaulin was set on fire and the beer tent brought down. On 4th October, the 1934 **drinking fountain** was ripped from its stone pedestal and broken; it is thought it was never repaired.

Based upon the costing allowances from October 1959, at the December 1961 KUDC meeting, Surveyor G A J Edmundson submitted his final report expanding upon his proposals for the **future development** of the Abbey Fields, *'arrived at after a study that has been going on a long time'*. Improvements at the swimming pool (new changing rooms and kiosk) had already been decided upon but he now added a toddlers *'paddling pool adjoining the swimming pool adjacent to the filtration plant'*. He continued by suggesting a pavilion overlooking the swimming pool area and the Oxpen Meadow, which in turn should be converted into a lake and have a *'tarred limestone footpath bordered by shrubs and other foliage'*. Shelters could be added as could trees to the northern side of the lake to provide *'a pleasant background, and shield it from High Street'*. He suggested that the *'stream'* from Forrest Road could be piped in and the hedges removed to give a much larger expanse of usable ground. The next suggestion was for a miniature golf course and there was ample room *'on the south side of the stream between the swimming pool and bridge which could be provided with the usual hazards and be quite free of obstructions of any other attractions'*. Then came the main brook which needed to be properly graded after which stratified rock could be added to parts of the banks to help stabilise them and *'beautify the area'*. And finally, the public conveniences needed to be upgraded in conjunction with the swimming pool improvements. Such was the workload in looking after the Abbey Fields and its developments, for 1962 an extra £1,000 was allowed for labour costs.

Over the winter of 1961-62, the permanent flooding of the **Oxpen Meadow** was more seriously discussed. The recently formed (in May 1961) Kenilworth Society supported the scheme and suggested it was kept throughout the year for boating *etc* and Councillor Whiteman was amongst those who commented favourably, *'It would be a most welcome added amenity'*. Although in early 1962 the meadow was drained as normal, the council said that a scheme was to be prepared for permanent flooding for the following year. Quickly off the mark was a Mr Fulham who in February 1962 applied to operate a boat on the lake once it was made.

But then in the autumn of 1962, the Kenilworth Society returned with a new scheme, made in conjunction with members of the local ornithological society, for the Oxpen Meadow to become a wildfowl sanctuary, or *'high class duckpond'* as the *KWN* reported it. One of the society commented that boating pools are available all over the district and the boats do little for wildlife; Kenilworth should do the reverse and have a wildlife lake with no boats, a view contrary to that prevailing for the previous 80 years.

In February 1962, arrangements were made once more for the **grazing** rights in the fields; however, the grazing area was about to be reduced again due to the proposed **pitch & putt** course on the 'Rosemary Hill field and Abbey Hill field', that was included in the estimates for the coming financial year. Mr Hubbard paid a reduced rent of £175 for using the remaining 35 acres (probably the whole area west of the north-south path, see plan page 83), down from £250, with the agreement terminating on 25th March 1963. The entire question of grazing was to be reviewed the following year.

In April 1962 the pitch & putt course was approved and a suggested course was discussed at the 6th June meeting. Remarkably, the course opened just ten days later; a player of the time recalls that it was of 9 holes and covered only half of the south eastern, Abbey Hill, quadrant of the fields. It cost 1s 6d a round, including the loan of two clubs, and although no deposit was required for the loan of playing equipment it was insured against loss, and burglary; the tennis and putting green attendant in the Pavilion had the course added to his responsibilities. The speed with which it was constructed was due to there being no excavations of any sort; tees were shown by numbered metal pointers in the ground, and greens were just neatly mowed, mostly circular, spaces. From the pavilion, players had to cross the Iron Bridge and turn left on to the course and play up the hill and back down twice to complete a round near the central hedge. It was said a more direct access from the putting green 'will soon be provided'. It was open from 9 a.m. to 1 p.m. then 2 till 9 p.m. on weekdays, but on Sundays the mid-day break started at 10.30 a.m. Every ball lost cost the loser 2s 6d, and in the first week only one was. *'The natural contours add to the interest and authenticity'* but several objections were raised to the course 'in its present position' and insurance cover was only given if 'all reasonable steps (are) taken to prevent balls being sliced or driven in the direction of public highways or private property'; there is no record of the course subsequently being altered.

Days after the course opened, the Parks Superintendent was laying out a clock-golf course that would cost 6d a round, but there is no further mention of this attraction.

Due to the pitch & putt course 'on the Abbey Hill field' occupying the usual spot, the question of parking cars for the agricultural show was raised in May 1962. The show was to be held on the Forrest Road and Memorial Fields as before, with the Abbey Hill area available as a parking area. Stock vehicles were permitted entrance only at Castle Road and then had to proceed by road to the Rosemary Hill field. The society were given permission to 'widen the bridge over the ditch in Abbey Fields', presumably the cattle bridge over the Luzley Brook that also linked the football pitches. Its new deck was of railway sleepers.

After the opening of the pitch & putt course, it would seem likely that **Punch** was moved to only occupy the field between the central dividing hedge and Rosemary Hill, but in July 1962 it was suggested in any case that the 'hedge between the two fields fronting Abbey Hill could be removed and the ditch filled with rubble and soil', and it was, immediately, but established trees were left. This was the boundary of the pitch & putt course (was an extension to 18 holes being considered?) but was an obvious move in any case to open up that area of the fields now that grazing there had more or less ended. Towards the end of the year the question was raised as to renovating the pitch & putt greens and it was suggested the course could be made more interesting by the introduction of bunkers, but 'an opinion was expressed that forming bunkers on this course is not desirable'; one reason being given was that they would interfere with tobogganing.

On 15th September 1962, the *KWN* published a photograph of a frail looking Punch in his Abbey Fields home; the only horse allowed for some years, he now had a permanent if unlikely companion, a *'small red cow'* even though this area was supposedly closed for cattle grazing. With his age catching up with him, 25-year-old Punch was offered a new home in the town to see out his last days, but the *'town pet'* who was *'one of the leading residents of Kenilworth'* was unfit to travel; the veterinary surgeon that had treated him for years advised that he was put down, and he was in the first week of October 1962. His passing was marked in the pages of the *KWN* as a front page news item, an editorial, and a poem. He was the last of countless horses to call the fields their home.

Punch and the *'small red cow'* in the Rosemary Hill field *(SaT)*

At the March 1963 council meeting, 'The question of allotting **grazing rights** in the Abbey Fields for the year 1963/64 was considered. No provision had been made in the rate estimates for 1963/64 for any income from this source', and it was resolved that 'no arrangements be made for grazing rights to be let in the year 1963/64'. With the termination of the agreement with Mr Hubbard on 25th March 1963, after centuries of use as pastureland for animals, grazing was finally brought to an end; Punch's passing had ended the council's own necessity, and his bovine friend was amongst the last animals to graze the fields.

The original retention of grazing in 1884 was to use the income for the repayment of loans; in the 20th century it was to be the potential loss of income added to the necessary increase in expenditure in having to cut the grass that ensured grazing continued. The loan repayments ended during the second World War but wartime necessities demanded the fields continued in use for food production, but why grazing was not ended soon after remains unexplained, although the useful income is the most likely reason. How fitting that problems with one recreational facility (cowpats on football pitches) and the introduction of another (pitch & putt) that had become popular in the later Victorian years, had contributed to the entire Abbey Fields at last becoming solely a park, 79 years after they were purchased for that purpose. Did the modern council know of the 1889 approval by the Local Government Board in Whitehall that the fields could be let for grazing only until it was 'advantageous to turn them into a park'?

Soon after the start of the new 1962-63 season, the **football** changing rooms were wrecked by vandals, or as the *KWN* reported, were *'raided by rotters on the rampage... as part of their bout of hooliganism'*. The Kenilworth FC portion (formerly the RNA club) had its windows smashed after the heavy covers were torn off, whilst next door the Legion club's changing rooms were ransacked and broken up, a paraffin heater smashed, lining torn from the walls, and empty beer bottles left strewn around. It was again the football clubs that carried out the repairs, although the council patched the roof several times. No equipment could be left in the rooms for fear of theft and so anything required had to be taken to the park for each match.

Inside it was damp and following more complaints from visiting clubs, Kenilworth FC put up fresh plaster board and *'sinks were installed, tables and other odds and ends were scrounged, matting obtained to put on the concrete with which the club members had covered the original cobbles, Tilley lamps installed for lighting and heating, and various ways of brewing tea (including primus stove) improvised.'*

Due to the extraordinary weather of the 1962-63 winter, there was a backlog of local football matches and the KUDC allowed the use of all football pitches on a Sunday for the first time; they stressed it was just to clear the backlog and the season was extended to 19th May. In the summer of 1963, a new football club, Abbey Rangers, was formed and joined the Leamington & District Football League. As many of its players were involved on Saturdays with employment or school teams, they asked if they could use an Abbey Field pitch on Sunday afternoons for an entire season, and this was granted; they were allocated the Forrest Road pitch and also allowed to use the changing facilities at the swimming pool.

After the winter break, the **putting** green re-opened in May 1963 (but soon closed again after rain made it unplayable) but the re-opening of the pitch & putt course was delayed some weeks as tobogganing had left little grass in some areas that had subsequently become muddy. The number of pitch & putt course users dropped when the weather was poor, but on a good day as many as 90 played the course, over a season more than compensating for the loss of income from grazing rights. Annually for a week in July, known from 1963, the carnival had exclusive use of the course for a competition.

When pools of water remained in the **Oxpen Meadow** in May 1963, it was once again decided to investigate its drainage. Perhaps surprisingly, considering how often it had been investigated and attempted, it was discovered that it was not possible to carry out any sustainable drainage scheme owing to the fact that the level of the adjoining brook into which drains had to connect was higher than the meadow. However, the water that had accumulated in several areas the previous few months had dried by evaporation and there was no nuisance from it. In April 1965, the 1961 proposals to make a lake with footpaths alongside appeared as a short-term policy for the KUDC; Mr Fulham again quickly applied to have a boat for hire once it was made, and equally quickly was again refused.

Whilst the question of the Oxpen Meadow was under discussion in May 1965, the Ministry of Works, who were carrying out extensive work at the Castle, were contacted about the possibility of somehow connecting the attractions of the Castle and Abbey Fields. In replying, the Ministry revealed that they had a long-term plan to reinstate first the water defences of the Castle and then at least one of the Abbey ponds, that which was where the Oxpen Meadow now was, and at no charge to the KUDC. However, they did stress that this would be some years away as they were heavily committed to the repairs at the Castle. The following year the KUDC intended to have the cost of creating a lake for consideration in the year's budget.

A variety of events continued to be held in the park. In 1963 the Kenilworth detachment of the Army Cadet Force held a drill and demonstration at the end of May, the Riley Register (a club for owners of pre-war Riley cars) held a national rally on 7th July, and the Massey Ferguson Car Driving Club held a safe driving competition in aid of the Freedom from Hunger campaign. Kenilworth **Round Table** held what became an annual Sports Day; they did not fence off any area but simply marked out a running track.

Perhaps the most interesting event at this time was the visit on 1st and 2nd of November 1963 of Bob Fossett's **Circus**; this was its 150th anniversary, and its first ever tour had started in Kenilworth. After it was founded in 1813, the town was its over-winter home and the circus set out from Kenilworth on its journeys. In 1813, the travelling show was hauled around the country by teams of 6 or 8 horses, and eventually up to 80 horses were used solely for this purpose. It was booked to appear on the rough ground at the rear of the tannery on 1st & 2nd April but heavy frosts were followed by rain during the time heavy vehicles involved in the tannery demolition were traversing the field; the site became flooded and the 3,500 seat big top could not be raised and the circus had to postpone its visit. Due to existing bookings around the country, the circus could not arrange a replacement visit to Kenilworth until November, so instead of starting the tour from Kenilworth as it had 150 years before, it was decided to end the anniversary tour in the town; even to accommodate that, two days had to be dropped from its planned week-long stay in Birmingham. The performance in the Abbey Fields was televised as it was claimed to be the country's oldest circus and was worthy of celebration. Amongst the many trapeze and acrobatic acts, high-wire walkers and the world's smallest strongman, were animal performances which included chimpanzees, lions, leopards, pumas, jaguars, baby elephants, camels, Welsh ponies, Arab stallions, zebras, and 'sacred donkeys'.

In 1962, the surface of the **tennis** courts was replaced with a 'bituminous material' and the maintenance contract with En-tout-Cas was cancelled. The headmistress at Abbotsford School asked if the new surface was suitable to be used for netball; enquires had to be made.

Beginning in November 1962, the lamps in the park were converted from gas to electricity. In December 1963, East Midlands Electricity offered to supply free power to lighting columns near the kiosk and Pavilion provided the council donated £50 for putting in the cables, which they did. The following year the gas lighting inside the Pavilion was replaced by electric.

By late 1963, 50 years after they built the facility out of their own funds, the **Bowling Club** had condensed to only twelve members, and in October an agreement was reached whereby the KUDC finally took over the maintenance and control of the green, and ownership of all the equipment. The club members however were still allowed free use of the green, and allowed to use lockers in the Pavilion for their own woods. Charges for the public playing bowls under the KUDC were at the Club price of 9d an hour, a reduction on earlier charges, perhaps reduced to attract customers. Over the winter of 1965/66, extra drainage was installed for the green and putting green.

The area around the **War Memorial** needed tidying up and there was also a problem of **cars** gaining entrance to the park at that point. In September 1963 the Parks Superintendant submitted a plan for improvements to the area and this was implemented; a length of fence behind the memorial was removed as was a length of hedge, and a row of posts was installed to stop the cars. Nearby, spring bulbs (in preference to the originally suggested flower beds) were planted along the Abbey Hill border. Six seats were purchased for the Abbey Hill 'frontage' in 1965.

From the end of 1963, the area from Forrest Road to the swimming pool received attention. First it was suggested that the hedge should be removed, but this was decided against as it would mean filling in the adjacent ditch. Then, with the hope of eventually improving the drainage of the **football pitches**, soil tipping and levelling alongside Luzley Brook was begun; a year later soil had been dumped at the side of the path but the path itself was damaged by the work necessitating repairs. The source of the soil is not known but there were many house-building projects across the town at that time.

In September 1963, a representative of Dr Barnardos Homes asked if it was possible to mark the organisation's centenary by laying out a flower bed in the park; the council replied that the Abbey Fields was 'not a suitable place for a flower bed' but a tree could be planted instead.

In September 1964, arrangements for the next three carnivals were agreed; the request was due to the carnival caterers wishing to have a three year contract.

The council had been in contact with the Ministry of Works suggesting something ought to be done to improve the appearance of the Tantara Gatehouse and other **Abbey ruins** which had become 'very tatty' in appearance. In January 1963 one councillor suggested that the Barn could become a café, or perhaps have some other use. All were agreed that the ruins were worth preserving but the Ministry again stated that they could not take the Abbey ruins under their guardianship due to their many other commitments, but were willing to advise. After an on-site meeting they recommended it would be wise to fence the Gatehouse, remove ivy from the Barn and to cover over the visible excavated remains with soil and grass leaving only the *'upstanding remains protruding above ground level'*, taking care not to damage them.

In April 1963, a history group was formed within the two-year-old **Kenilworth Society** (KS) with

Rev J A Thomson at its head; in July he said that the decision to fill in and cover the remains was not the best thing to do and he wished the site could be dealt with in a *'more ambitious way'*. The council said the only alternative would be *'excavation, consolidation, preservation, and subsequent maintenance, and would thus be expensive'*. The History Group had volunteers who would clear away the weeds as a first step even though it would have to be immediately followed with proper treatment of the stone; deterioration would be unavoidable if the stonework was exposed and not consolidated. Also the Gatehouse required work as it was in a dangerous condition and needed to be fenced off with notices. The council would be guided by the Ministry, but it was pointed out by the clerk that the council did not own the land the Gatehouse stood on. (*Note:* The plan included with the conveyance, WDC 131 reproduced on page 28, clearly shows that the land on which the Gatehouse stands *was* included; perhaps the clerk intended to refer to the land immediately around the Gatehouse.)

The History Group began work by clearing the undergrowth around the Chapter House wall, and were given permission to catalogue all the relics that had been collected in the Gatehouse and Barn. In October 1964 the group, numbering 34, broke away from the KS to form the **Kenilworth Historical Society** (KHS); they successfully filled the void left by the wartime demise of the Friends of the Abbey and its Surrounds, almost a quarter of a century before.

That summer, a Ministry spokesman dropped in at the Abbey Fields whilst working at the Castle and reported that the tidying had shown a great improvement, but what would happen next was dependant upon funds; if there were none then the current work must be maintained, if some became available he would arrange a site meeting. He continued, the grass needed to be kept cut, the railings around the ruins needed repair, and the Gatehouse was now beyond 'first aid' and needed proper conservation costing about £2,500, but the Ministry had no funds and wouldn't until at least 1968. The spokesman suggested the County Council may partially fund the work but the KUDC would have to find about half. The council decided to leave the entire question in abeyance 'until such times as the Ministry reconsider their decision not to accept the guardianship of the whole of the ruins', but in December the Ministry again reiterated that they could not take guardianship of all of the Abbey; they had over 700 monuments in their care, many of which needed urgent repairs, but their funds were limited and the Kenilworth remains were 'not in that high category.'

The **car park** was not without its problems. In March 1963 at the end of a particularly bad winter, there was much damage when the ground was wet for several months and part of it was closed to allow it to dry out. In June 1965 there were complaints of cars causing a nuisance when parked directly adjacent to the path to the church and alongside the church wall itself; unnecessary noise caused by those parking was disturbing church services. It was decided to contain the parking and install a low post and chain fence across the end of the area 16 yards from the church. A notice was also put up asking parkers to be more respectful of those at church.

Price increases were introduced at the **kiosk** for the 1962 season. Tea went up from 4d to 5d, Bovril 5d to 6d, minerals 7d to 8d, and coffee was now 5d, sandwiches 7d or 8d, hot dogs 7d, but still drinks remained at 7d. Ice cream price increases saw briquettes rise from 4d to 5d, dairy cones and vanilla tubs from 6d to 7d, splits 6d to 7d, and Snowfruite and Snocreme 3d to 3½d. It seems the kiosk facilities had become inadequate and it was again suggested in early 1963 that as a temporary measure the Barn could be utilised as an extra outlet, but in March the financial estimates for the forthcoming year included the cost of repaying a loan to be raised for the new pool buildings and this would include a purpose built kiosk.

In September 1963, with the financial go-ahead approved, final plans based upon those from September 1960 were prepared for improving the **swimming pool** area including the pool's surrounds, changing facilities, a turnstile entrance with pay offices either side, ladies and gents changing facilities, lockers and footbath entrance to the pool, changing facilities for winter sports, toilets, sunbathing deck on the roof, and an enlarged catering kiosk with a storeroom, kitchen, shop and counters both inside the pool and out. The estimate was £15,000 for the pool's improvement, and £2,500 for the kiosk. All were approved with precise costing to be carried out by quantity surveyors. In January 1964 tenders were invited for the work, although construction would have to wait until the end of the approaching season.

On 21st April 1964 the lowest tender for the construction of the kiosk, that by Kenilworth builders Hurst & Aitken for £3,567 15s 8d and well above the estimate, was signed but the estimates for the rest of the work were taking longer. It was hoped that work on the kiosk could start straight away alongside the existing kiosk but it was delayed as two trees needed felling; it was suggested that as two others needed felling for the later work that they should be sub-contracted together, and they were. Work finally started on the kiosk on 1st October.

On 15th September the tenders were opened for the main building work, and again it was Hurst & Aitken who had the lowest, at £23,854 *(£440,000)*; again, well above the original estimate. The agreed dates for completion of the work were 9th April 1965 for the kiosk and 28th May 1965 for the changing rooms. A late alteration to the plans saw the storeroom at the kiosk converted for use as a first aid room and equipment was purchased. The loan for construction was approved and was to be taken over 20 years. On 26th September 1964, the 1935 lido closed for the last time; presumably work started soon after.

The terracing has been removed and foundations dug for the new changing rooms; between the pool and the footings for the new buildings is the space created for a future enlargement. The encroachment into the park on the left necessitated the diversion of the footpath. At the far end are the originally thatched timber-framed changing rooms built in 1935, its plinth and the terrace it sat on were left and still survive; to its left at the end of the fence was the original entrance near the Iron Bridge *(JHD, KL)*

With work underway, in December 1964 the swimming club wrote saying they were disappointed the improvements did not include heating or covering the pool; the council's response was what one would expect: it was 'not possible to carry out all desirable improvements at the present time for financial reasons', but the council was anxious to make the pool 'as attractive as possible' and developments must be 'phased over a number of years'. It was clear that they thought of this as the start of a long-term plan to provide a heated, covered pool; they had looked into heating the pool by electricity, it would need a mains cable and substation at a cost £4,707, and electricity consumption at £570 a year. Alternative methods of heating were to be explored and reported later.

Two-tier terracing was provided either side of the cascade and required the clearing of the hedges, the last remnant of the original pool. It isn't known for certain when this was built; although during this rebuild is most likely, it is not specifically mentioned in reports.

The north-eastern corner of the new facilities. The plinth of the old changing rooms survived, left, as did the chute, 5-stage diving boards and the spring board; stairs lead to the sunbathing deck on the roof, that replaced the 1935 terracing *(ST)*

A view from the new roof sunbathing deck, showing the cascade with its new terracing, and the plinth left by the demolition of the 1935 changing rooms. On the hill can be seen a set of goalposts on the War Memorial pitch *(FF)*

The prices at the swimming pool had not been altered since 1958; new charges were introduced to coincide with the re-opening after the alterations. Child entrance remained at 6d but an adult swim doubled from 1s to 2s, as did the price for all swimmers after 7 p.m.; Sundays for all went up from 1s 6d to 2s 6d, and the cost for schools increased from 2d to 6d a child. The kiosk was ready to open at Easter 1965; exactly when the pool re-opened has not been discovered but until August, the *'high class changing facilities attracted few customers due to the goose-pimply conditions'*, but then the crowds began to flock as in the past and in particular children on their holidays from school. The new kiosk too had great patronage but it had until this point apparently operated without a cash register; two were decided upon but only one was ordered due to the cost, £154 each. The kiosk was open at weekends as winter approached but then was closed, re-opening at Weekends from Easter then daily from the Whitsun weekend.

The council decided it was time to assemble both short and long term **policies** for the development of the park and in July 1964 these suggestions were listed: a) heating the swimming pool's water, b) a children's paddling pool at the baths, c) chairs and tables adjacent to the kiosk, d) renovation of the exterior of the old barn to make it look more attractive, e) provision of a lake in the Oxpen Meadow and a central car park (the car park was deleted in a later council minute), f) drainage of marshland to bring it to proper use, g) improving the brook course from the ford to the swimming pool with a view to making it a more attractive feature. This roused the Kenilworth Society who conceded that 'as some development is inevitable' they would submit their own suggestions; the council replied saying they would be considered when the time came.

The facilities, **tennis**, **mini-golf**, and **bowling**, closed on Sunday's between 10.30 a.m. and 2.00 p.m., but as from the start of the 1965 season the break was reduced to between 1 and 2 p.m., and not closing until 9 p.m. The swimming pool had similar times, but an extra half-hour break and closure could be made in the evening if it was becoming overcrowded, to allow for new entrants.

As from the summer of 1965, all **football** teams were allowed to use the new changing facilities and the cost of using them and a pitch was £1 per match; Abbey Rangers were now in their third season.

In December 1965 it was noted that A E Dencer, the last surviving original member of the Bowls Club Committee, had left the town (he had been employed as Secretary of the Water Company at the time of the 1913 typhoid outbreak) leaving E Shrimpton as the last original member. The crown green produced little revenue for the KUDC; a December 1966 suggestion that a flat green would be more popular was turned down on the proposed cost of £1,498 plus £600 if Cumberland turf was used; the alternative of an additional new green, despite there being no obvious site to have it, would cost about £3,000. Crown green bowling was described as 'more sporting'.

An idyllic scene; a gentle game of bowls and a more energetic game of tennis as seen from the new sunbathing roof of the swimming pool. The putting green is to the right. The thatch on the pavilion was replaced in 1960

In January 1966 it was the turn of the Parents Committee of Kenilworth Abbey High School to plead for the swimming pool water to be heated and the pool covered, so that schoolchildren could receive proper tuition all year round. The town clerk replied saying that it 'would be a good thing' but 'quite expensive', and as the council had 'other priorities' and 'economic difficulties', it would not be possible 'in the near future'.

The way in which the town was developing had led to calls in the summer of 1963 for a specific use

An early 1966 view from near High Street showing the Oxpen Meadow in flood, and part of the original Plot 6 garden ground of Abbotsfield. The cow-path across the land donated by Gertrude Evans in 1938 splits with one part entering the Oxpen Meadow at the former field boundary, the other part heading towards the play area *(JHD, KL)*

of the Abbey Fields for **cycling**. Many children of the new estates in the Malthouse Lane area attended the new Clinton School on the Oaks Estate, and it was suggested that a cycling route across the Abbey Fields should be tried; starting opposite Malthouse Lane, down the rough cow-path created by use since Gertrude Evans donated the land, on to the children's play area, and then following the path to Forrest Road to give the children access to Brookside Avenue. It would be restricted to use by schoolchildren, and would avoid parents having to *'risk their children's necks on the Castle Road route notorious for its daft drivers'*. (That year, an attempt to convert Ford House into a hotel failed due to traffic concerns.) Despite the involvement of the Kenilworth and County councils, as far as is known not even an experiment was tried.

Then in January 1966, a Mr Drinkwater of Berkeley Road wrote to the council saying an increasing number of children from the Clinton Lane and Malthouse Lane area went to the Priorsfield and St Nicholas schools and suggested that the same diagonal path from opposite Malthouse Lane to near the children's play area should be properly made up; it was still just a worn trackway. The council agreed, £300 was allocated to tarmac the narrow path, not to the play area but to near the Tantara Gatehouse, the path diverting along the course of a former field boundary. This completed the current layout of hard surface Abbey Fields paths.

It was suggested that the diagonal path from Bridge Street to Abbey Hill should be lit; it was 370yds long and saved walking an additional 130yds along the roads but the cost and lack of electricity supply prevented it. To light the entire Abbey Fields paths satisfactorily would cost £4,000 and require 43 lamps.

A year after the new swimming pool buildings opened, the inadequacies of the adjacent **public conveniences** built in 1923 were discussed; they were subjected to regular bouts of vandalism and by the autumn of 1967 many of the fittings were in need of replacement. A scheme was drawn up and provision for new conveniences costing £8,500 was made in the 1968/69 budget, as was more drainage of the tennis courts and putting green for £1,100.

A **tree planting** programme was to be implemented over a number of years and to this end the County Land Agent was asked to prepare a report which he submitted in September 1965. The report had no mention of costs, as it would be spread over time and costs would rise, but £1,000 was to be allowed based upon 'current cost of young trees, labour, stakes, and replanting due to vandalism'. The *Kenilworth Weekly News* of 1st October 1965 reported about the Abbey Fields, *'There are several schools of thought as to how they should be treated, or left alone'*, before then outlining the proposed tree-planting scheme laid out by the County Land Agent on behalf of Kenilworth's General Purposes Committee. It suggested *'the choice of exotic foreign species should be discouraged to retain the effect of parkland rather than pleasure gardens. Heavier tree growth, with undergrowth to provide sanctuaries, may help to encourage more birds and wildlife. The main stream and its tributary are pleasant to walk in the summer and should attract more* *bird life if small adjoining areas are planted for places of sanctuary'*. Small sanctuaries along the brook *'at intervals'* should be created; he suggested weeping willow, ash, beech and liquidambar, and that when these were established the existing alder and *'erect'* willow should be felled. The plan also showed Scots pine along the Gertrude Evans border with High Street, conifers around the swimming pool, Indian horse chestnut along the path from Bridge Street, and horse chestnut round the entire southern boundary from Bridge Street to Borrowell Lane.

In response, the 24th December 1965 *KWN* printed the sketched plan from the Kenilworth Society dated 4th April 1964 that they had earlier submitted to the council *'in view of the rumours about possible development of the Abbey Fields'*; they believed the real amenity of the fields was its *'value as a pleasant and unspoiled open space'*. The plan showed clumps of trees around the edges of the fields *'arranged not to interrupt views from neighbouring houses or to cut up the main open spaces'*, a lake not to be used for boating, gardens near the swimming pool on the south side of the brook, a car park off Castle Road, and twenty feet wide canals replacing the Luzley Brook.

As in the past, the suggestion of planting trees along the southern boundary of the fields brought many protests; in January 1966 a petition was submitted signed by most of the residents of Abbey Hill, Abbey End, Rosemary Hill and Forrest Road saying that planting should be limited to replacing decaying trees and screening the swimming baths. The council resolution passed exactly that, and Jack Drew was to provide a report at a later meeting.

The *Kenilworth Weekly News* of 11th June 1965, had a feature on the soon to be demolished barn changing rooms once shared by Kenilworth FC and the British Legion, now out of use due to footballers being allowed to change in the new facilities at the **swimming pool**. The new changing premises were *'as up to date as their predecessors were unacceptably out of date. The old brick structures hold many memories, but the clubs concerned had few if any pangs at closing the doors for the last time'*. Despite the vandalism risks, the building had continued in use as a store but towards the end of the 1965-66 season, the clubs were asked to move their belongings somewhere else to allow demolition; the dilapidated building was not demolished until 1968.

In June 1966, the Working Men's Club applied to use the War Memorial pitch on Sundays; they already used it on Saturdays. The request was declined as the KUDC had to 'manage the fields in the best interests of the town as a whole. More extensive use of football pitches on Sundays could not be allowed'; Sunday playing was restricted to the pitch by Forrest Road. A similar request in December from the Kenilworth & District Boys Football League received the same answer. However, in 1966 the Leamington & District Sunday League was formed and the playing of Sunday football matches in the Abbey Fields became the norm; in a review of **byelaws**, that which prevented the Sunday playing of football and games other than in designated areas was deleted in December 1966.

In the summer of 1966, Jack Drew laid out 'various **cricket** strips' in the Forrest Road area, but had to stop boys playing cricket between Bridge Street and the tennis courts. This resulted in a request for clarification on the playing of cricket in the fields. 'It is essential that the playing of cricket with hard or semi hard balls should be confined to certain areas of the fields so the game could be played without giving rise any undue danger or inconvenience to other users of the fields'. Jack Drew did his best to cut the grass short frequently but could not 'carry out anything like the maintenance that would be necessary to ensure a good playing surface'. This is the first reference to 'permanent' cricket facilities being provided in some form, some 80 years or more after a cricket ground was first promised.

With the ending of grazing, the **agricultural show** became the only time cattle were allowed into the fields. The show in 1966 attracted 256 animals for the estimated crowd of 10,000 to enjoy. Flower, bird and dog shows were still included, and for further entertainment, *'Land-Rover Polo'*. The show was still on August Bank Holiday Monday despite that date having moved to the end of the month in 1965; the organisers thus had only days to clear and repair the field so it could be prepared ready for football matches the following weekend. In December 1967, iron fencing alongside the 'ditch with thick mud at the bottom' from Forrest Road to the swimming pool was removed.

The remaining exposed **ruins** and deteriorating condition of the Tantara Gatehouse continued to cause concern; its 18th century thatch had long gone exposing the clay seal and over time this had encouraged growth of bushes and even trees which in turn created fissures in the stonework allowing water in, and some parts were so badly affected that stones were loose and likely to fall. The repairs needed were threefold; clearance of foliage, repairing the stonework, and sealing the top. In June 1966 the council contacted the Kenilworth Historical Society to discover if they intended to carry out any more work, but their reply was

The fenced overgrown Abbey ruins with the path to the swimming pool and, top right, the Chapter House wall *(KHAS)*

that proper maintenance work was required, and the exposed excavated ruins should be covered over. A second opinion obtained from the ministry told them exactly the same, with the addition that removing the vegetation from the top of the Gatehouse was vital but then it would need 'capping'; the structure was so unsound the capping itself could be enough to bring parts of it down. The only solution was a full restoration for which it would be necessary to remove all the vegetation, followed by the 'rubble to be removed from inside the walls, the walls washed out and the rubble replaced, pointing, grouting, work on the vault, the main rib taken out and reset, much roofing work and a lot done inside the premises', at a minimum cost of £7,000. With no money available for the work, a fence for the safety of the public was hastily erected around it and the footpath diverted.

Towards the end of 1967, the fenced-off exposed but overgrown ruins around the Chapter House that extended to the choir and eastern end of the Abbey church, were finally covered with soil for their protection; some landscaping followed and the area was re-seeded the following spring. This created a second terrace that can still be seen as quite distinct from the flatter one created in 1928, and gives a good indication as to the area of ruins that had been uncovered for about 45 years.

In early 1963, the Kenilworth Aeromodelling Club, comprising almost exclusively male teenagers, asked the council if they could use the Hyde Road air raid shelter as a clubroom to store their models and equipment; they were turned down, but the council had to re-contact them in the following weeks as the flying of their powered models in the Abbey Fields was causing a noise nuisance to residents of Bridge Street. As a councillor was president of the club, it was hoped the problem could be sorted amicably, and a letter was written asking the boys to ensure the noise did not become a nuisance. The club replied apologising and hoping that their activities would not be suspended.

In early 1967, the council were trying to alter their **bye-laws** to ban the flying of powered model aircraft in the fields, but the Ministry of Health asked that first they investigate allocating an area of the fields specifically for the hobby; the council replied that it would be impractical due to the use in general of the whole fields being 'Public Walks and Pleasure Grounds' but should another model aero club be formed at some time in the future they would endeavour to find somewhere to accommodate them, implying the earlier club was now defunct. The bye-law was added later that year.

The council's provision of **sports facilities** was often discussed. In October 1966, the Kenilworth Sports Advisory Committee (KSAC), composed of representatives of various sports organisations and schools, prepared a report for the council about the existing and required accommodation for local sports teams. Those that had no ground of their own needed 29 acres to provide 6 football pitches for 12 teams, and

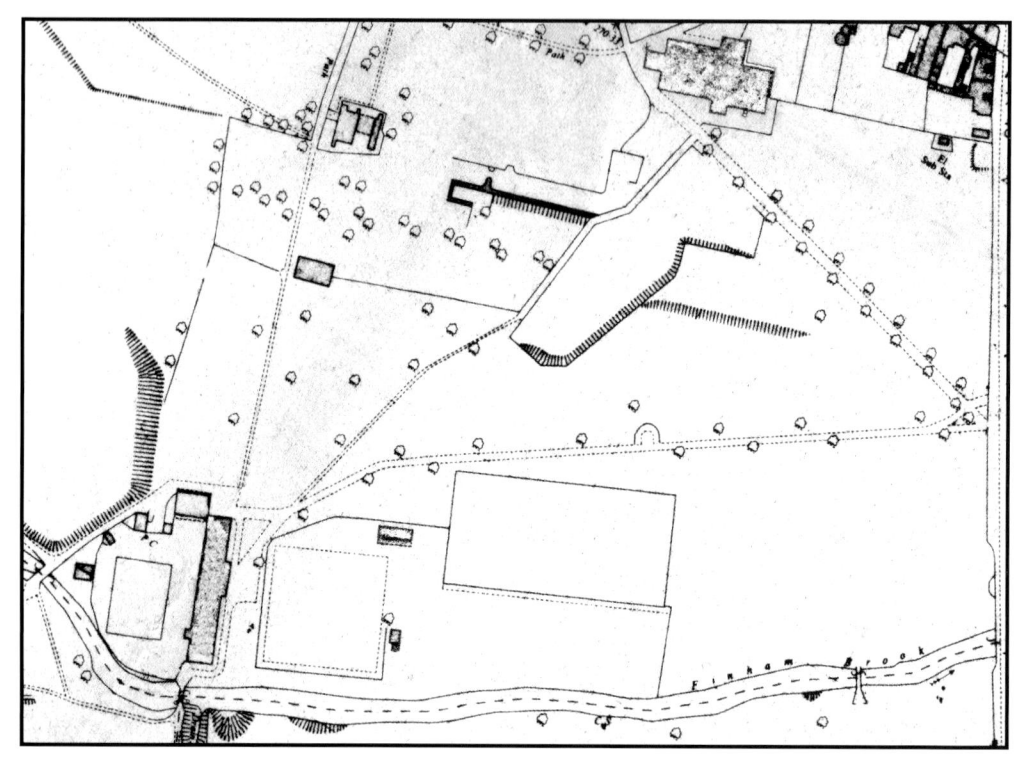

The swimming pool area greatly extended into the park with the building of the new changing facilities and kiosk, and the pathways needed to be rearranged. The covering of the Abbey ruins has produced a second terrace *(OS, 1966)*

a rugby pitch, and other facilities such as parking areas. The Abbey Fields were *'unsatisfactory as playing fields... and ought to revert to and remain as an open space for use of the general public'*. The report also suggested that swimming provision was *'not quite adequate'*, public provision for tennis was *'ample'*, and cricket and hockey were *'well catered for on private grounds.'*

The council's subsequent investigations revealed two areas where such sporting facilities could be provided; one to the south of the town, thought to be part of the Thickthorn estate, was not immediately obtainable and had gradient and access problems, but that south of the Castle on Castle Farm was 'readily available' and had an acceptable gradient. Until the 1930s it had been the home of Kenilworth Golf Club. A bonus was that there were two short stub roads already built (for intended later housing estates) at the end of John O'Gaunt Road and off Fishponds Road that could provide access. The total cost for 29 acres plus several more for areas not used by pitches was estimated at about £95,000, but grants availability was said to be 'somewhat remote'. Included in the same financial budget was a town Assembly Hall for £75,000, and both were put on the list of proposals that were 'shelved'. At this time the council was criticised for having a total of £1½ million in loan debts of which only £4,732 was for all its parks.

With progress on relocating the Abbey Fields sports facilities seemingly unlikely, the KSAC recalled an earlier idea and suggested to the KUDC that *'the swamp'* should be filled with industrial rubble then surfaced to provide sports facilities perhaps with a running track around it. *'In hot weather it emits a stink, and for hoards of flies and creepy crawlies it provides a maternity ground'*. There were also letters from residents opposed to such a scheme, and a reference back to a council minute in 1965 saying the Abbey Fields should retain its semi-rural state save for the making of a lake. The KSAC were told that there would be no further areas set aside for sports facilities in the park and in November 1968 the *KWN* reported that attempts to turn the marshy Oxpen Meadow into a sports field were *'bogged down'*; the Parks Committee confirmed *'The Abbey Fields will remain in their semi-rural state and that no further areas shall be set aside for sports'* but there was increasing pressure to provide new sports pitches.

Starting in 1967 the **Carnival** held a six-a-side football competition and was granted free use on two Saturdays of initially one pitch 'on the northern side of the footpath (from) the Forrest Road pitch', but later two pitches. Use of the fields for the usual carnival attractions were continued to be agreed in batches of three years; 1968-1970 was granted in December 1967. The carnival organisers continued to use the pitch

& putt course for a week-long competition at least until 1971; the only known loss or damage was in 1966 when a 'putting iron was broken in unusual circumstances' and the Carnival Committee was absolved from responsibility.

A new piece of children's **play equipment** was installed in May 1967; an eight-seat horse-rocker was set in concrete several feet thick. The rocker could be locked at night to avoid vandalism. The following year a safety cage was installed at the top of the 1953 slide at a cost of £33. Vandalism continued to be a major problem and in 1967 the police agreed to keep a closer watch on the fields in the evenings, but more destruction led to a dog-handler carrying out regular patrols; an Inspector gave assurances that the fields were receiving 'special attention'. Two years later the police reported they had caught no vandals but had made several prosecutions for bye-law infringements.

In 1968, the Central Council of Physical Education arranged for **tennis** lessons on three courts on one night a week for 6 weeks in May and June; this was repeated the next two years. The Kenilworth Youth Centre hired two courts one evening a week for ten weeks in the summer, and the Kenilworth Tennis Club arranged block bookings for winter use. Abbotsford School pupils continued to enjoy the courts on Tuesdays throughout all the months they were open. In 1968 the price of 10s was set for a pensioner's season tickets for **bowls**; this caused much outrage and the following month it was reduced to 5s, and **pitch & putt** and **putting** were included.

In 1968 the total income from the Abbey Fields amenities was £5,812, a drop of £809 on the previous year. This was blamed mostly on the weather and it was no coincidence that the swimming pool also took precisely £809 less than the previous year, a fall of a third to £1,453. Catering receipts were £3,327 and the largest sports income was from the newest attraction; miniature golf took £464, tennis £308, putting £203 and bowls just £50. Income from the hire of football pitches was not mentioned.

The **kiosk** was burgled again in September 1966, leading to improved security. Before the 1967 season, the letting of it to private contractors was discussed as was the staff's wages; the seasonal part-time employees were to be paid 5s an hour, as were the similar employees at the swimming pool.

In June 1966 Mr Long paid for a **seat** in memory of his wife; it was placed at his request near the War Memorial. Five poplar and two oak **trees** were felled near to Ford House due to their dangerous condition; they were not replaced as there were many trees in that area of the fields, many paid for by Mr Phelps in 1923. On Sunday 27th November 1966, more commemorative trees were planted. Two English oaks from Blenheim Palace were planted between the War Memorial and the Abbey Hill bus shelter in memory of Sir Winston Churchill who died in January 1965; when he visited Kenilworth in June 1945 he drove along Abbey Hill past that very spot and made a speech at the clock tower. By planting two it was hoped it would ensure at least one would survive but in fact both do. Councillor Mrs Adcock shovelled a dozen or so spade-fulls of earth for the one which today displays the Churchill memorial plaque. Either side of the bus shelter were planted two maples, one to mark the centenary of Dr Barnardos Homes, planted by Sir Alfred Owen, the president of the organisation, and the other to commemorate the Jubilee of the Boy Scouts, planted by the Earl of Aylesford; aluminium plaques to mark these two cost £17 15s and again both trees survive. Planting commemorative trees did not receive the same opposition as earlier mass-planting schemes in the same area. At this time, the swimming pool was screened with a dozen pine trees and a couple of maples, and a dangerous poplar alongside Forrest Road was felled and replaced. In late 1967, the redundant fence along the brook from Forrest Road to the swimming pool was removed.

In 1968, the National Children's Homes asked if they could create a floral display in the fields, and this first led to a general discussion resulting in displays being created along the Abbey Hill frontage and around the War Memorial, and then to suggestions to the County Council for the planting of the traffic islands at The Square and St John's which were adopted.

In April 1967, rotting timbers caused the closure of the **bridge** donated by the fairground people to the council in 1960 at the Bridge Street end of the brook. It was made entirely of wood and much was removed leaving only the framework and handrail. It was fenced off, and repaired or replaced at an undiscovered date. That month, there was a senior cross-country race held in the Abbey Fields with 14 competitors. There was a much better turnout the following week for the junior race which had 40; finishing second was 13-year-old Barry Powell who later played football for Coventry City, Wolverhampton Wanderers, and England. Two circuits of the course were required and included running through the brook due to the bridge closure. The runners were from the Parkfield Athletics, St John's Boys, St Nicholas Boys, and the Baptists Boys clubs.

The local Girl Guides held Abbey Fields late-summer Field Days (known in 1966 & 1967), but were refused permission to have a camp and BBQ. The agricultural show had become the main fixture in the calendar; in 1966 the wet weather again resulted in much repair work being needed to the **showground**.

In April 1967, the Kenilworth British Legion hosted the organisation's Annual County Parade which this particular year included the dedication of the women's branch; they were given permission to use the area around the War Memorial and the plateau, or terrace, near the church.

The new buildings in 1965 were set back from the pool leaving space for future developments and necessitating the diversion of the path (top right). Of interest is the sunbathing deck on the roof and the new kiosk, top left, but the 1923 conveniences remain (see photograph, page 76). The plinths of the 1935 changing rooms are retained as terracing at each end but a new fence leaves an inaccessible section over the brook *(KWN, 13th August 1971)*

Despite the major improvements at the **swimming pool**, the facilities were far from ideal as highlighted by Kenilworth Swimming Club when it announced in January 1966 that it was moving its gala to Leamington where the facilities were better; it was indoor and above all, heated. Harvey Pugh the president of the club said he did not want to see children standing shivering on the side of the pool between races any more, the water was so cold that some failed to finish their races and others reported feeling ill. As mentioned, the club had transferred to Leamington for the autumn and winter weekly meetings some years before and the attendances had been tremendous. *'For a town of Kenilworth's size, not to have an indoor pool is ridiculous'*, and attendance at the Abbey Fields pool in the previous summer was claimed to have been very poor despite the improvements in the changing facilities and kiosk.

In November the same year, the KSAC suggested that the pool should be covered and heated, a conclusion reached after contacting pool users. It was added that as Warwick University had no pool, a covered pool at Kenilworth would be used by students daily for training and polo matches. Kenilworth Swimming Club commented that it would also provide better facilities for schoolchildren and learners. The growth of the town meant very many more swimmers in Kenilworth were travelling to Leamington or Coventry to swim; those who only enjoyed a cold swim followed by lying in the sun in the summer were in danger of becoming a minority.

The KUDC discussed the possibility of heating and roofing the pool in February 1967, but deferred serious consideration until they had received the 'observations of the Kenilworth Sports Advisory Committee'. Having contacted consultation engineers, in March 1967 the KSAC submission claimed it would cost £10,500 to roof and heat the existing pool and its Chairman Derek Pickering had put together a dossier of the work involved. It would need £6,665 to roof and £1,200 to heat, with additional money needed for lighting and other equipment. He envisaged a steel frame with a roof 10ft off the ground, bricks making the first 5ft of the walls with asbestos sheets filling the gap. The roof would have a 10 degree slope, and would be of fibreglass and asbestos which would let in the light, but would not be high enough to spoil the view across the fields, a major consideration. The pool would cost £5 7s 6d per day to heat by gas, £3 15s by oil, and £6 9s by electricity. Of the thirty letters sent to organisations and schools, half had said they would use the pool if heated, and two were already swimming elsewhere. Derek Pickering urged the KUDC to heat the pool as soon as possible, and then roof it when finances permitted. However, there was a counter argument that the pool as it stood was unique in the area, and covering it would end the *'pleasure of fresh air and sunshine.'*

The KUDC minutes show that on 1st April 1967 the council resolved that 'heating of the pool is desirable but it would be an expensive operation, and in view of other priorities and the present economic difficulties such a scheme must be left in abeyance for the time being.'

Simultaneously with its submissions for covering and heating the pool, in March 1967 the KSAC suggested flooding the **Oxpen Meadow** to an extra 1ft depth than its 2ft 6ins flooded winter level, to make a permanent boating **lake**; creating a weir on the Castle side and using a 6ins pipe would provide enough water. The bottom of the lake could be skimmed and the earth used to provide an island. It was also claimed that the scheme would solve a long-standing problem as *'undoubtedly the creation of such a lake would prevent flooding at the ford and the allotments at Mill End'*. Derek Pickering had contacted a sailing club who assured him that despite the lake being in a hollow there would be enough wind. He envisaged a boathouse near the swimming pool which could also serve teas, *'The people who enjoy boating would not leave litter'*. There was opposition due to the problems a stagnant pool could create, but controlling water in at the Castle end and out near the swimming pool would avoid this.

The KUDC were to be asked to consider it, but it seems they had ruled out any chance of there being boating on the lake should it ever be formed. In response to the KSAC they said that the lake was on its agenda but 'deferred in the present period of (financial) restraint' but it would be only an 'amenity feature'. Swans were regular visitors to the meadow when there was enough water.

On Saturday 30th September 1967, just minutes after returning home from a holiday, **Jack Drew** went for a walk around the cemetery but collapsed and died; he was 63. He was buried in the cemetery which for so long he had been in charge. Jack Drew was a straightforward, hardworking and sincere servant of the town, and *'He was one of the most knowledgeable people about Kenilworth's past, and the history made in his lifetime'*. He attended National Horticulture meetings on behalf of the council, and was a founder member of Kenilworth's Rotary Club; in October 1968, the club received permission to plant a copper beech in his memory on the corner opposite the Abbey Hotel and it survives with a memorial plaque. At some time the second Blenheim Palace oak planted in 1966 was dedicated to his memory. Jack's knowledge and learning of the town's history was continued by his son John H Drew who published numerous books and articles about the town and inspired many, including this author.

The new Parks Superintendant, one of four applicants and starting on 12th February 1968, was Alec Retberg from Morley, Lancashire; he was 46 years old.

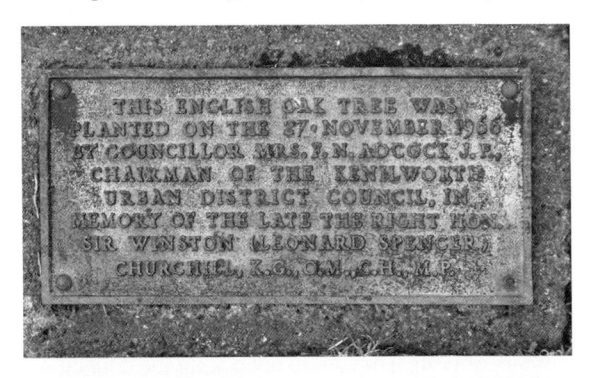

Above: The plaques for the two Blenheim Palace oak trees planted on 27th November 1966. One was later dedicated to Jack Drew; the later-added plate incorrectly says it was *planted* in his memory even though Jack was in a *KWN* photograph supervising the holes being dug

Left: The plaque for the copper beech tree standing on the corner nearest the then Abbey Hotel, donated and planted by the Rotary Club of which Jack Drew was a founder member

(All three photographs, 10th January 2017)

In February 1968, new **bye-laws** for the park were on the point of being introduced and were available for the public to inspect and raise objections. They had been largely unchanged since the 1930s, although as seen, there had been a couple of amendments. The fine for a first offence was raised to £20 and it was hoped that 'stricture measures will be enforced' to put an end to cycling in the fields by youths, mostly in the vicinity of the swimming pool. Of interest are the laws that prevented paddling in the brook and the catching of fish (both popular pastimes with children and apparently never enforced), a maximum of 15 minutes on any play equipment should there be someone else waiting to use it, and banned were the beating of carpets or hanging up of washing to dry; these latter points probably dated back to earliest versions of the bye-laws.

In December 1966, part of the unsurfaced **car park** 'triangle' was churned up by cars due to the wet weather; it was to be sectioned off until dry again. Cars entered and left the area via any of the gaps between the avenue of trees but in January 1968 a low chain fence and removable posts on the avenue were installed so cars could only enter and leave between the third and fourth trees; gravel repairs were made at the entrance. 'It was suggested that it might be advisable to convert the area into a proper car park by tarmacadamising the area and marking out parking spaces.'

In December 1968, parking restrictions were introduced in parts of High Street which created chaotic scenes further down where parking lay-bys were available. A bye-law had been introduced in 1951 allowing parking for three hours but this was often ignored, one car stayed for six days. In the spring of 1969, the Kenilworth Society, worried about proposed building developments on the north side of High Street, asked for assurances that it would not preclude the creation of a car park in that area as the Abbey Fields was the only alternative. The council's response, 'Car parking to the north of High Street would be preferable to using any part of the Abbey Fields for this purpose' was reassuring and gave rise to the society also stating that 'they are resolutely opposed to any extension of the car parking which already took place in the north east corner of the fields'. The council minutes show that they decided, 'Existing parking facilities in the Abbey Fields may be improved in the future but there are no proposals to extend these facilities'. The cost of temporary surface repairs to the car park was set at £850; it was to be considered when estimates for 1970-71 were presented.

The population growth (in 1961 the population was 14,427 and had since risen further, an increase of over 25 per cent in a decade) was creating a demand for more and improved recreational facilities; heating and roofing the pool, creating a lake and providing more sports pitches were making demands on the council at a time of national financial uncertainty.

It was perhaps inevitable that as soon as heating and roofing the **swimming pool** was discussed in early 1967, that particular summer would be *'one of the best attended for years at the pool, with its snack bar it makes the ideal centre during the school holidays'*. The *KWN* backed up the story with a collection of photographs showing well over 200, almost all children, at the pool. The following summer the swimming club offered to raise money towards heating the pool, but the KUDC passed a resolution not to offer any support, their three reasons being there was no public money to allocate to the project, the surveyor was short staffed, and he had in any case no time to prepare a scheme; *'It is not possible at the present time to offer any assistance in view of other priorities'*. Councillor Adcock was amongst those disappointed by her fellow councillor's attitude; *'Once in a while people are prepared to help themselves but this does nothing to encourage them. This resolution is just about the end'*. Councillor Spencer Harrison who had stopped swimming at the baths, said *'It is deplorable to say we cannot offer any assistance. Heating and covering the bath should have a far higher priority.'*

Undeterred, in July 1968 a group was formed to raise money to heat the pool but not roof it; the **Heat the Pool Fund** was formed at a public meeting and was separate from the swimming club, although the club backed the scheme and doubtless there were many members of both. They were not asking the council for money, merely their approval, and they intended to raise all funds for the equipment and installation, and a cover to keep the heat in at night. There was of course one obstacle to their aims; *'The committee greatly regrets it cannot accept donations until the council gives permission for the fund to become an active venture. We are hopeful the council will give further consideration to the scheme.'*

Council minutes record that their committee had further considered the proposals to heat the pool, and that they supported the proposal 'in principle', and the raising of funds 'in principle', but that professional advice needed to be sought for costing, and this they did in July and August. Gas would be the cheapest installation at £1,650, and oil would need a 25-30ft chimney. 'At the appropriate time the council will give consideration to the installation of a gas fired boiler to heat the water'. *'Civic minded members of the public have had to launch their own appeal to improve the swimming pool with no guarantee that the council will maintain the heating system to be provided.'*

A typically busy summer's day in the pool still heated only by sunshine *(KWN, 1st August 1969)*

Despite the lack of encouragement from the council, Heat the Pool fundraising began and the first event recorded in the *Kenilworth Weekly News* was in mid-August 1968 when 14-year-old Sylvia Grantham of Finham Road swam 93 lengths at 80ft a length in one hour 20 seconds. With 100 lengths in sight she was advised to stop as the water was only 48 degrees (9 degrees Centigrade); it was so cold that she had the pool to herself. She had taught herself to swim at the baths just the previous year; her efforts raised about £30. Within a month, the 18 members of the Heat the Pool Committee began a door-knock with each doing 400 houses. Many children were now doing sponsored swims; a new duration record was set by Christopher Eddy at 2 miles and 3 lengths. With interest spreading, the swimming club set aside one club night just to host sponsored swims, and Kenilworth Cricket Club offered the free use of their pavilion for any fundraising events the appeal wished to have, and 17th January 1969 was the first, a ploughman's supper. Also a Christmas Fair was held at a shop in The Square, the donation of toys, was requested. Early in 1969, a Heat the Pool poster competition was started, dozens of entries were put on display at the Talisman Theatre, newly moved to Barrow Road. There were two categories, over 14's and under 14's, with two prizes in each category. A Water Carnival was held at the pool.

One drawback of the new buildings at the pool was that the catering had to contribute to the building loan repayments and due to this despite high income the kiosk now ran at an annual loss; from April to October in 1968 this amounted to £317. Each year the decision had to be made as to whether the KUDC should continue to operate it or to once again let the business on a contract; it remained a council run business but it was decided to reduce the overheads by having a shorter season in 1969, opening immediately before the Spring Bank Holiday in May rather than the usual April and closing about a month earlier on 27th September.

As a reminder of the dangers of the local waterways, and recalling many incidents in the past that had helped prevent the construction of a lake, in July 1969 a 4-year-old boy fell in the brook at the Odibourne Allotments and was rescued unconscious. He fully recovered and the following week was photographed with his mother having swimming lessons at the pool.

In June 1969, ten months after its inaugural meeting, the Heat the Pool fund had reached £1,000 of its target of £1,475 as quoted for the equipment by the Gas Board, and its committee approached the KUDC for some commitment to the cause. The response in July was positive; after complimenting the group on their efforts, the letter continued that they 'can be assured that if the balance remaining can be raised by the end of

1969, the council will have the heating equipment installed and in operation for the commencement of the 1970 season'. In October, the West Midlands Gas Board revised their quote for the equipment upwards to £1,736, and said they needed four months notice to carry out the work. Arrangements were made immediately and work started with the hope of re-opening the following spring.

The newly heated pool was opened on Saturday 23rd May 1970. Heat the Pool Chairman Derek Pickering handed over a cheque for £1,769 13s 3d *(£25,000)* to KUDC Chairman C E Webster; this was £31 more than was required and at the request of the fundraisers two coin-operated hairdryers were provided. The KUDC also promised to install a plaque, commemorating the fundraising. The warm waters were an immediate success; *'Once they are in they just don't want to get out'*. On the next Tuesday it was noted that there were 100 in the pool whereas previously there would have been barely a dozen.

Very quickly there was a major problem; during a warm spell in June it was so popular with children after school that they stayed for several hours and overlapped with the adults that tended to swim later, leading to complaints from the grown-ups that the children were ruining their swimming time. The sheer numbers of swimmers caused problems with 'dangerous overcrowding' to the extent that on Monday 8th June the pool attendant had to close the pool at 6.15 p.m. so it could be cleared, and others could be let in at 7.00; the intervention became daily.

Safety consultants were called in and it was decided to limit the numbers at any one time to 400 swimmers; it makes one wonder what the numbers were when the pool was 'dangerously overcrowded'. A system of issuing 400 wrist bands was introduced that effectively restricted admissions; when any were returned, new admissions could be allowed. Also, in a move to placate the adults, the early evening break was made permanent, after which any children would be charged the same as adults, but this created new protests; now the youngsters complained that it was they who raised the majority of the heating funds, and the adults were taking advantage of their efforts!

The problems led to a review of the bath's operation. Until this time, there was one full time employee who was responsible for admissions, running the machinery, and cleaning the bath and its surrounds seven days a week; two persons were employed to help look after the lockers, and in school holidays only, another part-time attendant patrolled the pool area, but from the next season there were to be two full-time attendants for the whole season. The number of swimmers prevented the swimming club from being able to give instruction to youngsters and they asked for exclusive use for that purpose on Saturdays, which was declined as was a request for them to have two nights a week, and from St John's Boys Club for a canoeing session. Kenilworth's Youth Club members were allowed a discount of 25 per cent for swimming and tennis on certain evenings.

In August 1968, Kenilworth's councillors took on their staff in a sports day arranged by the members belonging to the NALGO union; taking advantage of the Abbey Fields facilities, at least **bowls** and **putting** were played, and the event was followed by a BBQ afterwards, not in the Abbey Fields, of course, but in the grounds of the KUDC offices at Wilton House.

With the backdrop of the Pavilion, Councillors and staff enjoy their bowls match *(KWN, 9th August 1968)*

Also in the summer of 1968, the Council organised, but Kenilworth's senior school pupils hosted, sporting play-sessions in the park for youngsters during school holidays. About 200 children at a time took part in cricket, football, netball, softball, rounders, tennis, and volleyball, or for the youngest just simply balls to play with. A photograph in the *KWN* shows shinty sticks being handed out! This was repeated the following year with the addition of a session in the swimming pool.

As mentioned, the provision of a bus lay-by and other work on the **Abbey Hill** and Rosemary Hill junction in the early 1950s left the road from the bus shelter to near the War Memorial without a pedestrian footpath on the Abbey Fields side. It was suggested in 1968 that such a footpath should be provided for reasons of safety, but with narrowing the road out of the question, it would involve a minimum 5ft wide incursion into the Abbey Fields. The covenant for the area allowed for the widening of the adjacent roads and this was seen to include its footpaths; however, the idea received widespread criticism even from within: *'It would be a continuation of the slow rape this authority is inflicting on the Abbey Fields'*, and the *'common sense view'* was that the path should not encroach into the fields.

But the final decision to do so was made in late June 1970 and work began almost immediately; this is the most recent loss of Abbey Fields land. There was still a row of beech trees along the boundary, those that had been mentioned regularly since the days of Henry Street; one, towards the War Memorial, was dying and was removed to make way, and the new path had to go around the two remaining beech trees and so encroached further into the field at these points. Much of the path had been constructed by the end of August but by the end of October the fence had yet to be reinstated; the council were having discussions on the subject as the surveyor had suggested it should remain unfenced. The Kenilworth Society added their opinion that the removal of the fence had 'considerably improved the view across the fields' and asked that it be permanently left down, and even the County Planning Officer weighed in saying the fence 'detracted from the general view of the Abbey Fields'. But once it was pointed out that the absence of a fence gave children the chance to run straight out of the fields and into the road, there was to be only one outcome and sensibly the fence was reinstated late in the year.

In January 1969, the council received a circular from the Home Office saying that all surviving **air raid shelters** were to be retained unless they were unsound, a danger to health or in the way of development. This led to those at Hyde Road (known to be 'unhygienic' even before it was bricked up) and the Arthur Street-Spring Lane junction (partly above ground and inconveniently sited) being demolished, allowing the sites to be grassed over. The three in the Abbey Fields were not seen as being a problem and so survived in case they were needed as requested by the Home Office, as did another in New Street.

In July 1966, the Clerk of the KUDC was instructed to approach the Charles Randall Trust about the land behind Little Virginia (field 381), a remnant of the original **Area C** that Randall had bought in October 1918, 'so it might be acquired and added to the Abbey Fields', but no response is recorded. Under the Warwick County Council Civic Amenities Act 1967, parts of Kenilworth were to become conservation areas; included in the eventual official notice dated 14th May 1969 was, 'The whole of the Abbey Fields and properties fronting the area', which included Little Virginia.

Then in May 1967, the KUDC refused permission for three bungalows to be built on the garden ground of Abbotsfield, now number 43 High Street, which was also part of the original **Area C,** incorporating the original building plots 2-6. There was a resistance to any form of residential development on the gardens as it would *'seriously injure for all time the special amenities of the Abbey Fields. To permit extra dwellings on this site would be inappropriate'*. The council made their opinion known to the County Planning Officer. In November 1968 there was a new application for a solitary bungalow and an offer to the KUDC to buy the *'remainder of the land'* to add to the Abbey Fields; the council was adamant that the *'amenities of the area should be preserved in their entirety'* and that a compromise allowing even one bungalow was not acceptable. A petition against any building on the land was under way. On 2nd December 1968 Abbotsfield and its accompanying 2.4 acres of land was sold by Sydney Robert Holbrook to H W Whiteman & Son Ltd, one of the largest building contractors in the Midlands; in a new twist, the head of the firm was Herbert William Whiteman, a Kenilworth councillor. Apparently empty for some time, Abbotsfield now had barbed wire on the access gates and fences around its Abbey Fields and High Street boundaries.

As the Abbotsfield story was developing, also in 1968 the KUDC was contacted by an agency asking if they would like to buy both the Little Virginia cottages and field 381 of 2.133 acres at the rear having a frontage to Castle Road; this they were reluctant to do as the houses were listed as 'sub-standard' on their unfit properties register compiled in 1965. The land behind was already allocated as an 'open space' on the

Town Map and so safe from development, and all was in the conservation area as designated by the County Planning Office just months before. The renovation costs stopped the council from buying the properties but they contacted the trustees and offered to take just the field on a tenancy. In the autumn the council were informed that negotiations were at an end as one of the trustees had died; this was Charles Randall jnr who died on 5th September 1968, a bizarre coincidence reflecting the death of his father during similar, and eventually fruitless, negotiations in 1933 over the same piece of land. In 1969 the council took it upon themselves to rehouse the Little Virginia residents, many of them were elderly.

The Charles Randall Trust were promising renovations and some started, but they were again approached by the KUDC in late 1970 asking if they were now prepared to let field 381; this time they were informed that the 'question was in abeyance' as they were considering adding a strip of it to Little Virginia.

The Little Virginia cottages were, as mentioned, included in the conservation area, fully adopted in August 1970, and this protected them from redevelopment or alterations other than those necessary to preserve them; however some were in such a poor state that they needed immediate work if they were to be saved. By August 1971 less than half the 15 cottages were still occupied and 13 were considered to be in a poor way, and the site was becoming an eyesore. The *Kenilworth Weekly News* featured an appalling but occupied cottage that had a leak through the thatched roof, and even after the addition of two tarpaulins rain water still flowed, running down the bedroom wall. The occupants went to bed with plastic sheets at hand should they be needed; they were amongst the few still waiting to be rehoused. The health authority had been informed.

In late 1969, the original 1923 **conveniences** alongside the pool were planned to be replaced the following year at a cost of £7,500; provision had earlier been made for £8,500 in the 1968/69 budget as a continuance of the changing rooms rebuild. It was not to be until October 1970 that plans were finally submitted for them; they were to be 'at an angle' to the kiosk to avoid further incursion into the park (see photograph, page 138) and on the site of the existing ones, preventing work from beginning until September 1971. In the meantime 'a modest scheme' to decorate the interior of the existing conveniences was carried out. As this was progressing, in June 1971 the building of a **paddling pool** was again discussed and £2,500 for it was added to the list of capital expenditure works for the year 1973-74, as was £6,480 for the lake. The KUDC continued to receive occasional letters asking for the swimming pool to be covered; the answer was always the same, 'The council have considered it but having regard for other financial commitments the council have not been able to include such a project in a capital programme.'

Six firms were invited to tender for the construction of the conveniences and the contract was awarded on 7th September 1971 to L S West Ltd for £11,301. However, two months later they informed the council that they could not proceed and so the work was awarded to the next bidder, Hurst & Aitken for £11,366, even further above the budgeted estimate. In January 1972 demolition of the 1923 conveniences, the town's first, had been completed and after investigating the cleared site it was decided to reposition the new ones so as to be in line with the catering kiosk and not at an angle as originally shown on the plan. By doing so it encroached further into the park but ensured space was kept at that end to allow for the expected future extension of the pool itself. Security of the site during the work left a lot to be desired: *'Despite the contractor's commendable efforts, an old age pensioner could get into the baths never mind a young hooligan with his hood up'*, and the inevitable happened; a *'wrecking spree'* resulted in the empty pool having objects thrown in damaging some tiles, the wooden steps to the diving board were smashed, the footbath was a *'total wreck'*, and pipes and doors attacked at the new incomplete toilets. Three 12-year-old boys later appeared in court for causing £200 of damage.

In January 1971 a **small slide** was installed in the **play area**. There were now two slides, a climbing frame, two sets of swings (probably the original swing frame from 1919 and the coronation swings), the horse-rocker, and still the 'giant stride'. In October 1971, a roundabout was bought from Wicksteed's for £189, and another new attraction for the area was a tree trunk recovered from the common and laid horizontally. At this time a firm of specialists were consulted over repairs to the 'giant stride', or 'maypole' as it was often called, who said spare parts would be difficult to find; if that was the case a replacement was to be ordered as it was now 52 years old. The **Kenilworth Round Table** wished to donate a 'play scheme' to the play area, 16ft by 10ft by 7ft high, but the council declared it was 'aesthetically unacceptable', but were to discuss with the organisation supplying an alternative scheme; there is no further mention of this in the council minutes.

Letting the **kiosk** was again discussed in 1970, but once more decided against; part-time employees were now paid 6s an hour. The pre-decimalisation prices included tea 7d, coffee 9d, sandwiches 9d, ice lollies from 3d, cones and wafers 7d, Raspberry Slice 9d, Wiz 6d; and post decimalisation, tea was 3½p (8d), coffee 5p (1s), cakes 3p (7d), and sandwiches 4p (9d).

The slide, left, with the climbing frame beyond and new swings close by installed for the Coronation. Extreme right is a small slide, presumably that installed in 1971 *(Undated, LAG&M)*

In 1970, Councillor Stansfield suggested that a **footpath** should be made from the swimming pool, following the brook, all the way to the common; a feasibility study was authorised, which raised concerns as most would be on land the council did not own. Two years later there had been little in the way of progress but there had been several letters published opposed to the, apparently, *'revolting idea'*.

The Round Table sports day was still a fixture and in 1970 band concerts returned to the park on three weekends, on the condition that no bandstand was erected and no seats set out.

The Kenilworth & District Boys **Football** League held a 6-a-side competition on 'all the Abbey Fields pitches', thought to be three, on 8th May 1970, a Friday evening. Despite the new changing rooms being used by **football** teams, it appears these were not permanently available and footballers often left the fields after a match in whatever state they ended the game. In October 1970 one Leamington team turned up in a very smart coach, but at the end of the game they were in such a mess that the driver wouldn't let them on, and arranged for an old coach to come and pick them up!

In September 1970, a letter from the National Council of Women of Great Britain asked for an area to be fenced off for use as a **dog toilet** in an attempt to keep the rest of the fields clean, and mentioned that just such a scheme had been a success in Bath. It was pointed out that cows had been banned from the fields for the very same reason but the *KWN* remarked that in comparison the cows had much in their favour as they *'kept the grass down, and the sort of fly they attracted did not then head for sandwiches as dog flies do. Cowpats were also much less offensive and more visible'*. Footballers and their coach drivers are likely to have disagreed.

At the end of 1970, the **tennis courts** were resurfaced at a cost of £2,100.

A request that was turned down, in 1971, was from the BBC wishing to hold and televise an edition of their very popular and legendary 'It's A Knockout' programme, featuring a competition between Warwick and Leicester Universities. The reason given was that it was 'unreasonable to restrict the public from the fields on days in addition to those allocated to the carnival and agricultural shows'; this author thinks that in fact, the public would have been immensely pleased to have seen the spectacle.

In late November 1971, the cost of a round of **putting** increased from 3p to 4p. The green was still used by the carnival fundraisers for an annual competition as was the pitch & putt course, and a carnival swimming gala was still held (all until at least 1972).

In the autumn of 1971, more problems were caused by **vandals** and cyclists, and other **byelaws** were regularly being broken. After complaints, the police were asked to specifically patrol the park on Friday and Saturday evenings, and Saturday afternoons. For the first time 'No Cycling' was painted on the ground at all entrances to the park, and it was suggested that perhaps the park should have a regular 'Ranger' to keep a check on activities. It seems the extra police patrols had the desired effect as in January 1972 it was reported their 70 extra visits resulted in 'little cause for complaint at the present time'. Dogs fouling the playground area was the next problem discussed; in response to a letter the parks committee stated 'The council are aware of the problem but under existing legislation there does not appear to be a solution to the problem.'

In 1972, the Warwickshire Lawn Tennis Association held coaching sessions on the courts on summer Tuesdays evenings; it was an 'enormous success' and was repeated the next year.

The Kenilworth & District Boys League continued their springtime **football** coaching sessions, and for the 1972 season the charge for use of a pitch and changing rooms was reduced from £1 to 50p. Litter was being left around the pitches and clubs were sent letters but it was soon established that the litter was left by casual users of the field and not the clubs. At the end of the season the West Midlands School Meal Supervisors held a ladies football match and made a collection for the Ridgeway special school. In 1973, clubs were told they could not hold matches in the fields on Remembrance Sunday. At about this time, the KUDC took a large step towards football being removed from the Abbey Fields by finally purchasing about 29 acres of **Castle Farm** for £16,000; the decision had been made in 1972.

In 1967, a virulent form of Dutch Elm Disease arrived in Britain; in 1970, a failing weeping elm **tree** near the park's Bridge Street entrance was felled, it is not known if it was diseased, but it was replaced by a semi-mature beech. In 1971, the disease claimed its first certain Abbey Fields victim; an elm tree near the swimming pool was felled, its bark removed to stop the disease spreading, and the trunk cut and left in the play area for children to play on. The Parks Superintendant Alec Retberg attended a seminar on the disease. Probably due to the potential loss of all elms, the tree planting scheme proposed by the County Land Agent in 1965 was revisited; this led to a more modest scheme of planting being planned over the next few years: 'Trees where space permitted in the avenues from Abbey Hill to Bridge Street and from Bridge Street to the swimming baths, screening of the swim baths, planting of weeping species at irregular intervals along the brook and in the Oxpen Meadow, and trees in the areas near the ford.'

In 1971 Kenilworth Soroptimists planted a tree to commemorate the golden jubilee of their International Association. In April 1972, a copper beech was planted to commemorate the 50th anniversary of the British Legion in 1971; the hole was dug in the wrong location opposite the end of Southbank Road, but today a tree with the golden jubilee plaque is near the War Memorial.

President of Kenilworth's Royal British Legion Branch, Major B H Thomas performs the ceremonial spadework at the wrongly located hole. Major Thomas was responsible for much of the work carried out by the Friends of the Abbey in the 1930s *(KWN, 14th April 1972)*

After around 25 million elm trees died nationwide, the government introduced a national scheme 'Plant a tree in 73' and several local organisations took up the challenge; other than the National Federation of Women's Clubs planting a tree to mark their silver jubilee, the groups names were not recorded.

The new **conveniences** were ready in time for the 1972 season, but that summer a chemical imbalance of the **swimming pool's** water gave it a murkiness. Excess chalk to treat the water caused problems with combing hair even after several washes; there was an excess of chlorine at the same time.

Despite the heated water, the pool only regularly attracted large numbers on fine weather days, it was either *'chock-a-block or empty'*, but its attraction was obvious; one Monday alone in the 1972 school holidays saw long queues and no fewer than 1,312 visitors to the pool. Sadly, later those same school holidays, a nine-year-old girl drowned in the pool. She came with her aunt and two sisters as part of a coach party of 20 youngsters and 10 adults from Birmingham not intending to swim but she borrowed a costume. She had just eaten egg sandwiches and biscuits and had a fizzy drink before going back into the pool for *'one more paddle'* but her aunt did not see her enter the water. The life guard on duty said most of the children were at the shallow end, a boy told her someone was on the bottom and she recovered the girl from 6ft 9ins of water and tried resuscitation, but was hampered by food in the girl's throat. The girl's aunt said she had no idea why she was in the deep end; a medical expert said that eating before swimming could cause cramps. The verdict was misadventure. She was the third fatality in the pool.

In January 1972 the **footpath** from the swimming pool following the brook to the common first suggested in 1970, was agreed 'in principle'; a landscape architect was to be hired to produce a plan, and the Parks & Cemetery Committee were to investigate the purchase of the land that the council didn't own. The estimated cost was £8,000 but it was expected to rise as by taking allotment land they would have to provide a replacement area. Eventually in 1974 it was decided the path would stop at Washbrook; the length through the Abbey Fields was also dropped from the scheme leaving just that through the School Lane Meadow, not finally completed for at least fifteen years.

In May 1973 it was reported that several owners of the adjacent properties had built entrance gates from their gardens into the Abbey Fields. 'Difficulties in other areas show it is always wise to take steps to prevent encroachment on the council's property' and so it was decided to erect a fence along the line of the council's boundary. Within months the Parks Committee backtracked, and allowed a Castle Hill resident to have an access from her garden to the Abbey Fields on payment for a licence, of just 5p a year.

The roundabout purchased in 1971, and in the background can be seen the Giant Stride in its 57th year; its eventual demise has not been discovered. Left background are the new conveniences *(KWN, 23rd April 1976)*

A permanent **car park** for and in the vicinity of High Street was needed and discussions continued into 1972; the proposals then were for the *'area set aside for car parking in the Abbey Fields'* as the obvious choice, but also suggested was a new car park created at the highest point of High Street on the Abbey Fields area donated by Gertrude Evans. This would have contravened Gertrude's insistence that the area *'shall forever hereafter be preserved and kept as nearly as it may be in its natural condition as open grass land'*. The fence separating High Street from Gertrude Evans' donated land was in need of repair; taking it down was considered, but it was repaired instead due to safety reasons, and it preventing cars parking on the fields.

The pressure from High Street businesses for the provision of a car park resulted in the November 1972 resolution by the Health & Highways Committee, 'that a properly made car park be provided with separate entrance and exit on the land set aside for parking in the Abbey Fields'; it seems the promise of a dedicated car park on the north side of High Street had been dropped in favour of a virtually cost-free alternative. In January a pedestrian entrance to the car park from Bridge Street was proposed to ease the access to High Street; it was to be a 'ramped pedestrian entrance from the car park to Bridge Street in the position of the existing air raid shelter, such shelter to be removed'. This was not pursued, the retention of the air raid shelter possibly being a contributory factor. Also suggested, but not pursued, was the 'opening out' of the driveway from Bridge Street to the church to provide facilities for the turning of vehicles such as those for funerals and weddings; this presumably would have meant the felling of several trees.

The KUDC expenditure programme for 1972-73 included £1,200 for Abbey Fields drainage and £4,000 for creating a **lake** and this was discussed in detail at the 30th November 1971 meeting. Surveys of the levels of the brook, fields and of water flow were needed before lake planning could start. However, the project was classed as 'non-urgent' and thus expenditure on the surveys for a non-urgent scheme could not be justified, and yet again the decision was made not to begin the process to form a lake.

Towards the end of 1972, Derek Pickering suggested a permanent lake could be created quite easily by using machines that were close at hand - the diggers constructing the Kenilworth by-pass. About 10,000 cu ft of material needed to be removed and would cost about £2,000, take a week, and produce a lake 3ft deep of an area of about 350 by 150 yards. *'It would become a pool as it was in Kenilworth's earlier history, its importance to modern Kenilworth would be its wildlife, including fish and fowl, of sailing and canoeing facilities'*. The removed earth could be deposited to make an island and to enhance the banks.

From 1960 to 1974, Derek Jones was responsible for maintaining the water system that flooded and drained the Oxpen Meadow. Water flowed down an underground conduit from just west of the Castle Ford to an inlet to the meadow about half way to the swimming pool and 20ft from the path. It would take about 48 hours to fill to a depth of about 1ft. The inlet could be closed by blocking with a sandbag. The main outlet was near the pool and fed into a drain that exited into the brook a short distance east of the Iron Bridge. The age of this system is unknown. (A detailed account can be read in *Kenilworth History 1995*, published by the Kenilworth History & Archaeology Society.)

On 9th June 1972, the *KWN* reported that a seven-year-old boy had found that fish in the **brook** had died; he was pictured with his fishing net under the headline, *'Who killed all the bullyheads?'* A ten-inch trout was also found at the spot near the Iron Bridge. The *'fish killing stuff'* had entered the water further upstream and steps were taken to ensure that no more did; the boy said he always returned his caught fish to the water.

Annually discussed, the council decided to retain the **kiosk** operation for 1973, opening for a few days over Easter but daily from the end of May. Tea was now 4p and coffee 6p. In 1973, glass bottles from drinks sold at the kiosk were becoming a problem, being left around the fields; it was decided to charge a deposit to encourage their return.

By March 1971, Abbotsfield was described as *'long empty, surrounded by barbed wire'* and becoming an eyesore, coinciding with the nearby dilapidation of Little Virginia. Whiteman & Sons had put in three applications for the site, each involving the demolition of Abbotsfield. Warwickshire County Council supported the 'no building' decision by the KUDC; the last application involved the building of 12 houses, 4 maisonettes and 2 flats on the site and the applicant appealed to the Department for the Environment against the refusal. Whiteman's representative at the appeal made a necessarily biased case: he said Abbotsfield was *'quite impracticable for use as a dwelling house, it has three storeys and a cellar basement. It needs servants to keep it up and few people today can afford servants. The building is not attractive, to some it would appear ugly. There is absolutely nothing to commend the building's preservation'*; it was in a conservation area but one zoned for residential development, was being vandalised and the barbed wire around it gave it the appearance *'of a PoW compound'*. The council's view was the development would *'detract from and be detrimental to the visual amenities of the area. To retain and enhance the character of the Abbey Fields, no more development should be allowed'*. When viewed from Abbey Hill across the fields, *'the High Street frontages are enhanced by the informal open contours of the Abbey Fields so that the introduction of a residential development would intrude'*. The petition opposed to any development on the site had received 1,200 signatures.

In May 1971, the Environment Secretary dismissed the appeal as the development would *'Deeply intrude'* into the *'park scene of the Abbey Fields'*, and be *'quite out of place among a group of old, mellow listed buildings.'*

A further planning application to convert Abbotsfield itself into offices was opposed by the KUDC as it was in the conservation area and the council also opposed the commercial use of premises in a residential area, but in July 1971 the KUDC relented and allowed the conversion of Abbotsfield to offices on the condition that the external appearance was retained; it was the *'lesser of two evils, the alternative being demolition'*. In a new move, the KUDC simultaneously agreed to buy an acre of the land if it became available to add to the Abbey Fields, perhaps suggesting a deal of some sort had been arranged.

Also, a planning application was submitted for number 41 High Street (built in the grounds and east of Abbotsfield before WW1 and formerly occupied by an employee of Holbrook's) for alterations and enlargement of both the dwelling and outbuildings. The application was by H W Whiteman & Son, and Councillor Whiteman declared his interest and left the room during deliberations. Mr Whiteman moved into number 41 once it was altered.

Despite having turned down the chance to purchase the Little Virginia cottages in 1968, at some point the KUDC decided upon compulsory purchase and were in 1971 making slow progress in the legal process; one councillor was quoted as saying, *'If something isn't done soon about Little Virginia, hooligans will reduce it to a rockery'*. One former resident was *'staggered and horrified to see the cottages looking like they do now'*. Although they had made promises of renovation, the Charles Randall Trust had done little work and in October 1971 put the cottages up for sale rather than carry out the rebuilding themselves.

Following an enquiry in November 1971 from an individual who was interested in purchasing field 381 between Little Virginia and the Abbey Fields to preserve it as a meadow and grazing area, the KUDC replied 'that in the public interest the land should be incorporated in the Abbey Fields and for this reason the council intend to acquire it.'

By July 1972, the cottages had been sold to William Sapcote & Sons, perhaps the country's leading renovators of old buildings, who set about the building work in April 1973. Having sold the cottages, the Charles Randall Trust then offered the land behind, field 381, for sale separately; the KUDC made an offer which was refused, and on 30th July 1973 the land was bought by Sapcote's. At some point, a strip of this land was added to Little Virginia; it is not known (to this author) if it was included in the July 1972 purchase of the cottages, or after the July 1973 purchase of the land. Sapcote's however were willing to negotiate with the council over the remaining land and the District Valuer was asked to do this.

The Little Virginia renovations were not to everyone's taste; it was remarked that they would become *'homes for the rich'* when completed and there would be no chance of the long-established elderly residents returning. The work of course created a lot of interest; amongst the finds were a cannon ball, floorboards with Latin inscriptions, a 50ft well, and a stone marked 'R' (similar to one at the Castle) that was later added to the end wall of one of the cottages.

Sapcote's rebuilt the fifteen Little Virginia cottages into ten. The former numbers 5 & 7 became number 1; 9 & 11 became 2; 13 became 3; 5, 17 & 19 became 4 & 5; 27 & 29 became 6; 23 & 25 became 7; 31 became 8. The first were advertised for sale in December 1973; numbers 4 & 5 backing onto the Abbey Fields were available for £26,500 *(£294,000)*, and numbers 7 & 8 endways on at the bottom of Castle Hill for £22,500 and £22,750. Every property had garage facilities in blocks at either end of site. Sapcote's won an award for the rebuilding work and despite two substantial rebuilds in 60 years, enough of the original fabric survived for the cottages to be listed. Perhaps due to their involvement with Little Virginia, Sapcote's were contracted in 1973 to repair the war-damaged top of the clock tower.

The most interesting items from the **Abbey** excavations were now loaned to the County Museum or on display in St Nicholas church, but the Barn retained some and was still described as *'a museum'*. However, it was not open to the public and a specific request had to be made to view the relics; by January 1972 there had been no such requests from societies or individuals for some years. Part of the Barn was again in use for the storage of tools for work in the fields but rather than clear these out to once more create a museum, Parks Superintendent Alec Retberg suggested the opposite; remove the relics so that park staff could use the Barn for storage and to carry out repairs. The Parks Committee agreed and were to contact the **Kenilworth Historical Society** (KHS) about how to pack and store the artefacts.

The KHS were then asked to carry out an inspection and prepare an inventory of the Barn relics and in 1973 were also given permission to remove the ancient clapper gate from its place in the Tantara Gatehouse to the Barn so it could be repaired; its future was to be discussed later. By now, the park superintendant's wishes had been overturned, and the KHS suggestion for an eventual museum prevailed. Harry Sunley later wrote, 'When we first had access to the Barn it was in a dreadful state, with all sorts of rubbish mixed up with bones, bits of metal, goal posts, and, most of all, sand eroded from the walls'. In a corner, buried under it all, was found a pile of hundreds of Abbey glass fragments uncovered during the excavations. By now the society had prepared a scheme and started negotiations with the KUDC for the future opening of the Barn as a museum.

The worsening condition of the Tantara Gatehouse continued to cause great concern; the St Nicholas Parochial Council said that if it could not be made safe then demolition ought to be considered; the KHS not surprisingly pushed for renovation. The D of E were once more contacted and they now set the cost of repairs as at least £10,000, and likely to rise by at least £100 for each year it was postponed.

On 16th April 1973 the KHS renamed themselves the **Kenilworth History & Archaeology Society** (KHAS) and immediately put to use the talents added to their title; Sapcote's welcomed members to their building site at Little Virginia and, within certain limitations of course, were very supportive in helping the Society undertake investigative work across the site. Though not certain, the logical conclusions to their investigations were that the cottages are of 17th century origin, and that a layer of stone chippings suggested the site was likely to have been the work-area of stonemasons in the past, the obvious conclusion being when the Castle and Priory were under construction.

The **Kenilworth Lions Club,** formed in early June 1969, held Abbey Fields play-sessions over the Easter weekend in 1971. It was suggested that the council needed to form a policy to deal with requests for use of the fields for large events and opening up areas for parking on specific days but it was decided to continue assessing each on its own merit.

In 1972, events in the fields included at least two scout & guide activity days, the Lions Club continued their play leadership events at Easter, and the Kenilworth branch of the Children's League held a 'waggers walk' which was a sponsored walk with dogs around a circuit of the Oxpen Meadow. Three bands performed as well; the Burbage Silver Band on 11th June, Bedworth Silver Band on 25th June, and the Bulkington Silver Band on 6th August. In 1973 the District Scouts held an International Day with two scout bands performing. The council had formed a policy for these smaller events in that they could not result in the 'exclusion of others' using the fields nor 'interfere' with general activities; for example, no areas could be roped off. It very much relied on sensible use by the applicants and goodwill by the general public and this author has found no complaints were ever received that the fields were being mis-used or the events created any difficulties, to the credit of all concerned.

The Lions Club took a bold step in fundraising when planning to hold a gymkhana and jumping show at Thickthorn in June 1972. The rain kept visitor numbers down to about 100, although some money was made by having a guess at how much the rain would fill a water gauge! With a profit of £200, the club were determined to put on another show the following year and in October 1972 asked the council for use of the agricultural society-created **showground** in the park on the following 9th June for an expanded 'Grand Show'; permission was given. The agricultural show organisers had agreed to Monday 29th August for their show but discovered that the Town & Country Show at Stoneleigh was to be expanded and now coincided; initially they asked if they could use the Abbey Fields on 29th July instead, but before an answer was given they re-contacted the council to say that they had arranged to hold the show at Thickthorn, their original home. Their last Abbey Fields show had been on 28th August 1972 and after 25 years of using the park and creating its showground, the Agricultural Society left for good, saying they had felt 'very much at home.'

On 24th May 1973 with the show just two weeks away, the Lions Club added a request to include a free-fall parachute display and also to use part of the Abbey Fields for parking; the former was agreed the latter was not, but on the same day as the show the Reverend Bull had arranged for half of the Abbey Fields parking area to be fenced from the public due to a wedding. It seems common sense prevailed as after the show the Lions thanked the council for allowing use of a field for parking. Disappointingly, the *KWN* chose not to report on the show. It was a curious coincidence that as the Agricultural Society left, another Kenilworth organisation held a very different type of show and thus continued the use of the showground.

After some years of debate under both Labour and Conservative Governments, the Local Government Reform Act of 1972 heralded the demise of the Kenilworth Urban District Council. In June 1972 the council was advised that Kenilworth would be part of a new District Council, later named after the county town, to come into power on 1st April 1974. On that day, the responsibility for the Abbey Fields would pass from the hands of Kenilworth although the new Kenilworth Town Council would be a statutory consultee on planning matters, but with no special standing legally.

By May 1973, the KUDC was receiving requests to use the fields on dates after its impending demise; the **Lions Club** wished to repeat their successful first show, and the **Round Table** asked for a field to hold a Donkey Derby. As the council would not then exist it could not give permission but in any case thought a Donkey Derby was 'inappropriate use of the fields'. But at about this time, in readiness for the reorganisation less than a year away, interim committees were being formed to deal with such matters. That dealing with parks had at least two members of the KUDC Parks Committee on it and it seems it sat to discuss these requests as in September 1973 the KUDC announced that both the Lions Show and Donkey Derby could go ahead after all, with Abbey Fields parking arrangements for both days. At the same time, the **swimming club** were given permission to hold a carnival gala in 1974, and the **Carnival** Committee was given its usual three-year permission to use the Abbey Fields until 1976. A degree of urgency was required to see several projected schemes come to fruition whilst the KUDC still existed; the **footpath** to the common, the **paddling pool**, and a **lake** on the Oxpen Meadow 'need to proceed as quickly as possible', but time restrictions saw all these fall by the wayside.

As work on the Little Virginia cottages was nearing completion, the now reduced field 381 behind was again offered to the KUDC and the District Valuer began negotiations; this time, by January 1974, agreement was reached upon a price of £4,500 *(£43,000)* plus legal fees for the 1.42 acres; the money was to be raised by a loan, a decision that had to be ratified by an interim committee. The conveyance is dated 30th March 1974 (the KUDC ceased to exist the following day) and included the covenant:

> '(The) purchaser will not at any time build or permit or suffer to be built or erected on the land hereby conveyed any building or buildings of any nature whatsoever'. The land was acquired 'for the purposes of the 1906 Open Spaces Act', and the purchaser agreed to 'observe and perform the restrictive and other covenants' that existed as they 'are still subsisting and capable of being enforced.'

This refers back to the covenants in the documents dated 10th October 1918 when Lincoln Chandler sold the premises to Charles Randall, which unfortunately do not appear to survive, but included confirmation of the building line restriction of the Syndicate's separation agreement of 15th October 1888.

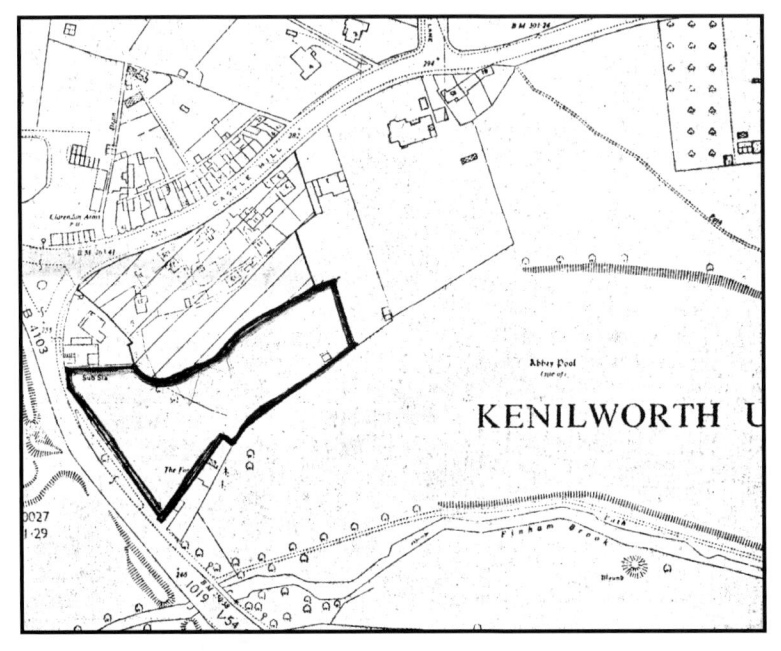

After perhaps 60 years of trying, field 381 was finally conveyed to the KUDC on 30th March 1974; part of the field had been used to extend the grounds of Little Virginia. Note also at the western end the two plots sold in 1898 and 1905 for the Castle Café on the corner, and Oakdale Villa

(WDC 147)

The conveyance is made out to the Kenilworth Urban District Council and has the signatures of E S and Stuart W Sapcote, but the council seal on the document is unmade and no council representatives signed it, an oversight caused no doubt by the council rearrangement. It is dated 30th March 1974 and so at the very last possible opportunity the KUDC finally secured the piece of land they had been trying to add to the Abbey Fields since at least 1932, and possibly 1914.

Whilst the negotiations were in progress, Mrs Clements of 3 Castle Hill asked if under council ownership she would be allowed to keep her donkey, pony and foals in the field and permission was granted for one year; and so when the land changed hands, grazing returned to the Abbey Fields, albeit in an area not yet open to the public. The land had acquired the nick-name 'the donkey field', but became known as the Paddock.

In January 1973, it was suggested that part of the garden of Abbotsfield in High Street (seen in the photograph on page 134) owned by Councillor H W Whiteman, could be purchased to be added to the fields. The clerk advised the owners that the council were prepared to exchange a triangular area of land of about 7,500 sq.ft, for an equivalent area belonging to the council between Abbotsfield and 39 High Street, now the home of County Councillor Jack Bastock; this was the narrow trackway strip, Clarendon's 15ft wide roadway, purposely acquired to provide access to the park that had not become a fully made-up path as may have been expected.

The upper part of the strip of land, Clarendon's 15ft way, providing an access from High Street and, behind the wall, the entrance to the 1867 churchyard extension. The kissing gate is likely Victorian *(3rd April 2017)*

By September 1973, the Town Development & Policy Advisory Committee agreed that 'the piece of land with a frontage of 100ft to High Street' (the original Plot 6), should be acquired, but left the decision about swapping it for the other area to the Parks Committee. A proposal by Councillor Mrs Dore and seconded by Councillor Evans that the Abbey Fields land was kept was defeated on a vote at the October Parks Committee meeting. It seems that by now there were two considerations as to the land to be acquired; either a rectangular plot of 2,611 sq yds with a High Street frontage of 100ft, or a triangular piece of it of 833 sq yds, and negotiations were to be on the basis that either way the council were to sell 600 sq yds of the Abbey Fields. The Parks Committee voted 5-2 in favour of what would be losing a small area of land on one side of Abbotsfield and gaining a much larger area on the other, with the council to pay an unrecorded amount of cash for the extra land. The attitude of councillors who were opposed to the idea was described by another as being like a *'dog in a manger'*; the area to be lost was of no use but the area to be gained could be of great value.

On 3rd October 1973, the Health & Highways Committee discussed a letter from Jack Bastock, the owner of 39 High Street; the footpath from High Street to the 1867 churchyard extension had been incorporated into his property and he asked the council if they were willing to divert this footpath from his land, to over the other side of the boundary wall and thus onto the thin strip that Councillor Whiteman was trying to buy! It was said that the footpath was useless for young mothers with prams as it had a kissing gate at the exit into the fields. It was marked as a pathway on maps (see opposite).

As the strip of land was used as an occasional access, it was gated at the High Street end and it was further suggested by Councillor Bastock that perhaps only a six foot wide strip could be lost and a four foot wide strip could be retained as a permanent surfaced entrance to the fields, particularly as mothers with prams had no usable access to the northern side of the fields save for a walk through the churchyard.

At the next H & H meeting two months later, it was decided that if the path was moved 'it would be necessary due to the gradient to grade the footpath down'; the cost of this, the path and fencing would be £580 and so it did not happen. Jack Bastock pointed out that he had not suggested the blocking up of the footpath but merely a more convenient line for those who used it, that coincidentally would block the land-swap and ensure a gap to his neighbours was maintained, securing his privacy.

However, the Abbey Fields-Whiteman land-swap proposals had been before several committee meetings and one of the full council before it was realised at the 27th November 1973 meeting that such a deal could not go ahead, the grass trackway was of course subject to the covenants preventing it from being anything other than a public open space; no explanation was forthcoming as to why this had not been realised at the outset. '*The recommendation was withdrawn without comment. From somewhere floated the word, embarrassing*'. The earlier stance by Councillors Dore and Evans that received adverse comments was justified. There are clear parallels but a different outcome to the land swap involving Mr Phelps and The Bungalow in 1912; had the current Earl of Clarendon, the 7th, George Frederick Laurence Hyde Villiers, been contacted, would he have been able to waive the covenant as had his grandfather?

The owners of Abbotsfield were to be informed of this realisation, but also that the council still wished to purchase 'the western portion of the garden land containing 2,600 sq yds', probably all of plot 6. The owners of Abbotsfield then made two offers, one was the whole rectangle of land with a High Street frontage of 75ft and a 235ft depth into the fields and covering 0.406 acres at a cost of half the value of the land, or the triangle of 100ft by 150ft as a deed of gift, on the understanding that the council puts up the fences, does not try to acquire any more of the land, and would hold it in perpetuity as an open space as already applied to the Abbey Fields. The council responded by saying they could not commit to never asking for more of the land, and asked for a 95ft frontage to High Street in place of 75ft.

Finally, on 19th February 1974 negotiations to purchase any land ended with the decision to accept the smaller triangular piece as a gift, 'to the intent that the said land shall form part of the Abbey Fields and forever be used as public walks and pleasure grounds'. The council was to erect a 6ft fence of oak boards, the fence to become the property of Abbotsfield; that was the last entry by the Parks & Cemetery Committee in the KUDC minute books, it had ended on a notable achievement to further extend the park. The conveyance includes:

> The owner is desirous of conveying by way of gift to the local authority the land in trust for the perpetual use thereto by the public for exercise and recreation purposes pursuant to the provisions of the Open Spaces Act 1906... subject to the building and other covenants and conditions contained in an indenture dated the 24th December 1884 made between Joseph Holland Burbery, William Evans, Samuel Forrest and Luke Heynes.

> The local authority hereby covenants with the owners not to use the piece of land for any purpose other than those permitted under the provisions of the Open Spaces Act 1906 and in particular that no building whether temporary or otherwise shall be erected or suffered to stand on the said piece of land or any part hereof.

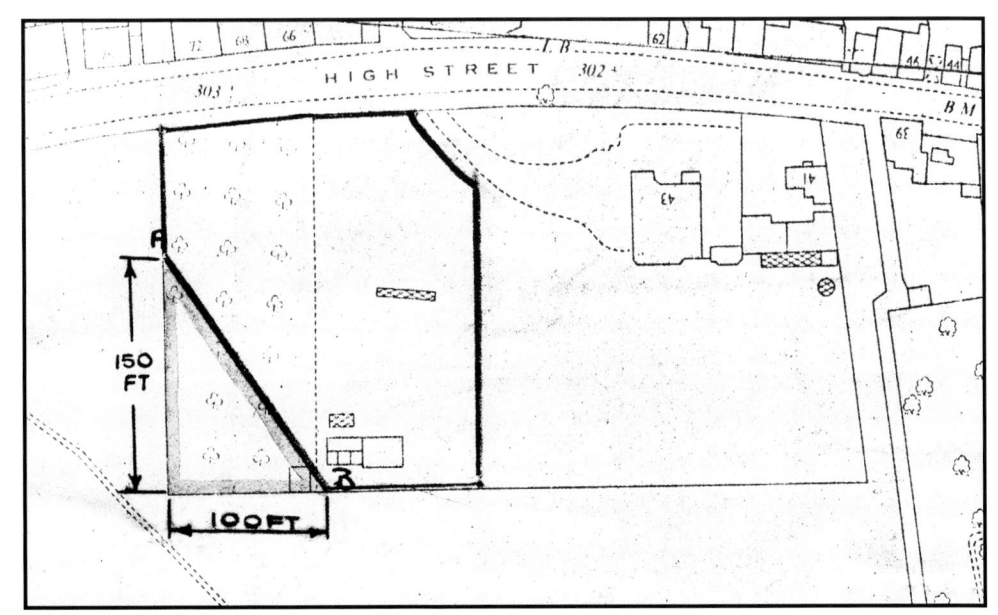

The corner of the original Plot 6, and a tiny corner of Plot 5, conveyed to the Kenilworth Urban District Council on 30th April 1974. Charles Randall's piggery and cow-house is alongside. Number 43 is Abbotsfield, number 41 the home of Councillor Whiteman, and number 39 the home of Councillor Bastock. See photograph, page 133 *(WDC 124)*

The handing over of the conveyance, dated 30th April 1974, was a low key affair at a council meeting in contrast to the gushing words spoken at past similar events; *'Quietly and with no more ceremony than if he was offering someone a light for a cigarette, Councillor Whiteman passed across the table the conveyance for the land, to Kenilworth, from him and his wife'*. The recipient, Councillor Kenneth W Hogarth, said *'On behalf of the town I would like to thank you very much for your gift'*. And thus, another 833.3 sq yds was added to the area of the fields. These two pieces of land, the Paddock of 1.42 acres (1 acre 2032 sq yds) and from Councillor Whiteman of 833.3 sq yds, added to that already incorporated in the fields (64 acres 2634 sq yds) brought the final total of acquired land to 66 acres and 660 sq yds, or 66.136 acres.

And so on the very last day that the Abbey Fields were under the direct control of the town and its inhabitants, the park area increased to all but 12 of the original 78 acres under offer. When taking the preservation and restoration of Little Virginia and 81-85 High Street into account, comparatively little of the original estate had been lost to development, a great tribute to the foresight of the originators of the scheme in the 1880s.

By the end of its reign, the Kenilworth Urban District Council had finally ended grazing and fulfilled almost all of the desires of the Victorians that had paid so much for the privileges of future generations. The KUDC had provided in the Abbey Fields football and hockey pitches, grass and then hard tennis courts, a putting green, bowling green and pavilion, occasional cricket pitches, built and then rebuilt twice the outdoor swimming pool and heated it, a refreshment kiosk, created a pitch & putt course, a children's play area, had an area altered to provide a showground, and removed hedges to create more open space. They had allowed the use of the fields for countless events from children's races and games, group parties, the annual carnival and fair, occasional circuses, agricultural and many other shows; it had instigated the major investigation into the remains of the Abbey ruins, and their preservation, and had allowed the Barn to be used as a museum by an amateur volunteer group. They had planted numerous trees, sometimes controversially, but also allowed many to be planted in commemoration of events, notable people and anniversaries. The fields played a part in both World Wars, and had become the focal point on so many occasions, or just for casual strolls or paddling in the brook, and were indelibly stamped on the minds of generations as a place of enjoyable times throughout their life. It was a park that all had become proud of.

The management of the Abbey Fields passed from the people of Kenilworth, ninety years all but a dozen days after the 5th Earl of Clarendon sold his 78 acre estate on 12th May 1884, but could the new Warwick District Council maintain the momentum, continue to provide what the people of Kenilworth wanted from their park, and what part could those people play in the future of their Abbey Fields?

The Agricultural show of 1970 on the showground created in 1954

Chapter 4: *A municipal park, or rural open countryside?*

The Warwick District Council's takeover of the KUDC's Abbey Fields did produce a problem; **Area B**, that alongside Abbey Hill and Rosemary Hill, was not owned by the KUDC but by the St Nicholas Churchwardens, at least that is the position as stated by the only available deeds to the land. Warwick District Council seems to have realised this and investigated as there is an undated document included with the conveyance recording its findings:

> The land which was conveyed to the Church Wardens… now vests in the District Council. Under the Local Government Act of 1894, Section 52, the powers of the Church Wardens… could be transferred to the Urban District Council. Under the Local Government Act 1933, Section 269, the functions and liabilities of the Church Wardens… were automatically transferred to the Urban District Council.
>
> It is not possible to tell from records immediately available whether the transfer of the Abbey Fields to Kenilworth Urban District Council took place under the 1894 Act or the 1933 Act.

This author too has found no confirmation of this particular area of the fields becoming owned by the KUDC, although at some time under the 1933 Local Government Act is the most likely; this is the Act that was replaced by that under which the WDC was formed.

No sooner had the WDC taken possession of the fields than the question of a lake in the **Oxpen Meadow** once more arose. In May 1974 the committee organising the following year's commemoration of Queen Elizabeth's 1575 visit to the Castle, hoped to display *'water frolics'* and offered the labour to form the lake out of *'the smelly and fly-breeding... swampy area'*. It was fully discussed at a WDC Recreation & Amenities Committee meeting. Whilst there was agreement in general, there were great reservations about the proposed lake's future after the celebrations, in particular the likelihood of canoeists and others taking to the water. It was suggested that after the commemoration it could once again be drained, but others suggested its retention although *'the only thing permitted upon it should be wildlife'*. It was also mentioned *'how touchy Kenilworth dwellers are on the subject of the Abbey Fields... so jealous of the current appearance... they resist even the introduction of flowers. If you get boating or a miniature railway, the people would be furious'*. The recommendation was in favour at this particular meeting but by the time of voting just two weeks later, opinions had changed and only three on the *'big committee'* voted in favour, largely swayed by unrealistic

The Oxpen Meadow *(23rd March 1986)*

proposals from *'the 1575ers'* (far from needing volunteers with shovels, professional excavations costing over £5,500 would have been required) and opposition from the Kenilworth public as ascertained by Kenilworth councillors. It was the appearance of the fields themselves that seemed to carry the strongest argument: *'Did they want children to inherit a municipal type park, or the rural open countryside present-day appearance?'* The danger of drowning was also raised, as was the cost of preventing boat use, and the subsequent necessary moves to provide a car park nearby *'to the further detriment of the Abbey Fields'*. The opinion was that the 1575 Committee had also over extended itself with ideas; *'A more woeful tale you never did hear'*.

In February 1978, the flooded meadow froze and dozens of skaters took to the ice; even ice hockey players appeared in photographs taken at the time.

In September 1975, the wooden **High Street** fence bordering the land donated by Gertrude Evans was becoming rotten and a part was missing. It was suggested that it could be dismantled and the access to the fields left open, but this was opposed both on grounds of safety, with the possibility of children running out the field and into the road, and providing unopposed access for parking cars. The cost for the initial repair was £40. At some unknown time after this, trees were planted alongside the boundary, including Scots pine as suggested in the County Land Agent proposals of 1965; strictly speaking, this was contrary to Gertrude Evan's covenant stating that the area should remain open grass land, and eventually they blocked the view from, and of, Clinton House, negating the reason that the land was originally acquired by Mary Draper.

The Abbey Fields continued to be used for **sports** although some activities were frowned upon. In July 1976 the area behind Ford House, which once had strips mown for cricket playing, was regularly used by several locals for hitting cricket balls and also, despite the nearby pitch & putt course, golf balls; action was to be taken if it was warranted. Another sport photographed in the fields by the *KWN* that year was summertime skiing using roller-skis. Kite flying too was gaining popularity, and large radio-controlled gliders hand-launched down the slope near the War Memorial also made regular appearances.

The park as inherited by Warwick District Council, photographed in 1973. The bowling green, pavilion, tennis courts and putting green provide a backdrop to children making their own entertainment in the brook, on steps perhaps forming a short-cut to the pitch & putt course. The steps in the bank are no longer discernible but the stepping stones survive in disarray *(KWN, 12th July 2006)*

The 29 acres at **Castle Farm**, bought in the later days of the KUDC, were in 1975 no closer to providing sports facilities due to the lack of funds. The *KWN* claimed that Kenilworth's rugby and cricket teams were well catered for on their own private grounds and that now there were *'hardly any'* football teams; it was suggested that some of Castle Farm should be converted to much needed allotments. Others claimed that football pitches were badly needed as those in the Abbey Fields were so poor, and also that Kenilworth Cricket Club had three teams but only one pitch meaning one team never played on its home ground. The full cost of providing facilities at Castle Farm was set at £140,000 *(£1 million)*, and included an access road necessitating a bridge to cross the Luzley Brook; there was a drainage pipe crossing it, with a drop of five feet or more, which was used by children for access to the fields.

By 1977 the widely held view was that extra sports fields were not required as there was little need, but the decision had been made to go ahead although at a slow pace in stages over a number of years. A children's play area was established with a slide, climbing frame and see-saw, and a wooden footbridge built from the Fishponds Road 'stub' to give access. In 1979 the long-term proposals were in disarray as the first stage of the planning application, the approach road and bridge, was thrown out after claims that an access road for motor vehicles from Fishponds Road would be too dangerous.

The loss-making council **catering** at the kiosk ended once the Abbey Fields came under the control of Warwick District Council. The business was let to Gilmans Catering of Leamington in April 1975, who kept on Mrs Warner as manageress; now in her 17th year in the job, she recalled her first days when the enterprise was in *'little more than a garden shed'*. A greater range of items was introduced, and opening times were 2 to 7 p.m. every day.

February 1976 saw the return of complaints in the local newspaper about the amount of **dog fouling** in the fields, which the writer suggested would become worse when the evenings were lighter and warmer. *'The old style KUDC who banned cows from it, never did anything to confine or restrict dogs'*, and nor had the WDC in its short tenure; the following week an article was published about the diseases that could be caught from dog droppings.

The **tennis court** nets were not put up until the end of April 1976 despite the weather being warm and the courts at other WDC facilities being in use. The reason given was that there was no attendant at Kenilworth and it would be uneconomical to have one.

Although now used less frequently, the **bowling green** still had a collection of regular players, most of which were elderly. When the price of playing for an hour was increased in 1977, letters were written to the WDC and *KWN*; *'30p, yes 30p! How can pensioners afford that?'*; there were now no reductions for pensioners at any of the Abbey Fields amenities.

The newly formed WDC had responsibility for numerous parks and open spaces across its district and **bye-laws** needed to be drawn up for them all. These were more or less standardised for all parks and were introduced in 1977; they remain virtually unchanged to this day. Of interest is that paddling in the brook is still forbidden but the taking of fish is not prohibited, and although one still cannot hang out washing to dry, it appears that beating carpets is no longer specifically forbidden, although it may be covered under Byelaw 19 concerning 'annoying' other users.

In late 1974, the Kenilworth History & Archaeology Society (KHAS) was instrumental in setting up the **Kenilworth Abbey Advisory Committee** (KAAC), its initial aim being to halt the deterioration of the **Tantara Gatehouse** described as 'on the verge of final irreversible collapse'. Three KHAS members were on the original committee, Irene Potter, Basil Lund and Harry Sunley, and also representatives of WDC, Kenilworth Town Council and the Kenilworth Society; Alfred Gardner FRIBA was appointed chairman. The necessary consolidation work on the **Gatehouse** had been held up for over a decade by lack of money, photographs show it to be perhaps two-thirds covered in vegetation. The Department for the Environment now put the estimate for repairs at £20,000; an appeal committee was formed within the KAAC with KHAS members prominent, and by March 1977 £3,500 had been raised by local appeals. The D of E offered a 50% grant making it possible for work to start, which it did on 18th April. Preliminary work began with the clearance of vegetation and in September restoration work proper started under the County Archaeologist assisted by members and friends of the KHAS. The revised estimated cost was now £16,500 *(£94,000)*, the balance coming from the D of E and WDC who offered a large contribution and in July the latter took over responsibility for the work as well as the funds. Work began by digging down 5ft or so to view the foundations which in itself was of great interest. The work was completed by December.

By June 1976, the KHAS had spent close on three years restoring and cleaning the Barn, and had turned their collective hands to some other restoration work, this time it was the object known as the 'ducking stool'. The society finally opened the Barn as a museum in early June 1977, but unlike their predecessors, the Friends between the wars, allowed free entry. Displayed were artefacts from local industries as well as of the Abbey, and included those that had been on show inside St Nicholas church with the exception of the half-ton pig of lead that remains in the church to this day. In 1979, a 'modest' electricity supply was installed.

Attention then moved to the comparatively overlooked Chapter House wall, itself also covered in vegetation and crumbling to the extent that demolition seemed the likely outcome. Such was its condition that *'once the Department of the Environment approve'*, the KHAS volunteered to dismantle it then store the stone in the Barn, even though there was little space. However, after so much time and effort had gone into restoring the Gatehouse, it would have made little sense to then demolish the Chapter House wall and in

Clinton House overlooks the area donated by its former occupant Gertrude Evans; the young trees today block the view both of and from the house. Mr Whiteman's corner, lower centre, has been planted with trees *(21st June 1981)*

February 1979 the D of E said it should be preserved and offered £250 of the required £750 to make it safe; the rest was paid by WDC, a small sum when compared to the Gatehouse work.

In September 1977, it was suggested at a Kenilworth Town Council (KTC) meeting that **flower beds** with seating could be introduced between the bus shelter and War Memorial. It was described as a *'charming'* idea as people used the area for picnics, but comments against included that the Abbey Fields were *'completely rural, not like a flower-planted bit at Warwick or Leamington. If there is to be any alteration to the fields it should be a lake in the Oxpen Meadow'*. The KTC vote, by a slight majority, was to recommend the beds, however the Warwick District Council Amenities Committee turned down the idea; *'Flower beds would be an intrusion into the beauty of the Fields. There is no money available anyway to do the work.'*

Subsequently, the **Kenilworth Society** let its views be known; *'The fields are public grounds that should not be marred by a lot of new planting'* adding that the small beds around the bus shelter enhanced the area, but the proposed beds of 40m by 2m or more *'would defeat the whole idea behind the donation of the Abbey Fields to the residents of Kenilworth as a public open space'*. Councillor J Wilson added, *'Leamington is the place for flower gardens, not Kenilworth'*; another Kenilworth councillor disagreed, saying, *'If some people had their way the Abbey Fields would still be used for grazing cows. A few flower beds would look very nice'*. This discussion about simple flower beds, approved by one council then rejected by the other, demonstrated not only the differing entrenched views as to precisely what the Abbey Fields were, but also the developing difficulties in their management.

In March 1979, rose bushes donated by a building society were planted near the War Memorial, but three more elms said to be over 100 years old succumbed to disease and were cut down, the good wood was to be used for making park benches, for Newbold Common. In November 1979, trees *'planted ten years ago'* were vandalised; three 20ft tall red oak trees were cut down to 2ft with a bow saw, a willow tree by the brook was destroyed and *'the new cedar-wood bridge over the brook'* was damaged. Within two weeks, a replacement red oak was provided by the *Kenilworth Weekly News* editor and planted alongside the brook, and another was planted in an unspecified location in memory of former Councillor Harry Potts who had died a few weeks before. In July 1982 a tree was planted in the park to commemorate the birth of Prince William; Mayor and Mayoress Bill and Doris Wozencroft were helped by Town Clerk Harry Sunley and schoolgirls Debbie Carroll and Claire Marley. (It appears that the tree died and has been removed.)

In July 1982, the WDC Recreational & Amenities Committee (R&AC) decided to create an artificial lake at Newbold Common, much to the dismay of Kenilworth's councillors still trying to have one approved in the **Oxpen Meadow**. The Kenilworth scheme had failed to materialise due to opposition and lack of finance, it was said, and yet the Newbold Common scheme was likely to prove more expensive, or be of *'minimal cost'* depending upon which side of the argument was being reported; potentially, it was to be partly paid for from outside sources. By the end of the meeting it had been decided to again consider a lake in the Oxpen Meadow at a later meeting, as had often been the case for almost a century.

An **army** recruitment display in the Abbey Fields during the last week of September 1977 showed off weapons, and children were allowed to handle, amongst others, a mounted machine gun and a field gun.

In September 1981, reflecting the lapsed tradition started before the Abbey Fields were sold by Clarendon, the Kenilworth **Fire Brigade** organised a fire engine rally in aid of the National Fire Service Benevolent Fund. Held on the levelled area alongside Bridge Street, more than 30 preserved engines appeared; the oldest was a steam Merryweather similar to Kenilworth's late Victorian Queen Bess, and the largest was a United States Air Force crash tender brought from Upper Heyford air base. Soon after the show started, the Kenilworth brigade was called away to a fire, and left the field with lights flashing and siren blaring! The show included demonstrations of fire fighting and equipment, a cowboy display by the Warwick Westerners, a parachute drop, and the Kenilworth Guides marching band.

The event returned and for the following years was held over two days; a parade of vehicles through the town, marching bands, motorcycle display team, and accident and fire fighting demonstrations were all included in the programme. It moved to Thickthorn but ended a couple of years later.

A car fire demonstration performed by the Kenilworth brigade. In the background is the set for the Wild West display, cars parked on the Rosemary Hill field, and the fairground bridge over the brook *(1st September 1984)*

In June 1976 the **swimming pool** heating was being turned off once a week to save costs, but then *'the saving became much greater than anticipated, because it has conked out'*. Large, roughly rectangular, pipes carried the water which was then heated by gas before circulating back into the pool, but the boiler was suffering from pinholes. It was said repairs could take some time; it was particularly difficult for the many schoolchildren learning to swim.

Inevitably, roofing the pool was a repeated suggestion as it would make it usable throughout the year *'instead of only during alleged summers'* and it gathered support in the summer of 1977 from, amongst others, the Kenilworth Safety Committee saying the more opportunities there were for children to learn to swim the better. However, a roof was always met by *'powerful protesting by residents who oppose any addition to* the buildings in the Abbey Fields and are particularly against a roof on the assumption that it would be out of place and a disfigurement impossible not to see', and who thought it would *'create the appearance of a building out of keeping with the landscape that is regarded as the essential feature of the Abbey Fields'*. The Town Council could of course only make suggestions as it was down to WDC to make the decisions, but as a result of the movement, the WDC Recreation & Amenities Committee allocated £15,000 in their budget for a 'Kenilworth swimming pool cover' sometime in the 1978/9 to 1982/3 financial years.

A town meeting to discuss the issue was called for 9th November 1977 but only 12 people turned up, and 6 of those were councillors; with something of an understatement one said, *'We shall need further evidence that this is what the people want'*. At this time there was a proposed district pool and the Town Council agreed to ask the WDC and Warwickshire County Council (WCC) to build it in Kenilworth.

In November 1977, a WDC working party was formed to investigate all pool requirements at Kenilworth, Warwick and Leamington, the latter being the only one with a covered pool. Some would say it was unsurprising that Leamington, that already had an enclosed pool, was chosen to be the site of the proposed district pool, but in January 1978 a *'detailed look'* was underway into Kenilworth's swimming necessities. Adding into the story was the closure of the small indoor pool at Thorns School as a cost-cutting exercise; pupil's parents hoped to raise enough funds to keep it open but this suggestion was rejected by the school.

Showing just how popular Kenilworth's pool was at this time, in the Whitsun holiday in 1978 an astonishing 5,500 used it, a claimed record, and compares say with the entire year of 1907 when only 2,038 used the baths.

But in October 1978, as a result of the *'detailed look'*, it was announced that covering the existing Abbey Fields pool had been ruled out; in addition to the *'National sized'* pool at Leamington there would be one other covered pool with several sites suggested at Warwick and at the planned sports facilities at Kenilworth's **Castle Farm**. The decision to keep the Kenilworth pool heated but uncovered was *'to satisfy the continuing demand for open air swimming'*. Roofing the pool was now said to cost £400,000, and there were also planning difficulties due to it being in *'part of an outstanding conservation area'*. With no promise of any changes at all to the facilities in Kenilworth, one councillor was outraged: *'If it were not for the* (council) *reorganisation, all the towns would have provided new pools for themselves. It's a case of Kenilworth being fobbed off again'*. There were critics elsewhere too and, after a vote, the following month the Policy & Resources Committee (P&RC) were instructed to re-examine the pool options, but initially they confirmed their earlier conclusions.

By April 1979, the P&RC had found a solution for Kenilworth's swimming accommodation by retaining the outdoor pool in the Abbey Fields and investigating the provision of a *'modest sized pool'* at Kenilworth School in Leyes Lane that would be available to the public outside school hours. By September, the committee's swimming pool working party recommended spending £350,000 on a 20m by 10m indoor pool at Leyes Lane, and confirmed there were no plans to close or alter the open-air pool in the Abbey Fields. There was however a proviso to the suggested Leyes Lane pool, *'if finance can be made available'*. A Kenilworth councillor said, *'There is not a snowball's chance in hell'* of getting the pool as the money was not there. This compares to the unanimously accepted plans to build the £2.3 million district pool at Newbold Terrace in Leamington.

Then in January 1980 government restrictions on spending were the given cause of all plans being *'put into storage'*, and now priority was being given to a major facelift to the existing Leamington pool. The Kenilworth plan was still for a joint-use pool at Kenilworth School, for a now reported cost of £700,000, double the estimate of the previous April; the boiler would also be used for heating the adjacent school sports hall and it was unrealistically suggested that a start could be made in October. It wasn't.

In March 1981, WDC advanced the proposals for sporting facilities at **Castle Farm**. They had by now constructed an entrance road from the Fishponds Road stub for access to the children's play equipment but now attention turned to the playing fields. In September the proposed layout was published and it included a pavilion with squash courts, football pitches and a rugby pitch, a hockey pitch alongside a new path connecting the facilities to the Abbey Fields, a 250yd banked cycle track and at last a permanent cricket pitch, an idea dating back to the purchase of the Abbey Fields in 1884; perhaps the 'pitchless' Kenilworth Cricket Club 3rd XI were expected to use it (in 2017, the team still plays its home matches 'away' from home, at Harbury). The plans were approved. The first phase of the *'ambitious Castle Farm project'* was given the go-ahead in September 1981 starting with £10,000 to spend on drainage and earthworks in 1981-2, and £60,000 in 1982-3. The whole scheme was now projected to eventually cost close to £½ million.

As 1981 progressed, so did the **swimming pool** story. In March the County Architect was drawing up plans for a pool at Kenilworth School in Leyes Lane, at a newly revised cost of half a million pounds, but in June the scheme was given *'a low priority'* with a pool at Warwick being seen as a greater necessity; the Warwick outdoor pool was in a poorer condition than Kenilworth's. The final decision in July was that a pool at Warwick had a budget of £800,000 and at last an indoor pool for Kenilworth was promised, but with a 1986 target and no confirmed location.

This was, almost inevitably, followed by a heat wave with Kenilworth's outdoor pool having queues *'around the block'*. The fine weather continued but the pool closed on 6th September much to the disbelief of many; in contrast to the days of the KUDC when the pool closed at the supervisors discretion based upon the weather, under the WDC the *'dates were fixed at the start of the year in accordance with an approved budget and coincided with the return to school of children after the holidays'*. Meanwhile there were arguments and complaints concerning the siting the new Warwick pool on Warwick Park's crazy-golf course: *'If Warwick doesn't want their pool, we'll have it'*, observed Councillor Butler.

One on-going story at this time was children getting sores and blisters on their feet when using the Kenilworth pool. The District Council was unable to afford tiling, at a cost of £25,000, but spent £700 annually in maintenance, much of which was on resurfacing the pool's floor and sides with a mixture of paint and cement, but every year a combination of chlorine and feet movement made it flake off, apparently causing the cuts to the feet of users, who were mostly children. Looking for a long-term solution, a visit was made by a pool specialist and in April 1981 the *KWN* covered the story of two workers under the Youth Opportunities Scheme chipping the paint off the sides and bottom of the empty pool in preparation for another re-surfacing; this was to no avail, in June once more there were stories of children again getting cuts when using the swimming pool.

At the season end, council officers concluded there was *'no evidence that the sides and floor of the pool are responsible for the complaints of cut feet'*; they believed it was caused by soft feet getting blisters going in and out of the pool and then bursting, perhaps explaining both why it was children only who were affected and why the problem was at its worse in the early season. However, before the following season a rather more severe maintenance programmes saw the walls and bottom sandblasted to remove 4 layers of rubberised paint ready for a new coating. The pool re-opened on 25th May 1982. The unemployed now had free use of the pool on Wednesdays but on other days had to pay the child rate of 25p.

The outlook from the Abbey Hill houses, one reason this area of the fields was saved, is about to change due to the planting of a number of trees. At least five seats, probably those installed in 1965, are provided for visitors to enjoy the view. In the distance is the beech tree felled *c*2000, leaving a recess in the pavement *(Autumn 1985)*

Once again, in June 1982, **cars** were being driven across the fields to the swimming pool; the police were informed and WDC installed barriers near the Bridge Street entrance to stop it. *'These people are spoiling a valuable amenity and this cannot be allowed to continue'*. Then, due to congestion caused by haphazard parking in the existing **car park**, the following month the District Amenities Officer suggested building a new car park alongside the tennis courts. It was then pointed out that *'Kenilworth's car parks are almost empty at weekends'* and since the Abbey Fields were there for exercise, *'visitors could park elsewhere and walk'*. The Recreation & Amenities Committee turned down the new parking idea for which there was no allocated money in any case, but decided to look at improving the access to the Bridge Street car park.

In June 1982, it was announced that Warwick District Council was to raise about £140,000 by selling several freehold properties it owned (inherited from the KUDC) at the corner of the Talisman Square precinct, along with some of the car parking land immediately behind it. It was recommended that the money should be *'considered to be earmarked for the **swimming pool***'. The pool was now described as a proposed indoor Kenilworth pool and planned for 1986 at a cost of £750,000, but within the Town Council there were concerns at selling the land at all, let alone what should be done with the money. As an indication of the financial situation of the time, the *KWN* ran a feature that they called 'Sign of the times' showing numerous empty Kenilworth business premises that were available for letting.

It was in the 11th February 1983 *KWN* that the public could see plans for a Kenilworth indoor pool for the first time, it was in the Abbey Fields. The proposals were by the Kenilworth Town Council, and were to be forwarded to the District Policy & Resources Committee for appraisal. As seen, the re-building of the changing rooms and kiosk in 1965 had deliberately left a large area at the northern end of the pool for any future development, and it was in that space that it was proposed to build an 18m by 9m pool, with a low flat roof with a sunbathing deck in keeping with the existing buildings. Its cost had not been finalised but was expected to be less than half of the £800,000 for the proposed new Warwick pool. The sale of land at Talisman Square, it was argued, should be put towards the pool in addition to £60,000 already set aside; half the cost was thus already met.

By August, a working party was looking at the two sites for a new Kenilworth Pool, the Abbey Fields and the Kenilworth School site in Leyes Lane; the developing facilities at Castle Farm does not seem to have been seriously investigated. It was now being said that if it was sited away from the Abbey Fields it would probably mean the closure of the existing outdoor pool for financial reasons, but choosing the school site and its shared use could enable it to stay open. That same week, the outdoor pool was in the news as it was once again closed as soon as the school holidays were over at the beginning of September; in earlier years it had stayed open for at least another month. A petition signed by 200 adults had no effect; the reasons given for the early closure were the losses made by the later closure date in the 1970s, and that *'it would not be fair on the staff'*. The KUDC had given greater importance to providing a service.

Over 100 clubs, societies and schools in Kenilworth and the surrounding area received a questionnaire sent by the Amenities Department in July 1983 to judge the likely use of an indoor pool, but by November just 20 of them had replied. There were alternatives to KTC's pool plans in the pipeline; an early estimated cost of £850,000 was now thought to be excessive and had fallen to £600,000, but no details were yet available of these alternatives.

At this time, the facilities in the Abbey Fields were under scrutiny; WDC had decided to hire a private contractor to run the **tennis, pitch & putt, putting and bowling green** but this had been a disaster. At off-peak times, such as evenings when there would be little income from them, the contractors simply closed up and left, whereas in the past the council's own seasonal staff kept the facilities open. On occasions the tennis courts were simply left unlocked allowing free play by anyone, and they were often taken over by youths *'hogging the courts'* and keeping others from playing. The attendants were, it was said, too young to cope with the youths that congregated around the Pavilion, and rode bikes and played football on the bowling green; damage had also been caused to paving, the tennis nets and telephone cables. There had been many complaints from the public; *'The summer has been a miserable time for the councillors due to the number of complaints'*. WDC decided to revert to direct labour the following year, although contractors remained at Jephson Gardens in Leamington and St Nicholas Park in Warwick.

In February 1984 it was being reported that a Kenilworth swimming pool, now a proposed 25m long and at a cost of £650,000, had been saved in a round of project cost-cutting, as had the proposed pavilion at Castle Farm. Just £100,000 was to be spent there on changing rooms and other facilities, and not the full £300,000 scheme; because the access road, car park and football pitches had now been completed, the rest was described as 'urgent'. The Abbey Fields was still the likely site for the indoor pool but there was no official confirmation; it was said that the existing pool could be closed for the 1985 season and the new to open in 1986.

With the Town Council's design still being the only one to view, Councillor Michael Coker said that *'great care will be taken to preserve the environment'* if the Abbey Fields was chosen as the new pool's site. *'It is understandable that people may fear the fields would be spoiled by the building of a new pool. Abbey Fields is the preferred choice as it would be easier to build within the tight budget guidelines and preserve the existing outdoor pool. It will be like an extension of the existing buildings around the current pool and not be an eyesore. What we envisage is that it would be no higher than the existing frontage and take up very little space outside the existing confines.'*

Leading campaigners supporting the best interests of the town at the time was the Kenilworth Residents Action Committee (KRAC) who asked for a town meeting to discuss the proposals; the Abbey Fields *'are an historic rural heart that provides a retreat of peace and calm at the very centre of the town. That could be threatened by a new pool that would generate a need for better lighting and increased car parking, which would further destroy the charm of the Abbey Fields'*. Their request was not granted despite gaining support from a number of councillors. One reason given was, *'If we started having public meetings on everything, there would be very little point in having us elected.'*

The roofs of the 1965 buildings were lower than their 1935 counterparts, councillors allayed fears that the proposed pool in the 1980s would be more intrusive. Clinton House is top left. Compare to the photograph on page 123 *(Summer 1984)*

Another controversial Abbey Fields project took place in April 1984. A pedestrian access was made from the **car park** through the boundary wall into Bridge Street, as near to the traffic lights as possible, a clear indication that the car park was now accepted as being for the High Street area and not just the Abbey Fields as initially intended. With part of the wall demolished, work was halted by the intervention of the D of E who suspected the wall may be covered in the Ancient Monuments listing; they claimed they should have been consulted before the work began. The wall had been rebuilt in about 1925 but clearly using ancient stone, presumably from the Abbey and including some from the excavations of the early 1920s. The work was delayed whilst the removed stones were inspected for any historical value, and it was not until October that work resumed.

At the end of May 1984, the **swimming pool** working party finally announced the Abbey Fields had been chosen as the preferred site. The announcement included a few details that the current pool provided between 20 and 40 per cent of the *'total recorded swims in the District'* but the *'old and broken down plant at the pool will have to be replaced in the near future. That would be financially impossible without the support of the new pool; the two can run using the same plant and same staff'*. The new pool would be *'carefully blended into the surrounding area.'*

Immediately there were concerns that the new pool would necessitate extra parking spaces and despite an assurance from the District Amenities Officer that no such extension was envisaged, people were not convinced. Another view claimed, *'The outdoor pool is very well used, and not many people are expected to* use the new facilities'. *'The majority of people think of the Abbey Fields as an oasis to be preserved; the new pool should be at Castle Farm where as many sports as possible are on one site.'*

But within weeks, doubts arose about the future of the entire project; the District Treasurer announced that no go-ahead would be given for the pool or further Castle Farm development until the government's expenditure target for 1985-86 was known, despite capital for the two projects having been allocated in February.

The announcement coincided with a seminar organised by KRAC to celebrate 100 years of the Abbey Fields. This included eloquent and passionate speeches covering the history of the fields, the Abbey, and the need to protect them. It was lamented that the area covered by the Scheduled Ancient Monument listing did not reach the swimming pool area. Judging of a photographic competition closed the proceedings. It was something of an oversight that there was no official marking of the anniversary.

Arguments continued at the Town Council meeting in July, the views polarised more or less down party lines. *'The Abbey Fields is being chosen because it is the cheap option and to keep the outdoor pool; if the funds are not there, we should wait until they are. Let's leave the Abbey Fields alone'. 'Unless the covered pool is sited next to the old one, there would be no safeguard for the retention of the open air pool'. 'Opposition might endanger the whole project. If we are split, there is a danger of losing it; we are on a knife edge as far as money is concerned'.* A vote backed the working party's proposals.

Also in July, a petition against the Abbey Fields as a site for the pool was organised and quickly gained hundreds of signatures; by the end of August it numbered over a thousand and demands were being made for a referendum on the subject. Councillors were quoted dismissing the organisers as *'ignorant… they don't know what they are talking about… they are a joke'*, and *'If the present proposals are blighted by the petition, it will be many years before these funds become available again, if ever.'*

The swimming pool in May 1985. From the left is the male changing rooms, entrance, female changing rooms, and refreshment kiosk all built in 1965, with the wooden-clad 1935 filtration plant building behind, and right, the public conveniences built in 1971. In the foreground is a recently installed sprung see-saw (which replaced the horse-rocker in the same location), a child's climbing frame and the 32 years old 1953 slide. The two trees can discerned on page 76

The attractions of the existing pool proved too tempting for one group early on the morning of 17th June 1984. Five men and a girl with wet hair were spotted by a police officer at 3.25 a.m. climbing out over the pool's fence. Each was charged with offences such as *'Entering the pool by improper means'* and using the pool without a ticket. Fines were of £10.

The Kenilworth **Swimming Club** and its 300 members had an exceptional year. They concentrated on the enjoyment and teaching of youngsters and more than 50 had taken their first strokes that year, but some 'senior beginners' were taught too; 181 certificates had been issued and 46 other awards. The coaches included Derek Pickering, the long-term campaigner for the pool to be heated and covered. But with the 1984 season now over and the outdoor pool about to close, the club were transferring their activities to Leamington's indoor pool.

At the beginning of September, WDC announced it was to ignore government guidelines on capital spending and press ahead with constructing the indoor pool, and facilities at Castle Farm; it was the last barrier for both. That same day KRAC announced it was to again ask the Town Council to hold a public meeting about the proposed pool, and said if they didn't then they would arrange their own and invite councillors to attend. *'There is so much concern in the town about the pool proposals, it is only right people should be allowed to put their views and have their say'*. The council unexpectedly agreed and set the meeting for the hall at St Francis in Warwick Road for Thursday 25th October.

But then the week before the meeting it was announced that the outdoor pool would not open the following year as the repair work was urgent and needed before it could be used again; £30,000 had to be spent immediately to prepare the boiler and filtration plant for further use, and another £70,000 for other repairs such as to the changing room roof. It was then said that the money would only be spent if the new pool was sited alongside. This was a similar situation to 1934 when the original pool closed needing a filtration system that resulted in the lido being built, and as in 1934 Kenilworth now effectively had no pool; it would be pointless to replace the equipment with the development plans close to fruition.

Just two days before the St Francis meeting, the District Council Policy & Resource Committee backed the chosen site in the Abbey Fields, the last stage before submitting a planning application. *'The council's solicitor has examined the covenants contained in the council's deed relating to the Abbey fields, and says these are compatible with the proposal'*. It was also accepted that no money should be spent to ensure the outdoor pool could re-open the following year, confirming its closure.

With the decisions made in the preceding days, not surprisingly, the meeting room at St Francis was *'packed to capacity'*, but the public were restricted to just asking questions. Again the council stated that the outdoor pool would not be repaired unless the indoor was sited alongside; *'Money would not be available to keep the outdoor pool open'*. *'The end result would in no way spoil the beauty of the Abbey Fields, in fact it would be an improvement'*, and, *'It is only the last few months I have become aware of any feeling of unacceptability over the siting of the pool'*. Another councillor said that Kenilworth *'was being fobbed of with a cheap pool'* and should wait until finances were available to build a substantial pool on another site. *'If the Abbey Fields is the only feasible proposition, then we should wait until the economy improves.'*

Following the meeting, one councillor, Bob Butler, was not convinced by the closure of the outdoor pool; with work on the new pool (if finally approved) now not set to start in any case until the autumn of 1985, he was sure something could be done short term to have the outdoor pool open the next season, even if unheated. A free evaluation offered by an independent company was refused, and it was simultaneously stated that a start on the new pool would be made early the next year. One letter writer to the *KWN* described siting the pool in the Abbey Fields as the *'biggest act of vandalism ever perpetrated on this town.'*

With the go-ahead finally confirmed, designs were invited and nine were submitted. That chosen was by Hamilton Bland, a former British Olympic swimming coach. In the early 1980s he began a career as a swimming pool equipment consultant and developed an impressive exhibition centre at his Leek Wootton home The Paddox where he had a pool built, set in neoclassical surroundings. *'He took an early interest in the plans for the new baths at the Abbey Fields and District Councillors were invited to The Paddox for a presentation. Later the consortium to which he was a consultant won the contract against some stiff opposition with a slick presentation and a value for money development'*. The pool was to be the first venture of his newly set-up Construction Consultants International Ltd. *'He is now faced with one of his biggest challenges in providing Kenilworth with a competition sized pool that will not look out of place in the Abbey Fields'*. Hamilton Bland said *'I am delighted because of the importance of the site and the challenge it represents as designers of indoor pools.'*

When the plans were finally revealed in February 1985, drawn by architects The Gillinson Partnership of Leeds, they were nothing like those the Town Council had proposed earlier that were in keeping with the existing buildings and stayed more or less within the existing boundaries; the new buildings would encroach into the Abbey Fields further than had been expected, and had a paved area beyond that, and the building had a pitched roof of almost three times the height of the existing buildings at the northern end of the site. On top of that, the outdoor pool was to be noticeably reduced in size by perhaps a third and altered to an irregular 'kidney' shape and would include *'a large 12 inch deep shallow end'*. The cost had also risen to £805,000; £730,000 for the new pool and £75,000 for the refurbishment of the outdoor. The changing rooms and cafeteria too were to be refurbished, and the rooftop sunbathing deck was to be kept. The potential start had been pushed back at least to the autumn, which would be a year after the old pool had closed. A councillor was quoted as saying, rather hopefully, *'I do not expect criticism, it does not need defending.'*

In early April 1985, 398 people took the opportunity to vote on the issue in a poll organised by KRAC in Talisman Square. Only 34 per cent agreed to the pool being built in the Abbey Fields with 43 per cent saying other sites should be re-investigated, and 23 per cent saying the whole project was a waste of money in the existing financial climate; most of those opposed to the site repeated the oft heard *'Leave the fields alone'*.

Eighty three voters said the pool should be at Castle Farm, and many voters of all opinions deplored the lack of a public debate on the options. KRAC urged people to write to councillors to make their views known. *'Within 5 years I think Kenilworth will have lost something quite unique as a result of building the pool.'*

At about this time, the 20-year loan for the 1965 rebuild of the changing rooms was paid off.

By the end of May the plans looked set to go ahead after backing from the Town Council despite the strong criticism of the design and location which was noticeably different from their own suggestion; quotes from councillors confirmed the opposing views: *'The outdoor pool looks like a big kiddies paddling pool and the indoor building looks like a warehouse with a hole in it'. 'It looks like an elongated cow shed'. 'Cramming it into a small space makes it a white elephant'. 'It is far too small, a lack of real thought has gone into this necessary development'. 'The whole thing has been well thought out and is a planning gain'. 'I am positive it will enhance the appearance of the Abbey Fields'. 'If we don't site it in the Abbey Fields, it might not go anywhere at all'.* The arguments were not made easier by the realisation that Leamington had an indoor pool of 3,000 sq ft, Warwick of 2,500 sq ft, and that Kenilworth's would be only 1,700 sq ft.

Two views from the same vantage point, the top of the 1953 slide.
Upper: The kiosk has been demolished to create an entrance *(27th October 1985)*
Lower: The new structure rises high over the excavation for the indoor pool. Dwarfed by the new roof, much of the 1971 conveniences are retained for refurbishment, the roof frame was later extended over the conveniences. Part of the former female changing rooms survived as the new cafe area; the 'V' shape cut in the wall matches the modern windows. The visual intrusion compared the earlier buildings is clear *(24th November 1985)*

There was also fierce criticism of the design of the *'outdoor leisure pool'* being like *'a glorified paddling pool'* with its odd shape and shallow depth. Towards the end of August 1985 a new design was unveiled showing it now to be a squat 'L' shape and with more deeper water, and at last a separate small paddling pool had been added, an idea first suggested 47 years previously in 1938. Both would be incorporated within the existing pool excavation. Now, 89 per cent of the new outdoor pool would be deeper than 2ft 4ins allowing for *'swimming as opposed to just splashing about'*; it would still only have a surface area of two thirds of the existing pool, and a water volume similar to the orignal 1896 pool, but inclusive of the new indoor pool the overall water area would increase by 19 per cent.

With the town not having had any pool for over a year, on-site work finally started at the beginning of October by Wincott Galliford Ltd, the official ceremony being at noon on 14th October. It was intended to be completed by the following June. As excavations began for the new pool in late October, the spoil was tipped nearby at the edge of the Oxpen Meadow, where some spoil had been tipped after the digging of foundations for the 1964/5 rebuild. It was suggested that this extra spoil could interfere with the drainage of the meadow but *'Council Officers'* said that the opportunity will be taken to repair the existing drainage system; despite the assertions, the Oxpen Meadow draining system as outlined on page 148 was interrupted.

Two views from more or less the original entrance to the swimming pool. On the left is the plinth of the 1935 changing rooms retained as a sunbathing terrace. Compare to the photographs on pages 89 and 112.
Upper: The conveniences are partially demolished, the new shape of the outdoor pool is in preparation, and slabs from the far end are stacked for re-use *(27th October 1985)*
Lower: The indoor pool building takes shape, the outdoor pool lining is complete, rubble from the site is being used to infill parts of the 1935 pool, the cascade and terracing are being removed *(December 1985)*

By the time photographs of construction appeared in the *KWN* in May 1986, the work was being quoted as costing £840,000 and the opening had been delayed. The outdoor pools had been filled but had debris floating in them and rubble all around, whist inside scaffolding was up allowing work on the roof.

The new pool was filled for the first time in the first week of September 1986; unlike the two previous such occasions in 1896 and 1935, the fire brigade were not required. It took two and a half days for the 75,000 gallons to be pumped into the pool from three jets (the 1896 pool held 60,000 gallons); the outdoor pool had already been filled. A hoist, part paid for by Warwick Avon Rotary Club, to enable disabled swimmers to enter and leave the pool, had arrived the same week. In conjunction with the work, the path from Bridge Street had to be rebuilt, partly through damage caused by construction machinery. The pool was handed over to the WDC on 12th September and they set an opening date at early October. *'It is something the town can be proud of. It surpasses anything that could be imagined when the idea was first mentioned'*, but criticism of the appearance and location was still not far away; *'Where once you could see trees there is now a brick wall. It looks like a large warehouse'*, and graffiti had already appeared.

On 5th October an open day was held for the public when *'hundreds'* had their first look at the pool. The following day a number of Kenilworth School Priory Hall pupils were the first to officially use the pool, and the public were allowed in for the first time at 12.30 p.m. on Wednesday 8th October. On the following Sunday, an impressive 800 paid to swim, but a problem meant the water was cooler than it should have been. The following Tuesday was the first, and well patronised, Mum's & Toddlers session.

The Official opening by the then Sports Minister Richard Tracey took place on 31st October 1986. It was said to be the country's first indoor/outdoor complex opened in a decade. Chairman of the Swimming Pool Working Committee, Michael Coker, who had started the *'journey'* four years previously by commissioning the original design said, *'The Abbey Fields is an area we hold dear and must not be spoilt in any way. This is a particularly sensitive area but this building is one to be proud of and does not detract from the area'*. The final cost of the work was now put at £860,000 (£2.3 million).

The 1971 conveniences, with the door, were incorporated into the new structure and demonstrate the height difference between old and new *(6th February 2017)*

Being opened in October, it is quite likely that outdoor swimmers (if indeed that pool was actually open) despite having been without their pool for over two years, were few; by the time the warm weather returned, swimmers would have become very used to the more agreeable indoor conditions and the outdoor pool had a greatly reduced patronage when compared to the summer holidays of the 1960s and 1970s.

The rebuilding did not destroy all of the earlier incarnations of the swimming pool. Much of the male changing room area is the structure from 1965 and the rooftop sunbathing area was retained. Part of the new café area was formerly the female changing rooms with the toilet being in the same place (I am told). The public conveniences outside the pool (the part that had been used by pool users was removed) were refurbished from the 1971 structure and the differing brickwork at the western end is clear. The slabbing in place around the outdoor pool was kept, and some could date to 1935. At the brook end, the plinth of the 1935 changing rooms survived as does the terrace on which it was built. But gone completely were the slides, diving boards and spring board, and the cascade, and with them much of the fun. Also, the shorter length, curved end and greater area of shallow water made length-swimming less attractive.

Just four months after the opening, Hamilton Bland's trio of businesses were in liquidation after the failure of two other firms that had been wound up with debts of over £300,000. He had sold The Paddox but vowed *'I will start up again'* and he did, becoming involved in a number of council pool developments across the country.

By June 1985 the new sports hall, and thus changing facilities, was going up at **Castle Farm**. It was opened that October and so far as is known the first football pitches were put to immediate use. Thus it was at about this time that organised Abbey Field's **football,** started in 1926, was finally ended but not before this author, having earlier retrieved a ball from the brook following a wayward shot in the warm-up and playing the match with saturated boots, managed to score twice in a 3-2 win for Leek Wootton reserves over Kenilworth Saints on the pitch formerly known as 'The Swamp', on one of its soft rather than muddy days. The Saints were probably the last Kenilworth club to call the Abbey Fields football pitches 'home'. Trees were soon planted on the War Memorial pitch, today there are about sixteen.

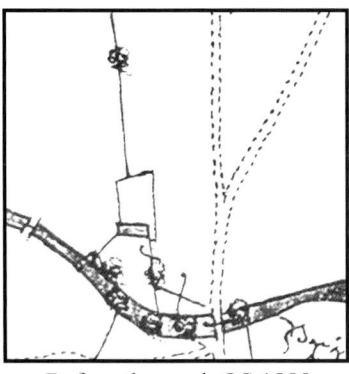

Before the pool, OS 1888 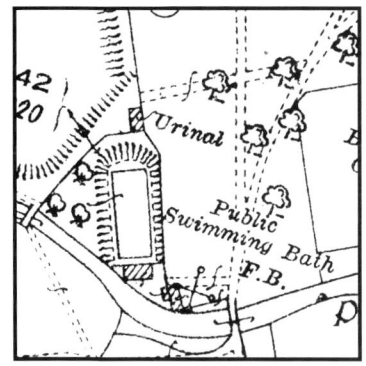 | The first pool of 1896, OS 1925 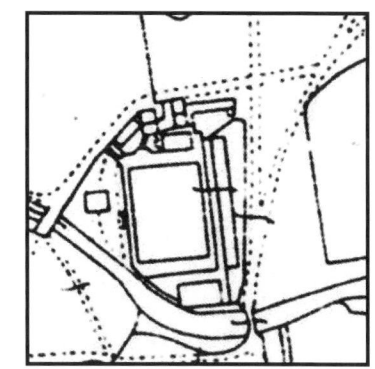 | The 1935 lido, OS 1938

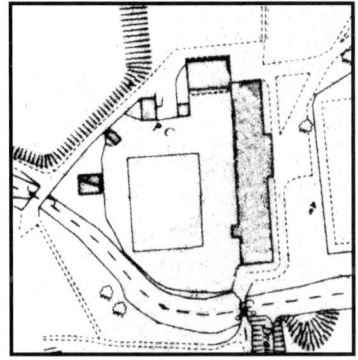

New changing rooms, OS 1966 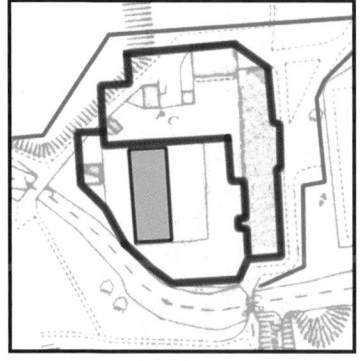 | Modern

The development of the swimming pool as recorded on Ordnance Survey maps.

The modern layout, left, is superimposed upon the 1966 map.
The black outline marks the buildings, the thinner line is the approximate extent of hard surface paths.
For comparison, the site of the original pool is included

In July 1984, the summer **Play Leadership Scheme** in the Abbey Fields was still going strong. Aimed at 7 to 14 year-olds, it ran daily throughout the school holidays from 10 a.m. to 4.30 p.m. with an hour's lunch break. Included this particular year were rounders, cricket, 5-a-side football, skipping, group games, stilts, tennis and swimming. The not so energetic could do drawing and painting, mask making and kite making, and it was hoped to arrange treasure and scavenger hunts, a nature trail and perhaps even a visit to a place of interest. The *KWN* also showed some youngsters attempting angling in the brook.

One unusual event, held annually for several years until about 1985, was an Abbey Fields pram race organised by charity fundraising regulars of The Royal Oak. Competitors had to push the pram's occupant, an adult, around a course. Prams were highly disguised as such diverse machines as the Magic Roundabout, a tank, and a bi-plane.

The subject of **dogs** in the fields, how they behaved and in particular what they left behind, continued to be a regular cause of discussion, which occasionally became rather heated as each side told stories of their experiences; the dog fraternity were as outraged at the general slurs as the complainers were at some owners lack of responsibility. A dog toilet area was a regular suggestion as was a fence around the children's play area. The seriousness of the accusations and 'tales' back and forth was lightened by one 'wag' in this 1985 letter to the *KWN*: *'I see your letter columns have fallen foul of a new topic. Following on from such partisan discussions covering the town's heritage, your correspondence are now dropping lines on a more down to earth matter – doggie do's. Once again the Abbey Fields is the centre of the debate and as muck-raking becomes plastered across your pages, the suggestion of a 'canine relief area' is again put forward. Now this idea must not be pooh-poohed, and 'Ladies' and 'Gents' may soon be joined by 'Dogs', but in my experience at least, many dogs cannot read and so may have difficulty in finding the chosen spot. However, the vision of an intelligent animal following its nose and bounding across the fields with his master in tow, whilst trying to keep its hind legs crossed in an attempt to reach its allotted patch before it is too late, is an entertaining one. Sooner or later the entire business will fall into the laps of the Town Councillors, they are the ones to sort out this mess. Let us hope that they can take positive steps without putting their foot in it.'* (Reproduced with the writer's permission.)

Bins were eventually provided. This was a subject often on the letters page of the *KWN*, and continues to be so to this day, although it must be said that today's dog owners take far greater care than in days past.

The entrance to the park from Borrowell Lane and the 1885 footpath; Luzley Brook is hidden behind the undergrowth to the left. Where the footpath curves past the tree, is the location of the gate in the photograph on page 46 *(16th August 2016)*

Whatever the arguments over the pool and its siting, there is no doubt it was responsible for bringing the whole future of the park and its uses into focus; the Gatehouse had been saved from collapse and the swimming pool built, but for ten years the rest of the fields had slumbered along with little change under the WDC. This was an extraordinary time in Kenilworth with the loss of historic buildings (The Poplars, The King's Arms and the railway station) and concerns about another (Kenilworth Hall), the building of houses on a flood plain (at School Lane) and the loss of a few acres of Crackley Woods, whilst hanging over the entire town was the threat of a coal mine being built nearby. It was perhaps a wake-up call for Kenilworth and its future direction, and as it often seems to be in town affairs the Abbey Fields was at the forefront.

A straightforward question asked in 1985 of WDC by KRAC member Gerry White led to an extraordinary outpouring of views about the use of the **Paddock**, then being grazed by Mrs Clements' two ponies, two foals and a donkey. As reported in the *KWN*, Mr White asked why the field had not been opened to the public as part of the park as intended when purchased by the KUDC; the reply was that there had been no demand to which Mr White countered, *'People are not aware that it is part of the Abbey Fields and so of course there has been no demand'*. This was interpreted as being an attempt by KRAC to have the grazing animals removed. As seen, Mrs Clements had been allowed to continue her lease for one year when the land was bought by the KUDC; despite the intention for it to become part of the park, they of course had no time to form any long-term plans for the field and the WDC had simply continued with the annual licence review for ten years. Mrs Clements said that she and her husband still paid for everything to do with the field, including cutting and weeding, and fence repairs. *'This field has never belonged to the Abbey Fields and the future of* (my) *pets would be in jeopardy if the field was ever opened to the public'*. Alec Retberg, now the Warwick District Parks & Recreation Manager, added, *'There was never any question as to whether the land was available to the general public as it was felt the 25-year-old donkey and ponies were an added attraction for everyone to enjoy. In fact it is the type of amenity we would wish to provide by way of a Pets Corner.'*

Quotes from letters in the following week's KWN included, *'Mr White's proposals are ludicrous, plain daft'*; *'KRAC have turned their wrath on a corner of Kenilworth that is so beautiful, their reasoning defies understanding'*; *'How upset I was at the possibility of the donkey and ponies being deprived of this home and perhaps having to be put down because someone has discovered that piece of land belongs to the Abbey Fields'*; *'Mr White's attack is more likely to alienate support for KRAC than to attract it.'*

KRAC's position was defended and explained by Chairman Avril Redman the following week. KRAC had been formed as part of a campaign to save the School Lane Meadow (effectively a continuation of the Abbey Fields 'open space' along Finham Brook) from development and they saw the Paddock as another piece of open land that may in time be lost. *'Our concern is the protection of both these meadows and of the Abbey Fields as a whole. As part of this concern we have sought consistently to establish the legal position regarding the Covenants of the Abbey Fields and so one of our members wrote privately to WDC asking for clarification of the position. So far, the WDC has never publicly clarified its legal interpretation of the covenants. KRAC seeks such an explanation as protection for the future. The KWN misrepresented our major concern on this issue with the result that those with little knowledge of our aims seem fit to attack us. We simply ask whether we are right in supposing that the WDC's present interpretation of the Abbey Field's covenants means that any other part of the fields could be privately let?'* Avril had already apologised personally to Mrs Clements for any distress caused.

The following week, Councillor Gerry Guest on behalf of the District Recreation & Amenities Committee was quoted as saying there were no plans to terminate the grazing licence and that the grazing animals were an *'attractive feature'* appreciated by many. How the private correspondence between Mr White and the WDC came to be reported in the first place was not publicly explained but the arguments obscured the purpose of the original letter - the WDC had still not stated their interpretation of the covenants.

Helping to promote interest in the Abbey and its fields, in 1985 the KHAS re-published Eustace Carey-Hill's 1937 fund-raising work, *The Abbey of St Mary*, with additional information credited to Richard Morris.

The **Kenilworth Inset Plan** was published in 1989 and included proposals for the future management of the Abbey Fields and churchyard. Referring to the map below: Area 1, which included the Paddock, was to be retained in its present form for informal recreation and the existing pitch & putt course, Area 2 to be the only area where development for formal recreation would be permitted, Area 3 to be subject to a project to restore and preserve the churchyard and Abbey Ruins, Area 4 to be flooded permanently and landscaped, and Area 5 to be retained as a permanent car park, re-laid and landscaped. The paragraph below these proposed outline plans stated:

> The Abbey Fields are a central and attractive feature of the Kenilworth Conservation area. They are subject to pressures for recreational use. The above proposals aim to strike a balance which will retain the Abbey Fields' character while continuing to meet legitimate recreational needs. The types of recreation referred to in Area 2 are sporting activities for which formal facilities (eg, buildings, pitch layout, or changing rooms) are required and play areas provided with non-mechanical play equipment. Area 4 will be developed simply as a landscape feature, not as a source of recreational activity. Area 5 will be retained as a permanent car park, re-laid and re-landscaped.

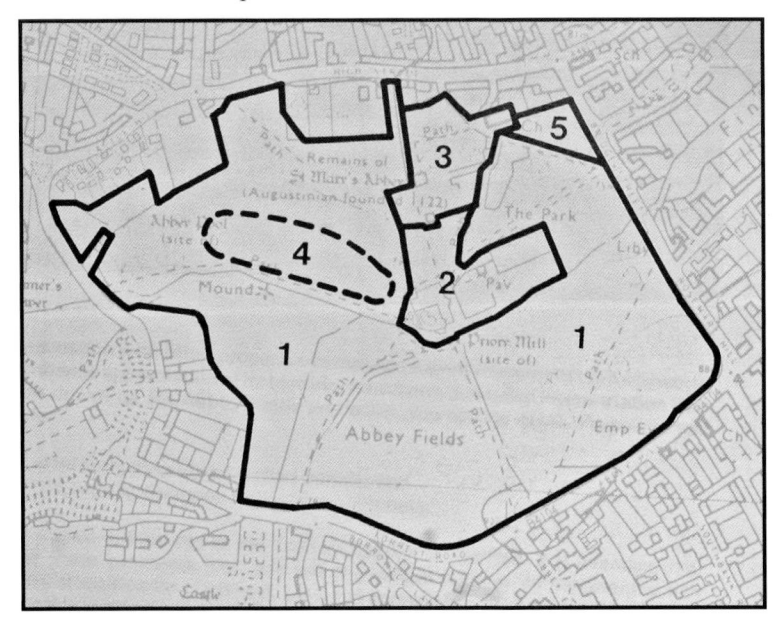

The car park area is shown larger than that in existence, but no extension was planned. The report also outlined proposals for a detailed Interpretation Plan for the Abbey and its remains, 'to enhance the appreciation... of Kenilworth's rich historical attractions'. The path from the Abbey Fields to the Common was at last to be built, but without the originally intended path alongside the brook inside the fields, and the car park re-surfacing and landscaping was to be 'in a fashion appropriate to this attractive location... to ensure its visual impact is acceptable.'

In February 1989, Severn-Trent Water (S-TW) began laying a water pipe from Abbey Hill to High Street across the fields; the course included an area on the south bank of the brook opposite the baths, close to the site believed to have been that of a mediaeval mill. As expected, the trench digger broke into archaeological remains close to the surface and Warwick Museum was alerted. The Museum and S-TW reached an agreement for work to halt in that specific area for seven days to allow an investigation to be made, and KHAS volunteers began a dig in 'freezing blizzard conditions'. Part of one building uncovered, in conjunction with the adjacent earthworks, was thought to be up to 20 yards long; several flagstones from its floor were still in place. There was nothing to suggest it was part of the Abbey mill, marked on Ordnance Survey maps as on the swimming pool site, and being 150 yards away from the known nearest ecclesiastical buildings made interpretation difficult; its use remains unknown for certain but a farm building is the most likely. Smaller finds (including 96 nails, a buckle, iron hoop, door hinge, animal bone, 21 floor and 703 roof tile fragments, and 223 slate roof fragments) helped to suggest a date for the building to perhaps the 12th or 13th century with use into the early 16th, the time of the dissolution and the Abbey's closure.

Also in 1989, two small square pits were dug for the installation of a new piece of play equipment; one revealed a sandstone surface, perhaps a courtyard, just 10ins below the surface, but further investigating did not take place.

The excavations in February 1989 by Severn-Trent Water, and the uncovered archaeology

Starting in about 1991, after consultations with Warwickshire Wildlife Trust, WDC took a different approach to managing the **Oxpen Meadow**. Drainage was carried out later, towards the end of April, and slower, taking a number of weeks to fully empty; so slowly in fact that the amenities officer suggested more would be lost through evaporation than drainage. The meadow could now be managed as a wildlife habitat and this had an immediate positive impact on the aquatic birdlife, and nests began to appear. Visitors to the park quickly became attached to the new feature to the extent that complaints began to be made that it was being drained at all. *'Draining of the Oxpen Meadow has begun to the annual chorus of alarmed voices'* is how the *KWN* reported the slow draining of the area on 29th April 1994. At the time there were nesting swans and moorhens, regular visits from a heron, and a collection of ducks, one pair of which had produced 13 ducklings in a nest built in a bush near the outdoor swimming pool. Letters were written to the *KWN* and the local MP was now getting involved too, questioning the decision. The explanation for the draining was quite straightforward; as there was not a continuous flow of water through the meadow it would become stagnant, and draining would also allow for at least one cut of the meadow floor to ensure it did not become overgrown. It was this careful management that had noticeably increased the wildlife diversity.

Not all Town Councillors were convinced; *'I can't believe anyone could consider pulling the plug'*, *'I think it is silly to start doing it now while the swans are nesting'*. A letter writer to the *KWN* pleaded, *'Please save this most beautiful and most excellent sanctuary for bird-life for us all to walk round and enjoy. Kenilworth looks right with this amenity. The lake looks heavenly. How could anyone consider unplugging it?'*

Just at this time, an **Abbey Fields Consultation** was being carried out by the Recreation & Amenities Committee; a questionnaire was printed in the *KWN*, and copies were available at three schools, Kenilworth Library and at the newspaper's office. More than 600 forms were filled in, apparently two or three times the normal number of such questionnaires.

The questions were wide ranging and the interim report revealed that 38 per cent of those using the car park went to the swimming pool but 'significant numbers' used it for shopping, visiting the theatre, visiting food outlets and going to church; it was now well-established as a free car park for the whole of northern Kenilworth. A third thought cycling should be allowed on some Abbey Fields routes, but although few admitted to cycling in the park , 'many' complained of the nuisance caused by youngsters on mountain bikes. The most popular feature with 84 per cent was the brooks. Two thirds were in favour of a permanent lake, as of course had just about every previous generation back to Victorian times, with a third favouring the retention of the recently introduced managed system. 'A lake of some sort has been almost universally welcomed. What has to be decided is the main purpose of a lake and how best to achieve it'. 'Favoured features' recorded at about 60 per cent were the historic remains, grassland and valley character, Park Rangers being employed, and 'no change' when it came to gardens and flowers; a third thought the latter were inappropriate. Two thirds also thought the Abbey Fields should be left as they were, the rest split more or less half and half in preferring careful change or 'the Abbey Fields should be as it was years ago'. The least enjoyed activity was bowls at 6 per cent; there was no mention at all of tennis, putting or pitch & putt.

The conclusions contained the paragraph, 'No change is signalled on a number of issues by a large majority: people like the Abbey Fields as it is: a natural area, although many of its features are man-made or are as a result of people's actions in the past. A greater emphasis on naturalness is a growing trend in urban parks. In seeking no change to the Abbey Fields, Kenilworth folk are proving themselves to be at the Vanguard of modern thinking'. However, another paragraph appeared to interpret 'no change' rather differently, as if it was predetermined; 'Change is surely allowable if it enhances the character that people want: if some features detract because they are incongruous then removing them is a change, presumably for the better', despite only 15 per cent of those in the survey favouring any change at all.

When the final results of the survey were available at the end of August 1994, the *KWN* headline was very succinct; *'LEAVE THEM AS THEY ARE'*. The report, composed by Amenities Officer Dale Best, outlined four guidelines for long-term management of the park: 1) The Abbey Fields should be maintained and enhanced as a setting for historic Kenilworth; 2) The area should have a natural character; 3) The history and archaeology of the area should be more evident and be the council's primary concern; 4) Recreational uses will be important but secondary. Dale Best was quoted as saying, *'No change is signalled by a large majority on a number of issues; people like the Abbey Fields as it is. We understand that people don't want a further shift towards the character of a traditional town park. Given the strong wish of people for the Abbey Fields to be natural, the presence of some recreational elements could now be questioned. Their location may also be at odds with other objectives and uses.'*

Only a third thought more visitors should be attracted, and just as few thought more should be made of the Abbey site, which hardly supported the statement number 3 above that the history of the site should be more evident and the council's primary aim with recreational facilities to be secondary. Despite the oft repeated phrase 'no change', it was evident that changes were planned and the future of the pitch & putt (if indeed it was still open, it was still there in 1988) on safety and inconvenience grounds, and the little-used bowling green, was immediately in doubt. The Amenities Officers were to have a series of walkabouts in the fields and further public consultation was promised.

At some point in the mid-1990s, a group calling themselves **The Friends of Abbey Fields** (FoAF) was formed. At its head, and probably also its instigator, was Jonathan Newey, a well-known and respected Kenilworth estate agent (who was not related to the long-standing Kenilworth family of Newey mentioned elsewhere). Finding details of their activities has proved elusive, but it seems the group limited themselves to observations and opinions.

The Barn forms a backdrop to the unused area of the 1884 churchyard extension with Leonard Hughes' avenue of trees from c1910 on the right (14th May 2013)

Undoubtedly driven by Harry Sunley, the **Kenilworth Abbey Advisory Committee** was re-constituted in 1987, and has functioned continuously ever since. This time, added to members from the KHAS, KS, KTC and WDC, was the vicar of St Nicholas, David Rake. The Gatehouse was once more in need of work, but now attention also turned to the Barn and the resurrection of a 1980 proposal to reinstate the first floor, missing for centuries, to improve the only museum of the town's history. Also the committee thought that the Abbey should become a greater attraction in itself and discussions were held as to how best to achieve this, the first idea being to somehow mark out the extent of the ruins on the ground. Funding of course was always the problem with such schemes, £15,000 being the estimate for the new floor in the Barn.

By 1994 the local MP James Pawsey had been added to the group. It had raised over £5,000 for the project which could now begin. Chairman Harry Sunley said, *'The Abbey Fields, given by previous generations to the residents of Kenilworth for their pleasure, will now have an exhibition centre which will be both an asset for educational purposes and a specific tourist attraction'*. On 19th September 1994, contractors moved in to install the upper floor of the Barn, work which took about three weeks. All the relics had been moved to the Tantara Gatehouse and the rearrangement created a perfect opportunity to once more catalogue all the remaining Abbey stonework, and this was carried out under the supervision of Richard Morris; WDC installed racking in the Gatehouse so the stones could be better stored.

The extra space in the Barn induced the WDC Heritage & Arts Manager to investigate creating an Abbey interpretation centre on the ground floor. With National Lottery funding, a combined project by WDC, KHAS and Warwick University culminated in the April 2001 opening of a fine new display that still allowed for the ground floor to be used for meetings. In addition, display boards detailing the Abbey's history were placed at several locations around the park, and in September 2002 thirteen ground-level information plates were installed at various places over the Abbey remains to give visitors a chance to follow what is buried below their feet. In 2003, protective railings were placed around the remnants of the Chapter House wall to deter climbers.

As part of the National Science Week in March 1997, Warwickshire Museum Field Services arranged to carry out a resistivity survey in part of the Abbey Fields, specifically for the public to become involved. The area chosen was a substantial 60m by 80m rectangle on the south bank of the brook opposite the swimming pool, with a northern boundary of the path to Forrest Road and an eastern boundary of the path to the War Memorial; the area included the buildings uncovered by the Severn-Trent Water pipe-laying of 1989 and so was bound to show results. Over two days, over 160 children and adults took the opportunity to 'have a go' and a number of straight-line anomalies indicating structures were found, but the lack of clarity on the available print-out makes certain analysis difficult.

With the new arrangements for the **Oxpen Meadow** gaining widespread praise and acceptance, problems arose in 1995 when the lake failed to empty; it was presumed there was damage to the drain and suspicion fell on the swimming pool work a decade before, but this was never substantiated. The meadow became a quagmire with large wet marshy areas remaining throughout the summer, and at times of heavy rain becoming a small lake. Action needed to be taken, and it was.

At the beginning of March 1997, all but one of the WDC Leisure Committee voted in favour of finally making a properly constructed permanent **lake** in the meadow; at least 112 years after it was first suggested. The public consultation with two-thirds in favour was a determining factor; *'We had one of the best reactions to a consultation, this will further enhance the beauty of that natural open park. This had been talked about since 1930, how much more time could we possibly need to talk about this'*, said one councillor, obviously unaware that the talking had been going on for 45 years longer than he realised!

The one councillor who voted against wondered what the money would be spent on; it looked like a lake already and would look the same when completed. However, it was estimated that 15,000 tons of material needed to be moved, and water would be allowed to flow through the lake; leaving it as it was the water would become stagnant leading to excessive weed growth and algae, making it little more than a *'wet bog'*. It was also said that the area would subsequently hold more water in times of flooding. Work was to begin in September to minimise the effect on wildlife, and a budget of £70,000 was allocated.

At the Town Council meeting the same week there were concerns that the scheme had been rushed; arguments were split mostly down political party lines at a meeting of *'angry exchanges'* lasting 90 minutes, but still leaving some councillors unhappy at not being allowed to speak. *'I am not averse to the plans but I want to know more'* was a typical quoted comment.

Not all of WDC's attempts at providing wildlife habitats were popular or successful. The summers of 1996 and 1997 saw large areas of the fields left unmowed in an attempt to create a **wildflower meadow** and give the fields a *'natural'* look. It was claimed in some quarters that this returned the fields to its past as meadowland, but others pointed out that it was previously pastureland and had never looked like a meadow. By September 1997 it was clear the *'experiment'* had failed; the long grass was used mostly as a dog's toilet and a place where rubbish collected, and it looked a *'mess'* and a *'shambles'*. Town Councillors had been trying to have mowing re-introduced in the areas for some time; one leading councillor was quoted as saying, *'I do not think we need another nature area in Kenilworth, we need the Abbey Fields mown and looked after and restored to how it used to be. It is an absolute disgrace and the majority of Kenilworth people do not want this. We want the grass cut to a level suitable for its traditional use'*. *'We have a real dog's breakfast here; let the Abbey Fields go back to what it was for years and years.'*

Jonathan Newey of FoAF said, 'Our members are split 50/50 whether or not it should remain as it has over the last two years. However, the committee is more strongly in favour of it remaining, mainly because of the wide variety of wildflowers that the areas have attracted since the scheme began'. The scheme was brought to an end the following month, but as shall be seen, 'seeds had been sown' that were to have a lasting impact.

Warwick District Council in their handling of the formative lake and attempted wildflower meadow had obviously decided it was the right time to take the park in a new direction. They teamed up with the Environment Agency to carry the lake scheme forward and work started in early November 1997; it was expected to take about 6 weeks. Water had already been drained as much as possible and the area was fenced off; the removal of silt was about to begin as was an inspection of the damage to the drainage system. Jonathan

Newey said, *'It looks a mess at the moment but will be wonderful when it is finished. I was staggered by how much silt has built up over the years, and the lake would have been a complete wreck in a few years if this work had not been done.'*

Liz Galloway, landscape artist for the Environment Agency, explained how the shallowness and by being allowed to dry to a quagmire had led to a build up of weeds, but now the end near the swimming pool was to be excavated deeper; the shallow margins and existing vegetation were to be kept.

There is no discovered record of any repairs to the drainage systems nor the discovery of any springs, channelled or otherwise, being found and by mid-December the excavation work was more or less complete; the removed soil had been tipped on land behind the Castle. Work on the inlet and outlet of the lake was about to start and the lake was already half-full due to rain. The workmen were no doubt relieved that the Abbey Fields conveniences re-opened that week after being closed for a month for a £20,000 refit.

However, in the new year wet weather brought the final landscaping work to a halt; heaps of mud and soil were left piled behind plastic mesh fencing. In mid-February Jonathan Newey said *'It looks a complete and utter mess; I have had a load of phone calls from people with similar views'*. Another worry was the approaching nesting season. The parks manager said that landscaping while it was so wet would *'do more harm than good'* and asked the public to be patient. Work resumed the following week and was completed in early March. A gravel path was made around its northern bank, but a perfect opportunity was missed during landscaping work to provide a place for a planting scheme to conceal the western end of the swimming pool buildings, simply achievable by having a slightly shorter lake.

The originally named Oakdale Villa, the Castle and Little Virginia form a backdrop to this view of the lake, a similar view to that on page 155 *(22nd November 2012)*

The oft repeated claim that a lake would be helpful in time of flood was tested perhaps sooner than had been anticipated. Just weeks after the lake was completed, extraordinary rainfall on Good Friday 3rd April 1998 caused widespread problems and the Abbey Fields flooded as it had many times before. The **swimming pools** suffered from much floodwater; they were subsequently emptied due to the vast amount of silt that had entered the system as there was a danger of damaging the filters, but this caused a major problem. The water pressure in the ground surrounding the pool caused the tiles of the empty indoor pool to start coming off leading to speculation that the pool itself may crack. It needed quickly refilling and there was only one solution; at last the modern fire brigade had the opportunity to emulate its predecessors of 1896 and 1935 and fill Kenilworth's newest pool! This time the nearest source of water, the brook, was used but this obviously brought silt with it and the pool ended up back where it had been after the flood, full of muddy water only now with the added problem of missing and damaged tiles.

Although it was hoped the outdoor pool could be quickly readied for use, the indoor pool could not be emptied for repairs until the water pressure subsided, and that was predicted to take weeks or even months. Two bore holes were dug in the pool's surrounds so water levels could be monitored. It was not to be until 13th May that it was safe enough for the pool to be emptied and pool staff were photographed in Wellington boots cleaning out the sludge that had settled at the bottom, reminiscent of the first, hardly filtered, incarnation of the pool. The outdoor pool re-opened in mid June by which time replacement tiling had been completed at the indoor pool but extensive grouting was needed in many areas leading to a delay of about a month.

The swimming pool was not the only Abbey Fields facility to suffer. By bad luck, an overhaul of the tennis courts was underway when the floods struck, delaying the completion of the 6-week contract also until mid July.

Over a period of time more buildings were constructed on the **Abbotsfield** site and plots, and Charles Randall's piggery and cow-house was also converted into a dwelling, despite it being on the wrong side of the building line for a residence. Perhaps after all, in 1968 the KUDC should have accepted the offer of just one bungalow on the site in return for a greater addition to the park.

At some unknown time, WDC stopped maintaining the path from High Street alongside the churchyard (see map, page 153) but the access via the kissing gate remained.

The Kenilworth Skateboarders Action Group had long campaigned for a **skatepark** in the town and had raised £3,000 to build one, but siting it inevitably caused problems. Seen as a place where teenagers would cause unnecessary problems, suggestions it should be in the Abbey Fields created a huge number of vitriolic complaints: *'I play tennis and skateboarding and tennis is not compatible'*; *'The Abbey Fields is dedicated to dog walkers, wild birds and people playing tennis. There's already a lot of kids riding bikes around, teenage drinking and stuff like that. It would just escalate'*; *'It would be the start of erosion of this very beautiful part of Kenilworth'*; *'The thin end of the wedge being driven in to the idyllic Abbey Fields'*. Others supported the idea as the Abbey Fields was created as a park and recreational place for all, but after design consultations with the youngsters, £1,000 was given by KTC and £10,000 was allocated by WDC, and the skatepark was built with the other sports facilities at Castle Farm.

In December 1998, Chairman and spokesperson of the **Friends of Abbey Fields**, Jonathan Newey, died at the age of just 51, and it seems the group disbanded.

By 2002, one subject had overtaken dogs as the most written about aspect of the park, and that was litter. *'Thousands of people visit our historic grounds each year and they don't want to see all the filth, bottles, and cans, paper wrappers, etc, all over the place. We should be proud of our beauty spots, not disgusted by the amount of litter lying around'*. There was just one litter bin in the most populated area around the children's playground and picnic tables, and it was regularly overflowing with rubbish. The following week, 19th April 2002, Sandra and Peter Whitlock wrote a letter agreeing, but theirs was to change the course of developments in the park; *'There are things that could be improved; in addition to tackling the litter problem, the wildlife value could be enhanced, vandalism reported promptly, the toilets kept clean and well maintained. It is because of these concerns that a small group of us are trying to re-start the Friends of the Abbey Fields'*. Anyone *'who would like to play a part in protecting and improving this lovely area'* was invited to make a phone call and join.

Sandra had many phone calls over the next few days and about 15 voiced genuine concerns. These were invited to a meeting a couple of weeks later at The Bakery in High Street (formerly the business premises of the field-renting Fancott family); rather more than 15 turned up and the room was severely cramped. The major concerns raised were litter, anti-social behaviour, poor maintenance of the conveniences and a general feeling that the park could be better managed and cared for. About half a dozen committed themselves to taking the group forward; an interim committee was formed with Sandra in its chair, and plans made to hold an AGM the following year for committee elections. It was agreed to revive the name Friends of Abbey Fields (FoAF), not as a continuation of the original group but a continuation of Jonathan Newey's idea. To increase membership and awareness, mail-drops were made in the streets around the fields and these had the desired effect. Despite being the figurehead, Sandra is very quick to praise the input of Adrian Rowe-Evans, and his wife Pru, who became a Friends' stalwart; in addition to his enthusiasm, his talents included great knowledge and experience as to how to approach projects, problems and difficulties, and in finding solutions. Adrian was on the committee from the beginning.

Early on, the committee realised that to achieve anything they had to have the support of Warwick

District Council. Responsible for the Parks Department was Jon Holmes, the great great grandson of William Holmes, that most enthusiastic of tree-planters in the early 20th Century; a meeting with him was arranged with Adrian Rowe-Evans and Pam Vaughan being the Friends' representatives. Jon Holmes was, not surprisingly, a little wary, but a first co-ordinated project was arranged for November 2002; cowslips, meadowsweet and purple loosestrife supplied by WDC were planted by a small team of Friends at the Castle end of the lake. The *'enhancement of the wildlife value'*, as Sandra had said in her letter, was quickly to the forefront.

In early 2003, Sandra established a newsletter for members only, and she was allowed to use the noticeboard at the swimming pool to announce activities and meetings. Members were asked to make donations towards bat boxes; these were made by the Warwickshire Bat Group who assisted when WDC installed them. Bird boxes soon followed. With growing confidence in the partnership and their influence, the FoAF asked Jon Holmes to leave the established hedge from the Iron Bridge to the War Memorial uncut to produce blossom and berries, and havens for insects and birds in particular; until this point, the hedges had all been kept neatly trimmed.

The first AGM in July 2003 saw Sandra elected as Chairman. That autumn, gaps in the hedge from Forrest Road to the Iron Bridge were infilled by 'an army of volunteers'; the Friends donating £100 to the cost of saplings. In the autumn of 2004 it was the hedge bordering the Paddock, which was still not part of the park and continued to be leased for grazing, that received attention; after clearing deadwood, 575 saplings were planted with the Friends again contributing £100. For the autumn of 2006, attention returned to the hedge from the Iron Bridge to the War Memorial, now much increased in volume after the lack of cutting; this time gaps were infilled, including the site of the old barn changing rooms that had probably stood for a couple of centuries until demolition in 1968, and the following year the hedge at the top near the memorial was restored. With increasing funds, the Friends contributed £1,000 to this.

From the outset the Friends declared aims included liaising with the District Council to ensure the Abbey Fields are kept in its semi-natural state, to enhance the park as a habitat for wildlife, to raise public awareness about the historic, aesthetic, wildlife and amenity value of the fields, and to encourage the public to participate in its protection for future generations. To ensure independence, serving councillors could be members but not elected onto the committee. Sandra Whitlock stood down as chairman after three years.

English Heritage carried out a major review of all the listed Ancient Monuments in its care in the early part of the 21st century. This was to have a great affect on the Abbey Fields as it was decided to now include the whole of the park, as well as the churchyard and the area split from the Paddock to become part of Little Virginia. This whole area became subject to Scheduled Ancient Monument listing number SM 35115, which is dated 8th September 2003. It was not until Christmas that it was in the newspapers and the quoted councillors seemed more excited that it appeared to have resulted in the listing of the field's three air raid shelters, and this led to confusion as to exactly what was now under the protection of English Heritage. The listing in fact covers 'The known surviving standing, earthwork and buried remains of Kenilworth Abbey and its wider Monastic precinct'. There is also a list as to what is excluded, such as the swimming pool, play equipment, grave markers in the churchyard, and surprisingly the Abbey Barn too (although the ground below them all is protected) but in December 2016, English Heritage confirmed to this author that the air raid shelters are indeed listed with the same Ancient Monument status as the Abbey remains. The War Memorial is shown as outside the listing area.

Because the whole of the Abbey Fields were now classed as an Ancient Monument, it meant that virtually no development of the park could take place without specific agreement by English Heritage and thus was created another layer of protection, or difficulty depending upon your point of view.

In response to the rescheduling, the **KAAC** extended its remit to include the entre Abbey Fields and consequently produced the *Conservation Plan for the Abbey Fields*, launched in December 2005. Its aims were, 'The conservation and enhancement of the Heritage merit of the area' to be achieved by 'protection against adverse change, interpretation of the site to the public, provision of high quality public amenities, research into its history and archaeology... to advance Kenilworth Abbey as a tourist attraction, with emphasis on the general setting: to cultivate Kenilworth Abbey as an educational facility: to encourage and assist the KHAS in promoting use of the Barn and Gatehouse as a public asset: to promote the maintenance of the fabric of the Gatehouse, the Barn and the Abbey ruins to an appropriate standard: to manage such funding as becomes available through grants and other sources'. The superbly constructed and presented report, mostly the work of Dr Geoff Hilton, remains the most thorough assessment of the Abbey Fields and highlights the continuing but unavoidable conflicts of the operation and use of a public park and its variety of recreational facilities and uses, whilst simultaneously preserving and interpreting the Abbey remains. Its conclusions as to the necessary policies to achieve this cover no less than four pages. The report was adopted as the major reference and foundation for future Abbey Fields policies of the WDC and English Heritage, and a dozen years after publication it is still essential reading for anyone with an interest in any aspect of the park.

There is no doubt that the **Kenilworth History & Archaeology Society** has gained a deserved high reputation for their work in investigating and recording the Abbey and its remains. Supported by the KAAC, WDC has allowed much investigative and other work to take place.

At the end of National Archaeology Week, on 24th July 2005 a 3m wide excavation was made immediately against the south face of the Barn by members of the KHAS; permission was obtained after months of negotiations with Warwick District Council, as site owners, and English Heritage. It was carried out mostly in rain and despite the best efforts of the volunteers to keep out the weather using umbrellas and a gazebo, the bottom of the pit, which owing to the conditions had been reduced to just a few feet square, became a quagmire. Not much of interest was found, the best being broken Victorian pottery and glass; there were many nails from the Barn's 1972 re-roofing. It is quite probable that the upper layers of soil in this area have been landscaped several times in connection with the churchyard extension, Abbey excavations and work to improve the levels around the Barn when the path was built and the step altered by the original Friends in the 1930s.

From August 2005, the KHAS set about carrying out a resistivity survey of the entire Abbey Fields; they had hoped to involve members of the public as much as possible but the licence from English Heritage short-sightedly demanded that only society members were involved, an opportunity missed, for example, to involve schools. It required the fields being marked out in 20m squares, and then dividing each into 1m wide strips; only one square needed to be marked out at a time. The results showed a wide variety of buried features including modern sewers, probable rocky outcrops near the War Memorial, and ancient paths and buildings, of which some were not where any were expected, including a large rectangular building discovered across the path from the car park, and others across the brook from the bowling green. It was hoped that these discoveries of previously unknown buildings would lead to an excavation, if only a couple of small pits, but more than a decade later this is still to happen. (For a full analysis of the surveys, see the KHAS publications *Kenilworth History* for 2006-07 and 2007-08.)

The **KAAC** had discussed the possibility of storing some of the duplicated or poorer quality stone from the **Abbey** in one of the three **air raid** shelters around the park's perimeter, and/or perhaps even making one an attraction in itself. This required a survey of the shelters and their condition and so in 2006 the KHAS received permission to inspect the inside of the shelters. As far as is known, it was the first time anyone had been inside since they were closed off in 1952.

The bricked-up doorways were left intact as each shelter has an access hatch; that on the Rosemary Hill shelter proved immovable and so it was not forced, but the other two were opened. The Forrest Road shelter was found to be knee-deep in water, the problem encountered when in use as a changing room in 1948, but that in Bridge Street was found to be in good condition. About 18ins of soil covers the shelter.

Inside, the shelter is 30ft long and 7ft wide and high, and ten steps lead up to the ground level of Bridge Street. It was constructed from concrete panels with mortar infilling and has a solid concrete floor which was covered in debris and mud. There were the remnants of an electricity supply with a conduit, lamp and switch, and an angle-iron framework covering much of the inside.

Despite the obvious interest in the structures, it was decided that the accessible shelters were unsuitable for either use initially suggested without renovation and a large outlay of funds. That at Rosemary Hill is potentially the driest due to its location, but the seized hatch would probably need to be destroyed to gain entry that way; perhaps one day the bricked-up entrance could be removed for an investigation as it would in any case need to be opened should it become an amenity at some time in the future.

The Society produced a leaflet about Kenilworth in World War 2 that included photographs taken inside the shelter, and installed an information board on the outside wall of that in Bridge Street.

In 2008, an area across the brook from the swimming pool, where the 1997 resistivity survey took place that included the archaeological remains uncovered by Severn-Trent Water in 1989, was found to be becoming wet. Investigations revealed a broken drainpipe was to blame. In contrast to decades of attempts to improve the drainage of the fields, some two years later a decision was made not to repair the drain at a cost of about £8,500, but to let the water create a permanent wetland, *'to increase biodiversity'*. One resident summed up the thoughts of many: *'There is a stream within 50yds and a lake within 100yds surrounded by wetlands. More diversity is not required by allowing a perfectly good drained amenity area to be turned into festering marshes'*, and he was photographed standing with the marsh halfway up his Wellington boots. Today bulrushes are established and an area some 50 yards across is left unmowed; potential damage to the known nearby archaeology which is likely to extend to the wet area does not seem to be a concern.

In the foreground is the marshy area created by a broken drainpipe. The indoor swimming pool is now screened by trees, as is Clinton House. Compare to the photographs on pages 123 & 163 *(12th January 2017)*

In 2003, the Lee family acquired the **Paddock's** licence to graze, and took the field in a new direction. At their suggestion it became managed partially as a wildflower meadow. With several animals grazing only at certain times of the year, annually the wildflowers recovered. As mentioned, in 2004 the FoAF reconstructed the hedgerow on the Paddock's parkland border. In 2009 it was said, *'The horses in the field are really popular; as they are bringing such enjoyment it made sense to keep them in the field for a little longer period of time'*. However, WDC now seemed to think that the field's biodiversity instigated by Mrs Lee was the priority and that perhaps only one horse should be allowed, and so laid down stricter guidelines; *'Officers became aware that the field was being heavily grazed and for far longer than would normally be the case'*. The Lee family asked for more flexibility than the new guidelines allowed but none was forthcoming and so in 2009, after six years of *'investing a lot of time and money'* in the field, they regrettably terminated their agreement with WDC. The WDC spokesman stressed there were no plans to end temporary grazing in the field and intended to make the license available to others, but as no one came forward once again there were no grazing animals in the Abbey Fields.

One rather unusual use for the Abbey Fields is the annual Boxing Day charity **Duck Race** held by the **Kenilworth Lions Club**. Starting in about 1990, 1,500 numbered yellow plastic ducks are released over the bridge at the Castle Ford for 'a bracing swim of 200 metres' on the flowing water to the finish line near the swimming pool. The speed of the race varies remarkably, dependant of course upon the flow of the brook from a gentle trickle to a fast-flowing stream.

One particularly memorable occasion was the 1997 race. By now, each duck had several backers, 4,000 tickets were sold and each winning backer would receive the full amount for a top-four place, but the fast-flowing stream caused problems. Firstly, one of the organisers 'launching' the ducks, that day numbering 2,000, lost his footing in the water and fell, and then hundreds of ducks escaped past the barricade put up to stop them near the swimming pool. The passing ducks distracted those attending a cycling event on the common, one man stood in the brook for half an hour catching them, dogs were useful in retrieving others; even the following day a schoolboy living in Lawrence Gardens collected 40 from near his back garden. Some were said to have eventually entered the River Avon at Stoneleigh. An appeal was made for the safe return of any further competitors.

After one popular tourist website ranked the 'quirky' event alongside the Welsh Grand National, the Stonehenge Winter Solstice and the Padstow Christmas Festival as a major Christmas attraction, the 2016 race saw a *'remarkable'* turnout to watch as the ducks were tipped out of four dustbins into the brook. Spectators lined the banks for an unusually slow race, *'the crowd was very patient'*. In a quarter of a century or so, the event has raised over £80,000.

The play area and equipment in its traditional location, much of which was installed in about 2000. The three-segment see-saw *(upper left)* is on the site of the 1953 slide; the sprung see-saw *(upper centre)* can also be seen on page 164. The swings *(lower right)* are on a replacement frame of unknown age on the site of earlier swings *(Both, 17th June 2008)*

    A new Abbey Fields event is the **Kenilworth Arts Festival**. Started in 2005 as simply the Kenilworth Festival, it has evolved into a week-long collection of art, film, theatre and literary events and workshops culminating in a free 'Fiesta' in the park; in 2016 the Abbey Fields hosted live music and a theatre group of acrobats, storytellers, musicians and puppeteers, with many stalls and sideshows.

    The **Friends of Abbey Fields** conducted a survey of the trees in the park and in 2010 produced a leaflet listing 64 types. Some of the oldest oaks, of which five species are represented, are up to 300 years old but the vast majority of trees date from the Edwardian years onwards. In the area bordering Abbey Hill in particular, numerous trees have memorial plaques, many of which are mentioned in the text.

    In 2011, WDC gave permission, later ratified by English Heritage (EH), for the FoAF to create a wildflower meadow on the lower part of the Abbey Hill field, once part of the pitch & putt course. Its boundaries were the now thriving hedge alongside the path from the War Memorial, the diagonal path to Bridge Street and the course of the hedge from Abbey Hill to the brook, removed in 1962. It was to be left unmowed for much of the year, save for cut pathways through it, and a wide variety of native wildflower seed sown, creating 'a place of interest and beauty while also promoting valuable wildlife habitat for a range of small creatures including butterflies, moths, frogs and toads… enabling our wildlife to have a small refuge now that so much agricultural land no longer provides those habitats'. It was certainly more successful and popular than the similar venture tried by WDC alone in 1997. In late 2011, the Friends planted 6,000 crocus bulbs alongside Abbey Hill. In October 2016 three exercise stations were installed, two alongside the tennis courts, the other at the western end of the lake, funded entirely by the Friends at a cost £6,500; the fields have become a popular destination for those on fitness runs.

Perhaps the least applauded of the Friends activities could be considered the most necessary, and that which probably had the most to do with their foundation; monthly litter-picks from April to October remove waste in bin-bags by the dozen. The litter-picks started in April 2009 after litter problems had again been highlighted in the *KWN* for over a year. Individuals had been seen picking up broken bottles, or collecting rubbish in carrier bags, with thoughtless youths late night socialising in the centre of the fields getting much of the blame. It was not now an absence of bins that was the problem but an absence of thought by park users. A WDC spokesman was quoted as saying that refuse contractors *'visit Abbey End (sic) and other parks on a daily, seven days a week basis, as part of their contract for picking up rubbish'*. Some of the rubbish is of course wind-blown, but the extent of the problem is demonstrated by the 2016 collections when 97 volunteer hours by the Friends resulted in 36 bin bags of rubbish being collected; how praiseworthy are their efforts, but how sad that they are needed.

The decline in use of the **bowling green** continued and by 2005, and perhaps several years earlier, was more or less out of use, for bowls at least; youngsters had begun to use the perfect surface for playing football. WDC announced that it would no longer maintain the green and there were protests but its days for bowling were passed; the date and players of the last game is unknown but it had lasted about 90 years. The putting green too was out of use and at about this time use of the tennis courts became free; this made the 1926 Pavilion redundant and it was boarded up.

The **play area** had been upgraded again in 2000; by now all the old apparatus was gone, the 1953 slide and climbing frame lasting until about 1993. As the decade progressed, a movement was begun by parents of young children, and some councillors, for a major upgrade and enlargement of the facilities which was limited by modern standards. The push for a great increase in the amount of apparatus gathered momentum, leading to the suggestion, probably originating from the Kenilworth Abbey Advisory Committee in 2010, for the use of the bowling green as a new site for equipment for younger children. It could be enclosed to ensure dogs, a regular cause of concern around the existing play area, could be excluded.

In great contrast to the longevity of much of the older apparatus, which was mostly constructed of exposed iron and steel, by 2012 some of the newer equipment with more 'user-friendly' plastic coated materials, was showing its age and already needed to be replaced; the oldest being used for perhaps twenty years, the newest barely a decade. Some *'popular favourites'* had even been removed and others cordoned off with orange netting; *'It's dangerous and looks shabby.'*

Although replacements were planned - *'WDC is aiming for the replacement playground equipment to be installed for the school holidays'* just weeks away - they did not materialise because a *'more all encompassing refurbishment of the play area is required'*. The Abbey Fields were not alone; a Play Area Review carried out by WDC across all its parks revealed £1.67m was required to bring all play areas up to standard; in the case of the Abbey Fields, a major investment of about £120,000 was planned, and most of the new equipment was indeed to go onto the bowling green.

The funding for the project was £100,000 from Warwick District Council, £20,000 from the Round Table and almost £4,000 from the Friends of Abbey Fields; much of the Round Table's contribution came from tickets sold and collections taken at the Guy Fawkes fireworks event at the Castle the previous November. The plans released in early 2013 showed that the 1926 tennis Pavilion was to be retained, but it quickly became reported that this was not the case, it was to be demolished due to it being a site of antisocial behaviour. Not surprisingly there was an outrage and many became involved at trying to save *'this important piece of park architecture'* as Patricia Cain of the Kenilworth Society called it in March 2013. *'We cannot pander to vandals, this is our heritage. It is irrational to knock something down due to antisocial behaviour rather than tackle the actual problem'*. Despite this, after the completion of the mandatory bat survey, on the advice of the police it was still intended to demolish the Pavilion the following month.

A backlash resulted in a back-track and a stay of execution, provided that an organisation could come up with a future use, and funding. Suggestions included replacing panels with glass and for it to be used as an arts display, removing the sides for it to become a shelter, or perhaps even a store and base for the Friends of Abbey Fields. Ideas had to be in by the end of May.

The 1926 tennis and bowls Pavilion designed by Sholto Douglas patiently awaits its fate *(22nd November 2012)*

Meanwhile, workmen moved onto the site in mid-March 2013; the bowling green had opened almost exactly a century before in April 1913. Apparatus for older children was to be on the established playground site but nearer the swimming pool, with the area immediately in front of the Barn to become a picnic area with tables, making an improved environment for the Barn, its museum, and the churchyard.

As the new play equipment was to be installed in an area of archaeological interest, consent was obviously required from English Heritage; a condition of this was a watching brief by Archaeology Warwickshire, 'to observe any groundwork associated with the scheme and record as far as possible the nature of the archaeological resource on the site'. At the beginning of March 2013, when the hedge alongside the pavilion was removed to increase the play area boundaries beyond those of the bowling green, a large quantity of handmade roof tile (suggesting a mediaeval demolition) was found less than a foot from the surface; the disturbed earth was subsequently levelled. As old play equipment was removed from its traditional place in front of the Barn, only topsoil with no finds was found to a depth of about 18ins.

Due to a communications breakdown, the on-site archaeologist stopped visiting the site once the initial clearance was completed but with a springtime opening widely promised by councillors, work continued without Archaeology Warwickshire being informed, in complete disregard of the agreed terms. Excavations and disturbance of the ground included the making of pathways, a pit for a trampoline, holes for equipment foundations, and a pit for a 'rain garden' which had not even appeared on the published plans. The play area included the excavated material being piled to form grassed play-mounds and from these, fragments of mediaeval roof tile were spotted by members of the public and retrieved, demonstrating that vital information had been lost.

With the hoped-for Easter opening date missed due to weather interruptions, the new play area was officially opened by the Mayor on 24th May 2013. Councillor Dave Shilton, portfolio holder responsible for the build, said *'I am delighted to see so many children enjoying this on the very first morning it is open. It is incredible that it is open now, and in time for the holidays'*. Rachel Shipman from St Nicholas School had won a competition to help design the layout and show the council what equipment the children wanted to have; she joined Councillor Shilton to cut the ribbon and declare the new facilities officially open. Councillor Ann Blacklock described it as *'beyond all of our wildest dreams'* and thanked all the parents who had been campaigning for the new equipment.

At the time of writing (June 2017), the future of the Pavilion is still unresolved.

The result of the absence of a sound archaeological investigation and inspection of the excavated material was brought home to this author when in January 2017, four years after the play area was constructed, he found a 3ins corner of a mediaeval or possibly Roman hand-made roof tile fragment *(left)* protruding from one of the play-mounds by an inch or more, in a position more than capable of injuring a playing child. It included an animal paw print. Other, small, fragments were close by but not so dangerously positioned. If it is confirmed as Roman, it is one of few such finds in the Abbey Fields and could be of great significance, but this is reduced by not knowing from precisely where on the site it was excavated.

The slide installed for the Coronation in 1953 and its safety cage added in 1968 photographed in August 1985; the same location in February 2017 with modern swings and climbing equipment. Trees and hedgerows have been lost

The well-used **parking area** off Bridge Street always had problems with its surface, being made of loose gravel, and its slope caused difficulties with water run-off creating gullies and drainage channels across it. It was resurfaced again in 2007, an occasion giving the KHAS a chance to complete their resistivity survey of the entire fields (the author can confirm much of this was done in pouring rain!) the result of which was inconclusive due to the compacted gravel surface being prohibitive for clear readings.

On 12th January 2012, Warwick District Council submitted plans to not only provide a more permanent surface, but to also introduce charges with the installation of 'Pay-and-display' machines; it was the last (by some years) of Kenilworth's large car parks to have charges introduced because it had ensured the free use of the park in which it was sited. The impending development was often referred to as 'pay and dismay'. One councillor, quoted as saying *'I doubt the charges will be more than 50p'*, was doubtless amongst those

The view from the swimming pool sunbathing roof, showing the wide variety of play equipment. The garden, foreground, was constructed by The Friends. Compare to the photograph on page 132 (21ˢᵗ February 2017)

disappointed at the announcement of £2.50 as the cost of parking for four hours or more. However, free parking would be allowed for 2 hours, supposedly to continue free use for Abbey Fields users, and passes issued for local residents with nowhere else to park. Vehicle bays would also be marked out, reducing the capacity by an estimated 30 cars to 109 but ending the problems caused by haphazard parking. English Heritage had always 'considered a hard surface unacceptable' (as stated in the KAAC *Conservation Plan*) on the grounds of the likely archaeological remains below, but had a change of mind provided a specific type of hard surface was used; they also insisted specified archaeological investigations had to take place, not of the car park area itself but of its surrounds where channels for cabling and kerbing needed to be dug. Two trees had to be removed to improve the entrance and others were to be planted elsewhere as replacements; these pits also created sites for investigation. The parking area was to be set back a little way from the St Nicholas church lime avenue to reduce potential root damage. The plans were passed in September 2012.

Work commenced in September 2013 (allowing for the summer season to pass), just a few months after the completion of the new play area on the bowling green. A durable but temporary rubberised surface was provided for parking 50 cars in the field opposite the car park, and another 40 spaces made available nearby at the closed Abbotsford School. The overall cost was set at £155,000, compared to £48,000 for its maintenance in the previous four years. The area covered was 3,500 sq.m (4,186 sq yds).

Once again, Archaeology Warwickshire carried out the watching brief under instruction from English Heritage, this time in the trenches dug around two sides of the car park for taking cables for the ticket machines, and in tree pits, both for trees removed and those planted. This was recorded in their report number 1417 issued in February 2014.

The pits left by the removal of two lime trees from the car park entrance contained a few odd pieces of handmade roof tile. The cable trenches revealed further likely mediaeval roof tile fragments, a 17ᵗʰ or 18ᵗʰ century ceramic wig-curler, and 18ᵗʰ or 19ᵗʰ century pottery and glass. One particular area had enough mediaeval roof tile fragments to suggest a layer of demolition material. Excavations for drains at the car park entrance revealed a fragment of mediaeval floor tile, a piece of moulded sandstone and floor tiles, one of which included the hoof print of a sheep. A hole dug for one of the new trees produced the oldest datable find, a rim-sherd of an early 13ᵗʰ century jug, likely to have originated in Alcester. But the most important discovery was that of two walls on the western boundary of the car park, which were running parallel to the boundary of the High Street properties and thus in alignment with the Abbey, and between them a north-south wall no less than 22ft long. A similar but shallower trench for kerbing revealed two more walls and an area of loose sandstone suggesting a demolished wall.

It is regrettable that due to the terms issued by English Heritage, further investigation of the archaeology (as happened with Severn-Trent Water in 1989) could not take place either by extending the depth or width of the channels which were restricted to the dimensions required for the new equipment. Digging machines were on site, an archaeologist was present, and experienced volunteers from the KHAS just a phone call away; further investigation just outside the car park boundaries would not have been difficult or expensive, nor interfere with the work, but there was no provision for this in the agreement. The conclusions drawn were that there is a layer of demolition debris, perhaps scattered across the whole site, and the walls are of a previously unknown part the Abbey complex and possibly link up with those found on the opposite side of the path during the KHAS resistivity survey. If they are related to the ruins, they may be either a high-status house one would expect to find associated with an Abbey, or a place of learning, the only buildings 'missing' from the confirmed layout. And so, the car park is known for certain to cover archaeology connected with the Abbey that will remain buried and uninvestigated; a great opportunity missed, and probably lost for some time. The north-eastern corner of the Abbey Fields is potentially the most exciting area yet to be investigated.

The indoor swimming pool as seen from the older children's play ground. Compare to the photograph on page 164
(9th February 2017)

Modern Abbey Fields, new play equipment on the former bowling green alongside the swimming pool
(17th January 2017)

The parking area is mostly on part of Area B that was saved for the town by public subscription and subject to the restrictive covenants that include the phrases: '... should forever remain unbuilt upon... for the purposes of the Recreation Grounds Act 1859. No building or erection shall at any time hereafter be built or erected upon any part of the premises... the said premises shall for ever remain as open public grounds for the purposes of the said act'. The car park also includes part of Area F that has the stipulation that it '... shall forever hereafter be solely used for public walks and pleasure grounds under the control of the council and the same shall not nor shall any part thereof at any time hereafter be sold leased or disposed of for any other purpose'. The reader is left to decide for themselves if WDC adhered to these covenants.

It is regularly stated that the Churchwardens are still consulted over Area B, presumably due to their one-time ownership of the land. Although they were involved in discussions regarding the car park it seems that this was due to them being an interested party; if any mandatory arrangement was ever in place it has now certainly lapsed, or at least, the current Churchwardens have no knowledge of such an agreement.

Three of the original ten Holmes Avenue trees of 1904 dwarf visitors to the park; the two on the left can be seen as guarded saplings on page 56. Today 28 trees form the avenue, including a cluster near the War Memorial *(26th August 2016)*

'Holmes Avenue', the diagonal path from near the War Memorial to Bridge Street, still largely comprised the ten trees with large gaps left after the concerns of 1904, but with a few additions mostly at the Abbey Hill end. In early 2015 another ten lime trees were planted to fill the gaps; responsible of course was Jon Holmes, the great great grandson of William after whom the avenue received its unofficial name. Present for the occasion were a group of William's descendants.

As the new century entered its second decade, Kenilworth was facing dramatic changes in its future. The building of HS2 just outside its boundaries, and having to find space for 2,000 new houses and then accommodate their occupants within the town's facilities, posed many questions. To judge the townsfolk's thoughts on a wide ranging number of subjects, in early 2013 the Town Council instigated a questionnaire as part of its Action Plan, which in turn would contribute to Warwick District Council's Local Plan for the following 15 years or so; rumoured to be included was the moving of Castle Farm Sports Hall to the site of the outdoor swimming pool as part of a re-assessment of all WDC leisure facilities.

The questions relevant to the Abbey Fields received between 1,663 and 1,787 answers, by far the most numerous of any known survey, and almost three times that of 1994. For each question there was an option to strongly agree, agree, disagree or strongly disagree; for this summary the results are condensed to agree or disagree. Not surprisingly 98.2 per cent thought that the Abbey Fields are a recreational asset and must be preserved and protected; 79.4 per cent thought the area vacated by the old play equipment should be used as an enlarged picnic area and have a hard-standing for musical and other performances; 66.2 per cent disagreed with the suggestion the outdoor swimming pool should be closed in favour of a sports hall; 81.3 per cent thought the annual fair for the carnival should move from its traditional spot to the Forrest Road showground; and 77.5 per cent agreed that a cycleway should be provided alongside the brook from Bridge Street to Borrowell Lane (more about this, below). Apart from a question asking if the lime avenue from the church to Bridge Street should be retained (after eleven decades, it needs replacing or expensive pollarding), there was no other directly affecting the park in the 38 questions; an opportunity was lost to gauge public opinion about the growing importance given to wildlife habitats and their extent, the provision of additional recreational facilities (other than the cycleway), and current opinions of the importance of the preservation, display and even investigation of the Abbey itself, all relevant for planning for a greatly increased population.

The Kenilworth Greenway, a cycleway from Kenilworth Common to Berkswell along the former railway line and with a branch to Warwick University, opened throughout in 2011 and instigated calls for a cycle path through the Abbey Fields. From the common, the cycle route continued through The Close and then along the School Lane Meadow path to Bridge Street; an extension under the bridge and through the park was an obvious next step, with an exit at Borrowell Lane that could allow continuance along the path to the Castle Farm recreational facilities. In the park the obvious route was to first follow the north bank of Finham Brook to the central area, suggested as a footpath by Councillor Stansfield in 1970, and after crossing the brook, the route could follow the 1885 path to Borrowell Lane.

The Town Council's own position was made clear in its (19th July 2012) 1st Action Plan response: 'The Town Council would object strongly to the provision of a cycle route through the fields, as this is contrary to the use envisaged for the fields since they were dedicated to the Town', followed up in its (undated) 2nd Action Plan response, 'The Abbey Fields were dedicated to the Town over a century ago with a view to their being for recreation and outdoor use and they have been limited in all that time to pedestrian access. We are therefore clear that there should be **no** use of the fields for a cycleway as this would disturb the traditional use of the fields for walks and exercise on foot, and we could not conceive of a cycleway that did not disturb this use without the construction of separate roadways which would be contrary to the original dedication'. The numerous historical errors in these statements are clear.

However, by the time the Action Plan questionnaire was formulated there had been a commendable change of position; 'Cycle access: The Town Council objects to any mixed use of the pedestrian footpaths in the Abbey Fields. A dedicated cycleway should be routed…' before continuing with the already suggested route as its proposal. But the damage was done, their original but superseded declarations continued to be quoted in discussions about the cycle path, notably in the *KWN*. As mentioned, three quarters of those that filled in the survey answered 'Agree' to the proposal. This position was confirmed in the Town Action Plan draft dated December 2014.

Warwick District Council and Warwickshire County Council commissioned Sustrans, a charity whose major project is a national cycle network, to plan a route in detail. Its major criteria were: a) Minimise potential for conflict between pedestrians and cyclists, particularly around the children's play area and near the swimming pool; b) Minimise visual intrusion of the route on park land; c) Avoid impact on local archaeology and historic features of the park; d) Provide good connections to surrounding residential areas and adjoining cycle routes.

The plan was eventually revealed in late 2016. The hard-surface path is shown as 3m wide and after passing under Bridge Street, follows the brook to where cycle-parking would be provided on the swimming pool side of the new play area, destroying the neat garden area provided by the Friends. From there it crosses the brook with a new bridge, three times the width of and replacing the elderly but sound Iron Bridge, before turning right initially onto the existing path before following the southern side of the hedgerow to Borrowell Lane, leaving the 1885 path on the other side of the hedge for pedestrians. Its cost was estimated at £663,000, and about 70yds of the route was superimposed on busy existing pedestrian paths near the swimming pool.

This author believes a better route, particularly when taking into account criteria points a) and c), would cross the brook perhaps 50 yards to the east of the Iron Bridge (avoiding the busy pedestrian area near the swimming pool and saving the destruction of the Iron Bridge), so the cycle path could then, *via* the existing hedgerow gap, cross the War Memorial path giving only that one point where pedestrian paths and the cycle path would co-exist. There are concerns of buried Abbey remains being somewhere in the vicinity of the bridge; an acceptable surface such as that installed on the car park could be used, and a watching brief as in other recent developments should ensure no damage occurs, provided its terms are carefully considered, and executed. At the time of writing, a final decision has yet to be made.

The Iron Bridge still shows signs of earlier attachments, including a gate across the middle. Originally the path continued in a straight line until the building of the new changing rooms in 1965; the railings between the bridge and changing rooms is the site of the original pool entrance. Just visible is the wall alongside the brook protecting the swimming pool. The bridge is under threat from the current cycle path plans *(17th April 2016)*

The former Abbey ponds area levelled with material from Rosemary Hill, Hyde Road and Abbey excavations, is used annually for the carnival fair. The proposed cycle path would be on the left parallel to the brook which is now hidden by the undergrowth on its banks *(17th October 2016)*

Following a policy as stated in its *Conservation Plan* of making the Abbey history more accessible to the public, in the later 2000s the **Kenilworth Abbey Advisory Committee** devised a scheme to renovate the **Tantara Gatehouse** and its two chambers, suitably for putting its own and other Abbey artefacts on display to the public. This would also ensure the Gatehouse, the most important of the surviving Abbey ruins, would be maintained in a better state of preservation. The scheme was instigated and driven by its Chairman, Abbey authority and Kenilworth history stalwart Harry Sunley; sadly, Harry died in 2011 leaving Dr Richard Morris at the head of the project which he suitably renamed 'The Harry Sunley Memorial Project'. For this to come to fruition, the roof needed a more permanent seal, electricity had to be installed, racking and other displays built, the internal fabric of the building renovated and of course the Abbey stones to be sorted and catalogued, again, cleaned and made presentable. The projected cost was about of £50,000. The KAAC kept English Heritage informed for advice and approval.

Weather-proofing the Gatehouse was the first priority; in 2014, the roof was covered with a damp-proof membrane and turf laid on it and allowed to grow providing a 'soft topping'. To decide a route for the underground electricity supply (to be taken from that at the swimming pool) that would cause the minimum damage to any archaeology, in 2015 a small excavation on the western side of the Gatehouse was carried out, largely by KHAS members. Well preserved stonework was discovered extending several feet below the surface as well as floor tiles similar to those of earlier excavations; less expected were mineral bottles made for the Leamington Spa Aerated Water Company, one of which was dated 1913. (A full report of the excavation appears in *Kenilworth History 2015*.) At the time of publication, this project is ongoing and funds eagerly sought.

All the above-ground **Abbey** ruins will inevitably continue to deteriorate. Of particular concern is the remnant of the Chapter House wall; much of the visible remains are the original rubble core devoid of most of its outer layer and thus it is particularly susceptible to weather erosion; stones still regularly become displaced. Its eventual demise is more or less unpreventable without a vast amount of expenditure.

According to their website the KAAC comprises: from Warwick District Council (1 councillor, and 3 officers representing Conservation, Property Services and Arts / Heritage); The Parochial Church Council (2 members or representatives); Kenilworth Town Council (2 councillors); Friends of Abbey Fields (2 members); The Kenilworth Civic Society (2 members); Kenilworth History & Archaeology Society (2 members); Historic England (formerly English Heritage, 1 official, usually the Inspector of Ancient Monuments responsible for the site); an archaeologist from Archaeology Warwickshire (WCC); and co-opted members as needed. It meets several times a year but almost unavoidably other commitments restrict the attendance of several members. Its AGM early each year is open to the public.

In April 2015 English Heritage had split into two; the original name was retained by a new charity to look after the National Heritage Collection, and the new Historic England provides 'expert, constructive advice to owners, local authorities, and championing the wider historic environment.'

A storm in February 2017 felled the top of a yew tree in the churchyard, dislodging the top of a length of the boundary wall built in the 1880s. It revealed what appears to be worked Abbey stone used as rubble infill *(8th March 2017)*

The area once occupied by the **putting green**, between the tennis courts and the brook, was transformed into a wildflower 'summer meadow' by a three year establishment plan with the FoAF again heavily involved, and is now fenced on three sides; in late summer 2013, a large wooden sculpture of a mole emerging from the ground was added.

A year after the initial plans were postponed at the last minute, the **swimming pool** was closed towards the end of 2011 for a refurbishment of the changing rooms, drainage, new tiling, and an improved reception area. It was officially re-opened on Monday 30th January 2012. The annual number of swimmers was steady at a few hundred either side of 20,000 until 2014 when 28,607 was recorded, increasing to 49,695 in 2015, falling to 42,985 in 2016; the Kenilworth Swimming Club, Kenilworth Masters Swimmers and swimming lesson attendees were not included. It is notable that the initial increase coincided with the opening of the new children's play area; the closure for much of 2017 for refurbishment of the pools at Warwick and Leamington are likley to give another boost to the figures. The Pool Manager told this author that 80 simultaneous outdoor swimmers was a particularly good day in the weather-wise often disappointing summer of 2016; the days of 400 in the outdoor pool whilst others formed lengthy queues are long past. The outdoor pool is heated to a minimum of 19 degrees Centigrade, often to the low 20s; the indoor is nominally 29 degrees.

As mentioned, WDC is carrying out a review of all its leisure activities and at the time of writing (April 2017) Warwick's and Leamington's swimming facilities are receiving major upgrades; the review results for Kenilworth are awaited but will *'focus on improving the current facilities at Abbey Fields and Castle Farm'*. The Kenilworth Wardens Cricket Club seems to be on the move to Castle Farm, again raising the fear that the Castle Farm sports hall may be moved onto the Abbey Fields outdoor swimming pool site. An online petition to retain the outdoor pool started in the autumn of 2016 quickly gathered 2,000 signatures. Its originator suggested increasing, and better publicity for, its opening hours, evening swims with added attractions of music and barbecues, and fun sessions for juniors.

In 1985, the indoor pool was built in the Abbey Fields to ensure the outdoor pool was retained, in preference to keeping the sports facilities together at Castle Farm; how ironic that 30 years later, to have the modern sports facilities together the Castle Farm sports hall may be moved to be alongside the indoor pool resulting in the outdoor pool's closure. Castle Farm was purchased specifically to provide municipal sports facilities and to enable those in the Abbey Fields to close; today the reverse could happen.

Kenilworth's outdoor swimming pool is listed in amongst about 140 remaining in the UK; another 15 have closed or been demolished in the last decade or so; its nearest outdoor neighbours are at Chipping Norton (30 miles distant) and Cheltenham (45 miles).

The swimming pool today. Compare to the photographs on pages 89, 112 & 167 *(21st February 2017)*

Despite the demise of grazing in the **Paddock** in 2009, the public continued to be denied access and it was managed purely as a meadow as started by the Lee family in 2003. Such was its developed and managed biodiversity that in 2015 WDC designated it a Local Wildlife Site. In 2016, grazing returned for short periods with rare-breed sheep, a situation to be reviewed annually. The Paddock becoming open to the public as part

Thirty years on, the stark ends of the swimming pool buildings sit incongruously in their surroundings with no attempt at blending or concealment. A decade passed until the lake was constructed, time enough for landscaping, and trees to have been planted *(6th February 2017)*

The outdoor pool covered for the winter. To the left is the 1935 terracing, the plinth for the changing rooms is narrowed by the 1986 boundary wall. The water treatment plant, top right, is partially on the site of the original. The 1965 sunbathing roof terrace is still open *(21st February 2017)*

of the park as intended, since at least the 1930s and perhaps back to 1914, until its eventual purchase in 1974, seems unlikely in the near future.

The Abbey Fields documents deposited at the Land Registry has the Paddock as separate from the rest of the park. The Abbey Hill bus shelter is not included within the park boundaries and is now considered part of the highway, but the War Memorial, deliberately built on a highway extension, is included within the park.

The Paddock and Oakdale Villa *(9th January 2017)*

Historic icons in the Abbey Fields. The 13th century Chapter House wall protrudes from the terrace constructed in 1968, the flatter terrace stretching away to the right is from 1928, the lime avenue was planted in 1902, the drinking fountain was built in 1934 next to the path constructed in 1897, and all have a backdrop of St Nicholas church, existing by 1291
(6th February 2017)

The area of the Abbey Fields is today always said to be 68 acres, and yet, as has been seen, up to 1974 the total area of land bought and donated only amounted to 66.16 acres; it isn't known when or by whom the figure of 68 acres was calculated. The disparity could be explained if the original land sale did not include the area of the brooks that are apparently about 1.7 acres (although they are shown as part of Area A on the conveyance which does not mention any exclusion). Alternatively, perhaps a more modern calculation has shown the originals to be inaccurate.

However, using the original figures, the fields have never been even as large as 66.16 acres because areas were lost before the 1974 additions. The total acquisitions prior to 1974 totalled 64 acres 2634 sq yds (reached with Gertrude Evans' donation in 1938) but from this must be subtracted 34 perch (1,028 sq yds) due to the Abbey Hill widening for Forrest Road in 1884, and an estimated (by this author) 1,500 to 2,000 sq yds for other incursions by Rosemary Hill and Abbey Hill in 1913/14, 1939, 1950, and 1970, reducing the area to under 64 acres.

To this then is gained Mr Whiteman's corner, but perhaps now the Paddock (1.42 acres) should be discounted as it is not accessible to the public and unlikely to ever be integrated into the park, and of course 4,186 sq yds has been lost due to the now permanent car park. Taking these areas into consideration, the accessible park can be said to be as low as about 63 acres 1595 sq yds, or 63.329 acres.

The entrance from south of the Castle Ford. Behind the trees is the only area of the park lost for any reason other than road widening; it helped Mr Phelps reshape his garden in 1912 *(17th April 2016)*

As stated in the *Conservation Plan*, 'In the collective memory of people who were born in Kenilworth, childhood experiences and holiday outings form the foundations of their powerful attachment to the Abbey Fields. Incomers also are very appreciative of the Fields; it is one of the amenities that attracts them to the town'. With the population already increased by 40 per cent in 45 years and about to rapidly increase further, greater pressure will occur on the Abbey Fields with unavoidable additional usage and callings for new amenities and features. Kenilworth currently has less than 4.4 hectares of open space per 1,000 population, well under the district average of 5.46 and proposed minimum of 5.6; it is a figure more likely to fall than rise in the near future. Every square yard of the Abbey Fields most important recreational asset, its open grassland, will need careful management in the immediate future.

The operation of the Abbey Fields is now a complex affair. Although owned by Warwick District Council that has the major say on developments, none can take place without Scheduled Monument consent from Historic England and, in planning or listed building applications, statutory consultation with Kenilworth Town Council but no obligation to abide by its advice. There are also numerous departments of Warwick District Council involved including Neighbourhood Services (responsible for green spaces strategy, management of the Abbey Fields car park, and day-to-day maintenance including cleansing, refuse collection, grass cutting, tree pruning, weed control and footpath repairs), Cultural Services (responsible for the arts, provision of sports and leisure facilities including the swimming pool), Housing and Property Services (responsible for repair and maintenance of buildings), and Development Services and Business (responsible for planning controls, and guidance on conservation and historic assets).

The fields are also in a Conservation Area bringing its own limitations, and of course there are covenants to abide by. The Kenilworth Abbey Advisory Committee, Kenilworth History & Archaeology Society (about 80 members), Kenilworth Civic Society (40 members) and Friends of Abbey Fields (180 members) are routinely consulted, or offer their opinions, on most potential developments. On occasions these groups are at the forefront in suggesting and promoting ideas and schemes, contributing financially and seeing them to a conclusion. Sometimes members of the general public (22,413 in 2011) also have a chance to have their say in an official questionnaire. And so, despite the ownership now being in the hands of a district authority, there is no doubt that the people of Kenilworth continue to play a major part in the appearance and development of the Abbey Fields.

Under Warwick District Council the park has become a very different place to that they inherited from the Kenilworth Urban District Council in 1974. Some facilities have been lost; the sports pitches due to the opening of a better location, the pitch & putt due its inconvenience, putting and the bowling green due to lack of use. The indoor pool is well used but sits incongruously in its surroundings, and its outdoor neighbour is still popular with an enthusiastic but comparative minority. The extended play area has become perhaps the most popular feature and in addition to townsfolk attracts visitors from a distance. The ruins where possible are safely consolidated and protected, the Abbey history is displayed, and the Barn museum opens throughout the summer (and had over 3,000 visitors in 2016).

Once neat and tidy hedges are now left to ramble almost uncontrolled; acres are turned over to be wildflower meadows in the spring. There are now so many mature trees along the Abbey Hill frontage that it is difficult to even see the 1904 Holmes Avenue that itself was opposed as it obstructed the view across to St Nicholas church. In the 1994 survey the most important feature of the Abbey Fields were the brooks; today they are virtually invisible for much of the year along much of their length due to undergrowth giving a ten to twenty foot wide wildlife habitat to both banks; a generation is growing up having hardly seen them other than from bridges, never mind paddled in them as had their parents. In addition there is now a fenced rain garden and a broken-drain created marsh, and of course, the lake is now well-established and attracts a wide variety of, sometimes rare, aquatic birds.

However, difficulties are arising; a large proportion of the trees are now well over a century old and need either replacing or expensive pollarding before weakening branches become dangerous. The lake has developed water-flow problems due to the brook levels, as discussed in the past, and its plant life is in places becoming intrusive.

But perhaps the biggest problem with the Abbey Fields is that they have become so many things to so many people of different generations and backgrounds, producing a wide variety of views on its uses, amenities, and character. Despite the regular polls always declaring 'Keep the fields as they are', they continue to be changed and evolve. However many times there is a headline 'Leave the Abbey Fields alone', there is another announcing an alteration. For the better? A simple question that has complex answers, inevitably guided by personal preferences.

So what of the future?

It is this author's hope that whatever scheme, small or large, botanical or constructional, that may be projected and considered for the Abbey Fields, and whatever authority, group or individuals are involved, that the following are always given the prime consideration before any decision is made.

Firstly, the hopes, aims and intentions of the Victorians who acquired the fields to produce a large park with recreational facilities for the people of Kenilworth should be remembered. Secondly, the desires and wishes of those individuals who donated land and included Covenants restricting their use and development should be respected at all times. These two go hand in hand simply because without the foresight, commitment, determination and financial outlay amounting to the modern equivalent of £1¾ million by the Local Board and its members, and the later generosity of those individuals, there would be no park for us all to enjoy.

And thirdly, every opportunity should be taken, and also some created, for the investigation and protection of the known and yet to be discovered archaeology and history of the ruins. They are after all, the Abbey's fields.

The lake and associated landscaping adds to this view of Abbotsfield *(28th December 2016)*

The former cattle bridge over the Luzley brook *(17th April 2016)*

Addendum

On 15th May 2017, Kenilworth Town Council published its **Pre-submission Neighbourhood Plan**. The following is the extract relevant to the Abbey Fields:

' Policy KP14G: Design Management in Abbey Fields:

Development proposals in the Abbey Fields Character Area, as shown on the Policies Map, will be supported, provided they have full regard to the following design characteristics:

The area is primarily a recreational open space of national historic importance
There are significant views both north and south across the Fields
The Abbey Fields Lake is an important water feature
There is a significant historical relationship with St Mary's Abbey and its grounds
There is an important relationship visually and historically with the Castle
There are significant remains of St Mary's Abbey Gatehouse, Abbey Barn with adjacent picnic area, Chapter House Wall, Parlour remains and Lapidarian
St Nicholas Church and churchyard are within the fields, incorporating the Abbey remains
There is an important relationship between the church and the rear of houses in High Street
The War Memorial is a focal point at the junction of Abbey End with Abbey Hill
There are many important trees within the Fields, with over 70 varieties, including the Lime Walk, and also important trees in the adjacent gardens
Boundary treatments are important to the interface with the surrounding streets
The Town swimming pool and children's play area occupy a significant location with views from Abbey Hill
The 1925 Bowls Pavilion, within the play area, is an important example of municipal park architecture and should be retained for future use
Building materials are generally masonry, brick, render, timber cladding, slate, tiles

The Abbey Fields Conservation Area forms an integral part of the character of the town of Kenilworth, linking the Castle to the old and new Town centres, and should be preserved.

Abbey Fields is a Scheduled Ancient Monument, but it is also important to maintain non-listed buildings with original features. The car parking is almost at full capacity and consideration needs to be given to future car parking location. A link to the Castle needs consideration.

Any future development in or near to this Conservation Area, should maintain this historic site in full, retaining its unique atmosphere. '

Authors note: The map associated with the policy included a new car park in the Abbey Fields with an entrance alongside the Forrest Road air raid shelter. After protests by this author it was quickly removed; it had been included in error, but of course remains on printed versions.
Comments upon the proposals were invited, and could contribute to alterations before the final submission is published.

In May 2017, the avenue westwards from the door of St Nicholas church, dating from the 1880s, was heavily pollarded creating extra light and an openness to that area of the churchyard not seen for many generations. New lime trees were planted in odd gaps in the avenue.

In July 2017, the Warwick District Council Greenspace Development Officer published a report 'to consider bringing forward a tender to scope and consult on a Heritage Lottery funding bid for Abbey Fields' under the Parks for People scheme. This is the start of a process and it is likely to be some time until any specific project is discussed.

The Kenilworth Agricultural Society still holds its annual show, now at the Stoneleigh Park showground which has allowed a great expansion of the attractions.

This view of the swimming pool is undated but thought to be the 1970s. The spring board and 5-stage diving boards have been removed leaving only the slide from the 1935 equipment supplied by Wicksteeds *(LAG&M)*

In 2017, the indoor swimming pool is open Monday to Friday from 6 or 6.30 a.m. until 10 p.m., with each day split into as many as fourteen sessions, including ladies, lane swimming, schools, aquafit, adults, and Kenilworth, Kenilworth Masters and Baginton swimming clubs. Weekends are 7.00 a.m. until 8 p.m., Saturday includes junior lessons, and the final session on Sunday is for a canoe club.

The outdoor pool re-opened on 27th May for school holidays and weekends only from 10 a.m. until midday, and from midday to 7.00 p.m. dependant upon the weather. Weekend times are 10 a.m. until midday, then closed until 1.30 p.m. from when there is another weather dependant session. It is closed on weekdays during term time. The date of the season-end closure is not displayed.

Prices at the swimming pool for 2017 were £4 for an adult swim, and £2.50 for juniors and concessions (including over 60s and registered disabled). Spectators paid £1.30, and a family entrance was £11.90.

Since 1st June 2017, all WDC sports and leisure facilities are managed and operated by Sports & Leisure Management Ltd, trading under the name Everyone Active, but remain under council ownership. It is hoped the new managers will bring 'exciting new programmes and initiatives' to encourage sport participation; they immediately made, mostly small, price increases to those listed above, but also extended and simplified the outdoor pool times to 10 a.m. to 6 p.m. daily. WDC will 'continue to control a selection of prices for concession users'. The agreement lasts for ten years.

The catering kiosk prices for 2017 include tea for £1.30, coffee from £2.20, toasted sandwiches from £2.80, ice cream cones from £1.40.

In her will, Gertrude Evans left her home in Charmouth, The Poplars, to Mary Hogg, the daughter of her cousin Phillip Evans. Mary also had the benefit of all Gertrude's personal effects. Her chauffeur, Walter Spurdle, inherited her car(s) and former residence The Bungalow, also in Charmouth. Several charities received £50 donations and the rest was split between her cousins, or their children, in the Evans and Bagnall families.

On 8th September 2016, this author submitted to the Kenilworth Town Council that William and Gertrude Evans, George Marshall Turner, Joseph Holland Burbery and Luke Heynes should be considered as names for future Kenilworth streets, in memory of their involvement in creating the Abbey Fields park, and to complement Samuel Forrest and Forrest Road.

The cow-path from High Street to the Oxpen Meadow may soon be altered. Mr Whiteman's corner donated in 1974 is now completely overgrown. Compare to the photograph on page 133 (26th June 2017)

At the time of this publication, plans for improving the narrow 'cow-path' from High Street across the land donated by Gertrude Evans to near the Tantara Gatehouse, have reached the stage of a feasibility study and consultation with interested parties including Kenilworth Town Council, the Parochial Church Council, Friends of Abbey Fields, the Kenilworth Civic Society, Kenilworth History & Archaeology Society, Natural England, the Sensory Trust, and an archaeologist from Archaeology Warwickshire.

The path is approximately 260m long and has a drop in altitude of 11m/36ft, most of which is in about a quarter of its length. It is intended to widen the path to 1.2m (at an estimated maximum cost of up to £100,000) to make it more suitable for those with disabilities, including those driving disability vehicles. Alterations to gradients, and thus the route, may be necessary.

Also at the time of publication, the Earl of Clarendon's 15ft way access between 39 & 41 High Street has been closed to the public for up to a year for construction work at number 39, that also includes the permanent closure to the public of the footpath that once provided access to the 1867 churchyard extension (see page 10). Part of the wall and the kissing gate (see page 152) have been removed. The area closed for a year to the public is part of Area F bought by the Board from the Syndicate for £400 on 14th March 1889; as has been seen, in 1974 the KUDC came close to selling this strip of land before realising the covenant prevented any other use: '... shall forever hereafter be solely used for public walks and pleasure grounds under the control of the council and the same shall not nor shall any part thereof at any time hereafter be sold leased or disposed of for any other purpose inconsistent with the same being solely used as aforesaid. '

Just days before the text was due at the printers, the author was contacted by Shelagh Hubbard, the daughter in law of Phillip Hubbard, the Abbey field renter mentioned in the text. Cows were walked to the fields from their Malthouse Lane farm after morning milking and back again in the evening; the householders on the route sometimes forgot to close their front gates, with inevitable results. Only young cows grazed the southern Abbey Fields and were not removed for football matches, they simply ignored the games and spectators, and grazed elsewhere. Other details supplied by Shelagh have been squeezed into the text.

In March 2017, the author submitted this question to Warwick District Council under the Freedom of Information Act: 'What is Warwick District Council's interpretation of each of the eight individual Covenants that restrict developments in the Abbey Fields, and how much relevance does the Council put on these Covenants when making decisions?'

Several replies have failed to provide the desired answers; correspondence is continuing.

Index

Locations and people from outside Kenilworth are generally not included; nor are subjects in the Addendum.
Page numbers in bold type denote illustrations.

Abbey Fields Amenities:
Allotments **58**, 76
Aviary 115
Band performances 43, 80, 86, 94, 105, 110, 145, 150
Bandstand 65, 86
Bridges:
   Cattle bridge 58, **83**, 110, **196**
   Fairground bridge 122, 137, 159
   Iron Bridge 7, 12, 22-3, 32, 36, 43, **47**, 53, 73, 125, 188, **189**
   Other 79, 94, 102, 107, 121-2
Bowling green, & club 51-3, 55, 57, 60, 70-4, **75**, 77-8, 82, 84, 87, 93, 100-02, 105, 110, 119, **120**, 128, **132**, 137, **142**, **156**, 157, 162, 173-4, 182-3, **185-6**
Brooks:
   Finham 5, 7, 12, 15, 35, 42-4, 53, 65-6, 73, 78, 87, 90-1, 96, 99, 100, 107, 109, 125, 140, 148, **156**, 157, 173, 176, 180
   Luzley 7, **30**, **46**, 58, 73, 109, 125-6, 128, 134, 137, 156, **170**, **196**
Car parking 74, 82, 90, 93, 94, 96, 107, 113, **114**, 121-2, 126, 128, 129, 132, 134, 140, 148, 150, 161-3, 171, 173, 184-7, 194
Catering, & kiosk 96, 107, 113, 118, **123**, 124, 129, 132, 137, **138**, 140-1, 144, 148, 157, 165, 168
Conveniences 61, 73, **76**, 104, **123**, 124-5, 133, 144, **147**, **166-8**, 176
Cricket 11, 13, 24, 31, 38, 55, 60, 85, 103-4, 114, 118, 134, 156
Cultivation 36, 58, 99, 101-3
Cycling 39, 74, 87, 100-1, 110, 133, 140, 145, 173, 188-9
Drinking fountain **86**, 125, **193**
Exercise stations 182
Fishing 12, 42, 53, 61, 140, 148, 169
Flowerbeds 86, 111, 124, 128, 137, 155, 158, 173
Football 38, 51, 80, **81**, 93, 96, 99, 103-05, 107, 114, 117-8, 121, 127-8, **131**, 132-4, 145-6, 168
Footpaths:
   Abbey Hill – Iron Bridge - High Street 8, 39, 44, 47, 66, 94, 177
   Bridge Street – St Nicholas church 39
   Bridge Street – swimming pool 38, 40, 103, 146
   Diagonal, Abbey Hill – Bridge Street **3**, 44, 73, 86, 110, 133, 146, 181, **187**
   General, all 9, 23, 31, 37, 41-4, **136**, 145
   High Street – Gatehouse 37, 95, **133**, 134, **152**
   Iron Bridge – Borrowell Lane 8, 23, 39, **46**, 109, 121, 134, **170**
   Iron Bridge – Castle Ford 47, **76**, 86
   Other / proposed 8, 39, 73, 147, 151, 176. 188

Grazing/renting 8-11, 15, 20-1, 23, 26, 28, **32**, 36-8, **40**, 42, **46**, **56**, 60, **62**, **72**, 73, 81, **83**, 84, 93-4, 99, 101-3, 105, **108**, 117, 119, 121, 125-7, 134, 149, 152, 170-1, 178, 180, 192
Hockey 38, 104, 114, 121
Horse riding 82, 85, 87, 117
Income 41, 115, 119, 122, 137
Lake, see also Oxpen Meadow 171, 173, 175, **176**, 178, **192**, **196**
Land levelling 55, 64, 68, 70, 72, 128, **189**
Memorial Field 79, 85-6, 102, 107, 109, 117, **131**, 134
Mound, the **7**, 121
Netball 104-5
Paddling pool 96, 107, 125, 132, 144, 151, 166
Pavilion 65, 74, **75**, 77, 87, 93, 96, 105, 120, 122, 124, **132**, **142**, **156**, 162, 182, **183**
Pets corner 170
Pitch & putt 86, 124-7, 132, 136-7, 145, 162, 171, 174, 181
Play equipment 64, 80, 82, 87, 101, 112-13, 137, 140, 143, **145**, 146, **147**, **164**, 172, **181**, 182-3, **184-6**, 191
Putting 77, 86, 93, 100, 105, 113, 119, 122, 125, 127, **132**, 133, 142, 145, **156**, 162, 182, 191
Seating 38, 40, 58, 73, 96, 102, 110, **118**, 128, 137, 158, **161**
Shelters 86, 96, **111**, 112-3, 125, 158, 182, 193
Showground 109-10, 117-9, 121, 126, 134, 137, 150, 188
Skating 11, 24, 58, 63, 72, 109, 156
Sports, general 76, 80, 94, 99, 103, 114, 117, 121, 135, 136, 156, 171
Swimming pool, & club(s) 12, 23-5, 27, 34-5, 36-8, 43-9, 56-7, 61, 66, 75-7, 79- 80, 82, 84-5, 87-8, **89**, 90-1, 93, 96, 98-101, 104, **112**, 113-4, 119, **123**, 124-5, 129, **130**, **131**, 132-33, **136**, **138**, 140, **141**, 142, 144, 147, 151, 159-62, **163**, **164**, 165, **166-9**, 176-7, **180**, **186**, 187-8, **191-2**
Tennis courts, & club 55, 69-72, 74, **75**, 76-7, **78**, 82, **84**, 87, 100, 102, 104-5, 114-5, 119, 122, 128, **132**, 133, 137, 145-6, **156**, 157, 162, 176, 182, **185**
Terraces 79, 105, 132, 135, **136**, 138, **193**
Tobogganing 58, 65, 73, 86, 126-7
Trees, inc planting 32, 38-9, 41-2, 44, 51, 56, 73, 94, 97, 101-03, 111, 128, 133-4, 137, 143, 146-7, 156, 158, 161, 181
Trees, memorial 63, 73, 83, 113, 120, 137, **139**, **146**, 147, 158, 181
Wetland, marsh 179, **180**
Wildflower Meadow 175, 181, 190
Wildlife 42, 74, 82, 125, 133, 139, 148, 155, 173, 175, 177-8, 182, 188, 192, 195

200

Abbey Fields Conservation Plan	178, 185, 194
Abbey Fields Consultation	173
Abbey Fields Estate sale & development:	13
Area A	15, **16, 17, 26,** 74
Area B	15, **16,** 18, **19, 26, 114,** 155, 187
Area C	15, **16,** 20, **21,** 25, **29, 30,** 33-4, 53-5, 91, **95,** **116, 123, 133,** 143, 148, **151,** 152, **153, 158,** 176
Area D	15, **16,** 17, 23, 25, **29, 30,** 33, 49, **50, 194**
Area E	15, **16,** 18, 25, **29, 30,** 54, 58, **59**
Area F	15, **16,** 21, 27, **28,** 50, 74, 187
Area map	**16**
Preservationists	15-6, 19, 25, 114
Syndicate	15-8, 21-3, 25-7, 29, 55, 116, 151
Abbey Hill widening	18, 86, 97, 110, 143, 194
Acts of Parliament	6, 13-4, 20, 28, 60, 95, 150-1, 155
Barns (other than Abbey Barn)	25, 44, 99, 104, 117, **118,** 134, 178
Boy Scouts	65-6, 79, 104, 112, 119-20, 137, 150
British Legion	66, 79, 104, 114-5, 118-9, 121, 127, 137, 146
Bye-laws	38, 78, 82, 87, 101, 103-4, 107, 112-4, 117, 134-5, 140, 145, 157
Castle Farm	136, 146, 156, 160, 162, 164, 166, 168, 177, 187-8, 191
Conservation area	143-4, 148-9, 171, 194
Covenants	16, 19, 20, 28, 30, 36, 47, 55, 58-9, 62, 66, 95, 97-8, 107, 110, 143, 148, 151, 153, 165, 171, 187, 194
Department for the Environment	148-50, 157
Dogs	87, 145-6, 157, 169, 177, 182
Earl of Clarendon: First creation	6
Second creation:	
1st Thomas Villiers	6
2nd Thomas Villiers	6, 9
3rd John Villiers	9
4th George F W Villiers	9, 10, 17
5th Edward Hyde Villiers	10, 12-7, 19, 50-1
6th George H H Villiers	51
7th George F L H Villiers	153
English Heritage	178-9, 181, 183, 185-6, 190, 194
Events:	13, 82, 104, 107, 125, 127, 137, 145, 150-1, 155, 159, 169, 175, 179, 181, 189
Agricultural Show	105, **106,** 108, **109,** 119, 126, 134, 137, 150, **154**
Carnival	79, 80, 83, 93-4, 98-9, 101, 104-5, 112-3, 115, 119, 122, 125, 127-8, 136, 151
Circus, Bob Fossett's	128
Circus, Sanger's	99, 104
Civil Defence	119
Duck Race	180
Edward VII Coronation	40
Elizabeth II Coronation	109, 113
Empire Day	61
George V Coronation	51
Gymkhana	105, 108
Kenilworth Festival	181
National Union of Railwaymen	61
Peace Celebration, 1919	63
Play sessions	143, 150, 169
Queen Victoria's jubilees	25, 38
War-time	100-101

Fire Brigade & engine	11, 36, 39, 44, **51,** 65, 75, 77, 79, 83, 86, 90-1, 99, 102, 104, **159,** 176
Flooding	7, 9, 34, 52-3, 55, 64, 72, 77-9, 84-5, 93, 96, 119, 122, 124, 139, 176-7
Football Clubs	80, 85, 103, 104, 114, 117-8, 127, 132, 134, 156, 168
Forrest Road (Abbey Hill Rd)	18, 22, 54, 58, **59,** 60
Friends of Abbey Fields (1)	174-5, 177
Friends of Abbey Fields (2)	177-8, 180-2, 185, 190, 194
Friends of the Abbey	81-2, 92, 98, 129, 146, 157
Garden Café	34, 55, **151**
Girl Guides	65-6, 79, 83, 104, 112, 119, 137, 159
Houses:	
Abbotsfield	32, 42, 52, 55, 61, 64, 73, 91-93, **123, 133,** 143, 148-9, 152-3, 176, **196**
Belmont / Manor House	29, 30, **33**
Bungalow, The	33, 49, 58, 73, 76, 80, 99, 103, 133, 153
Clinton House	20-1, 54, 58, 94-5, **109, 123,** 156, **158,** 163
Crackley Hall	69, 70, 81
Ford House, see Bungalow, The	
Gables, The	52, 80
High Street, 39	37, 73, 93, 152
High Street, 81-85	13, **21,** 26, 55, 95, 115, **116**
Kenilworth Hall	14, 33, 35, 69, 170
Montague House	33, 51
Montpelier House	**41,** 119
Oakdale (Villa)	34, 55, **151, 176, 193**
Sion House	13, 15, 17, **18,** 32
Spring, The	14, 54, 119
Thickthorn	49, 69, 105, 119, 136, 150, 159
Thornby House	69
Virginia	91
Wantage / Hillcote	53, 55, 95
Wilton House	92, 104, 142
Kenilworth, New Jersey	82
Kenilworth Abbey Advisory Committee	157, 174, 178, 182, 190, 194
Kenilworth Action Plan	187-8
Kenilworth Aeromodelling Club	135
Kenilworth (Civic) Society	125, 128-9, 132, 134, 140, 143, 158, 174, 182, 190, 194
Kenilworth Cricket Club (modern)	141, 156, 160
Kenilworth History (& Historical) Society	129, 134, 149-50, 157, 174, 178-9, 184, 186, 190, 194
Kenilworth Inset Plan	**171**
Kenilworth Lions	150-1, 180
Kenilworth Local Board formation	12
Kenilworth Residents Action Committee	163-6, 170-1
Kenilworth Round Table	127, 144, 145, 151, 182
Kenilworth Safety Committee	159
Kenilworth Sports Advisory Committee	135, 136, 138-9
Kenilworth Town Council formation	151
Kenilworth Urban District Council formation	34
Lake (see Oxpen Meadow)	
Litter	139, 146, 177, 182
Little Virginia	5, 7, 8, 13, 17, 29, **30,** 34, 55, 61, 91, 143-4, 148-50, 154, **176**
Ministry of Works	78, 81, 92, 110, 115, 122, 124, 127, 128-9, 135

201

Monarchs, visits	6, 7, 11
OS Maps	24, 36, 43, 58, 74, 90, 136, 169
Oxpen Meadow / pre-lake	6, 11, 20, 24-5, 31, 39, 42, 53, 63-6, 72, 74, 84-6, 94, 96, 99, 105, 106, 107, 151, 108-9, 110, 118, 121-2, 124-5, 127, 132, 133, 144, 146, 148, 150, 155, 156, 159, 167, 175
Paddock / field 381	55, 91-2, 143-4, 149, 151, 152, 154, 170-1, 173, 178, 180, 192, 193

People:

Adcock, Cllr F	137, 140
Addison, G A H	14, 16, 27
Aitken, James, Mrs	44, 47
Asplen, Dr	61
Bagshaw, John	13, 15, 23, 25-7, 29
Barrow, Alfred, Samuel	94
Barwell, C	72, 74-5, 78
Bastock, Jack	152-3
Bates, Thomas	119
Best, Dale	173
Bland, Hamilton	165, 168
Bostock, G	109
Bostock, W	88-9, 103, 108
Bourne, Edmund	32, 34-5, 37, 40, 45
Brewer, Charlotte,	48
Burbery, Joseph H	13, 15, 18, 23, 25-6, 29-30, 33, 153
Butler, R	161, 165
Cain, Patricia	182
Carey-Hill, Eustace	67, 69, 81-2, 92, 124, 171
Chandler, Lincoln	33, 51, 52, 55, 57-8, 61, 91, 151
Church, George	15, 17, 32, 34
Clements, Mrs	152, 170
Coker, M	163, 168
Crouch, J,	52, 59, 62, 65, 67-8, 69, 72
Crouch, Nora	57
de Clinton, Geoffrey	5, 92, 103
de Montfort, Simon	65
Dencer, A E	52, 120, 132
Dencer, Cllr	73-5, 78
Dennison, Charlotte, Ethie	53-5
Dilworth, Frances E	77, 96
Docker, Frank D	33, 52, 57, 60, 80, 82
Douglas, Sholto	45, 48, 52, 57, 60, 63-4, 67, 74-5, 79, 183
Draper, E H	10, 20, 54, 91
Draper, Mary	20, 31, 36, 42, 54, 95, 156
Draper, W H	91
Drew, Jack	80, 93-4, 100-04, 109, 111, 113, 118, 121, 134, 139
Drew, John H	139
Dymond, George P	52, 60, 78, 100
Eagles, J G	35, 37
Edgar, Ted	109, 119
Edmundson, G A J	102, 119, 124-5
Ellis, Arthur, Alice,	53, 55
Evans, Beatrice	14, 54, 115, 116
Evans, Gertrude	14, 49, 54-5, 58-60, 69, 81, 94-5, 108, 115, 116, 148, 156, 158
Evans, Percy	14, 54, 58, 116
Evans, Philip	54, 116
Evans, Sarah	14, 54, 116
Evans, William	13-6, 18-20, 23, 25-7, 29, 30-2, 34, 54, 116, 153
Fancott, family	9, 11, 43, 61, 83, 96, 108, 171
Faxon, F, Mr	76, 93, 98, 116
Forrest, Samuel	14, 16, 18, 22, 153
Fox, Percy	81, 83
Fretton, Mr	27, 31
Gardner, Alfred	157
Gee, Edwin, Mr	43, 44, 76, 81, 83, 86, 88, 99, 103
Griffiths, Cllr	88, 96-8
Growse, Dr	49, 58
Hacking, Andrew	52, 58, 65, 76-7
Hadow, E F	75-6
Hawley, Thomas	13, 26, 31
Heynes, Luke	10, 13, 15, 18, 22, 153
Hibbert, Maj J	109
Hilton, Geoff	5, 178
Hiorns, Mr	88, 94
Hogarth, W	154
Holbrook, Sydney	92, 143, 149
Holmes, Jon	178, 187
Holmes, William	12, 37, 38, 41, 42, 178, 187
Hubbard, J, E, P, Mr	83, 94, 99, 102, 108, 119, 126
Huckvale, Alan	108, 112-3
Hughes, Leonard, Rebecca	56-7, 174
Hurst & Aitken	129, 130, 144
Ingram, W	49
Jackson, James E	34, 36-8, 41, 44, 45, 47, 52-3, 62, 65-6, 70, 72, 81, 85
Jackson, T G	81, 82, 85-6, 88, 92, 96, 98, 103, 107
Jarvis, J A	45
Jeacocks, Mr	37, 44
Jeffcoat, Rev Thomas	29, 59
Jones, Derek	148
Judd, John	13, 22
Kimberley, Sam	61
Lawrence, H W	82
Lawrence, J H, Mr,	53, 70, 73, 75
Lee, family	180, 192
Loasby, G L	103
Lockhart, Walter	13
MacQuilkin, Robert, Mary	48-9
Mander, Edward H	13, 15, 22
Martin, Austin	57
Martin, Helen, Percy	60, 119
Morris, Richard	171, 174, 190
Newcombe, Freda	94, 99
Newey, Arthur	36
Newey, Harry, H	48, 76
Newey, Jonathan	174-5, 177
Nixon, E	60-1, 65, 70
Norris, Mrs	112
Paxton, Charlie	116
Pears, W T	14, 31, 35-6
Phelps, F R M	49, 50, 73, 80, 99, 103, 137, 153, 194
Pickering, Derek	138, 139, 142, 148, 164
Poole, W S, family	10, 14

Porter, Charles	110, 123
Postins, Mr & Mrs	107, 113
Pratt, L W	60, 74-5, 89
Prince, H	87, **100**
Purnell, Edward	34-5
Quick, Harry	67
Randall, Charles	46, 61-3, 65-7, 69, 73, 76, 81, 83, 91, 151, 176
Randall, Charles jnr	91, 144
Randall, Charles, Trust	143, 144, 149
Randall, George	91
Randall, Mrs	60, 73
Redman, Avril	171
Retberg, Alec	139, 146, 149, 170
Riley, William	34-5, 37, 40, 45, 47
Robbins, Richard, Mr,	11-13, 15, 17, 20
Roberts, Joseph	11, 19, 22, 27, 31, 34, 37, 42, 51, 73
Rotherham, K	60
Rowe-Evans, Adrian, Pru,	177-8
Sapcote, W & Sons	149-51
Satchwell, family	43
Schintz, Dora	49, 53, 57
Schneider, Louis, Auguste	43, 48
Shard, W	40
Shaw, Eli	87-9
Sheepy, George	48
Shelswel, Ellen	48
Sherwin, Thomas	52
Shilton, Dave	183
Shrimpton, E	**100**, 132
Siddeley, J D	80-3, 92-3
Skelscher, Harry	48
Slade, Frederick	13-4
Smalley, Dr L	88, 94, 96, 108
Smith, E B	107-8, 112
Smith, Edward, & Son	15, 26, 31, 35
Smith, Joseph	31, 35
Smith, Rodney 'Gypsy'	82
Spicer, Arthur	62
Stansfield, Cllr	145, 188
Street, Henry	15, 31, 33-4, 36, 37-8, 41, 45
Street, Arthur	41, 44-5, 64, 66-7
Sumner, S	40
Sunley, Harry	150, 157, 159, 174, 190
Swain, William	12
Taylor, R	44-6
Thomas, Mr	43-4
Thomas, Maj B H	81, 92, **146**
Tipson, Thomas, Mrs	79, 115
Tisdale, George	81, 82, 85, 87- 91, 94, 96, 101
Trepplin, C, E	15, 23
Trunkfield, Henry, Sarah	47-9
Turner, George	13, 15, 20, 23, 25-6, 29, 30, 32, 34, 41, 53-5, 91
Waites, Kathleen	**53**
Ward, John James	45
Warner, Mrs	120, 157
Watling, Major H R	85, 88, 95, 108, 119-20
Watson, Mary, family	48
Watson, Maud	**95**, 115
West, Enoch J	33
Whateley, R, H	31-2, 40
Whitley, Thomas	31, 65, 69
Whitlock, Sandra	177-8
Whittaker, Mr	95
Whiteman, H W	125, 143, 148-9, 152-4, 158, 194
Whittindale, Ada, James, Edgar	14, 17, 33, 85
Winstanley, Harold	70
Wynter, Dr D	10, 13-5
Population	9, 11, 26, 57, 66, 91, 103, 119, 140, 194-5
Punch	116-7, **126**
Rabbits	87
Red Cross Hospital	57, 60
Rifle range	46
Rosemary Hill widening	55, 97, 111
St Mary's Priory / Abbey	5, 6, 8, 17, 21, 62, 115, 174, 178, 185-6
Ancient Monument listing	71, 115, 163-4, 178
Barn, the	8, **22**, 38, 61, 68-70, 78, 81, 92-3, 99, 103, 128, 129, 149-50, 157, **174**, 178-9
Chapter House	25, 68, **69**, 70, **76**, 79, 129, **135**, 157, 175, 190, **193**
Excavations, ruins, relics	10, 12, 26, 27, 31, **57**, 64-7, **68-9**, 70, **72**, **75**, **78**, 81-2, 92, 103, 124, 128, 129, 134, **135**, 149-50, 163, 171, **172**, 175, 188-90
Lake	7
Mill	7, 9, 91, 172
Surveys	175, 179, 184-5
Tantara Gatehouse	6, 8, 10, **11**, **22**, 26-7, 31, 39, 81, 124, 128-9, 134, 150, 157, 170, 178, 190
St Nicholas Church	6, **32**, **40**, 49, **56**, **57**, 62, 64, **68-9**, 82, **84**, **114**, 149, 157, **193**
Churchwardens	13, 19, 27, 50, 65, 114, 155, 187
Churchyard	6, **10**, 12-14, 21-2, **23**, 26-7, 31, 49, 50, 54, **56-7**, 58, 81-2, 92, 98, 102, 152, 171, **174**, 178, **190**
Schools	44-6, 49, 76-7, 85, 96, 101, 104-5, 113-14, 128, 131-2, 134, 137, 160-2
Sewers	12, **32**, 94, 110, 124
Skatepark	177
Swimming (other than at pool)	12, 22, 72
Toll Road	**9**
Unemployment	24, 34-5, 65, 66-7, 69, 73, 76, 85, 89, 161
Vandalism, thefts	45, 61, 77, 104, 107, 117-8, 123, 125, 127, 133-4, 137, 143, 145, 148, 158, 164, 182
Volunteer Training Corps	47, 58, 61, 63
War Memorial	62, 65-6, **67**, 78, 128, 158, 178, 193
Warwick District Council formation	150
World War 1	57-62
Spoils, cannon	62, **63**, 78, 99, 102
World War 2	99-103
Air raid shelters	97, **98**, 103-4, 110, 143, 148, 178, 179
ARP	96-8
Youth Club / Centre	107, 114, 137

By the same author:

Kenilworth's Railway Age (1985)   92 pp (A5), including 12 pages of illustrations, out of print

Kenilworth's Engineering Age (1995)   64 pp (A5), including 20 illustrations £3.95

    The rise of engineering firms as they replaced established industries, such as brickmaking and animal skin processing. Of particular note are their origins in stables, outbuildings and sheds and the subsequent transition to purpose-built industrial estates.

Rails to Kenilworth and Milverton (1999)   88 pp (A4), 50 illustrations and 3 layout plans £7.95

    A more detailed look at the origins and early days of Kenilworth's branchline, the 150th anniversary celebrations, rail-workers' reminiscences, newspaper reports of incidents and a detailed account of the origins of the rail system of Leamington and Warwick to which the branch was joined.

    The above titles published by The Odibourne Press.   www.Odibournepress.co.uk

Victorian Kenilworth and its People (2006)   199 pp (A4), over 100 illustrations £9.95

    A comprehensive account of the many changes that took place in Kenilworth during the reign of Queen Victoria that laid the foundations of the modern town. New roads and buildings, the construction of the gas, sewer and water utilities, new industries, philanthropists and villains, high unemployment and mass emigration, and the establishment of the fire brigade are amongst the many subjects included in detail.

Kenilworth People and Places, Vol 1 (2011)   154 pp (17cm x 24cm), over 120 illustrations £.9.95

    Included are detailed histories of Kenilworth's cinemas, Kenilworth's own football trophy, The King's Arms, Kenilworth Hall, Rouncil Towers, Crackley Hall, The Globe Hotel, the clock tower and its benefactor, Chesford Grange, the Bourne family, early pilots, a little-known bicycle pioneer, the early days of Kenilworth's Scouting and Guides movements, The Towers, Parkfield, the chemical industry, Eykyn's Garage, *etc.*

Kenilworth People and Places, Vol 2 (2013)   160 pp (17cm x 24cm), over 160 illustrations £9.95

    Continuing the themes of Volume 1, this records the histories of more estates including those of Thickthorn, Elmdene, Woodside and the Cay family, Wilton House, Thornby House, Worcester Gardens, as well as the history of the Library, the Water Tower and reservoir, Kenilworth Boys College, and early Kenilworth photographers. Of particular interest are the origins and first 25 years of Kenilworth's Carnival, and the development of the town's early council housing up to 1940.

A Portrait of Kenilworth in Street-Names, Third Edition (2015)   72pp (A5), 25 illustrations £5.00

    In association with, and continuing the work of, Dr Geoff Hilton, this third edition is fully revised. It explains the origin of every Kenilworth street name, and explores the development of Kenilworth's street naming back to the 18th century.

    The above titles published by Rookfield Publications.   www.VictorianKenilworth.co.uk